AMERICAN PANORAMA

American Panorama

ESSAYS BY FIFTEEN AMERICAN CRITICS ON 350 BOOKS PAST AND PRESENT WHICH PORTRAY THE U.S.A. IN ITS MANY ASPECTS

EDITED BY *Eric Larrabee*

New York University Press

WASHINGTON SQUARE · 1957

Library of Congress catalogue card number: 57-11743

Printed in the United States of America

The Contributors

Jacques Barzun, writer and professor of history, is dean of the graduate faculties at Columbia University. He is the author of *Teacher in America, Berlioz and the Romantic Century, Music in American Life* (No. 21), and other books.

Lyman Bryson, professor emeritus of education in Teacher's College, Columbia University, is the author of *The Next America* (No. 43). He is familiar to American radio audiences as the moderator of the program, "Invitation to Learning."

Carl Carmer is an authority on American folklore. Among his many books are *Listen for a Lonesome Drum, Stars Fell on Alabama,* and *The Hudson* (No. 49).

Clifton Fadiman, though best known as a radio and television personality, is a writer and literary critic as well. From 1933 to 1943 he was book editor of *The New Yorker,* and he edited *The American Treasury* (No. 106).

Cary T. Grayson, Jr., of the Carnegie Corporation staff, was specially charged with the planning and execution of the project from which this volume derives.

Frank E. Hill, writer and educator, is co-author (with Allan Nevins) of *Ford: The Times, the Man, the Company* (No. 232).

John A. Kouwenhoven, professor of English in Barnard College, Columbia University, is the author of *Made in America* (No. 175) and *The Columbia Historical Portrait of New York* (No. 174).

Eric Larrabee, a co-author of *Creating an Industrial Civilization* (No. 288), is associate editor of *Harper's* magazine.

Russell Lynes, managing editor of *Harper's* magazine, is a journalist and essayist. He is the author of *The Tastemakers, A Surfeit of Honey,* and other books.

Elting E. Morison, historian and professor of history at Massachusetts Institute of Technology, was editor of *The Letters of Theodore Roosevelt.*

Paul Pickrel is both managing editor of the *Yale Review* and chief book critic of *Harper's* magazine.

John Andrew Rice tells of his own career as a writer and educator in *I Came Out of the Eighteenth Century* (No. 254).

Lionel and Diana Trilling are both distinguished literary critics. Mr. Trilling is also professor of English at Columbia University and the author of *The Liberal Imagination* (No. 308) and *Middle of the Journey* (No. 309).

Mark Van Doren is the author of *Nathaniel Hawthorne* (No. 314) and many other works. In 1939 he was awarded the Pulitzer Prize for poetry.

Foreword

Carnegie Corporation, as a philanthropic foundation whose purpose is "the advancement and diffusion of knowledge and understanding" in the United States and certain areas of the British Commonwealth, has long been aware of the enormous difficulties faced by anyone who looks for a well-delineated portrait of the United States. The country's very size, its physical diversity, the heterogeneous backgrounds of its 170 million people, and the rapidity of social change have made most portrayals seem more in the nature of caricatures. The project to which this volume is both introduction and guide is an attempt by the Corporation to provide, through a varied selection of writings about the United States, a picture of present-day American civilization and its origins. Sets of the 350 books selected for the project have been distributed to the Commonwealth countries where the Corporation is active. Each set was accompanied by a copy of *American Panorama.* This volume in itself we believe can serve as a guide for all those, both at home and abroad, who are seeking a broader comprehension of the U.S.A.

The task of drawing up a suitable list of books turned out to be formidable. Nothing quite like it had been done before. Other efforts, both governmental and private, to devise lists of American books had special limitations of one sort or another.

What we sought was a list of three to four hundred books illustrative not only of good American writing but of the entire range of American thought and behavior, books which taken together would present a kind of portrait of America—its past and its present, its daily life and its dreams, its avenues and its alleys, its economy and its art. We began to look upon the whole venture as something of a gamble. Was it possible with this number of books—a limit determined by practical considerations—both to portray contemporary American civilization and explain its origins? Would we encounter significant areas of American experience that could not be represented adequately through books simply because the volumes had never been written? These and other problems plagued us. Nevertheless, we accepted the challenge and went ahead with our plans.

We began by talking with qualified individuals in all parts of the country about the project. These consultants were of varied backgrounds and interests; each was chosen for his capacity to throw light on some facet of the project. Some of them were book reviewers. Some were librarians. Some were authorities on specific regions of the country. Some were specialists on art, music, the theater, history, economics, industry, education, and so forth. Approximately 140 people gave us advice at this stage—advice which proved invaluable.

By this time, we had a fairly clear notion of the categories which we would have to cover if the books were to form a reasonably comprehensive portrait of the United States. We chose experts who had special competence with respect to these categories and asked each of them to prepare a list of books within his category. Some sixty such lists were obtained.

It is impossible to thank individually each of the men and women who prepared lists for us, and all the others who gave so generously of their time and advice, but we do wish to give collective recognition to their important help. The willingness of highly qualified and busy men and women to devote long hours to a project of this sort was a significant factor in encouraging us to press ahead. And I must express our special gratitude to Lewis Gannett, distinguished former member of the New York *Herald Tribune's* book review staff, whose thoughtful articles on problems of the overseas dissemination of American literature did much to stir our interest in the subject.

We created an advisory committee of five members whose task it was to use the special lists and their own wide knowledge of American writing to draw up a draft list of selections from which the Corporation's officers could make a final selection. Lyman Bryson served most ably as the chairman of this committee. Other members were Jacques Barzun, Carl Carmer, John A. Kouwenhoven, and David Riesman. The high praise due this imaginative and distinguished committee cannot be overstated.

One of the recommendations of the advisory committee was that a short critical introduction be prepared for each selection on the list, placing the book in perspective and in effect saying why it was chosen. The writing of these introductions was done in part by the members of the advisory committee themselves and in part by the following scholars and professional writers: Clifton Fadiman, Cary T. Grayson, Jr., Frank E. Hill, Eric Larrabee, Russell Lynes, Elting E. Morison, Paul Pickrel, John A. Rice, Diana Trilling, Lionel Trilling, and Mark Van Doren.

These individuals are the authors of this volume, which is a collection of the introductory pieces for all the items on the bookshelf. The introductory pieces have also been printed and pasted inside the covers of all volumes to be sent overseas. Again I must express the deep appreciation of Carnegie Corporation for the ready understanding which these writers showed of their task and for the spirit in which they carried it out.

The New York Public Library agreed to collect and ship the books. The cooperation shown by John Mackenzie Cory, Chief of the Library's Circulation Department, and William Stern, also of the Library's staff, and the latter's skill as general supervisor of the entire operation, deserve our special thanks and praise. Our gratitude is also due to those publishers who because of their interest in the project supplied books at special discount rates.

Cary T. Grayson, Jr., was asked by the Corporation to take special responsibility for the planning and execution of the project. From the earliest conversations to the preparation of the final list, every phase of this long and arduous task received the stamp of his competence and good sense. The tactful and able manner in which he has marshaled the many resources and talents that have gone into this project deserves particular note.

I must express, finally, our warm thanks to Eric Larrabee for accepting the editorship of this book. His experience, judgment, and taste have combined to produce more than a competent guide and introduction to the bookshelf. His thoughtfully edited volume stands as a new contribution to the literature which *American Panorama* represents.

JOHN W. GARDNER, President
Carnegie Corporation of New York

June, 1957

Contents

AMERICAN PANORAMA

Introduction

The United States is no easier to describe to its inhabitants than to people of other lands. While this book, as John W. Gardner has said, is primarily intended for readers in the British Commonwealth, both its sponsor and its editor believe that it will have a comparable usefulness at home, or wherever there exist those kinds of curiosity about America that printed words can satisfy. Though conceived as an adjunct to a selected library of 350 American books, it can be used independently as a condensed and interrelated survey of the culture from which those books have come. It is a handbook, or tries to be, in the favorable sense of that word.

It represents, first, the conviction that there is such a thing as the American culture. The contributors assume that there is an identifiably American civilization. Moreover, they regard it as the total activity of Americans, not merely our literature or fine arts. They treat its books, like those considered in the pages that follow, as a by-product of the American experience rather than its substance. Hence this collection is not put forward as a literary monument. In making up the list there has been no attempt to include the ten best, or 100 best, or even 350 best American books in terms of objective merit. This is, rather, the best selection of books which its compilers could make, within the limits of availability and their own knowledge, to convey the breadth and depth of America to a relatively uninformed, but interested, reader. Others might well have chosen differently.

It is a partisan list, and the essays collected here about the books are partisan. They reflect a clear-cut image of America, if a variegated one, and they are colored by affection for that image. Their writers belong to the small minority of Americans who are actively interested and informed about the indigenous culture, and sufficiently free of imported standards of value to judge its achievements in the appropriate, local terms. Not that these writers are unaware of their nation's faults—there is much criticism of America, some of it savage, in the books they describe—but that their awareness of its *virtues* is a new and precarious thing. American civilization is still—in fact, is increasingly—a self-conscious study. In spite of centuries of effort to disentangle ourselves from European influence, this generation of educated Americans is no more free than its predecessors of a set of built-in comparisons—where is our Bach, our Shakespeare, and so on?—and can arrive at a sympathetic view of itself only by deliberate effort. The American culture does not consist of a body of commonly accepted, or even tacitly acknowledged, masterpieces. There is no "official" viewpoint, and even if there were this book would not propose to reflect it.

What its contributors attempt to do instead is to locate a given book in its proper context. In a sense, they suggest why the book is on the list in the first place; but, more than that, they establish it within a set of relationships, not only to other books on the list but to those overarching American themes that in each instance seem most relevant and illuminating. In some cases this means telling a great deal about the author; in others, little or nothing. In some, it requires description of the time and circumstances of publication; in others, less so. But in every example the effort is to place the book against some kind of background, preferably that which the unfamiliarized reader—American or foreign—will find most rewarding to know about.

Early in our labors these prose introductions acquired the inelegant name of "blurbs," from publishers' slang for the advertising copy printed on the dust jacket of a book, and "blurbs" they have remained. It is an unusual art form, one in which none of its present practitioners is wholly comfortable, and we have all attempted to make it serve more than one of several contradictory purposes. As editor, I have tried where possible to effect an over-all community of tone and balance without sacrificing the individual personality—often strongly defined—of the contributor. Some readers may find this a disability in the book, since they cannot count on finding exactly the same standards of judgment applied to each work on the list. On the other hand, the same standards do not necessarily apply to two such disparate books (two that are frequently mentioned in the "blurbs") as *Made in America* and *Lanterns on the Levee*. In most instances the books are commented on by a writer with a special competence or interest in the areas to which they belong, and therefore with some inherent prejudice. Perfect objectivity might be admirable but it would be uninteresting by comparison.

Certain shared points of view remain, however, and should be mentioned. As I have suggested, this book is relatively sanguine. It is not antipathetic to the twentieth century. It views the "great experiment" of American democracy —to borrow a title from the list—with considerable indulgence. It welcomes the agreeable aspects, while reserving judgment on the disagreeable, of a mass culture. Nor does it define "culture" as merely those activities classified as "cultural" by the educated upper class of Western Europe during the nineteenth century. It testifies to a belief that America, when and if its contribution to the planetary total is summed up, is just as likely to be judged for its popular and industrial arts as for its symphonies and frescoes. It says, in effect: we are what we are.

The list of 350 books itself has all the strengths and weaknesses of a committee effort. No one will have any trouble finding holes in it. The discerning observer will perhaps be able to detect the biases, stated or implicit, of the distinguished personalities who served on the advisory committee; an even more penetrating analysis might reveal the effects of their mutual barter and exchange. To such natural criticism, the editor—who had at best a negligible part in the selection—can only say that he saw enough of the task to appreciate its difficulty. He was, in the first place, appalled to discover how many desirable books, even those of recent provenance, could not be included because they were out of print. (Fortunately, many publishers have been willing to re-issue books on the list for this occasion.) In the second, it is easier to make a selection which satisfies one's own possessive view of America than to adapt to someone else's. It would be fair to the canon as finally agreed on to say that no one involved in it is satisfied and that all have been restrained from further tampering with it reluctantly, certain that if they were only given the chance a few discreet adjustments would result in marvelous improvements. To the would-be critic I can only say that this is more complicated than it looks, and ask you to take my assurance on a certain amount of faith.

In addition to the indexes, which are self-explanatory, there is one aid to the reader which should be described. Each book on the list is numbered and each essay numbered accordingly. There are then cross-references—that is, within a given "blurb" there will often be parenthetical suggestions, by number, of related books in which the reader might be interested. There are either too few or too many of these signposts. Their purpose is not to provide a complete network of relationships among subject matter having a common interest; often an obvious reference, especially where dozens would be obvious, will not be made. Our intention is another of our many compromises, in this case between guiding the stranger and insulting the friend. The aim here is that the student who comes to the list completely without preparation shall at the very least be encouraged to browse from one book to another. The references are intended to offer a trail for those who come with no particular plan of their own; as a catalogue or scholarly scheme of study the references are less satisfactory, and should be supplemented with professional guidance.

The main credit for this volume, as Mr. Gardner has indicated, devolves upon its contributors. Grateful acknowledgment should also be made to The Viking Press, Inc., for permission to quote Phyllis McGinley's poem "Blues for a Melodeon" and to e. e. cummings for "the Cambridge ladies" and "no time ago." I can only add my indebtedness to my father, Harold A. Larrabee, for helping to eliminate errors of fact and blunders of interpretation that might otherwise have slipped through.

Eric Larrabee

New York City
June 1957

1. *Yosemite and the Sierra Nevada*

by Ansel Adams *and* John Muir

The Sierra Nevada, a mighty range of mountains nearly four hundred miles long, rises in saw-tooth peaks that form a natural boundary between California and the east. In the center of the range and 150 miles directly east of San Francisco is a scenic area of pinnacles, waterfalls, lakes, streams, wildlife, and Big Trees known as Yosemite National Park.

The name most closely associated with this region is that of John Muir (1838-1914). Born in Scotland, he was educated at the University of Wisconsin and soon thereafter left for California and "the university of the wilderness." When he arrived in San Francisco in 1868, Muir lost no time in asking for the nearest way to "anywhere that's wild!" Thereafter he was "hopelessly and forever a mountaineer," starting off on a trip with only a notebook, a bag of bread, tea, and a blanket. For nearly half a century he took odd jobs in order to spend his time exploring, studying, speculating, and scribbling about the natural surroundings that fascinated him.

The journal he kept during his first months in the mountains appeared 41 years later, almost unchanged, as *My First Summer in the Sierra;* it constitutes the central text of this volume. For an introduction to Muir the reader will do well to turn to this section first. It is a tale of adventure, filled with the same enthusiastic delight in new experience and the same exactness of first-hand observation that is found in *Walden* (in No. 305). Muir, like Thoreau, had the capacity to live completely alone, absorbed by natural scenes, and yet retain a lofty vision of Nature's ultimate relationship to man. In this volume, however, there is little indication of his eloquence as a conservationist whose numerous writings set in motion a wave of popular interest in the preservation of wild beauty. The stamp of John Muir is found in many parts of the country, but he has no finer monument than the maintenance of Yosemite as a National Park.

Ansel Adams, noted Western photographer, has recorded nearly three quarters of a century later the same Yosemite and "range of light." His photographs, which constitute the second half of this book, are an appropriate complement to Muir's interpretation of the timeless realities of one of America's favorite wilderness regions.

C. G.

2. *The Selected Letters of Henry Adams*

edited by NEWTON ARVIN

Descended from one of the families longest settled in New England —a family which gave the country its second and sixth Presidents, an ambassador, and a Secretary of the Navy—Henry Adams (1838-1918) added luster to the name by means altogether different from his forebears'.

He too wanted political power and renown, but he had been born at the wrong time, and especially with the wrong kind of character. Aged 23 when the Civil War broke out, he went to London as secretary to his father, the American ambassador. The United States to which he returned as a journalist in 1868 was not a society run by codes and organized by classes. It was a helter-skelter grouping of old and new inhabitants, rapidly industrializing themselves under cutthroat competition.

For this free-for-all, Adams had no taste. He plunged into historical scholarship and teaching, for a time as assistant professor of medieval history at Harvard. He wrote the definitive account of the Presidential administrations of Thomas Jefferson and James Madison, and a series of brilliant sketches linked by philosophizing which he called *Mont-Saint-Michel and Chartres.* In later life his pessimism deepened, and his view of history was darkened by speculations on modern science. The second law of thermodynamics predicted a state of meaningless (and cold) equilibrium for all particles of the universe, and Henry Adams prophesied a series of violent crises which would end civilization even before entropy achieved its deadly work.

His bitterness and frustration were concentrated in *The Education of Henry Adams,* a posthumous account which made him instantly famous as he had not been while alive. It is full of memorable descriptions, such as the inauguration of President U. S. Grant ("a man of the old stone age"); but in it Adams indulges a kind of personal fallacy. He takes the view that he should have been "told" by his teachers, prepared for the decadent modern age which accepts multiplicity instead of seeking unity. At the apex of the unity, one is made to feel, there would have been an Adams.

Yet a diametrically opposite strain also runs through Henry Adams's work. It is evident in *Democracy,* one of two novels he published anonymously, and especially in the admirable letters of which a very small selection is given here. Further information about his career and antecedents will be found in *The Adams Family* (No. 4).

J. B.

3. *Relation of the State to Industrial Action and Economics and Jurisprudence*

by Henry C. Adams
edited by Joseph Dorfman

The Adams who wrote this book is not related to the Adams family represented in the preceding book or the one which follows it on this shelf of American books (Nos. 2 and 4). He is, by comparison, relatively unknown, though his mind and work were original and the influence of his pioneering thought has been increasingly recognized.

The introduction by Professor Joseph Dorfman, himself a noted historian of economic thought, makes plain the circumstances in which Henry C. Adams (1851-1921) worked when he directed the statistical work of the Interstate Commerce Commission, the first agency designed to curb the powerful American railroads' anarchical practices and disregard of the public interest.

In reflecting on the acts of the two great powers of modern times—the state and big business—Adams was led to formulate the first searching theory of their permanent and desirable relation. The fact that he was a liberal in the finest tradition lends special importance to his views, for it was the liberal swing away from total *laisser-faire* toward the end of the nineteenth century which produced the network of restraining laws and practices now in force throughout the free world. It rejects a thoroughgoing socialization, which would merge the power of the state and that of big business, believing that this merger multiplies the power of each by infinity; and it acknowledges at the same time that a complete hands-off policy is neither possible in fact nor defensible in theory. Adams's formulation of the equilibrium to be sought has thus the importance of both a fundamental charter and a prolegomenon to future speculation in these fields—for example, Adolf Berle's (No. 33), Peter F. Drucker's (No. 102), and the editors' of *Fortune* (No. 119).

J. B.

4. *The Adams Family*

by JAMES TRUSLOW ADAMS

It is almost possible to turn the genealogical chart of the Adams family into an outline history of the United States. At the table when the first drafts of the Declaration of Independence were prepared was an Adams; at the head of one of the great manufacturing firms in one of our largest industries today is an Adams. In between there have been Presidents, ambassadors, cabinet members, architects of new political parties, soldiers. For the most part, members of the family have put their energies directly at the service of the state; but among those with Adams blood in their veins have been distinguished historians, railroad presidents, sociologists, economists, and at least one man who wrote novels.

The over-all record of the Adams family, sustained for two hundred years in a highly competitive democratic society, is a singular achievement. What, in politics at least, makes it the more remarkable is that the Adams frame of mind was not one which ordinarily rouses public enthusiasm and support. Members of the family often enough belonged with those heroes Thoreau said serve the state with their consciences and thus, for the most part, resist it. The Adams conscience was imbedded in characters undecorated by the genial arts, pathologically shy and self-aware, with the New England skill in concealing the rills of inner passion behind outward embankments of granite. What the Adamses possessed was clear. intelligence, incorruptible judgment, and the Calvinist's extraordinary administrative sense, his feeling for the organization and application of power.

The earliest and greatest members of this family have come down to us cold and monumental like Roman statuary. In part, this is our own fault. The existence of uncommon individual power, as opposed to collective might, so disturbs us that even when we gaze back upon it with respect our glances tend to fix it safely, as with General Washington, in stone. But the Adamses also are responsible, in part, for they no more had the skill to command the popular memory than to win large majorities from their contemporaries. Yet they were living, fascinating men and James Truslow Adams (1878-1949) sets out to make them so again. He was no relation, but he was a student of the early times and he possessed excellent perceptions and a ready pen. From his pages emerge with engaging and informing grace the tribal customs, characteristics, attitudes, and personalities, public and private, of this remarkable tribe.

E. E. M.

5. *Grandfather Stories*

by Samuel Hopkins Adams

Grandfather Stories is a group of twenty-three tales of the past related by an old man for the edification and amusement of his grandchildren. With these stories, Samuel Hopkins Adams (1871-) has built a bridge between the American past and the American present. His grandfather's memories make vivid the early nineteenth-century days of the republic; and his own, the decades of the 1870's and '80's. Though the majority of the stories deal with the Erie Canal in western New York State, and the city of Rochester through which it passes, this is not a regional book in the narrow sense.

The robust, vigorous character of Grandfather Myron Adams is reflected largely in his ebullient speech, peppered with a pungent vocabulary of now-archaic words and idioms. The old man's command of nouns of vituperation alone would inspire the envy of a fishwife, and his grandson's rehabilitation of many rich folk expressions once in common use is a joy: a wind is "fit to blow a bespoken boot off a wooden leg"; an ignoramus "don't know enough to stamp dirt in a rathole"; and Grandfather "was not born in the woods to be scared by an owl."

The book covers a wide spread of significant American social history. Beginning with the "pribbles and prabbles" of Rochester high society, it continues with lavish and authentically detailed tableaux of a bygone age—circuses, transportation, literary clubs, national figures, chicanery, photography and the early cinema, ghosts, medicines, and competitive sports such as baseball, single sculling, and pie-eating. The result is a spirited literary re-creation of the colorful and active world which was America in the days when the republic was getting under way, and a picturesque summing up of the nation's progress through the first century and a half of its existence. The book also reflects Mr. Adams's sympathy with his grandfather's complaint against the present, which the old man calls "this thin-blooded age when loyalty is a dull spark and patriotism the echo of Independence Day rhetoric."

C. C.

6. *The Spirit of Youth and the City Streets*

by Jane Addams

Writing in 1909, a woman who thought of herself as a social worker but who spoke as a poet issued a quiet but deeply disturbing indictment of industrial life. The modern city and its growing industrialism, she said, were making a society which wasted the young, "caring more for the products they manufacture than for their immemorial ability to reaffirm the charm of existence." Most men and women, Jane Addams (1860-1935) believed, never learn to get an affirmation of the value of life from art or literature. They depend on "the young to equip it with gaiety and enthusiasm" and there was no chance for youth to do this work, to renew the joy in the wine of life, in a city like Chicago.

The alternatives to the enjoyment of their natural gaiety and happiness were vice and sorrow. It was the habit of moralists at that time, as it still is in some places, to blame the degradation of youth on natural viciousness. Jane Addams said that their surroundings, the misuse of the arts, and the dull apathy of authorities collaborated to frustrate the young in their drive for amusement and thus led to evil.

Jane Addams was not the founder of settlement work in industrial America, although Hull House (opened in 1899) was one of the first great centers of social work. There she and her devoted associates trained younger associates for devotion. But her great role was to put into words the deeper reasons for pity, the clearer understanding of human passion and frustration, and the more generous beliefs in human capacity that made work among the unfortunate a crusade for beauty and peace. She understood how a young girl might be driven by a desire for beauty out of an ugly home into a dangerous street, and how cheap theaters and dance halls might be romantic when romance was possible nowhere else. She put the issue boldly: "We may either smother the divine fire of youth or we may feed it." Jane Addams received the Nobel peace prize in 1931 in recognition of her stand for international tolerance and generosity, but that was only an incident in her lifework of salvaging civilization for the sake of youth.

L. B.

7. *Little Women*

by LOUISA M. ALCOTT

Although this children's classic is no longer widely read by children, the great reputation it won when it was published (in 1868-9) continued well into the present century and is lovingly sustained in the memory of an older generation. It is safe to assume that the book will always hold an honored place in the American literary canon. Indeed, one can guess that with the passage of time, when a new domestic culture is sufficiently established not to be embarrassed by reminders of the past, youngsters no less than adults will return to it with fresh enthusiasm as a charming and authentic record of New England life in the Civil War period.

The authenticity of *Little Women* derives not only from its genius for homely detail but also from the fact that its author was faithfully depicting her own family situation. The daughter of Bronson Alcott, the distinguished Transcendentalist educator and friend of Emerson and Thoreau, Louisa May Alcott (1832-88) omits from this autobiographical novel only the illustrious persons and the sense of spiritual and intellectual ferment which must have been part of her own early experience. For the rest, the home life of her March family is her own quiet, happy, affectionate home life. She is herself the Jo of the book, the literary sister and the most appealing of the four March girls, each of them characterized with such memorable precision. The drama of *Little Women* is the small, unsensational drama of everyday living, of an acute and tender imagination touching with magic the plain story of four girls growing into womanhood.

For the contemporary reader, what is perhaps most striking about *Little Women,* even more archaic than its social scene, is its overt moral emphasis. This is a gay household and an entirely human one, where the parents have a deeply tolerant understanding of the foibles and follies of their four dissimilar daughters. But it is also a household where no possible occasion is missed for communicating the appropriate moral instruction. It is surely as much a reflection of the emotional robustness in which Louisa Alcott was reared as an evidence of her own liveliness of spirit that this appeal to conscience throughout *Little Women,* instead of clouding the story and detracting from its charm, is one of its most amiable attributes.

D. T.

8. *The Big Change*

by FREDERICK LEWIS ALLEN

The "big change" is what happened to the United States in the first half of the twentieth century—its growth in industrial and military power, from which international influence inevitably follows, as a good many Americans have reasons—sometimes unhappy reasons—to know. But even the people of this country are still not fully aware of the change, and arguments go on at home, as they do abroad, about conditions and problems which no longer exist.

The Big Change is lively and brief, but it is solid too; and to find any other book that can tell us so much about the contemporary United States would be difficult indeed. The discontents which preceded the first World War, as described in Hofstadter's *Age of Reform* (No. 149), are summarized to make way for the arrival of mass production, of which the reader can find a full description in *U.S.A.: The Permanent Revolution* (No. 119). Then came the Depression and the second World War, which are seen to be crises instrumental in building the America of today. Frederick Lewis Allen (1890-1954) was primarily a social historian; he gives color and texture to our memories of the past in helping us understand the present.

Allen's changed America is no longer isolationist, no longer afraid of its own government, no longer willing to admire ruthless power in business nor to honor wealth for its own sake. In art and literature there is self-confidence, at last. The social community has a richer interchange of personalities and nearly everyone shares in the community of culture. The story is true, even though Americans themselves can scarcely believe it.

L. B.

9. *Only Yesterday*

by FREDERICK LEWIS ALLEN

Yesterday in this case was the decade between 1919 and 1929; or, to put it in terms of events, between the demobilization of American soldiers after World War I and the great stock market crash which ended a dizzy, free period of speculation and social experiment. The period is still known in America as "the Twenties," and many look back upon it as a strangely blithe interlude, a happy breathing space, before the two decades of depression and war that followed. It is already a mythical time; and this book, published as early as 1931, suggests that it was so thought of even then. For Frederick Lewis Allen (1890-1954) expected his readers, sobered by two years of financial and spiritual retrenchment, already to have forgotten in many details what yesterday was like. Perhaps it is always true that the most recent history seems the most remote, but Allen could count upon its being particularly true at the instant of time when he composed his narrative out of yesterday's newspapers and magazines (he himself was the editor of *Harper's* magazine), and out of the memories he shared with other intelligent men.

The decade of his record was in a number of respects less happy than the myth has made it. A revolution in manners and morals did, to be sure, cut the country free from certain timidities which a long isolation from Europe had fastened upon it like a provincial code. And this change—some thought it was for the worse—was abetted by a literature that pronounced scornful judgment on a people not yet grown up, not yet a community of the modern world. The people responded with what may now seem an amusing alacrity; the growing pains, real at best, were at the worst grotesque. But other extravagances of the time are not so pleasant to remember: the Red scare, the Harding scandals, the illusions of permanent prosperity, and the violence attending Prohibition. Nevertheless it was a decade like no other in the history of America, and by common consent this is the most humane account of it yet given.

M. V. D.

10. *The American People and Foreign Policy*

by Gabriel A. Almond

American foreign policy is the "hottest" subject on any side of either ocean. It is all wrong and all right, too ridden by isolationism and insidiously influenced by internationalists; it is unequal to America's potentialities, neglectful of her responsibilities, vitiated by imperialism, ruined by moralism, ludicrous in its naive charity, and so ruthlessly selfish as to leave one gasping. The fault is that it is a partisan affair, a bi-partisan affair, at any rate an affair which—as a whole—has no partisans anywhere.

All this you may gather from the newspapers and the "high-placed spokesmen" of foreign governments whom the newspapers report. None of this publicized opinion is exactly disinterested, and few of its utterances rest on any solid investigation of facts and possibilities. Hence the interest of this book by Gabriel A. Almond (1911-). It has no ax to grind; it does not "believe" or propound any thesis. It tries to reproduce the living thoughts of those who ultimately condition American foreign policy, namely the American people.

For it is one of the difficult things about democracy that what the country does on the world scene is subject to daily scrutiny and daily interference by those who think to advance their irrelevant domestic interest by shouting denunciation or feigning alarm. "Open covenants openly arrived at" is a tenable slogan only in contradistinction to perpetual backstairs intrigue. As Thomas A. Bailey (No. 16) would also suggest, democracies have not yet devised the suitable routine of alternation—private negotiation and public discussion. But Mr. Almond shows how far one democracy, at least, has gone in solving this common problem by making self-aware and explicit the ups-and-downs of mood and action in America's dealings with foreign nations.

J. B.

11. *Winesburg, Ohio*

by SHERWOOD ANDERSON

"Never did he succeed in getting what he wanted out of life and he did not know what he wanted." This might have been said of most of the people in Winesburg, Ohio, and the equivalent of Winesburg anywhere else in the Middle West: Edgar Lee Masters's *Spoon River* (No. 205), Zenith of Sinclair Lewis's *Babbitt* (No. 184), the university town of Dorothy Canfield Fisher's *The Bent Twig* (No. 111), the stop-over towns of Theodore Dreiser's *Sister Carrie* (No. 101). Even Chicago, home of James T. Farrell's *Studs Lonigan* (No. 107), was not quite certainly a city at the beginning of the twentieth century, as New York was, or London. Winesburg was part town, part countryside, with no line drawn where the town ended and the farms began.

The whole of the Middle West was then at a moment of transition and, to some, dismay. The pioneers and immigrants from the Atlantic seaboard and Europe had known what they wanted. They wanted land, and now they had it. It was then that another kind of hunger began to gnaw. It began in the town, where work was not of necessity continuous, as it had been on the farm. The farmer's day had no beginning and no end, and anyone who was not working was loafing. In the town it was different. The town-dweller found no name for it in his farm vocabulary, but what he had was leisure, and leisure is a seedbed of discontent.

Winesburg, Ohio, published in 1919, is a history of discontents. No one in the town is completely anything. Talents remain untested, dreams remain dreams, and even the drunkard has his sober moments. And yet one gets the feeling that it will not always be so, that another frontier is opening, that out of the discontent something good will come, something is sure to happen. What happened was Sherwood Anderson (1876-1941).

J. A. R.

12. The Living Lincoln

edited by PAUL M. ANGLE *and* EARL SCHENCK MIERS

Selections from the writings of Abraham Lincoln (1809-1865) are all but innumerable, and none of them fails to be interesting for the simple reason that Lincoln himself never failed in any speech, letter, telegram, or memorandum to reveal the character by which he now is everywhere known (see Nos. 98 and 272). His style is a mystery because it is so plain and yet so pungent, so apparently colorless and yet so manifestly personal. It is never eccentric, and yet no sentence of Lincoln's can be mistaken for that of any other man. The explanation lies deep within the temperament and the intellect he had, and he had an abundance of both. The present editors have chosen their selections in the interest of making an autobiography appear, and indeed one does appear, just as a great deal of history appears; but it is singularly true of Lincoln's written words that no matter what their subject or intention may be they end up by becoming portions of the testament he was ever composing.

The shock of his assassination in April, 1865, just as the Civil War was won and the nature of his plans for peace had begun to be known, assisted a process of canonization which still in a sense goes on. He had been obscurely born; he had taught himself; he was strong and kind; he spoke in parables; and now that he had crushed his enemies he was about to forgive them. The legend thus created is not untrue; yet it simplifies a career which gains rather than loses by being better known. The strength of Lincoln was indeed prodigious; perhaps no other man could have won the difficult war he fought side by side not only with generals but with politicians and fanatics. But the gentleness of his last years had been slowly and painfully acquired. The Illinois lawyer and politician had once been proud rather than tolerant of his power, and the tone of his voice had even been harsh with an uncontrolled sarcasm. Nor can there be any doubt concerning his ambition; it was ever-present, like his political acumen. Nevertheless he emerges as one who deserves his legend: incalculably complex, predominantly humorous and good, and, in spite of his insistence that he was ordinary, unique among both men and statesmen.

M. V. D.

13. *The Promised Land*

by Mary Antin

Mary Antin (1881-1949) fell in love with America when she was young, even before she saw the Statue of Liberty and Ellis Island, and her love lasted throughout her life. If she should return now and read again *The Promised Land,* she might be saddened at what time has done to it. For the story of her early years in Russia—sad, forbidding, near-tragic when it was written—now reads like nothing worse than discomfort, and her America has changed.

Her father had preceded the family, but he never found his promised land and he was obliged to lodge them in a Boston slum. Poverty, however, was familiar and no great burden in America where "everything was free," as she had heard in Russia. It was true. Street lights, music, and education, "the one thing he had been able to promise." Her account of her second day in America, when a little girl from across the alley, a stranger, took her to school, has the quality of immediate experience. But education, for her, was not confined to school. Undeterred by a blizzard, she plowed her way to a railway station to meet a wise man, and returned home through the blizzard with the warm assurance "that it was possible to live without knowing everything."

Yet freedom exacted penalties. In the confusion of the new world many ties with the old grew lax or were broken. Parents became the pupils of their children in learning to be Americans. Mary Antin saw a "sad process of degeneration of home life" in other immigrant families, but consoled herself with the reflection that it was "part of the process of Americanization . . . an upheaval preceding the state of repose." But she could not find repose when she saw her sister deprived of "the precious rights of an American woman: a long girlhood, a free choice in marriage, and a brimful womanhood."

J. A. R.

14. *The Conqueror*

by GERTRUDE ATHERTON

The tide of American popular interest has turned away from Alexander Hamilton (1755-1804) in the past fifty years, while the reputation of Thomas Jefferson (1743-1826)—his lifelong opponent—has been growing. Such reversals often happen, of course, and public opinion often reverses itself again. Hamilton was the constructive genius of economic and technological America. Hamilton saw more clearly the coming American fact; Jefferson (see No. 166) felt more deeply the American dream.

This "dramatized biography" of Hamilton by Gertrude Atherton (1857-1948) was first published in 1905 and since then has been steadily popular, even though her portrait of Jefferson is unjust and her partisanship for her protagonist sometimes excessive. Hamilton's illegitimate birth, his precocity, his passionate energies, and his achievements in a life cut off by the ritual murder of a duel when he was only 49, make him a hero fit for romantic exaggerations. Nevertheless, Mrs. Atherton founded her fiction on years of careful research, and her imaginary conversations, though stiffened with what the author took to be an eighteenth-century idiom, are more convincing than most such fancies.

The Conqueror is also more useful, as a picture of a time and a career, than many equally interesting historical novels, because the author successfully undertook to recount the public events in her hero's life as well as the intimacies and the imagined personal crises. This was perhaps easier to accomplish with Hamilton than with many public men because he lived with such intensity. His best-known writing, the papers he contributed to *The Federalist* (No. 134), are lucid and powerful, but they do not convey much of the vivacity of his character. He loved and hated and fought in politics and in the courts like a champion on the battlefield. Historians—as, for example, Frank Thistlethwaite in *The Great Experiment* (No. 303) and Morison and Commager in *The Growth of the American Republic* (No. 225)—offer the reader more balanced views of the part Hamilton played in building the United States. But no sober biographer has yet done him justice, and anyone who wants to understand American history may well read—with caution—*The Conqueror*.

L. B.

15. Congress Makes a Law

The Story Behind the Employment Act of 1946

by Stephen K. Bailey

Stephen K. Bailey (1916-) is typical of the best of the young Americans currently studying and writing about politics. Political scientists of the present generation have reacted emphatically against the older assumption that political science is properly concerned with theoretical problems; instead they have tried to get at the raw material of politics, to turn over the fabric of political life and to look—not at the symmetrical surface pattern described by the traditional textbooks—but at the seamy side where people really live and political business is actually transacted. Political behavior that their predecessors would have censured, because it failed to conform to an ideology, they often find less blameworthy than it once seemed.

In this attempt they have been immensely helped (and sometimes led astray) by a variety of new methods, such as new interviewing and polling techniques and new aids to analysis, especially psychiatry and semantics. Mr. Bailey does not employ many of these new methods, since they are inapplicable to the subject, but he very successfully epitomizes the spirit of the new political science. His book examines, in great detail, the process by which the mishmash of aspiration, fear, special interest, and political fortune-hunting somehow work through the American Congress and emerge on the statute books.

Possibly, in seeking to show how it became law, Mr. Bailey does not sufficiently emphasize the importance of his example—the Employment Act of 1946. To be sure, continuing prosperity and high employment in the decade since the Act was passed have not provided a test of its efficacy as a device for dealing with an economic depression, but nonetheless it has already had considerable effect. Writing in 1955, Mr. Alan Sproul, then President of the New York Federal Reserve Bank, said that the Act is now "the main guide to public economic policy in the United States."

P. P.

16. *A Diplomatic History of the American People*

by Thomas A. Bailey

Thomas A. Bailey (1902-) of Stanford University has written a study of American diplomacy in an unusually lively style. With it he revives the atmosphere of the public pressures within which the statesmen who controlled our foreign affairs have thought and worked, and his judicious selection of contemporary cartoons and illuminating episodes emphasizes the role that public opinion has played in the formation of American policy since the earliest days of the republic.

During colonial times and the early days of the nation, relations with foreign governments were vital to the United States. But by 1815 territory as far west as the Rocky Mountains was safely settled and the remaining land seemed certain to become American when it was needed. Public attention turned to developing this internal empire and, as concern with international affairs diminished, the United States became generally committed to a policy of nonentanglement and isolation. However, from their involvement in two world conflicts, most Americans have since learned, in Woodrow Wilson's words, that "we are participants, whether we would or not, in the life of the world. What affects mankind is inevitably our affair as well as the affair of Europe and Asia."

A Diplomatic History of the American People, like the contemporary study by Gabriel Almond (No. 10), stresses the part played by the American people in shaping this change in foreign policy. Often the observer from other countries finds it difficult to understand how a Henry Wallace, a Senator McCarthy, or a Hearst newspaper can be so vocal and yet not speak for the American nation. Dr. Bailey points out that as long as the United States remains a democracy, such voices will be heard and politics will be involved in foreign affairs; but it is his view that "American public opinion in the long run determines basic foreign policies."

C. G.

17. The Eyes of Discovery

by JOHN BAKELESS

In 1943, when *The American Land* (No. 312) was published, its author lamented that "what America looked like when the earliest explorers and settlers first saw it is by no means clear from the meager records they left." Seven years later these industrious researches by John Bakeless (1894-) proved the complaint to have been unfounded.

In this study Mr. Bakeless has displayed the deductive ability of a detective, the conscience of a scholar, and the creative imagination of a poet. From the early drawings and manuscripts he has been able to consult, he has succeeded in re-creating the sense of wonder with which early explorers—Dutch, Spanish, French, and English—looked out upon the New World. He has employed the words of the explorers themselves wherever he finds them effective, complementing them with reports of later visitors; and he has used his own clear prose to present the conclusions he derives from various original materials.

It should be added that not least of the virtues of this book are Mr. Bakeless's biographies of the explorers themselves. The hundred years from the mid-sixteenth century to the mid-seventeenth was a period of amazing adventure. Too often its enthusiasms have been attributed to Elizabethan England alone, when actually able men of all nationalities felt the compelling urge to penetrate the unknown reaches of the world. Columbus, a Genoese, became an explorer for Spain (see No. 223); Henry Hudson and his literate first mate, Robert Juet, were Englishmen in the employ of the Dutch; Estebánico, a Moroccan slave, was considered to be exploring for Spain, though before his death he seems to have been more concerned with advantages to be obtained for himself. Mr. Bakeless has done much to re-create for his readers the spirit of this age of discovery.

C. C.

18. *Go Tell It on the Mountain*

by JAMES BALDWIN

In one of his other books the Negro writer James Baldwin (1924-) says: "I hazard that the King James Bible, the rhetoric of the store-front church, something ironic and violent and perpetually understated in Negro speech—and something of Dickens's love for bravura—have something to do with me today; but I wouldn't stake my life on it." He might safely stake his life on it, for it is all there.

The King James Bible, its rhythms, cadences, its symphony, is heard in the writing of nearly every Southerner, and James Baldwin—though born and reared in Harlem—is Southern, as Southern as William Faulkner (No. 108). To read *Go Tell It on the Mountain* without knowing the King James Bible is like reading *Paradise Lost* in the same ignorance. God is of the Old Testament, ominous, violent, and worst of all just, which makes more gentle His gentle Son when He lifts the sinner from the dust of the threshing floor.

The store-front church of Harlem is also Southern, its like to be found on every countryside. But there in the South the worshipper may be Negro or white, for—Baldwin again, in his *Notes of a Native Son*—"It must be remembered that the oppressed and the oppressor are bound together in the same society; they accept the same criterion, they share the same beliefs, and both alike depend on the same reality."

But in speech the Negro is different. He conducts his speech, knowing exactly when to signal for the trumpet or the drum. Elizabeth: "I got woodwork in the dining-room for you to do. And you going to do it, too, before you set foot out of *this* house." Roy: "You won't know your old woodwork when *I* get through." And later, Florence: "I reckon the Lord done give them *those* hearts—and, honey, the Lord don't give out no second helpings, *I'm* here to tell you."

Mr. Baldwin speaks elsewhere of a "necessary dimension" in a novel about Negroes, "this dimension being the relationship that Negroes bear to one another, that depth of involvement and unspoken recognition of shared experience which creates a way of life." Here, in one volume, is that way of life.

J. A. R.

19. *Writing on Life*

Sixteen Close-Ups

by LINCOLN BARNETT

In *Life* magazine, where most of these sketches originally appeared, the short biographical essay is called a "close-up." In the *New Yorker* magazine there is a similar institution called the "profile." Whatever name it is given, the form has now established itself as one of the features of American journalism.

All of Lincoln Barnett's (1909-) subjects are celebrities, that peculiar product of this century of mass communication. Some of them—actors, directors, song writers—are distinguished for their achievements in the popular arts; others of them are, or were, important figures in the news. It was Mr. Barnett's assignment to write about these men and women in such a way as to answer the question: What are these people *really* like apart from their public function?

Such an assignment has, of course, unbounded possibilities for psychological exploration. But the writer of a close-up has little space and time allotted him and must select from the vast material of biography only those elements which convey the dominant impression he receives in interviews and journalistic research. It is Mr. Barnett's recognition of the manifold limitations surrounding his assignments that prompts the short prefaces to the essays in this volume. But actually these introductory discussions add little to the enjoyment of the sketches themselves. In fact, the high literary seriousness with which the author would wish to invest his work has the perverse effect of calling attention to the deficiencies of his medium, rather than increasing the reader's respect for Mr. Barnett's own skillful practice of a difficult and interesting branch of journalism.

D. T.

20. *God's Country and Mine*

by Jacques Barzun

Jacques Barzun (1907-) subtitles his book: A Declaration of Love Spiced with a Few Harsh Words. That is a fair enough summary, though naturally it omits any indication that the declaration is continuously witty and winning.

The main problem in writing about the United States is not that of being interesting. The main problem is to say something that will still be true a few years or ten or fifty after the words are first set down. The United States has a way of confounding its commentators, not by disproving them, but by dating them. We know that de Tocqueville alone (No. 90) has met this test with an almost absolute triumph; and many admirers of Mr. Barzun will wager that, though his work is hardly on a de Tocquevillean scale, what it has to say will bear reflection for years to come.

Mr. Barzun's master is William James (No. 163). His is the Jamesian cheerful pragmatic gaze, concerned with what is actually *there* and what actually seems to be *working*. He likes the United States because it is a pluralistic universe, in continuous process of change, open-ended, open-handed, crammed with choices, many of them silly, many of them noble. He is not fooled by the European café-society denigration of the American culture; he is too good a European for that. Nor does he assume that the good life has reached its fulfillment here; he is too good an American for that. He is balanced without being a compromiser; and, though amiably merciless in seeking out weaknesses, he keeps always in mind that many of them are the ubiquitous weaknesses of twentieth-century industrial man.

Whether he touches on baseball or advertising, Kinsey or children, doctors or intellectuals, the pressure of the machine or the deification of teamwork, our popular culture (which he thinks Germanic) or our highbrow culture (which he thinks French), he is always sane, humane, and never limited by the blinders of conventional judgment. What gives his book its wonderful quality of *lift* is his central conviction that "the man of ideas is rising among us as a power: that is why he is being attacked." As an intellectual's graceful but never superficial survey of mid-century America, this book may be recommended virtually without qualification.

C. F.

21. *Music in American Life*

by Jacques Barzun

In addition to the information it assembles so entertainingly, the mere fact of this book's existence tells much about the state of America's musical culture (see also No. 58). There is no better evidence of the cultural revolution Jacques Barzun (1907-) describes than the fact that a report written by the dean of the graduate faculties of a great university, for the Committee on Musicology of the American Council of Learned Societies, gives attentive and thoughtful consideration to juke boxes, jazz (compare Nos. 147 and 282), and the economics and aesthetics of phonograph recording, as well as to concert programs, musical education, and the principles of music criticism.

The recent "democratic and secular spread of music" which Mr. Barzun celebrates has been paralleled, of course, by the democratization and secularization of the whole idea of culture. "High culture" and "popular culture" now cross-fertilize one another as never before, and American intellectuals no longer draw an impassable line between them. (The reader might consult here the books of Miss Constance Rourke [No. 269], David Riesman [No. 259], and Lyman Bryson [No. 43].)

At the outset, Mr. Barzun suggests that America's growing appetite for music is in part a reaction against the machine, "an expression of widespread dislike for our own times, for work as we know it under technology." A similar explanation of the rise of summer camps is given in Morgan's *Summer's Children* (No. 222), and the anti-machine attitude is frequently expressed in much American fiction and poetry. But Barzun is aware of the irony in this observation; for, as he repeatedly stresses, the spread of musical culture has been directly (and not necessarily unhappily) dependent upon the technology against which it is in part a protest. As he effectively shows, "the disc, the film, and the vacuum tube" have made music portable and cheap, have improved musical technique and the judgment of it, have spread the demand for the "average" musical product, and have "opened the way to the diffusion of every kind of product," the best as well as the worst. For the reaction to the American musical scene of three composers, Aaron Copland, Charles Ives, and Harry Partch, consult Nos. 69, 71, and 243.

J. A. K.

22. *The American Faith*

by ERNEST SUTHERLAND BATES

When we are tempted to think of modern America as a place where conformity and standardization produce a desperate monotony, we must suspect ourselves of generalizing from insufficient data or superficial appearances. For the conspicuous fact about America since the landing of the Pilgrims in 1620 has been its ability to accept the most variegated collection of peoples since the Roman Empire, and to harmonize their passions and aggressions more or less peacefully, without changing the creeds or tastes or missions that propelled them to these shores.

Religion, as the most inclusive of the passions, continues to divide Americans into hundreds of sects without as yet splitting their national unity. The religions developed in the United States or transplanted to it are in fact so numerous that to deal with them all in one volume would produce merely a catalogue. Ernest Sutherland Bates (1879-1939) has consequently had to select and combine in order to give an idea of the main currents of American religious thought and feeling. His book gives merely a sampling, although one of great diversity.

In subdivision there is strength. From coast to coast may be seen churches of innumerable denominations boasting new recruits or announcing by a sign for the passing motorist: "Revival Now Going On." The older and larger churches remain solid but testify to the peculiar character of American religiousness by engaging in many "interfaith" activities, and a successful preacher like Harry Emerson Fosdick (No. 121) in a sense rises above denomination. Indeed this has gone so far that some persons of simple mind and strong faith have seen in the American cooperation of Protestants, Catholics, and Jews the "solution" to all the world's religious problems.

On the other hand, religious innovations continue to flourish in an atmosphere in which they are regarded as a right. Not long ago, a Mohammedan delegate to the United Nations in New York indignantly complained through the columns of a newspaper that the city had no mosque. And on the West coast, cults rise and fall in the freedom of the open spaces and the invigoration of the climate. Hindu theologies captivate notable exiles from Europe such as Aldous Huxley and Gerald Heard, while in reverse motion Billy Graham enthralls the English multitudes. It is against this background that one should read the sober scholarly treatment of the American faith by Mr. Bates as well as the satirical-realistic extravaganza of Sinclair Lewis's *Elmer Gantry* (No. 185).

J. B.

23. *New Art in America*

20th Century Painting, U.S.A.

edited by JOHN I. H. BAUR

Painting in America since the turn of the century has been characterized more by search than by discovery. There have been valiant efforts to discover new aesthetic truths, new ways of interpreting the American scene, new manners of coping with the relationship of visual experience to abstract design. There have been attempts to interpret the machine in our civilization, to achieve "social realism," to promote regionalism, to delineate the poetry or cruelty of cities and the cruelty and poetry of the landscape. There has been tremendous individuality, but there has not been the kind of originality of vision that could carry the influence of American art beyond its own borders.

The American art world has been in a constant state of revolt. In the early part of the century it was a revolt against the official academicism of the last century that led to the establishment of a school of social realists (Sloan, Glackens, and Prendergast). The Armory Show of 1913 (see Oliver W. Larkin, *Art and Life in America* [No. 180]) introduced the School of Paris to most American painters for the first time, and the revolt took a new direction into expressionism and abstraction (Dove, Hartley, Marin, Stella, Demuth). In the 1920's and '30's a different kind of social realism evolved, this time with political or regional overtones. And since the second World War the attempt to cope head-on with the problems of symbolism and abstraction has absorbed the attention of many of the most promising young American painters, so that today there is a revolt brewing among those who believe that abstractionism has become a new "academy." The atmosphere of revolt, of search and probing, has produced a half-century of extremely lively and vital painting; it has opened vistas yet to be explored; but it has not, on the whole, produced a school of painters whose influence is likely to be international. The paintings here reproduced are an American expression, considerably influenced by European aesthetic doctrines, of an era of boiling change, social conflict, and growth.

John I. H. Baur (1909-) has ably described in his three introductory chapters the nature of this changing artistic scene and the main artistic movements of the past half-century in America.

R. L.

24. *Revolution and Tradition in Modern American Art*

by John I. H. Baur

The title of John I. H. Baur's (1909-) book is to be taken more literally than most of its kind, which are likely to use "revolution" and "tradition" in a loose way to catch the eye rather than fill it with light. The author begins his story with the great overturn in the visual arts of 50 years ago, and shows how much more profound the upheaval was in the United States than elsewhere, because of our conservatism and unpreparedness for novelty. The New York Armory Show of 1913—which injected the French Fauves, Cubists, and Post-Impressionists into the mass of 1,200 American works—was a decisive event. Since then, American art (see also No. 256) has been cosmopolitan, and as such has shown the multiplicity of crosscurrents in evidence throughout the world.

After a period of feverish emulation came the reaction of the 1930's and '40's against a vaguely defined modernism. The theories of reaction—partly social, partly intellectual—are of interest as disclosing the ceaseless cultural ferment in this country and the reality of its influence on a host of painters and sculptors. Whatever may be said of their work, individually or as a whole, it cannot be denied that they have been, day in and day out, in the thick of the battle. By way of contrast and illumination, Mr. Baur winds up with a flashback to the American tradition of romantic realism and to the less firmly rooted Impressionism, both of which were dethroned by the revolutionists of the early twentieth century.

To say all this is to say that Mr. Baur is an excellent historian: his milieu is always well-drawn and unfailingly apposite. But he is also and pre-eminently a judicious critic, who can separate wheat from chaff in aesthetic theories, as well as characterize form, manner, and animus in painted or sculptured work. His possession of an eye is attested not only in words but also in the choosing of his two hundred illustrations.

J. B.

25. *The American Spirit*

by CHARLES A. BEARD *and* MARY R. BEARD

Charles A. Beard (1874-1948) was the most continuously interesting intelligence at work in the field of American history throughout the years of his long lifetime. Upon some occasions he succeeded in producing a change in the traditional interpretation of one or another of the great episodes in our past. On other occasions he investigated areas of great but overlooked significance. And with his wife, Mary R. Beard, he wrote a series of large volumes that, taken together, provide one of the most illuminating interpretations of our total national experience from the beginning to the present.

Part of his intellectual strength derived from the massive learning he had at his disposal. Part derived also from his willingness to peer beneath the myths and slogans that float to the surface of any nation's history. A large part, too, derived from the fact that he had all his life a central unwavering position which gave his historical activity added purpose. These things are revealed in this book—which is, as the title page says, a study of the idea of civilization in the United States. Using the text supplied by citizens from the earliest days of the republic to the present, the authors describe both the content of the American spirit and the process by which the content was put together through the years.

In the course of this account, the central intellectual position of Charles Beard betrays itself in sardonic asides, wry humor, and—from time to time—direct assertions. It was his assumption that the American spirit not only was a peculiar product of our national experience, unexportable in pure form —which is true—but also that this spirit could not be safely joined with what he called conceptions of Western or world civilization. In other words, in the constant debate among ourselves on the question as to whether the country can still retain a distinctive individuality while operating as an effective member of the larger community of nations, the Beards appear for the negative. In time, this attitude—so persistently held by too many Americans for whom Charles Beard, with all his great gifts, was an eloquent spokesman—may seem less a part of the enduring American spirit than itself a passage from an American dream.

E. E. M.

26. *The Declaration of Independence*

by CARL BECKER

The manifesto by which the American colonists announced to the world that they had separated from Britain and in which they gave their reasons, associated a philosophy of government with the founding of a nation. The nation has become a success, or at least a great power, beyond the possible dreams of the colonists of 1776. Does it still live politically by the eighteenth-century doctrines of natural rights? This essay by Carl Becker (1875-1945) contains a detailed examination of the text of the Declaration, which is necessary if one is to understand it as a political document. But most of his book is given to analysis of Thomas Jefferson's thinking, taking him as a typical liberal of the eighteenth century, and to a discussion of the subsequent fate of the doctrines. One is led to ask whether or not the strength of a nation is in any essential way dependent on its political philosophy—and then, more searchingly, to ask what happens to its spirit when its faith is eroded by events.

The people of the United States have kept in working order the principle which is to them most important; they maintain a government which exists by the consent of the governed. In fact, there is much wider suffrage now than in 1776; no race, no dispossessed persons, no sex, no partisans are legally excluded from the vote. The reasons may be more utilitarian than philosophic, but the fact remains. The principle was not conserved, however, without a struggle. The Americans have had to live through a revulsion against revolutionary ideas, influenced partly by immigrant scholars and immigrant notions. They have had to absorb the South's defense of slavery and withstand the coercions of a growing industrialism. Changes in political doctrines can be traced in Hofstadter's *The American Political Tradition* (No. 150), and the working of the slavery argument is described in Cash's *The Mind of the South* (No. 51).

Becker was the finest stylist among modern American historical writers, himself a true man of the Enlightenment, with a cool and elegant temper. He was also a steady believer in the ultimate America, though he would not undertake to prophesy its final shape.

L. B.

27. *Looking Backward, 2000-1887*

by EDWARD BELLAMY

The three decades that followed the American Civil War were distinguished by rapid industrial development. Men flowed off the farms and crowded into the cities where the mills were built. In the competition for the steadily enlarging markets new, sharp practices replaced the older, more humane procedures. Money and power were unduly concentrated in the hands of a few who felt responsible only for the survival and welfare of their own industrial enterprises.

The dislocations in the social structure, the distortions in the schemes of value introduced by the accelerating industrial process, disturbed or angered many members of society. Some merely assailed the existing conditions; others sought to offer new solutions. In *Looking Backward,* Edward Bellamy (1850-1898) tried "to reason out a method of economic organization" that would guarantee to each citizen "a livelihood and material welfare on a basis of equality corresponding to and supplanting" his political equality. His hero falls asleep in 1887 and awakens in 2000 to find himself in a commonwealth, a socialist state. Guided by an attractive young woman he sees everywhere cheerful, decent citizens sustained by goods and services distributed by the government.

It is Bellamy's skill as a novelist, no doubt, that largely accounts for his book's popularity. But the fact that over a million copies have been sold and that the work continues in print may be ascribed in some part to his concern, seventy years ago, with problems that still perplex any people engaged in the satisfactory ordering of the industrial process. And, in these pages, he was not content to believe that the equitable distribution of goods in quantity—the automatic washing machine in every kitchen, the car in every garage—would in itself prove a satisfying end. He spoke for many of his countrymen, now as then, in suggesting that the products of the industrial energy intelligently organized could be used as a device for obtaining a nobler future by eliminating, as he said, "the consequences of 'Man's inhumanity to man.'"

E. E. M.

28. *Patterns of Culture*

by Ruth Benedict

Probably no other book will serve better as an introduction to this collection of American books than *Patterns of Culture,* by Ruth Benedict (1887-1948). It provides a framework in which to view any strange society as a working entity. As Dr. Benedict points out, all societies rest upon certain assumptions about what is worth having and doing and being in life, and those assumptions shape any particular culture, from its way of disciplining its children (if it does discipline its children) to its way of waging war (if it wages war). These assumptions are not universal, however, and therefore societies differ.

Of course, the assumptions underlying primitive societies such as the ones Dr. Benedict describes have a simplicity and above all a coherence that cannot be found in American society, which incorporates all kinds of people from all over the world, many of whom have brought with them their own ideas about what society ought to be. Besides, American society has come into being in recent historical time; it is self-conscious in a sense that the societies here described are not, because it has consciously chosen, and indeed is still choosing, many of the principles on which it rests. Nevertheless, *Patterns of Culture* provides admirable practice in the kind of imaginative broadjumping that it takes to get from one culture to another.

The book is also a good starting point because it represents a way of thinking that has recently exercised a powerful influence on how Americans themselves look at other people. As Americans have found themselves in a position of world leadership, they have made a valiant if not always successful attempt to see the world from points of view other than their own, and books on cultural anthropology like this have been one of their chief aids. No work of scholarship published in America in recent years has sold as many copies as *Patterns of Culture*. In one large college it was chosen "book of the year" and all the students and faculty members read and discussed it. Some moralists have deplored the book as advocating cultural relativism; on the other hand it could be said that the history of the United States has been such as to require a considerable amount of cultural relativism on the part of its people.

P. P.

29. *John Brown's Body*

by STEPHEN VINCENT BENÉT

When *John Brown's Body* appeared in 1928 it was hailed as an American epic, and it was indeed the first narrative in verse to seize upon the greatest epic theme in our history (the American Civil War) and develop it with distinguished skill.

Back of Stephen Vincent Benét's (1898-1943) accomplishment lay a movement in American literature, from the 1890's on, to find more individual forms in prose and verse and to express more fully the national character. Through the poetic "renaissance" beginning in 1913, poets especially, Carl Sandburg (No. 273) and Edgar Lee Masters (No. 205) among them, had revealed the richness of American folk material and carried forward the liberation of American language which began with Walt Whitman (No. 333). Benét drew much from these forerunners and from the general sense of national maturity that was intensified by World War I. But his own experience as an Army officer's son—who in boyhood had known the South, the Far West, and the East—had given him a sense of the whole land and its quality.

Benét had early become a skilled writer of verse, publishing his first volume when he was only seventeen, about the time he entered Yale University. *John Brown's Body* was not in fact an epic—one critic justly termed it "a loose episodic narrative." In part its character grew from the plan Benét adopted, for he interwove stories of imagined characters, northern and southern, with an account of the war—its causes, personalities, and battles. Never a pioneer in poetic form like Pound or Eliot, he was a highly facile craftsman and assimilated what he found useful in earlier creators, turning to rhyme, free verse, ballad forms, and standard "blank verse" as he felt these appropriate. The result is an informality of style at times almost glib, but usually arresting because of flashing turns of phrase and a sure adaptation to the poem's theme. Benét's fiction is appealing but thin, his history authoritative and revealing. He deals impressively with such heroes as Lee, Lincoln, Stonewall Jackson, and Grant, and his account of the Battle of Gettysburg moves with sweep and power. Benét shows throughout his personal sense of the meaning of this war which divided the nation but steeled it for mature growth, as the reader will find in the concluding stanzas, which begin, "Out of John Brown's strong sinews the tall skyscrapers grow. . . ."

F. E. H.

30. *The Dramatic Event*

by Eric Bentley

Eric Bentley (1916-) once wrote a book called *The Playwright as Thinker*. He could himself be described by the parallel formula: the dramatic critic as thinker. For unlike most dramatic critics, Mr. Bentley unites general knowledge and wide reading to the normal equipment of special interest in the theater and technical information about it. This is why he has rapidly risen to the head of his profession in the United States. Born in England but now a naturalized American citizen, Bentley is at once dramatic critic for the political and literary weekly *The New Republic* and professor of dramatic literature at Columbia University. In the present volume are collected the best of his reviews of recent Broadway plays—the genre he himself anthologizes in No. 31.

In general, the application of ideas to the theater is resented by everybody—at least until playwright, actors, and audience are all dead, by which time academic treatment is accorded the few plays that survive. But Eric Bentley's mode of applying ideas to the living subject is very hard to shrug off. In the first place he uses ideas, not ideology; in the second, he speaks as a man of the trade, for he has directed plays in half a dozen countries and languages, so that his ideas *fit*. Lastly, he can cite proofs or examples from an immense repertory, thus disposing of the common excuse of "unpractical" to refute critical objections. If one adds that having lived in the East, the South, the Northwest, and the State of California, Mr. Bentley knows his America, it becomes clear that his social and cultural approach to the modern American theater is both instructive and of lasting significance.

J. B.

31. *From the American Drama*

edited by ERIC BENTLEY

As English comedy was firmly centered in the drawing room, so American comedy—at the time of the first two plays in this volume—was centered, less firmly, in the society column of the newspaper. Those whom Alexander Hamilton, making an equation, had called the "rich and well-born," might expect to find their names recorded there; but no actress, and that is the special seasoning of "Captain Jinks of the Horse Marines." The first-nighters were early assured that the captain, while for the moment out of funds, would after trivial vicissitudes get money and get his girl. What kept them on edge was how he would also, overcoming the dowager, get her into Society. The characters of "The New York Idea" were already in, and for good measure in *two* drawing rooms. Besides that doubling the only difference from English comedy was, in anticipation of Hollywood, the jolly treatment of divorce. Philip Barry's "Paris Bound," to be found in *Representative American Plays* (No. 253), is nearer home ground.

Thornton Wilder's "Our Town" (in *Sixteen Famous American Plays,* No. 284) and the Wilder play here included are pure American. The break with tradition is clean. First-nighters at a Thornton Wilder play never know what to expect, except a leaping imagination. There is no end to the play, no curtain. Rather, the imagination of the playwright has become the experience of the playgoer, and the people on the stage are his people. He knows them better than he knows his neighbors, better than he knows anyone, and they are not soon forgotten.

Eric Bentley (1916-) in quest of a word for his discernment of a similarity between Thornton Wilder and William Saroyan, winds up at the end of the alphabet with "zany." Perhaps. To some, Saroyan's work is surrealism with a strong infusion of sentimentality. The uncommitted reader will find another play of Saroyan's, "The Time of Your Life," in *Sixteen Famous American Plays* (No. 284), and in *Critics' Choice* (No. 78).

"Captain Jinks" now reads like a libretto, "Guys and Dolls" like a play. There are other differences. When Lieutenant Brannigan says, "Well! Well! An interesting gathering indeed. The cream of society," he is echoing the old society column. Nor do the newspapers now speak of "social climbing." That term has been subsumed under the sociologists' "social mobility," which still means "up," even for guys and dolls.

J. A. R.

32. *An Artist in America*

by THOMAS HART BENTON

In two books on this shelf, Henry Nash Smith's *Virgin Land* (No. 287) and John F. Kennedy's *Profiles in Courage* (No. 172), there are chapters about Thomas Hart Benton (1782-1858), the Missouri senator whose great-nephew and namesake (1889-) wrote this autobiography. Those chapters are worth reading as an introduction to the brand of Jeffersonian democracy which finds contemporary expression in the painter's work and in his writing—neither of which is "polite," both of which have a certain truculent vitality and swinging rhythm. The nineteenth-century senator's devotion to the West and South, and his distrust of the Atlantic seaboard's deference to Europe, are echoed in the twentieth-century artist's "Farewell to New York." Notice, too, that the "America" of the artist's autobiography, for all its hearty inclusiveness, does not contain New England—a region which some Americans think of as peculiarly an artist's province.

The reader who gets caught up in the restless movement of Benton's narrative (the verbal equivalent of the restless, syncopated curves of his drawings and paintings) will savor a good deal of the creative energy which was released, paradoxically enough, by the Great Depression of the 1930's. The regional movement in the arts, in which Benton and his friends John Steuart Curry and Grant Wood were significant figures, was a part of a visual rediscovery of America which is described (in somewhat unfriendly perspective) in Oliver Larkin's *Art and Life in America* (No. 180).

Benton tells us that his forbears were "an individualistic and cocksure" people who "nursed their idiosyncrasies and took no advice." The reader may suspect Benton, to the extent that he is not seeing them in his own image, of being molded in theirs. But his idiosyncratic and argumentative streak, as well as his appetite for the everyday actualities of American life, link him to many another American artist. Among the older painters, one thinks of John Sloan (No. 41); among the architects, Frank Lloyd Wright (No. 347); and among musicians, Harry Partch (No. 243).

J. A. K.

33. The 20th Century Capitalist Revolution

by ADOLF A. BERLE, JR.

It is often said by visitors who get a firsthand impression of capitalism in America that it is not much like the capitalism familiarly found in the political myths of the modern world. It differs substantially from the evil and oppressive system described in classical Marxist doctrine, and even among Americans there is vigorous dispute as to its true nature. Adolf Berle (1895-)—who is lawyer, economist, diplomat, and an original member of F. D. Roosevelt's "brain trust"—has previously published a number of studies which show the extent to which our productive energies are massed under the control of a few great stock companies. But, as he has watched the development of industrial power, Mr. Berle has concluded that while the corporations will continue to grow they have taken on—this was unexpected—a social role, one which will compel them to develop a social conscience. The decisions of their managers will be major factors in deciding what kind of community their workers will live in and indeed what kind of country we shall all live in together.

Mr. Berle was not among those who attended the Corning Conference reported in Eugene Staley's *Creating an Industrial Civilization* (No. 288) but he assumes, as did the Corning delegates, that an industrial civilization can work toward the good life. He assumes also, with much more confidence than most students of our economic life have as yet attained, that managers of corporations will have to carry a heavy moral burden in this achievement.

However, there will be no single monolithic ideology precipitated out of the thinking of executives and directors and no "central group which proclaims orthodox doctrine and punishes deviation." In any case, American business corporations are now giving more and more generously to the budgets of the universities. If there is a preventive against mass conformity, it is free thought; and corporations are now helping to endow this freedom. The business leaders will not create the philosophical and spiritual ideas of the America of tomorrow, but Mr. Berle believes they will have much to do with putting those ideas into effect.

L. B.

34. *The Collected Writings of Ambrose Bierce*

In the Midst of Life, like Theodore Dreiser's *Sister Carrie* (No. 101), was bound to meet hostile rejection. The American reader was not ready at the turn of the century to see things that way, preferring to judge every human act as dead right or dead wrong and the actor as good or bad. Elvira Barwell was a bad woman whom one did not care to meet, even in print, in spite of her satisfactory end, while Carrie was worse, being a success. War, any war, was still a glorious enterprise and every soldier a hero. Nobody was willing to see a raw recruit shoot his own father.

But in spite—if not because—of his rejection, Ambrose Bierce (1842-1914?) had a following that became a cult. By them, whatever he wrote was praised—on the general ground that he wrote superbly, on the specific one that he wrote on the West Coast and did not write in the effete East. The result was complete insulation from competent criticism and from companionship; for, by all accounts, including their own, he despised his idolators. Being therefore irresponsible, he spread himself thin. The collected works, printed in his lifetime, ran to twelve volumes, here mercifully reduced to one. H. L. Mencken suggested that this prodigality was an old man's bid for a hearing, but it may have been because he was unsure of himself. He did not think that he was a realist, nor a humorist, humor being "tolerant and sympathetic." As to wit, there is no question. In the midst of much that is cheap and shoddy, there are moments of brilliance. And as to his misanthropy there is no question, either. His definition of "man" might have been written by Mark Twain, or Ring Lardner, or James Thurber—after a bad night.

He could have been a new kind of lexicographer, for no American writer has had a keener ear for the latent meanings of words. For example, "commendation, *n.* The tribute that we pay to achievements that resemble, but do not equal, our own." He can also restore to a journalistic cliché its original lustre. In its setting "an act which made a deep impression on me at the time" fairly jumps off the page.

J. A. R.

35. *The Fireside Book of Favorite American Songs*

edited by MARGARET BRADFORD BONI

The songs Americans sing when they are relaxed—around a campfire with a guitar, or in a friendly house with a piano, or perhaps in a bus or on a train with no accompaniment at all—are of many kinds, just as they come from many sources. There will always be one man or woman, young or old, who knows more words and tunes than the rest; but he will not sing alone, for most of his companions will in time remember more than they had thought they could. Perhaps no person in the world is totally ignorant of the songs sung in his country.

In the United States these may be British in origin, or French, or German, or something else; they may be secular, they may be religious, they may be of some ancient folk not readily identified, they may be products of vaudeville or burlesque, or of that strictly commercial center in New York which is known as Tin Pan Alley. Yet all of them together add up to something national—a truly popular possession, familiar in every section of a country which on its surface bears few signs of uniformity or rule.

The 131 songs in this collection represent remarkably well the range of melody and theme which any study will reveal. Whenever they are known, the names of composers and authors are duly recorded; but with one exception—Stephen Foster—such names are rarely remarked by those who do the singing. The tribute is to the sentimental or the witty words, to the nimble or the dolorous air, rather than to the brains that once invented them. It is enough to be conscious that a certain song is a Negro "spiritual," or a cowboy lament, or a music-hall pleasantry, or a remembrance of home, or a ballad, or a satire, or a celebration of some river, some desert, some plantation where the singer perhaps has never been. Nor does the antiquity of any piece concern him; he may not know whether it is genuinely old or whether it is pretending to be so; if it sounds old, and the tune is irresistible, he sheds his own time like a shoe and participates in the one eternity he will ever experience.

M. V. D.

36. *The Genius of American Politics*

by Daniel J. Boorstin

One of the important questions Daniel J. Boorstin (1914-) poses in this book is, to put it too simply: Why does a twentieth-century American politician who wants his country to isolate itself from the outer world find it useful and necessary to invoke the support of George Washington's views as stated in his Farewell Address at the end of the eighteenth century? Certainly one of the most entertaining, and to others doubtless puzzling, things about the national character—so uneasy in the presence of theory and metaphysics—is its continuing need to place its contemporary "know-how" within the sanction of a larger scheme hallowed by history and tradition. Americans have beguiled themselves with the idea that their democracy rests upon a permanent doctrine, forever fixed some two hundred years ago, conformity to which is the first rule of survival. Fortunately, as Mr. Boorstin points out, this rapidly evolving society has been saved from the disastrous effects of this misconception by reinterpreting the doctrine, often unconsciously, to meet modern contingencies.

This is only one of the paradoxes caused by the collision between appearance and reality which Mr. Boorstin seeks to examine in this lively book. He throws out many ideas and generalizations that put particular aspects of the national character in different perspectives from those in which they have traditionally been perceived. Some of his conclusions are not wholly novel and others are not wholly convincing, but this is no great matter. The book has two excellent specific points to make. First, despite the absence of a logical method or any theoretical system, there is in American society an impressive continuity. Second (compare the Beards [No. 25]), American democracy is the product of a particular national experience evolving within a particular set of conditions and seeking to meet peculiar needs; it will not do to make the building of precisely this Jerusalem in others' green and pleasant lands an object of our policy.

E. E. M.

37. *Sidewalks of America*

edited by B. A. Botkin

Folklore grows wherever people choose to entertain themselves rather than be entertained. While city people, not so dependent on self-amusement as country folk, do not create so many legends and tales, even in such crowded towns as New York there have been ghost stories, songs of factory workers, fanciful characters—Paul Bunyans of the city streets. B. A. Botkin (1901-) has assembled, in *Sidewalks of America,* a vast potpourri of urban Americana, subtitled "Folklore, Legends, Sagas, Traditions, Customs, Songs, Stories and Sayings of City Folk." By creatively interpreting this diverse material on the theme of the city's impact on the American folk imagination, Mr. Botkin has given us, in his own words, "the mood of the city—as well as . . . a documented portrait of the city in the national picture."

The city presumes the survival of the fittest, and the folklore of its people is no exception. Individuals, songs, narratives, even jokes, must have especially compelling qualities to achieve any permanence or attract general attention in cities where the population is always changing and where even major eccentricities and unique events are sometimes ignored. In the country or a small town there may be but one "character" to delight the community; in a city such a man has many and strong competitors.

With materials that include the calls of street vendors in early New York and the advertising lingo of modern Madison Avenue, the ghost tales of the White House and the legends of Chicago gunmen, the lusty birth cries of the labor movement and the effete titter of high society, the gambling halls of the early West and the tall tales of the Hollywood tribe, the early jazz of New Orleans streets and the "bop" of Broadway, Mr. Botkin has fashioned a variegated pattern. Its diversity can be attributed to locale (coastal, river, farmland, and mountain cities; mining, factory, and trading centers), to rivalries and differences (between "hick" and "city slicker," between the flux of new immigrants and the static old guard, between the civic prides of competing cities), but most of all to the racial and national groupings, to the occupations, and to the struggles and accomplishments of the vast populations that inhabit American cities.

C. C.

38. *A Treasury of American Folklore*

edited by B. A. Botkin

The late Stephen Vincent Benét, author of many stories based on American folklore, once wrote: "It's always seemed to me that legends and yarns and folk tales are as much a part of the real history of a country as proclamations and provisos and constitutional amendments. The legends and yarns get down to the roots of the people. . . . You can explain America in terms of formal history; and can also explain it in terms of Rip van Winkle and Paul Bunyan, of Casey Jones and Davy Crockett." In this book, B. A. Botkin (1901-) has assembled a rich, colorful, and comprehensive collection of such lore, providing significant material for a broad reappraisal of the social background of the American people.

Here—in ballad and legend, tall tale and jest, ghost story and play rhyme—is the unconscious artistry of numberless, nameless men and women who have been moved to expression by creative impulses as old as the history of local human habitation. "Art," said the English stylist, George Moore, "begins in the irresponsible imaginations of the people." Native imaginings, which we know as "folklore," have their sources in the landscape, the migrations, the work, the play, the daily happenings of the people's lives; and in Mr. Botkin's panoramic anthology can be found the ever-flowing, every-changing springs of the folk fancy in America.

Knowledge of the folk tradition of a nation is knowledge of the creative workings of the minds of its communities. It is a key to their values. Wherever men plant and harvest that they may live, legends and yarns and songs spring up as an extra crop. At this elemental level of life men of all nations cannot fail to recognize their potential brotherhood. When they can find that their minds and hearts have woven similar patterns from mutual experiences, they will know that they understand one another. *A Treasury of American Folklore* provides, in addition to pure entertainment, an auspicious opportunity for such understanding.

C. C.

39. *The Tragic Era*

The Revolution After Lincoln

by CLAUDE G. BOWERS

This is the story of how the people of the United States, after the Civil War was over, tried to put the pieces of the country together again. It is, unhappily, a story which anyone who wishes to understand the American nation today should read. Things were done and left undone in the years from 1865 to 1877, in what Claude Bowers (1878-) calls the tragic era, that still profoundly influence the attitudes of Americans toward one another.

It was not a simple problem that confronted the nation at the end of the war. There was first the question of when and under what terms "the erring sisters," as Lincoln called them, should return to the Union. There was further the question of how the Negro emerging from bondage could most easily be assimilated by the society. The country was in no condition to think reasonably about either of these matters. The executive branch of the government had been tossed into confusion by the assassination of Abraham Lincoln and the elevation of Andrew Johnson—a confusion not greatly reduced by the subsequent election of U. S. Grant, who remained in office until 1877. In Congress the controlling (Republican) party was divided between the forces of forgiveness and the forces of vengeance, a division that reflected the mixed emotions of the citizens in the North. In the South there were the tangled feelings of anger and despair that attend any defeat of a people.

In such an environment it would be difficult to supply quick and satisfying solutions for the problems. In the event, it proved impossible. Things happened—the impeachment of a President, the military occupation of the defeated section, government by carpet bag, and terror by the Ku Klux Klan—that were in no way attempts to shape constructive policy. They were instead, as Bowers says, "desperate enterprises, by daring and unscrupulous men." Not until the passions aroused by four years of Civil War had been gradually discharged through twelve years of uneasy truce was it possible to reconstitute the political union, and the union of sectional feelings was still further delayed. An account of these years, says the author, a former Ambassador to the Spanish Republic and biographer of Thomas Jefferson and Andrew Jackson, contains "lessons that are well worth pondering." He examines these lessons somewhat more in sorrow than in anger, and with such lightness of touch as the record permits.

E. E. M.

40. *The American Character*

by D. W. Brogan

It would take a fairly spacious room to house all the stupid and misinformed books that visitors from overseas have written about America. It would take another room at least as large to house books from the same source in which ignorance is abetted by malice, or information is distorted by spite and preconception. Yet, for all this dross (much of it amusing), probably no nation has been better served by its foreign observers than the United States. The unsurpassed observations of American society by the Frenchman Alexis de Tocqueville (No. 90) are today, more than a century after their publication, not only more widely read, quoted, and admired than ever before; they seem also more pertinent. The Swiss Siegfried Giedion's analysis of our technology (No. 128) and the Swede Gunnar Myrdal's analysis of our race problem (No. 230) are only two of the many specialized studies in which the fresh observation of the outsider has stripped away for Americans the camouflage of custom.

D. W. Brogan (1900-), Professor of Political Science and Fellow of Peterhouse, Cambridge, stands in the very front rank of our contemporary observers from abroad. His knowledge of everything American is so enormous that even Americans who think they know something of their own country are tripped up by his amazing range of allusion; he is acutely discerning yet intensely sympathetic, with wit to point his criticism and charm to rob it of its sting. Not that all Americans would agree with everything Brogan says. He is himself so devoted a student of the Civil War that he probably exaggerates its significance for living Americans. His remarks on American love of talk should be balanced with some mention of American reticence and inarticulateness and distrust of words.

Mr. Brogan's theme in *The American Character* is the part that space has played in making Americans what they are. He does not apply this concept mechanically, for he knows that Europeans have encountered and conquered space elsewhere without producing the same style of life, but he uses the concept as a point of entry for a lively and illuminating account of American behavior.

P. P.

41. *John Sloan*

A Painter's Life

by VAN WYCK BROOKS

In the art of America, as in the art of most European nations in the past two centuries, each generation of painters has felt it necessary to revolt against what had come to be the entrenched academicism. John Sloan (1871-1951)—a man of independent spirit, talented, intelligent, but not facile—was one of a group of painters early in this century who tried to break the grip of the National Academy on the teaching of art and the selection of works to be publicly exhibited. The group, known as "The Eight," believed that they were establishing the first school of truly American art, independent of current movements in Europe and based in a truly American subject matter.

This was not, to be sure, the first such group; there had been painters in the nineteenth century who had been just as independent and just as American. But the fire of crusaders was in "The Eight" and they did, indeed, break the grip of the old academy, which had come to be a school of sentimental painters of story pictures, diaphanous nudes, and romantic landscapes. "The Eight" became known as "The Ashcan School," as some of them frequently drew their subject matter from the seedier side of metropolitan life. They were instrumental in bringing the Armory Show (1913) to New York, which was America's first introduction on a large scale to the new experiments of the School of Paris.

Whether John Sloan is as important a painter as Van Wyck Brooks (1886-) would seem to believe is a matter of dispute, but as a symbol of an era in which artists were often fighters for social as well as artistic causes, and in which the American artist began to discover his independence, Sloan is an excellent example. (Different perspectives on him will be found in *Art and Life in America* by Oliver Larkin [No. 180], in *New Art in America* by John Baur [No. 23], and in *Painting in America* by Edgar P. Richardson [No. 256].)

Sloan supported himself (as many American artists have) by commercial work which had nothing to do with his painting. He was a teacher of young painters whom he castigated but who loved his honesty and his concern for their welfare as artists. His life was long, somewhat tumultuous, continosly productive, and his work was ultimately recognized by the official art world with which he had always been at loggerheads.

R. L.

42. *The World of Washington Irving*

by Van Wyck Brooks

Van Wyck Brooks (1886-) has spent most of his life reading, thinking, and writing about the United States. Some years ago he conceived a vast project, a set of volumes that would describe the literary development of the country from the outset to the present. In that series, now completed under the general title of "Makers and Finders," *The World of Washington Irving* is the first volume.

The title is, in a way, misleading. What Van Wyck Brooks has put into this book is what he knows and feels about a great many people who contributed to the country's intellectual development in the days when Irving flourished, from about 1800 to about 1845. The knowledge the author brings to his task is immense; he appears, indeed, to know all the facts of life in the period under review. The method Mr. Brooks pursues in organizing all this information is first to establish the physical and social environment within which his authors —Cooper, Bryant, Simms and all the others—lived and worked. The effect, as he moves in leisurely fashion, north and south, east and west, is of a well-composed landscape painting, almost a montage, suffused in soft and subtle lights. Against these charming backgrounds, he introduces his writers. This is done by a kind of running litany in which may be discovered the personal history, the moods, and indeed often the words of the authors Mr. Brooks is describing.

After reading these pages, the reader is left with the feeling that he has been exposed to expert reminiscence. There is the warmth and lavishness of detail that goes with personal recollection. When Van Wyck Brooks writes literary history, he seems to be in a family circle, recounting for younger members the lives and fortunes of men in a former generation to whom he was bound in a long and close association.

E. E. M.

43. *The Next America*

by LYMAN BRYSON

The first World War catapulted the United States from relative self-containment into a position of international prominence; the second greatly increased both its power and its responsibilities. Lyman Bryson's (1888-) book is designed to help both Americans and others to understand the present and future the country now faces. Making a startling re-evaluation of the life Americans lead, the author asks how they can best deal with their own new problems and share in meeting the world's.

A graduate of the University of Michigan, successively a poet, journalist, discussion leader, and professor of adult education, Mr. Bryson is perhaps best known to Americans as a skilled moderator of radio and television discussion programs. But although he is a popular speaker and writer, he has portrayed *The Next America* with a degree of thoroughness which leads him to confront perplexing questions in history, philosophy, and government.

Mr. Bryson finds the great change in American life to lie in the substitution of "collectives"—political, labor, religious, social—for the participation of the individual in democratic activity. Many of the choices that the individual once made are now made for him by organizations. There are, to be sure, both checks and compensations, but the individual must struggle harder for the right to take a personal part in determining his destiny. The process of doing so is, in the author's opinion, the essence of democracy, and he examines democracy as an instrument of government and living in contrast with the Communist or other types of social control in which self-appointed leaders enforce uniformity and prescribe the citizen's role and rewards. Mr. Bryson's exploration of this area is close and revealing, and comprises one of the most thorough expositions of the democratic ideal, particularly in terms of contemporary life, that can be found. Few books about modern America give a clearer analysis of the nation's character, a more detailed and logical consideration of modern ideas affecting it, or a fuller articulation of its promise.

F. E. H.

44. The Spirit and the Flesh

by PEARL S. BUCK

In this volume are included Pearl Buck's (1892-) portraits of her father (*Fighting Angel,* originally published in 1944) and mother (*The Exile,* written in 1921 but not published until 1936). It is probable that these two books, together with *The Good Earth,* represent that part of her voluminous output which has the greatest claim to relative permanence of appeal.

The title *Fighting Angel* is a questionable one. It cannot be doubted that Andrew, Miss Buck's Presbyterian missionary father, was an embattled warrior for the Lord; but that he was an angel is a plausible notion only if one feels that such men as John Knox, Calvin, Ignatius Loyola, and Mohammed were angelic. Andrew was of their iron breed, a fanatical, pure-flamed converter of Chinese souls over a period of 50 years. The likelihood that he was interested in or even aware of the Chinese (not to mention his own family) as fallible human beings, laughing and loving and suffering, is at least debatable. He was, as his daughter so well puts it, a spiritual imperialist. For all his reverence for learning (he was an excellent Chinese scholar) and immaculacy of spirit, he seems to have had much in common with the primitive Fundamentalists who represent an important but not unduly attractive strain in the American character.

Pearl Buck's mother was made of different stuff. As depicted in *The Exile,* the better of the two books, she emerges as a woman of great courage, vitality, and charm. The point of view is not in the least objective; indeed, it is the author's heroine worship that gives her book its moving quality. The average reader will be torn between two emotions: admiration for the fine spirit of this exiled American, and rage at the fact that so splendid a character should have suffered needlessly (four out of her seven children died under heartbreaking circumstances) as the wife of a cold and pious egotist, and in a profession for which she had no real talent. *The Exile* is by no means good propaganda for the missionary movement. It bears witness to the old truth that missionaries fare forth sometimes to save others' souls, sometimes only their own.

C. F.

45. *Backgrounds of Power*

by Roger Burlingame

The author begins by saying that this is a book "for those who are more interested in people than in machines." But that does not mean that this is a collection of personality sketches of mechanics and industrialists. It does mean that the book tells how and why the sequence of machine operations known as mass production became a dominant element in American life, and what that has meant to the men and women whose lives it affects.

After a brief summary of the remote origins of certain concepts and principles underlying modern technology, Roger Burlingame (1889-) carries the story through chapters dealing with specifically American achievements in the organization of production (always seen in firm connection with developments abroad) and with the social and political movements which paralleled and interacted with these technical advances. There are chapters on mass finance, labor organization, the Ford revolution (see No. 46), and the spread of American technology to the rest of the world (a subject dealt with in illuminating and touching detail in *Challenge of the American Know-How* [No. 63]). Finally there is a chapter on the resistances which people everywhere have set up to counteract those aspects of mass production which appear to threaten their integrity as human beings.

Mr. Burlingame emphasizes the close relationship between the evolution of American mass production and the working out in practice of the idea of political and social democracy. Though there is valuable additional material on mass production technology in Allan Nevins and Frank E. Hill's *Ford* (No. 232), in Siegfried Giedion's *Mechanization Takes Command* (No. 128), and in Charles R. Walker and Robert H. Guest's *Man on the Assembly Line* (No. 316), no one has shown so clearly as Mr. Burlingame why there is a crucial distinction between mass production historically evolved, as it was in the United States, and mass production "expediently imposed," as it was in feudal Japan, in Stalin's Russia, and in the "rationalization" of German industry during the 1920's. Technology might be a purely neutral agent if it could be isolated from a socio-political context; but it cannot be.

J. A. K.

46. *Henry Ford*

by Roger Burlingame

In the character and career of Henry Ford (1863-1947) is the material for a great novel. His life poses our most interesting question: how does what we do relate to what we feel about what we do? In other words, what kind of culture, what sort of meaning can be attached to the American endeavor? Henry Ford was ignorant and without formal training, but he was intuitively an incomparable engineer, always seeking to fulfill the ideal morality of the engineer: the finding of the simplest, most direct, statement of a solution to a mechanical problem (see No. 232). That is why the Model T—his cheap car—stripped as it was of all irrelevant connotations, was a beautiful thing appealing directly to the American mind and heart. But it was also the Model T that got him into trouble.

Henry Ford had a truly remarkable insight; he could produce this car so cheaply and in such quantity that motor transport could be made available to most Americans. But it was this recognition that an automobile could be made a cheap consumer commodity that removed Ford from the safety of mechanical situations and placed him amid the confusions of the social environment, where the morality of the engineer did not apply. He had, first, to organize the human energies in his company to fit his exact purpose. This, he soon discovered, could not be done by voluntary association or persuasion; in the end he could achieve his simple and obvious end only by constructing his own industrial universe through the ruthless exercise of his will and authority. Then too, the car he put in the hands of everyone came to mean more than transport. Around the automobile a complicated scheme of values grew up—conditions of status, prestige, even personal security attached themselves to ownership. The simple direct statement of the Model T no longer served; the small cheap car had to look like a big expensive automobile.

Offended by the administrative and social implications of his great idea, Ford withdrew further into a world of his own. As he had brought the great factory under his absolute dominion, so he created a context he could control out of old wagons, blacksmith shops, and the reconstruction of colonial villages—in sum, out of collected relics from an unchanging past. By devising means for changing the conditions of American life, he succeeded only in putting himself out of touch with the meaning of the life he helped to create. In this biography the strength, the weakness, and some of the implications of that extraordinary life are set forth by Roger Burlingame (1889-) with an economy of means the subject would have greatly admired.

E. E. M.

47. *An Anthology of Famous American Stories*

edited by ANGUS BURRELL *and* BENNETT CERF

This anthology is generously representative: 73 short stories by 61 writers, from Washington Irving (1783-1859) to J. D. Salinger (1919-). It has a sound, standard quality; that is, the most generally acclaimed stories by the most generally recognized writers are included. The editors have not tried to make "discoveries" and they have successfully conquered any bias toward the experimental. Here is an honest sampling of the best work Americans have done in the short-story genre.

It can be argued that no American short-story writer equals Chekhov's copiousness or power of psychological penetration, or matches de Maupassant's intensity or velocity. But we have our own masters. In his own narrow field of moral allegory Hawthorne is still supreme. There have been many imitators of Poe, but "The Pit and the Pendulum" is still one of the best horror stories ever written. While it was only after the first World War that the American short story began in general to sound a deeper, sadder, Chekhovian note, we must remember that around 1890, in "Billy Budd, Foretopman," Melville had already written one of the great short stories of his century. And there are few more bitter tales in the language than Mark Twain's "The Man That Corrupted Hadleyburg."

The American range is wide, the levels are many. We excel, sometimes to our peril, in the "well-made" story which hovers between magazine fodder and literature. We are particularly rich (see the examples from Mark Twain, Bret Harte, Joel Chandler Harris, Mary E. Wilkins) in stories of local color and dialect humor. We used to like stories with rounded or trick plots; Fitz-James O'Brien, Frank Stockton, Ambrose Bierce, and O. Henry gave us such tales. Today the drift is toward the short narrative of irony, wry humor, or violence, and few writers are concerned with mere plot-carpentry. The prose itself, as in J. D. Salinger, Irwin Shaw, or John O'Hara, is apt to be economical and muscular—a far cry from Irving's comfortable chimneyside style. In general the American short-story writer seems to be developing a native, authentically American tone and technique, both of them largely influenced by the commanding figure of Ernest Hemingway (No. 143).

C. F.

48. *The Rise of David Levinsky*

by ABRAHAM CAHAN

The modern world has grown so tragically habituated to the spectacle of mass displacements of persons fleeing from religious and political persecution and the ravages of war that inevitably some of the edge has been taken off an earlier drama, the large European emigrations to America in the late nineteenth and early twentieth centuries (see No. 136). That movement of populations produced, however, a literature of great interest and force to document a time when people departed their native lands, not at the point of a gun, but in the hope of new and wonderful possibilities.

Of the many novels of Russian-Jewish immigrant life in the United States, *The Rise of David Levinsky* (first published in 1917) remains the classic performance, unrivaled for its honesty, its social comprehensiveness and clarity, the variousness of its social imagination, and the simple dignity of its presentation. The story of a young poverty-stricken Talmudic student, a typical product of the Russian ghetto, who arrives in New York penniless and alone in the mid-1880's and who in the space of a few years establishes himself as a millionaire clothing manufacturer, Abraham Cahan's (1860-1951) novel is acquainted not only with every feature of "the land of golden opportunity" but also with the high price its conquest exacts in terms of translated values. David Levinsky pays for his success by forfeiting the intellectual and religious preferences in which he had been reared; but his author understands that the culture of the homeland would have levied on him an equally high if different toll —there is neither bitterness nor sentimentality in Mr. Cahan's portrait of Levinsky's crude Americanization.

Although *The Rise of David Levinsky* is written in the first person, only its early sections can be supposed to be quasi-autobiographical. Mr. Cahan made his own distinguished career in the United States, not as a millionaire merchant, but as the highly honored editor of one of America's leading Yiddish-language newspapers.

D. T.

49. The Hudson

by Carl Carmer

Americans are extremely fond of their rivers, especially those which have borne the traffic of discovery and expansion. To them the Hudson, at whose mouth is New York harbor, is more "majestic" than the Danube, more "romantic" than the Rhine. Since Henry Hudson, seeking the Northwest Passage to China for the Dutch East India Company, first explored the river in 1609, millions of men and women have come to it from foreign lands in search of new homes in a new world. Some of them (the Dutch first of all) settled on the island of Manhattan to form the nucleus of America's greatest city; many others scattered to the west and south and some sought their fortunes to the north on the banks of the Hudson itself.

The Hudson is not a "great" river like the Mississippi (No. 311) or the Rio Grande (No. 154); it is not a long river, though it runs wide and deep for several hundred miles to the north. It is—and has been since the seventeenth century—a busy river, a profitable waterway and often the site of conflict. The first Dutch settlers lived on its shores sometimes peacefully, sometimes at war with the Indians. Tenant farmers lived sometimes amiably, sometimes at war with the great Dutch and British landholders. And the river played a dramatic part in the American Revolution. It has provided a livelihood for many—whaling fleets have had their home ports at cities on its banks, in the spring it yields millions of shad; tankers, freighters and barges, excursion boats and pleasure craft ply its waters. Its banks are dotted with villages and small cities and with the mansions of the great landowners of the past.

In *The Hudson* Carl Carmer (1893-) tells the story of the civilizing of a river valley—in microcosm the story of the civilizing of the American continent: the battle with the wilderness, the conflicts of commercial and agricultural development, the struggle by modest men against oppression by powerful men and organizations. Cultists seeking to establish utopian communities, inventors, aesthetes, heroic men and women, sea captains, and politicians and statesmen people this lively narrative.

R. L.

50. *Autobiography of Andrew Carnegie*

In his combination of shrewd practicality, optimism, and philanthropic idealism, Andrew Carnegie (1835-1919)—the poor immigrant boy from Scotland who was devoted to his mother, worked hard, and grew up to be the multimillionaire steel master—seems like the archetypal hero of the nineteenth-century success story. Yet his career differed in important respects from the careers of most of the other "moguls" with whom he is often grouped. Most of all, perhaps, he differed from them in being an affectionate and happy man, at least until the outbreak of the first World War, which, as his wife testified, broke his heart. For Carnegie was apparently quite free from the subconscious fears which drove so many of our fortune-builders. There is nothing in him of the repressed cruelty that scarred the nobility of John Roebling, for instance—another immigrant who built a great industry (No. 294).

Impelled by affection for his mother and the ambition to free her from poverty, and proud of his radical heritage from Dunfermline ("perhaps the most radical town in the kingdom") and his uncle and father, who had denounced "privilege in all its forms," Carnegie had a profound confidence that the fates would be kind to those who worked hard and lived honorably. Certainly they were kind to him. Starting as a bobbin boy at $1.50 a week, he was earning $2400 a year eleven years later and had already made investments which were netting him an income of over $47,000! "Earth," he later wrote, and firmly believed, "is often a real heaven."

After he had accumulated a fortune in steel, and began to realize (especially after the bloody Homestead strike) that he himself was coming to be regarded as a "creature of privilege," he decided that it was "a disgrace to die rich" and determined to begin giving his fortune away. Before he died he had given more than three hundred and fifty million dollars, and had set a pattern for disposing of surplus wealth which other rich men have subsequently followed.

J. A. K.

51. *The Mind of the South*

by W. J. CASH

There is no single book to serve as a better introduction to the American South than *The Mind of the South,* by W. J. Cash (1901-). Its theme is the need for, and the limitations on, Southern self-analysis; it portrays the South as a region where—partly because of external pressure, partly by internal necessity, and partly by choice—the defense of institutions has usurped the intellectual and moral energy that might have gone into reassessing and improving those institutions; where, in short, the need for rationalization has usually been so great as to make impossible the scrutiny of reason.

But *The Mind of the South* is a book sympathetically, imaginatively, and intelligently bent on destroying its own thesis, for it is an exercise in precisely the kind of self-analysis whose lack Cash deplores. In this it is not alone; in the years before it was written there had been an impressive growth in research on Southern problems, whose results Cash made use of in his book; and since then research has multiplied. Nor has the Southern literary renaissance, whose beginnings Cash relates, shown any abatement, and the imaginative writers have undoubtedly done as much as or more than scholars both to show the South its own image and to make the rest of the world aware of Southern problems and points of view.

There are some surprising omissions from Cash's pages, most notable being his failure to mention the TVA, the great multi-purpose engineering project undertaken by the federal government to improve the standard of living in a large section of the South along the Tennessee River. (Readers interested in this subject should consult David Lilienthal's *TVA: Democracy on the March* [No. 186].) But the chief shortcoming of the book is simply the fact that it was written in 1941. The second World War and its consequences have wrought important changes in the South and in race relations, most of which have had the effect of intensifying and speeding up the movements Cash recorded—further industrialization and urbanization, and the shift of Negroes to the North.

P. P.

52. *Death Comes for the Archbishop*

by WILLA CATHER

When *Death Comes for the Archbishop* appeared, in 1927, Willa Cather (1876-1947) was already a widely known American novelist. Her realistic portrayals of the American Middle West (such as *My Ántonia* [No. 53]) had appeared while Theodore Dreiser (No. 101) was in full tide of creation and Sherwood Anderson (No. 11) was becoming a force in American fiction. Her approach was as direct as Anderson's, her manner of writing less experimental; he dealt with the older, eastern area of the Middle West, she with her own more recently settled Nebraska, where she got her university education and her first experience in journalism.

The idea for a novel with New Mexico as a background and two Roman Catholic priest-pioneers as her heroes came to Willa Cather when she was fifty and had known the Southwest for some years. An actual biography (that of the Rt. Rev. Joseph P. Machebeuf) served to an extent as her model. Her book is a fictionalized biography rather than a novel in the usual sense, and it draws strength and color from the background of Spanish-Indian towns, the Pueblo Indians and their customs, and the nomad life of the Navajo. While its theme is the inspired struggle of Bishop (later Archbishop) Latour and his French compatriot, Father Vaillant, to re-establish order in their territory after the American conquest of 1848 and to push their faith into new regions, its background of Spanish discovery and Christianization, the persisting culture of the Indians, and the stark, vivid beauty of the land make strong secondary claims upon the reader.

The novel convinced many Roman Catholics that Willa Cather was one of them; this fact pleased her, but she remained a Protestant deeply sympathetic with a memorable Catholic experience. *Death Comes for the Archbishop* revealed her as a mature artist. It is one of the finest and most beautiful records of the American Southwest, and will give to readers abroad an understanding of that extraordinary region, the earliest territory in what is now the United States to have been settled by the whites, and one in which Indian culture, touched both by Spanish and American influences, has most fully preserved its essential character.

F. E. H.

53. *My Ántonia*

by WILLA CATHER

My Ántonia, first published in 1918, is an autobiographical work, in the sense that it draws its material from its author's childhood experience in Nebraska. It employs the transparent but effective device of a narrator, Jim Burden, through whose recollections of his youth on a prairie farm—and especially of Ántonia Shimerda, the vivid and lovable playmate of his boyhood—Miss Cather re-creates the post-pioneer culture in which she was reared and to which she remained tied throughout her career by the closest spiritual and intellectual bonds.

Many streams, Miss Cather would have us know, watered this culture. Jim's grandparents, on whose Nebraska farm the narrator passes his boyhood, were Virginians; their nearest neighbors are the Shimerdas, a family of Bohemian immigrants; close by are the Russians, Peter and Pavel; in Black Hawk, the prairie town to which Jim's grandparents move when they grow older, there are estimable Scandinavian friends. It is Miss Cather's purpose to celebrate this pluralism and to acknowledge America's indebtedness to her immigrant populations. And in its time, when national pride often tended to overlook the sources of national virtue, *My Ántonia* was a significant contribution to the general effort of social enlightenment. In our own day, however, we are likely to note that it is in her indigenous stock—Jim's family—that Miss Cather finally locates her truly unflawed and unfaltering moral standards—and this despite the fact that it is an immigrant girl, Ántonia Shimerda, who is the heroine of the book and its most compelling character.

Ántonia has her father's sensitivity, a delicacy which rendered Mr. Shimerda incapable of surviving transplantation to America. But she also has the qualities of endurance of her peasant forebears; she can work like a man in the fields, forgetful of the refinements learned from Jim's family. The struggle between Ántonia's capacity for absorption into the American culture and her ability to retrogress to a more primitive level of self-preservation, a conflict which is also shown as the conflict between womanliness and manliness, makes up the substance of Miss Cather's novel. But this schematization is happily obscured by the book's beautifully gifted prose, in particular its remarkable descriptions of nature, and by the informing charm of Ántonia herself.

D. T.

54. *A Stillness at Appomattox*

by BRUCE CATTON

The Civil War was a confession of failure, an admission that instead of union there was a nation divided. Nor, when the war ended at Appomattox, did its end heal the wound, the wound to pride. Though arms were stacked, the war continued, in words. For 50 years boys sat in parlors up North and on piazzas down South and listened. Every family or neighborhood had its veteran, eloquently one-legged, who told "how we whipped the Rebels" or "how we almost whipped the Yankees, if only we'd 'a' had . . ."—something. In the telling, places became as familiar as nearby towns or countryside: Richmond, Bloody Angle, Charlottesville, and always Appomattox. Generals came alive, as if they sat in the room: Philip Sheridan, George Meade, Stonewall Jackson, and always U. S. Grant and Robert E. Lee, at Appomattox.

At school the war as known at home became dry dull words in a book called history. Shrewd publishers could not even bring it to life again by their printing of one version for the North and another for the South. History was still dull. But some of the boys who had listened were not content. The veterans' war must be somewhere, if they could only find it, and they began the search in libraries, archives, and collections, in letters and diaries and obscure pamphlets. They published their findings, and history began to come to life again, but still not the history the boys had heard.

It had to wait for Bruce Catton (1899-), who has evidently read everything that has to do with the Civil War. He has also listened to the words on the page with a boy's ear. He is a reporter turned historian, and he is also innumerable one-legged veterans. *A Stillness at Appomattox* has the quality of experience, from the Washington's Birthday Ball to the moment when Sergeant George S. Hampton felt the first sharp pang of a wound beginning to heal.

J. A. R.

55. *An Encyclopedia of Modern American Humor*

edited by BENNETT CERF

There *are* classic anthologies, but anthologies of humor are not among them. They come and go. This one is better than most, which means merely that the present writer is so constituted that he laughs at many of the same things that amuse Mr. Cerf (1898-). It is hard to think of anyone with a sense of humor so personal that he will find *nothing* in this fat volume funny; but it is not impossible.

The operative word in the title is *modern*. Mr. Cerf, a model of the contemporary, includes Mark Twain and Bret Harte (out of piety, one feels), but for the most part the accent is on the smart, the modish, the up-to-date. This is sensible; even last year's jokes sound historical.

All the great names are here—Dorothy Parker, Robert Benchley, Frank Sullivan, E. B. White, Clarence Day, Ring Lardner, James Thurber, Franklin P. Adams, Ogden Nash—but Mr. Cerf has not stuck to the familiar, nor is his definition of humor bound by tradition. He comes up with diverting stuff by relatively new writers such as Mac Hyman and Shirley Jackson. He puts in a reflective essay by John Mason Brown and some social history by Cleveland Amory, quite rightly persuaded that they are just as diverting as humor of a more conventional variety.

From this volume there is no single conclusion about modern American humor that one can draw. We have left behind the old pioneer humor of exaggeration; we have almost abandoned dialect humor; and city-produced humor is dominant over rural. So much one can say; but there is not much more one can say except that "Dr. Kronkhite" and "The Night the Bed Fell" are both highly American, are both highly laughable, and have not the slightest kinship to one another. One of the features of the book is the collection of light verse, a field in which we are beginning to rival the British achievements of the nineteenth century. Mr. Cerf has room only for samples; but they are good ones.

C. F.

56. *The Blessings of Liberty*

by ZECHARIAH CHAFEE, JR.

One of the articles of American faith was most clearly defined by Thomas Jefferson in his first inaugural address in 1801. If there be those among us who wish to change the republican form of government, "let them stand undisturbed," he said, "as monuments of the safety with which error of opinion may be tolerated where reason is left free to combat it." In recent years there has been evidence that public faith in this proposition has been somewhat shaken.

Professor Chafee (1885-1957) of the Harvard Law School lists twelve "encroachments on the ideal of freedom of speech, press and assembly which have taken place [in this country] since 1945." Some of these are the result of Congressional legislation, like the McCarran Act which set up what was called a Subversive Activities Control Board. Some are the product of executive action, like the removal by the State Department of a mystery story from a set of American books sent to information centers in foreign cities because it had been written by an alleged subversive.

In this book Professor Chafee investigates some of the causes for the present weakening of confidence in the Jeffersonian doctrine, examines the mechanical operation of some of the encroaching influences, and discusses some of the general implications of the present condition of things. Because he is learned and clear, his book should dispel for readers both here and abroad much of the murk that surrounds such subjects as the current use and meaning of the Fifth Amendment of the Constitution or the conduct of Congressional investigating committees. Because Chafee is appalled by the prospect of what can happen when a society has, in Walter Lippmann's metaphor, fastened manacles upon its wrists to keep its hands from shaking, his book is also an affirmation of the necessity of liberty for human beings.

This book has obvious claims on the attention. It is an important study—seeking to clear away ignorance and fear—of what, in the long run, is the most important problem confronting the United States. The man who wrote it has an equal claim on the attention. He used the blessings of liberty to develop, as any reader will discover, a wise, witty, humane, and eternally vigilant spirit by the exercise of which he worked to procure those blessings for others.

E. E. M.

57. *The Selected Writings of John Jay Chapman*

John Jay Chapman (1862-1933) is almost unknown to American criticism and he is entirely unknown to the American public at large. Yet he is a vigorous and highly civilized mind, often profound and always readable, who will some day be "discovered" for the fourth or fifth time and will then take his place as one of America's great critics.

Criticism came as naturally to Chapman as breathing. Whatever institution or idea he encountered he took apart and judged with the deftness of a watchmaker and the judicious passion of a fastidious man committed to culture. Had he been more encyclopedic, less sheltered, and also better balanced emotionally, he would have been a transpontine Bernard Shaw.

As it was, his critical energies first displayed themselves publicly in the politics of New York City at the turn of the century. He wrote journalism, lectured and campaigned, and then published two books: *Practical Agitation* and *Causes and Consequences,* in which an unmistakable new voice could be heard. Unfortunately, from the start he was too patently of no party but his own. He belonged to the well-to-do and educated classes and did not turn his back on their culture but on their politics. He was really a radical and reformist, yet he did not speak the language of rabble-rousing. He was to his fingertips a man of letters though he wrote in a denuded idiom that had nothing in common with the genteel literary prose of the period. Agitation led him to study the figure of William Lloyd Garrison, of whom there is no better portrait than his. Yet here again, the length, the tone, and the concealment of scholarship prevent the book from falling into any convenient class.

Chapman was by temperament a universal abolitionist, and it is surprising that he has not on this account been taken up by the modern writers of the same bent. One reason may be that he was also an anti-obfuscator and a man of action. His remarkable act of symbolic penance for his fellow countrymen at Coatesville, where a Negro had been lynched, is something as alien to our collectivist tendencies as it was to the genteel ones of Chapman's day. Except as an incomparable essayist, he is not yet for us, but for the ages.

J. B.

58. *America's Music*

by Gilbert Chase

American music shares with American poetry and the other arts the advantage and the handicap of not having been born at home. Foreigners —and some Americans—keep repeating that the United States is culturally a young country, but this is of course absurd. The country is a young body with an old inherited mind. It was transplanted, like organs in modern surgery, from the body of Europe as soon as the Pilgrims landed at Plymouth ten generations ago.

The difficulty for such a culture is not to mature but to find its youth. If American music throughout the world means jazz, it is not only because that genre corresponds to something nagging in every modern urban man, but also because jazz (see Nos. 147 and 282) arose in America among a people capable of using naively and for their own satisfaction such fragments of culture as lay about them. The burden of outside critical thoughts did not lie heavy upon them.

All other American composers started with an incubus—from the conscience-ridden Puritans (who, like Luther, loved music next to godliness) to the men of the eighteenth, nineteenth, and twentieth centuries, all of whom had a duty to "the best that has been played and sung in the Western world." Stephen Foster, one of our most delightful melodists, may not have produced "genuine" folksongs, but he perceived by instinct that the only escape from stifling salon criticism was to make a manly stab at the merits of ignorance. The very criticism leveled at his work, that it is *his* work and not the song of that great lark, the people, shows what a pestiferous atmosphere of misplaced intellect hovered over our gifted men during three centuries of talented efforts.

Gilbert Chase (1906-) tells the story of American music from the misjudged Puritans to the great European influx after Hitler, with simplicity and scholarly detail. Nowhere does he try to inflate reputations or apologize for weakness. And though he limits biography to its just place in a cultural narrative, he does not content himself with a dry catalogue of names, dates, and concert halls. His book thus forms the sizable background to the revolution in taste which has lately made music in America (see No. 21) a great industry and a widespread passion.

J. B.

59. *A Goodly Fellowship*

by MARY ELLEN CHASE

This life story of a woman professor at Smith College shows the kind of career that was open in the first half of the twentieth century to an American girl of lively mind and resolute spirit. In her childhood, Mary Ellen Chase (1887-) knew only the New England of seacoast villages and stern landscapes, a country much like that described in the poems of Robert Frost (No. 125), in Edith Wharton's *Ethan Frome* (No. 327), and in a more kindly way in the stories of Sarah Orne Jewett (No. 167). She studied and taught, as a girl, in the crowded and ungraded schools and the little academies of that region, then ventured while still timid and provincial into the Middle West. She went thence to Montana and on to a state university, working in almost every kind of educational institution in the United States except the public school of the city slum and the racially divided school of the deep South. She came to know all kinds of administrators and all kinds of faiths, learning and advancing in her ambition to be a good teacher of English and, if possible, a writer.

Being a born teacher, she shows the bias against explicit method which is common to teachers who are gifted enough not to need it, but she is otherwise completely hospitable to ideas, to persons and to the values of widely different regions and classes of people. She is always a New Englander, however, and her approach to her lifework was very different from that shown in the autobiography of Alvin S. Johnson (No. 168), another devoted educator, but an immigrant boy, brought up in the Middle West. What she shares with Johnson and other Americans of her time is self-confident ambition and faith in the social mobility and freedom of democracy.

Mary Ellen Chase has not only her confidence in herself and in the democratic system; she has also, to a degree that might seem naive in a person less learned or less wise, an unshaken faith in the efficacy of education, as she has seen it practiced in many forms, to save men and women and to build a civilization. In this she serves, involuntarily perhaps, as spokesman for the teachers of the United States, especially for the dominant group of women in the public schools who are the builders of the constantly renewed American foundations.

L. B.

60. *Review and Reflection*

A Half-Century of Labor Relations

by Cyrus S. Ching

The relations between workers and managers must necessarily be the theme of many books about modern life, especially in a country so heavily devoted to large-scale business operations as the United States. Cyrus S. Ching (1876-) began as a workman and struggled to better his condition, a typical American ambition. But he bettered himself by becoming a masterly negotiator, and for a lifetime gave his skill and knowledge to the betterment of other workers as well. A serious accident taught him that his employers cared nothing for what happened to him. He survived to see the modern attitude of watchful toleration between labor and management developed by struggle and statesmanship.

After a few years on the worker's side, Mr. Ching went into management, thinking that more could be done for mutually trustful relations by trying from the manager's side to find some method of frank communication between the parties. Even in 1920 it was considered radical for any spokesman for management to admit in public that there could be "understanding" between a company and its employees. But it was for such an understanding that Mr. Ching campaigned, at last earning great influence as a mediator in the service of the Federal government. In the two decades between 1920 and 1941, he saw established the psychological conditions that made collective bargaining possible. How far American thinking has come in Mr. Ching's lifetime is indicated not only by his recollections but also by the concern for the welfare of the worker indicated in *The Man on the Assembly Line* by Charles R. Walker and Robert H. Guest (No. 316) and *The Social Problems of an Industrial Civilization* by Elton Mayo (No. 209).

In Mr. Ching's recollections, sometimes only implied but always evident to the watchful reader, will be found much of the explanation for the fact that there has never been a successful "labor party" in American politics.

L. B.

61. *The Index of American Design*

by ERWIN O. CHRISTENSEN

It took the Depression of the 1930's to produce the first extensive, orderly, and accurate record of the American folk arts. As a project designed primarily to give employment to artists and craftsmen, in a period when there was little or no other employment for them, the Federal government initiated a number of programs for artists. (Several are described in *Art and Life in America* by Oliver Larkin [No. 180].) One of these projects was a conscientious attempt to collect and reproduce (mostly by water-color techniques and photographs) the ephemeral, useful arts that America produced from its Colonial days to the end of the nineteenth century. That is not to say that many other collections have not preserved and catalogued American crafts, though America's interest in resurrecting and caring for its artifacts is a fairly recent preoccupation. The first collections date from the latter part of the nineteenth century, but in the 1920's there was a tremendous boom in the collection of Americana. *The Index of American Design* may be said to result directly from this popular movement, and this particular volume is an attempt to provide a sample of the kinds of arts and crafts that constitute the complete *Index,* which includes many thousands of items.

The useful objects of art—furniture, tools, textiles, figureheads, commercial signs, glass, clothes, toys, and such—created by Americans for their own pleasure are for the most part the work of untrained designers but highly skilled craftsmen—men and women who understood the properties of their materials and brought to their work a sense of pleasure and forthright artistry. This "vernacular" tradition is explored at some length in *Made in America,* by John A. Kouwenhoven (No. 175), but the text of the present volume and its admirable reproductions afford a quick and pleasant panorama of it. Those arts in America which developed independently of most contemporary European influences, and beyond the tentacles of aesthetic dogma, represent American popular taste far more accurately than the so-called American "fine arts" of the same period. They do not, on the other hand, reflect the taste of the millions of Americans who fell under the secondhand influence of a number of "tastemakers" who borrowed from Europe and attempted to lead Americans by the nose into the paths of "refinement."

R. L.

62. *The Doctors Mayo*

by Helen Clapesattle

Rochester, Minnesota, once "a little town on the edge of nowhere" is now synonymous to most Americans with the Mayo Clinic. It is a city whose transient population far exceeds its permanent residents, a paradox resulting from the work of three remarkable men whose lives span nearly a century of American life and medical progress. They have made Rochester an international center for training medical specialists, researchers, and educators, and for treating patients from every state and countless foreign countries.

"We were reared in medicine as a farmer boy is reared in farming," Dr. Will often said. But it was the cyclone of 1883, when victims around Rochester had to be sheltered and cared for, that set the course for the Old Doctor and his young sons. The Mayos' ability to grasp the exceptional opportunities of time, place, and volume of work to be done enabled them to secure talented assistants and expand their activities. Influenced by the example of teamwork set by Doctors Welch, Osler, Halsted, and Kelly at Johns Hopkins (see No. 116), the brothers had developed by 1914 a cooperative private group practice among clinicians, surgeons, and laboratory men housed under one roof. But above all the Mayo Clinic was influenced by Dr. Will and Dr. Charlie Mayo, who sincerely believed their father's dictum, "No man is big enough to be independent of others," and who nonetheless never ceased to be pioneers during an era of tremendous activity in medicine.

After repeated refusals to allow their biography to be written, the brothers finally agreed to make themselves and their records available to an author chosen by the University of Minnesota. The resulting account tells in straightforward and nontechnical language a great deal about developments in American surgery during one hundred years of spectacular growth for the Middle West. It is a particularly fascinating story of the evolution of frontier practice into one of the world's great medical institutions. Though no attempt has been made here to continue it beyond the deaths of the brothers in 1939, clearly the Mayo Clinic and the Mayo Foundation live on as very active memorials.

C. G.

63. *Challenge of the American Know-How*

by Pearl Franklin Clark

The unprecedented spread of technical-assistance missions throughout the world since the end of World War II has partly obscured the tradition to which they belong. The "development" of "underdeveloped" areas has been going on for centuries. America itself was still being "developed" by European funds and technicians as late as the first quarter of the twentieth century. But the rise of American technology had been accompanied by the conscious development of a workable doctrine, and increasingly the men skilled in applying it, the specialists in industrial efficiency to be found in far corners of the earth, were Americans. Already, in the 1920's, an international management consultant like Wallace Clark (1880-1948) would logically be summoned to France or Poland to introduce "American methods."

What these methods were is the subject of the deceptively simple and seemingly chauvinistic book Clark's wife has written. She is candid, curious, concerned—one can see her refusing to drop the marital dialogue over the nature of "know-how," in which she found herself engaged, until she had satisfied her doubts. Preoccupied with people and with "human values," as she thought a proper wife should be, Mrs. Clark (1886-) at first reproached her husband for concentrating so intensely on the mere physical conditions of work, the way it was organized, or the often trivial obstacles that held it up. Only gradually did she come to see that her "human values" were already embodied in his seemingly cold concern, tirelessly reiterated, that nothing interfere with the flow of work. Finally she came to appreciate, and to quote with awe, the remark of a Polish financier: "Let us follow the American methods. I believe in them as I do in God."

Her book can be read as a corrective to attacks on the "inhumanity" of mass production like Siegfried Giedion's (No. 128), but, most important, it must be read alongside Roger Burlingame's *Backgrounds of Power* (No. 45) as a wholehearted denial of the widely held idea that technology is a neutral instrument. "We want your productivity," Americans are frequently told, "but not your philosophy." Mrs. Clark perceives, as many more complex minds have not, that the two are inseparable. Where John Kouwenhoven, in *Made in America* (No. 175), has shown that industrial democracy possesses an internal aesthetic, Mrs. Clark has shown that it also contains a morality—and that in the absence of democratic beliefs the supposedly "neutral" machines will seldom produce as expected.

E. L.

64. Collier's World Atlas and Gazetteer

Most readers have had the disquieting experience of wishing to find at least one good map in a volume of history, biography, or even fiction. A reader of this shelf of American books will often experience a similar lack. Whether he seeks to understand the geography of *The American Land* (No. 312), to follow the vacation guide in *The Everyday Reference Library* (No. 68), to explore *Mormon Country* (No. 290) with Wallace Stegner, or to locate places mentioned in *An American Dilemma* (No. 230), he needs maps. This atlas with its excellent format, clear detailed maps, and wealth of supporting material will serve as an extremely useful aid to the inquisitive reader's orientation.

Despite its title, *World Atlas and Gazetteer* is a very American volume. Half of the maps are of North America or of individual units of the United States. A large portion of the central section is devoted to essays giving information for each state and such territories and possessions as Hawaii, Alaska, and Puerto Rico. In addition there is a major essay on the "Physical and Economic Background of the United States," and maps and tables which locate and describe the territorial growth of the United States, the National Park system, and American railroads, highways, and airlines.

The "World Index and Gazetteer" alphabetically arranges countries, regions, cities, rivers, etc., with identifying symbols so that they can quickly be located. More than five thousand cities and towns are included, with easy reference data on their geographic, historic, tourist, or industrial significance. Also in this section are detailed maps of the business districts of over fifty major cities in the United States, while the gazetteer lists nearly every town of any importance (here again the emphasis is on American communities; well over half the entries are from the United States). The reader who seeks the location of Upperville, Virginia, the size of Peru, Vermont, or the importance of Carmel, California, will easily find his answers here.

C. G.

65. *Theodore Parker*

by HENRY STEELE COMMAGER

Doctor Ripley took a look at the young man and said, "Don't be an egomite." But Theodore Parker (1810-1860) was already one by nature, as Emerson later testified, saying, "T. P. has beautiful fangs." He was an egomite also by inheritance. In the family home at Lexington, Massachusetts, where the Revolutionary War began, hung the musket of his grandfather. While he may not have fired from his musket "the shot heard round the world," John Parker had, by family tradition, fired a verbal shot by saying, "If they mean to have war, let it begin here." His grandson took this as a guide to future action.

He began with minor wars, with "vaulting self-assurance." First the church, for "where the spirit of the church is, there is slavery," and its ministers, his brothers, "anointed dullness." This was the Unitarian Church, creedless yet enslaved to creed. Then, attacking on the literary front, he proclaimed the German to be "the fairest, the richest, the most original, fresh, and religious literature of all modern times." Mere history, whatever others might say for it, was defective. "In telling what has been," Parker said, "the historian is also to tell what ought to be." There were others like him in New England, and presently he found himself a member of the "interlocking directorate of reformers."

Every cause, however, had the same flaw: there was something to be said on the other side. What he sought was a one-sided cause, of pure right against pure wrong. He found it at last, in slavery. Pitting one abstraction, equality, against another, slavery, was a logician's delight. Besides, slavery was not only immoral, it was down south. New England had long abandoned slavery; there was no money in it. There was also more money in trade with China than in transporting perishable cargo from Africa. There was now more money in the products of slavery, and Boston business was hostile to the cause of abolition, as William Lloyd Garrison (see No. 57) had learned. But Parker was not dismayed. Feeling, as he said, "like a Hebrew prophet," he moved, as prophets do, from conclusion to premise. Presently he was using the phrase "writ in blood," and listening with approval to John Brown's summons to civil war: "Without the shedding of blood there is no remission of sins."

J. A. R.

66. *Education and Liberty*

by James Bryant Conant

From Britain and from Europe the United States inherited the forms of educational institutions and some of their basic ideals. The American problems, however, have always been different from those in older countries, and the names for schools took on new meanings. The beginnings were very British. They were modified in the nineteenth century mostly by importations from Germany. Forms which did not fit American conditions have been distorted. The resulting complex system is described by Dr. Conant as a basis for suggestions for reform.

Dr. Conant (1893-), the former president of Harvard University, compares American school practices with the curricula, the enrollments, and the admissions policies, and also the relations to government and religious bodies, of schools in the other English-speaking countries. He keeps in view the fact that the high school, the most special of American institutions, has an open door for the whole youthful population and takes in about three out of four of them for some kind of "education." The intellectual, the dull, the gifted, and the plodding, they all go to the American high school and thence into life, either directly or by way of higher learning—the "liberal arts" college, which is also quite different from older European models. It is not professional even for scholarship.

Dr. Conant's most drastic suggestion is to advance the prestige of the new two-year colleges at the expense of the standard four-year institutions, "making a climate of opinion in which the length of education beyond eighteen is not considered the hallmark of respectability." He would leave the high school as it is now, a generous institution serving everyone somehow. He would provide better ways of helping able students.

The book has a copious set of appendices in which are given facts and figures. It should be compared with Alvin Johnson's *Pioneer's Progress* (No. 168) and Mary Ellen Chase's *A Goodly Fellowship* (No. 59), which will put humor and life into the statistical picture. The significance of Dr. Conant's book lies in the vigorous assertion, by the former head of the oldest and one of the most respected of American universities, that education in a democracy must be both for an élite of native capacity, wherever found, and also for everyone else, for each according to his powers.

L. B.

67. *The Leatherstocking Saga*

by James Fenimore Cooper
edited by Allan Nevins

Allan Nevins (1890-), professor of American History at Columbia University, has linked in one volume those five of James Fenimore Cooper's (1789-1851) novels portraying that most popular of American fictional figures, Natty Bumppo, known variously as Leatherstocking, Deerslayer, Pathfinder, Hawkeye, and *la longue Carabine*. The books are arranged in the chronological sequence of Bumppo's life rather than the order in which they appeared in print. In addition, Professor Nevins has judiciously edited the novels, selecting the passages primarily concerned with Bumppo and rejecting many of Cooper's superfluities. The result is a unified and artistically highlighted portrait of the simple and noble master of forest lore whom readers from nearly all nations of the world have long regarded as a supreme characterization in American literature.

Bumppo, the fearless frontier scout, emerges from these edited pages as "untutored but noble-minded . . . a being of great purity of character but of as marked peculiarities." In *The Great Frontier* (No. 322), historian Walter Prescott Webb makes the argument that as long as the frontier exists men of this description will continue to emerge from society as its natural leaders, and in *The Virgin Land* (No. 287) Henry Nash Smith adds that from the attributes which this woodland sage possessed, grew, both in America and abroad, an endless parade of imitative narratives in which Bumppo (as a type) played his familiar role.

Even more important today than Cooper's influence on literary history is his role as an American folklorist and poet. Through the Scout's mouth he reported the folktalk of his time and, as for poetry, Cooper said that Bumppo "felt, though it was unconsciously, like a poet." The author gave much of his own poetic expression the common touch by offering it in the unpretentious garb of an unlettered man's dialect.

An accomplished American stylist recently described the admirers of Leatherstocking and his ilk as "the cult of the sublimated roughneck." Allan Nevins has made answer; his removal of the unessential has left a worthy core. As a result, Cooper's genius has been so illuminated that it will need and receive many reappraisals both in his own country and abroad.

C. C.

68. *The Everyday Reference Library*

edited by LEWIS COPELAND *and* LAWRENCE W. LAMM

In any country dominated by a rising middle class there is a demand for books telling one how to behave, whom to emulate, and what to reject. In America, where the fluidity of classes is further complicated by physical mobility (few Americans live or die where they were born or remain in one place during their working careers), the proliferation of "self-help" books, etiquette books, and such has been enormous. A vast branch of the publishing industry turns out nothing but so-called "How-To" books.

The Everyday Reference Library is probably the most compendious example of these books, and is also one of the most widely distributed. Aimed as it is at the average middle-class family, it inadvertently provides a remarkable series of insights into the preoccupations, aspirations, and tastes of a large number of Americans.

In its emphasis on "usable" information, it is of course solidly in the utilitarian tradition which has been so marked a feature of American life since Benjamin Franklin's time. In its implied assumption that "experts" can tell one the proper way to bring up children, choose a career, or "acquire greater poise and charm," it is a reflection of the national faith in "book-learning"; yet, at the same time, the entire work presupposes the conviction that everyone can "do it himself,"—whether "it" is repairing a car, succeeding in business, or painting a picture.

As a direct source of information about what Americans wear and eat, what jobs they work at, and much else, the book is well-indexed and encyclopedic. Indirectly it is perhaps even more revealing. Notice, for example, the large amount of space devoted to (and therefore the interest assumed in) "business"; observe that questions of how to write good English are treated as a category of business information, and that "social correspondence" is obviously considered to be almost exclusively a feminine interest; and notice too the way the automobile dominates everything from house plans to vacations.

J. A. K.

69. Our New Music

by Aaron Copland

There is nothing like the words of the witness. Mr. Copland's book proves this once again, with the usual limitation that every witness needs a little cross-examining to sort out what he had the chance to know best from what he was told, mistook, or imagined.

This suggests that the reader of *Our New Music* might be well advised to yield to a natural temptation and begin with the author's autobiographical sketch near the end of the book. It is candid, truthful, engaging—and it permits a surer estimate of what precedes. Add to this the fact that much of the volume first appeared in a different form during the very time of creation that it discusses, and it is clear that what we have here is not a history or even a critical survey, but a fighting document.

Its role as such does not prevent its being mainly reliable, except the first section, which presents a distinctly jazz-age view of what happened in the late nineteenth century. To make Moussorgsky come out of a self-fertilized egg as a pioneer in music is to go against Moussorgsky's own testimony and his visible (audible) connection with his chosen predecessors.

Beginning with section two, however, the knowledge and judiciousness of the writer shine without blemish. It is in fact remarkable that one who was part of the new movement, and a prolific producer at that, should have had the time and the detachment to describe so justly the work of his generation and its immediate elders. As to the part of persuasion—about the reasonableness and emotional contents of the new music, about its theoretical bases and its public reception—Mr. Copland (1900-) repeats with unusual felicity and force the good old-fashioned things that have had to be said about art every twenty years since Cro-Magnon man first drew pictures in caves, some 25,000 years ago.

J. B.

70. *Joseph Henry*

by Thomas Coulson

It is said of American science that it aims at invention rather than discovery; that its chief concern is with the application of natural or mechanical principles rather than with a study of the principles themselves. Europe supplies the ideas and America makes the machines. If this is the rule, Joseph Henry (1797-1878) stands out as an exception to it. He was a true discoverer within the field of electricity, as Benjamin Franklin (see No. 313) had been in the century before him. But where Franklin went on to invent the lightning rod, Henry was content through his long life merely to investigate the subject of his choice. He was not even ambitious to proclaim the discoveries that grew out of his investigations; he was singularly indifferent to either fame or money. In certain of his researches he anticipated the great Faraday, and by the time of his death in 1878 he was famous throughout Europe; yet, although his funeral at Washington was attended by the President of the United States, the entire Cabinet, the Justices of the Supreme Court, the leading members of the diplomatic corps, and many scientists, he remains a relatively unknown figure among the people he served. Everybody remembers that Morse (No. 195) invented the telegraph; few have heard that Henry made the invention possible.

His career was wholly American, however, for he was a self-made man and scientist. Born in modest circumstances at Albany, New York, he managed first to study and then to teach in the local Academy, and at last to do both things so well that when he was called to be a professor of physics at Princeton University he had already made some of his most valuable discoveries. At Princeton he made still more, so that when the Smithsonian Institution was to be created in Washington the task of secretary and director fell to him. He went there in 1846 and devoted the rest of his life to the organization of American science. In a sense this was a sacrifice, since he was henceforth unfree to pursue his own pure studies in electromagnetism. Yet as an organizer he was magnificent too, and he did much to make science everywhere what it is today.

M. V. D.

71. *Charles Ives and His Music*

by HENRY COWELL *and* SIDNEY COWELL

An unsuspected connection between art and the career of insurance executive is exhibited by the lives and works of two important American artists recently dead: the poet Wallace Stevens (No. 295) and the composer Charles Ives (1874-1954). Both men seemed able to produce abundantly in spite of the strain of business, and even to draw from their skill at office work if not substance for art at least a steadying discipline.

Ives was undoubtedly the less appreciated of the two. Only toward the end of his life did his music begin to be played often enough to impress his name on the public mind. But his influence on musicians has been great, and he is now posthumously reaping the reward of his long and solitary efforts. As so often happens, the imitators have paved the way for the enjoyment of his innovations.

The present biography has in its co-author, Mr. Henry Cowell (1897-), another composer of advanced views who is now recognized as one of the grand old men of American music. His tribute to Ives is therefore authoritative, even if spoken from the vantage point of a different generation, and even if Ives seems by his choice of themes and methods to be closer to the national, "populist" tradition.

J. B.

72. *The Literary Situation*

by Malcolm Cowley

The best American literary criticism in recent years has not been in the nature of a survey, as the reader will see if he turns to such books as Lionel Trilling's *Liberal Imagination* (No. 308) and Randall Jarrell's *Poetry and the Age* (No. 165). Mr. Trilling and Mr. Jarrell are typical of modern American critics in their engagement with individual writers and texts, and when they turn to more general considerations it is not in the spirit of the calm historian, but (in Mr. Jarrell's instance) to engage in polemics or (in Mr. Trilling's) to examine broad social and political problems rather than those specifically literary.

Therefore it is useful to have such a book as Malcolm Cowley's (1898-) *Literary Situation,* which is for the most part a dispassionate account of the literary scene in twentieth-century America, with a good deal of emphasis on matters usually considered beneath the notice of the critic. Mr. Cowley's long experience in literary journalism and his association with a large publishing house enable him to give many illuminating details on the economics of publishing and the working habits of writers. He has read so many books in manuscript that he knows not only that fraction of the literary iceberg above water but also the far larger section that is submerged—the books that get written but never published.

Mr. Cowley is also well equipped to write such a book because he has moved with and been a part of the American literary scene for over a third of a century. In the 1920's when many American writers were expatriates, he was an expatriate. In the 1930's when many American writers were left-wingers, he was a left-winger. Now he has settled down as an elder statesman of literary journalism, with views on most matters appropriate to his station.

On the other hand, no writer—not even one so well informed as Mr. Cowley—could substantiate all the generalizations in this book. Some of it is pure autobiography; some of it is trivial. When, for instance, Mr. Cowley tells us that most American writers wear "mahogany brogues or loafers" in the country, he is not only dealing in trivia but he is also exceeding the limits of reliable information.

P. P.

73. *Guard of Honor*

by JAMES GOULD COZZENS

Unlike most American novels of World War II, *Guard of Honor* contains no scenes of combat. It takes place entirely within the continental United States, at an Air Force base in Florida, and its concerns are not those of battle. *Guard of Honor*—to the extent that it has a single subject—is about command, about the giving and receiving of orders, and about the way in which things get done or do not get done. It is a study of how the American military system, with its incredible compromises between authority and disobedience, manages to function at all. To this limited degree, it is not a war novel but a novel of American organization and administration—almost a novel of American business. The sense of caste and conduct which its characters bring to the Air Force has been learned elsewhere, out of a deeper and more lasting matrix in American life.

Yet James Gould Cozzens (1903-), who was himself an Air Force officer, has not misrepresented the impact of the second World War on his contemporaries. For successive generations of Americans, war has involved a startled discovery that organization is just as important as bravery; and World War II, for the majority, offered more experience with organization than they had previously known. In it they were confronted, like Mr. Cozzens' Captain Hicks, with the overlapping complexities of administrative situations they might previously have dismissed as simple. And the confrontation is dramatized, in *Guard of Honor,* by its overtones of politics and, more particularly, of race. The war came to America after a decade dominated by liberal convictions, and Mr. Cozzens has taken advantage of this to arrange events so that his liberals are not redeemed by their ideals, but behave very badly and cause more trouble than they save. Some of his critics have thus been led to characterize *Guard of Honor* as "conservative," and to accuse Mr. Cozzens of seeking to justify authority by ridiculing those who are insensitive to its perplexities. Some of his passages on the place held by the Negro in the American armed forces at the time he wrote (which has since changed, and is still changing) may seem unsympathetic. But the reader would do well to remember that it is one of the novelist's privileges to tell what is, as of the moment he perceives it, without having to tell what should be.

E. L.

74. *The Just and the Unjust*

by JAMES GOULD COZZENS

Law is a means toward an end, and in a democracy that end is justice. But law is an abridgement of freedom, which is at the heart of democracy. Law is also a protector of freedom. Law thus stands as mediator between citizen and citizen and between the state and the citizen, guarding the rights and enforcing the obligations of both, and that is justice. This is the theme, here drily stated, of *The Just and the Unjust,* brought literally to life in the account of a trial for murder.

The trial is held in a small northeastern town, where everybody knows everybody, and everybody's personal and family history. But the men accused of a brutal murder are strangers, outsiders, city gangsters, by their very appearance inviting extinction. The town, left free to act, would have been swift. In the center of the town, however, and of its life, stands the courthouse, grim, ugly, but there. Law, the mediator, enters—slow, cautious, cumbersome. The people grow calm. They trust law to render justice. But the trust is not complete. Sometimes law fails, for law must be administered by men. So they watch, and talk, about themselves, about one another, and again about the trial. They keep a critical eye on the judges, the presiding judge and his colleague, the jury (their peers by definition), the lawyers for the defense, the district attorney, and his assistant.

The young assistant has his troubles, and the story is of how he meets them, and how one trouble touches another until they are woven into the context of the town. There is one persistent question: how to be a just man. As the trial moves slowly toward its end, the town watches and the young man is anxious. The two old judges on the bench, and the young assistant's bedridden father, could tell them why, reassure them. They could tell them that of three stable institutions of our English mother country—crown, church, and court of law—America had chosen one, the court of law. A democracy needs stability, forms; and when the jury has rendered its verdict in proper form, it is the judges who speak.

J. A. R.

75. *An Omnibus*

by STEPHEN CRANE

When Stephen Crane (1871-1900) died at 29 he had written enough stories and poems to fill a twelve-volume edition of his collected works, and even that omitted a good many pieces still in manuscript or in the files of newspapers and magazines. The feverish productivity this implies was altogether characteristic of the young man whose genius blazed steadily until exhaustion and illness silenced it. *The Red Badge of Courage* (1895), by which Crane was best known in his time—and indeed it remains his masterpiece—astonished those who learned that its author had never been in battle; a marvelous rendering of fatigue and fear, and a document of the American Civil War which many readers still assume to have come out of firsthand experience, it is in fact no more—and no less—than an exercise of the imagination. Crane's imagination, like that of any narrative artist, is what interests criticism most; and criticism has been busy for two generations assessing and labeling the extraordinary faculties of a writer whose revolution in technique is variously called naturalistic, symbolic, and imagistic. A simpler term would be "intense."

Whatever Crane wrote, whether long or short, whether in prose or in verse, was intense to the breaking-point. The present selection shows the principle working not only in *The Red Badge of Courage* but also in *Maggie: A Girl of the Streets,* written at twenty and published two years later under a pseudonym, as well as in a number of shorter narratives which equally support Crane's reputation. "The Open Boat," justly celebrated as Crane's finest short story and as one of the finest in modern literature, begins with one of those sentences which are quoted as lines of verse are quoted: "None of them knew the color of the sky." "The Blue Hotel" and "The Bride Comes to Yellow Sky" are further specimens of Crane at his best. His best will always seem unique; genius is the right word, in his case.

M. V. D.

76. *Cartoon Cavalcade*

edited by THOMAS CRAVEN

This collection represents the work of 195 American cartoonists and covers the period from 1883 to 1943. Since the latter date there has been a considerable development in the fields of the political and the sophisticated cartoon, as well as a steady degeneration from the already repulsive norm established by most of the comic strip "artists." But this volume is typical and copious enough to serve its purposes.

Cartoons can be looked at in two ways, or both at once: as occasions for happy laughter, and as records of the preoccupations of the nation at a given time. While it is untrue to say that all of these cartoons are funny (many are damnably dull, some—particularly the strips—nauseating) enough of them retain their humor to afford the casual reader many hours of diversion. As a record of the risible and derisible in the life of the American people, they are even more interesting.

The trend from 1883 to our own time would appear to lie in these directions: greater sophistication (the mental innocence of the turn-of-the-century cartoonist, such as Charles Dana Gibson, is almost embarrassing); greater obliqueness of presentation; the growth of the zany, the macabre, and even the neurotic cartoonist; the emergence of the wonderful *New Yorker* school (No. 234), the slow decline of the crackerbox or folksy cartoonist; greater sexual candor; improved draughtsmanship among the straight cartoonists and worse among the successful comic strip artists; the triumph of the one-line caption, or even the captionless cartoon; in the strips the substitution of vulgarity and illiteracy for charm and fancy.

Mr. Craven contributes to this volume three long, solid, entertaining essays: "American Humor and the New Century," "World War I and the Impudent Decade," "The New Deal." Taken as a whole they constitute a sound, informal history of the American cartoon and of the social and political scene on which it has exercised its satire. Mr. Craven considers and judges the work of several dozen of our best comic draughtsmen from Homer Davenport to Walt Disney. His comment, though it may err a bit on the side of enthusiasm, is perceptive, witty, and based on a deep love and knowledge of his subject. The reader is advised to read Mr. Craven with care, for if he does so the rest of the book will have more to give him.

C. F.

77. *Letters from an American Farmer*

by HECTOR ST. JOHN DE CRÈVECOEUR

The "American farmer" was a French gentleman (1735-1813) who made a modest reputation by the publication of his letters, in 1782, though by that time his twenty years of happy wilderness enterprise had come to an unhappy end. He suffered heavily in the frontier warfare of the American Revolution. He ended his book with the description of a project, never attempted, to take his family into a wilderness still deeper than around his home in Pennsylvania, where the foolish and bloody quarrels of civilized men could not disturb them.

He began his explorations and farming experiments in the 1760's. His farming was not an amusement; he cleared and cultivated large properties in Orange County, New Jersey. This makes more remarkable the fact that his descriptions of life in the colonies were so glowing that he is given credit (or blame) for persuading hundreds of settlers to come over from Europe at a time when the practical Benjamin Franklin was warning immigrants not to expect an easy life.

Crèvecoeur did not mean to describe an easy life but rather an idyllic life for the man who was willing to work. In his chapter on "What is an American?" he speaks of the immigrant's escape from Europe—"From involuntary idleness, servile dependence, penury, and useless labor, he has passed to toils of a very different nature, rewarded by an ample subsistence." This was to be a new man and he was to act on new principles.

Descriptions of the wilderness, of the wild animal life, of the whaling islands off Massachusetts and the whaling, of early slavery in the South, gave the book its first success. Then it was forgotten for almost a hundred years. Now it is read as one of the first chapters in the long story of pioneers' progress, to be followed by the many novelists and historians of the pioneering tradition.

L. B.

78. *Critics' Choice*

New York Drama Critics' Circle Prize Plays, 1935-1955

edited by JACK GAVER

Successful plays are not always good literature. If they were, the libraries of the world would be vaster than is now the case. Since they are not, the printed drama is relatively slight in bulk. Every theater must have its play, but the audience does not demand of each such play that it be worthy of becoming a classic. Many plays serve temporary purposes, and do so with an intelligence of which later generations need never be aware. Nor is it easy at one moment in dramatic history to guess what contemporary plays, if any at all, will outlive their time.

Perhaps no member of the New York Drama Critics' Circle—the editor of the present volume is himself a member—believes that his vote for the best play of the year is a decision in favor of immortality. It is rather that the Circle as a group decides each year which play it has admired the most; and since its collective judgment is the best available, for the time being it is dominant. Jack Gaver's volume records the judgments of twenty years (1935-1955) and prints the texts of sixteen plays upon which agreement could be reached. These sixteen plays are therefore a significant revelation of what has been happening in recent years on the New York stage.

The playwrights whose names would stand out in any knowledgeable American's mind are Maxwell Anderson, William Saroyan, Lillian Hellman, Tennessee Williams, Arthur Miller, Sidney Kingsley, and John van Druten. John Steinbeck is better known as a novelist (No. 292), and the others have yet to produce a discussable body of work. The whole impression, however, is powerful, suggestive of a several-sided vitality in the current American theater. The chosen plays are by no means uniform. Some of them, like "Watch on the Rhine" and "Darkness at Noon," deal with grim events of their time; but William Saroyan writes like a happy child, Maxwell Anderson clearly aims at the classic effect, and Tennessee Williams sinks his attention into characters whose predicaments, while perhaps contemporary, are nevertheless something like timeless too.

M. V. D.

79. *Connecticut Yankee*

An Autobiography

by Wilbur L. Cross

The long life of Wilbur L. Cross (1862-1948) forms a bridge between the old New England and the new. Apart from his family, his two great loyalties were Connecticut, the state where he was born, and Yale, the college where he was educated. Both underwent remarkable changes in the years he loved and served them, and he played a leading role in their transformation.

When Mr. Cross entered Yale in 1881 it was a college of about 600 students. The president was a clergyman; the curriculum was prescribed and uniform; the emphasis was on the classical languages. When Mr. Cross was retired as Dean of the Graduate School at Yale in 1930, the college was only one division of a great modern university. The president was a psychologist; students were allowed to choose most of their courses from a large variety of offerings; the classics were being kept alive chiefly by the teaching of Greek and Latin literature in translation.

The state of Connecticut changed quite as much as Yale in Mr. Cross's lifetime. To be sure, the rural Connecticut of his boyhood was not altogether typical. The state had long been a leader in trade and industry—an insurance business had been started in Hartford in 1794, and in 1798, near New Haven, Eli Whitney built a gun factory which first used the key principle of American production methods: standardized interchangeable parts. Therefore industrialization was not new to the state, though it grew enormously in Mr. Cross's lifetime. Perhaps the greatest change was in population. The Englishness of his part of New England was dramatically diluted as large numbers of immigrants, especially from Italy and Central Europe, poured in. In the crucial years of the great Depression when Mr. Cross was Democratic Governor of Connecticut (1931-39), he took the lead in formulating advanced social legislation to protect the state's industrial workers, who were often recent immigrants.

Mr. Cross was distinguished as a scholar of English literature and as editor of *The Yale Review,* but his temperament was essentially political; the spirit of the shrewd and self-reliant boy depicted in the early chapters, who loved nothing quite so much as a good horse-trade, survived to the end.

P. P.

80. *Collected Poems*

by E. E. Cummings

Throughout his career as a poet, which by now is a long one, Mr. Cummings (1894-) has been preoccupied by the preciousness of personal, individual existence. In this respect he continues the great tradition of two classic writers of his native Massachusetts, Emerson (No. 105) and Thoreau (No. 305).

The predominant tone of Mr. Cummings's earlier poems is satirical. He deals fiercely and bitterly with the elements of civilization which frustrate and destroy personality and individuality—war, commercialism, genteel propriety. In his later poems, although he does not cease to exercise his satirical powers, the emphasis is on the joys of personal existence. He becomes one of the few modern poets who express *delight*—in love, in sexuality, in springtime and flowers, in stars and the sun and moon, in the dawn and the night; and he is one of the few modern poets who are frankly, and successfully, lyrical.

What everyone knows about Edward Estlin Cummings is that he spells his name e. e. cummings (though he does not do so on the title page of this edition) and that in general he plays hob with typography. It need scarcely be said that this typographical manipulation, which at first sight might seem arbitrary and meaningless, is never without its serious poetic intention. It serves many purposes, of which perhaps the chief one is to "explode" the conventional logic and syntax—in this it has affinity with the method of the great painters of the Cubist movement—and to leave it to the reader to combine them into meaning; the reader is thus invited (or challenged) to take a more than usually active part in the poem.

Mr. Cummings deals with language in as bold a way as he deals with typography. He makes use of extreme colloquialism, slang, dialect, and extravagant ellipsis in order to shock the reader out of his conventional "poetic" expectations. Especially in his later work he makes use of a linguistic device which seems strange until we perceive that we all use it most of the time: the use of one part of speech as if it were another. It is a characteristic of English that verbs are freely used as nouns and nouns as verbs: we walk or we take a walk, we use a hammer or we hammer. Mr. Cummings speaks of a man (his father) who moved "through sames of am through haves of give." A reader new to Cummings might well begin acquaintance with the poet by reading his prose Introduction to the volume *New Poems* (1938).

L. T.

81. The Enormous Room

by E. E. CUMMINGS

e. e. cummings (1894-) is an early American revolutionary who, born too late to be a signer of the original, takes any means to write his own Declaration of Independence. He believes, as finally as Jefferson himself, that he was born with "certain unalienable rights." But life without liberty is empty and the pursuit of happiness impossible. He was born to this simple belief. Concord, Massachusetts, where an earlier American revolutionary "fired the shot heard round the world," lies a few miles from Cambridge, his home. At the time of his growing up, Harvard University, in Cambridge, was the undisputed intellectual center of America. But intellect is not intelligence:

> the Cambridge ladies who live in furnished souls
> are unbeautiful and have comfortable minds
> (also, with the church's protestant blessings
> daughters, unscented shapeless spirited)

so,

> no time ago
> or else a life
> walking in the dark
> i met christ
>
> jesus)my heart
> flopped over
> and lay still
> while he passed(as
>
> close as i'm to you
> yes closer
> made of nothing
> except loneliness

His independence got him into trouble in France. Having gone there during the first World War as a volunteer ambulance driver, he presently found himself in what would in the next war be called a concentration camp. There he learned first-hand that "it takes a great and good government perfectly to negate mercy," that there was no sure connection between law and justice. *The Enormous Room* is a record of a poet's imprisonment, but it is also a gallery of memorable portraits.

J. A. R.

82. *The Sacramento, River of Gold*

by JULIAN DANA

Rivers were the moving water highways by which explorers first entered America. Traders followed the same routes, offering the Indians cheap tinsel in return for furs which would bring high prices in the markets of the world. Pioneers settled beside the navigable streams in order to be able to float their lumber, their grains, their fruits to the growing cities downstream. In writing the story of how the West was opened, Bernard DeVoto found the key to two of his books (Nos. 91 and 92) in a river, the wide Missouri.

Constance Lindsay Skinner, whose idea it was to tell the history of America through a group of books about its rivers, once wrote: "The natural rhythm moving the pioneer life of America forward was the rhythm of flowing waters . . . we began to be Americans on the rivers." Her project, which she planned to be more literary than formally historical, came into being as "The Rivers of America Series," and three of the volumes written for it appear in this collection—*Great River* (No. 154), *The Hudson* (No. 49), and *The Sacramento.*

The ambitious efforts of Spain, Russia, and England to acquire the vast and fertile lands that enrich the American West are not as well known, even within its own borders, as the simpler annals of eastern regions. Mr. Dana has summarized them with due regard to conventional history—the presentation of significant events in chronological order, the circumstances and motivations from which these events developed, the economic and social results that followed. He has added to these, as Constance Skinner recommended, the songs, the stories, the customs of a curiously heterogeneous people, in the hope that through these his readers may more completely understand his purpose as historian. A river has given his subject geographic cohesion; the inhabitants of its banks have given it historical distinction.

C. C.

83. *Two Years Before the Mast*

by Richard Henry Dana, Jr.

As the author's preface to the original edition (1840) of his narrative indicates, he was well aware that he was doing something new—presenting an account of life at sea from the point of view of the common seaman. Scott, Cooper, and others had written novels of the sea, but "a voice from the forecastle" had hardly yet been heard. That was what Richard Henry Dana, Jr. (1815-1882) proudly claimed to offer.

He was, of course, no common seaman. His father was a New England editor who wrote poetry and essays. Dana himself was a Harvard undergraduate, temporarily unable to continue study because of weak eyesight. Like many of his countrymen, however, especially those brought up under Puritan influences, he rejected the advantages that his birth and position could provide and deliberately started at the bottom, going to sea before the mast.

By nature Dana was a reporter, and he took pride in having "adhered closely to fact in every particular." But his book is more than mere reporting; it is journalism raised—perhaps for the first, but by no means the last, time in American experience—to the level of literature.

To some degree, of course, it is a work of propaganda. Dana wrote it, from notes written during the voyage, in fulfillment of a vow made after two of his fellows had been flogged—a vow that "if God should ever give me the means, I would do something to redress the grievances and relieve the sufferings" of his fellow sailors. As propaganda it succeeded; both in England and the United States it led to legislation benefiting seamen.

If that were all, the book would have died when the conditions it described were reformed. But, as D. H. Lawrence bears witness in his brilliant though erratic *Studies in Classic American Literature* (included in No. 337), Dana's "dispassionate statement of plain material facts" is also the record of "the great fight of the human soul for mastery over life and death, in knowledge." It is the record of a young gentleman's doffing his frock coat and learning what work is, what Cape Horn is, what the sea is. As Lawrence does not say, it is also an unconscious revelation, eight years before the event, of the inevitability of American expansion to the shores of the Pacific Ocean—the subject of Bernard DeVoto's classic trilogy (Nos. 91, 92, and 93).

J. A. K.

84. *The Wilson Era*

by JOSEPHUS DANIELS

Josephus Daniels (1862-1948), though he was never elected to an important public office, had the look and the sound of a "Southern politician of the old school." He frequently wore the "uniform," the broadbrimmed hat and the black string tie; he had the steadfast faith in ornate prose. But he also possessed a larger faith that set him somewhat apart from the main body of the old school. He did not lose himself, like so many of his fellows, in memories of a South before the Civil War that he had never known. Instead, as a newspaperman in his home state of North Carolina, he fought for 30 years to give the South faith in the liberal view and in itself.

His life is an impressive example of the strength and distinction so many Americans have been able to derive from the acceptance of what is best in the regional culture whence they have sprung. Yet it is also an example of the difficulties the essentially provincial mind can get into when suddenly confronted with great affairs and responsibilities. In 1913, when he became Secretary of the Navy, Daniels knew nothing of the conditions of life in the Navy, but he had a clear view of how life, in general, ought to be. With something of the zeal and complacency of the missionary to the heathen tribe, he set out to impose his views upon the naval service. Much that was surprising, and a little that was good, immediately followed. There followed also constant strife between the Secretary of the Navy and some of his ablest officers.

Daniels gives a shrewd account of his own doings in these struggles and also tells much of what went on in the Wilson administration from 1913-1921. He is an expert witness in his own and the President's behalf; the mood of aspiration that Wilson and his followers brought to public affairs is well described (see also No. 142). And one can forgive Daniels much; the lacing of his prose with all the platitudes of literature, the small vanities, such as his anxiety to have it known that though he never lost the common touch he had indeed walked with kings, his inability to expand his original stock of opinions—these can all be forgiven because he was, at the very bottom, both authentic and a pure type.

E. E. M.

85. Life in America

by MARSHALL B. DAVIDSON

Pictorial history can be extremely misleading, since it reflects style at least as strongly as it suggests content. It tends, of course, to simplify and prettify history, heightening it to romantic frenzy or leveling it to classical calm. It tends to make all pioneers into heroes, all sailors jolly, all landscapes beautiful or, in the hands of the satirist, precisely the opposite. Daily life is rarely drudgery, though it is sometimes squalor. Entertainment is always gay or vicious; it is never boring. Work is made to seem like fun, or uplifting. It is rarely just necessary. In *Life in America* Mr. Davidson (1907-) has balanced pictures with prose in such a manner that what emerges is as near to the truth as the historian, considering the material available to him, can make it.

The first volume of *Life in America* tells the story of Europe's discovery of the western hemisphere, the first settlements on the North American continent, and the struggles for survival. It describes life in America in the colonial period, the establishment of its independence from European rule, the opening of the West, and the expansion of American interests through trade beyond the seas. America as a primarily agricultural nation turns in the middle of the nineteenth century toward industrialization. The second volume of *Life in America* is more of a history of modes and manners, of how Americans have amused themselves, of how they have lived in their cities, and of how they have been welded into a nation with a unique social and political philosophy.

Life in America is an informative and entertaining primer of American history and culture. It makes no pretense at completeness, though it is the first successful attempt (and an ambitious one) to tell this particular story through a carefully contrived balance between pictures and text. For the purpose of establishing America in the eye of the mind, there is no other volume in this collection of books so useful as this one.

R. L.

86. Honey in the Horn

by H. L. Davis

To most people, Americans and others alike, the glittering Far West of the American dream is California. The northwestern states of Washington and Oregon are less familiar. But, as Bernard DeVoto points out in *The Year of Decision: 1846* (No. 93), this was not always so. Rival claims with Great Britain and the fame of the Oregon Trail (Parkman in No. 240 deals only with the eastern portion of the route) called attention to the Oregon territory and attracted settlers there while California remained relatively unknown. But the discovery of gold in 1848 started a flood of migrants to California (see No. 83); and since then the northern states have lived in the shadow of their big, rich, and influential southern neighbor.

H. L. Davis's *Honey in the Horn* is a fictional narrative of the open spaces of Oregon and its restless inhabitants in more recent years—the homesteading period of 1906-1908. Although the two principal characters are unappealing and unrevealed in action, their long string of adventures brings them into contact with sheepherders, horse traders, sawmill workers, hop pickers, wheat thrashers, storekeepers, real estate men, sheriffs, desperadoes, Indians, half-breeds, cowboys, and settlers of every variety. The author admits in a note at the beginning of his novel that at one time his ambition had been to include "a representation of every calling that existed in the state of Oregon" during this period; and he has done almost that. Before establishing a reputation as one of America's finest prose writers, H. L. Davis worked as a typesetter, cowboy, sheepherder, deputy sheriff, surveyor, folk singer, and poet. *Honey in the Horn* has the tang and force of real knowledge and experience, and the cowboys (whom he calls "vaqueros") and Indians are not of the romantic stuff to be found in most Westerns (see No. 130).

C. G.

87. The Best of Clarence Day

The place of Clarence Day (1874-1935) in our literature is minor but assured. And it would be assured even if millions had not met his most famous work through the classic Howard Lindsay–Russel Crouse play version of "Life with Father" (in No. 284). His claims are double: he is that rare animal, a philosophical humorist; and he is the portrait-painter, or perhaps only the watercolorist, of a way of life and a kind of character that have today vanished from the American scene. Vivid social history that is at the same time appealing humor: this is the unique hallmark of Clarence Day's three books of reminiscence.

Clarence Day is the only begetter of the literally hundreds of nostalgic family chronicles that have diverted or bored American readers during the past quarter of a century. His stories, however, are not merely the first; they remain the best. The elder Day has become the classic type of the heavy Victorian-American lovable family tyrant, as his wife has become the classic type of the fragile female who always wins. The background—that of a wealthy, self-confidently upper-class New York family from the 1880's well into the new century—has rarely been better explored, even in novels written with greater care and finish. And the tone, that of a gentle irony, so intelligent that it need never stress its own perceptiveness, has proved induplicable.

The more reflective Clarence Day is to be found in *This Simian World* and *The Crow's Nest,* the first of which is included in this volume. Day had a Voltairean streak in him, a tough-minded skepticism that combined engagingly with a basic American idealism. This aspect of his witty and nimble mind appears most notably in *This Simian World* which, though less familiar than his household chronicles, is probably his finest work. One should not forget too that he was a first-class writer of light satirical verse (see *Thoughts Without Words*) and that his impish drawings may have fathered a whole school of American caricature—compare, for example, James Thurber (No. 306).

America has produced many intelligent writers and many charming ones, but few who are both intelligent and charming. Clarence Day with ease contrived to be both. His work is small-scaled and in a way unimposing; but his touch was so sure that he produced no failures.

C. F.

88. *Indian Tales*

by Jaime de Angulo

Most Americans have misconceptions about the American Indian and scant knowledge of his contributions to the art and folklore of his country. As for art, elsewhere in this collection (*Indian Art in the United States,* No. 100) the reader will find much that may awaken his interest in and awareness of the Indians' creativity. As for folklore, as Carl Carmer points out in the foreword to *Indian Tales,* Jaime de Angulo (1887-1950) "has packed his book . . . with tall tales and jokes, ceremonial rituals and poetic allegories, gambling games, and hunting adventures." From the stories and myths of certain California tribes, among whom he spent forty years of his life, de Angulo has composed the series of incidents that occur during the prehistoric travels of the animal-human Bear family. With humor and pathos he has mingled a casual, happy tale with abstraction and poetry.

De Angulo wrote these stories and illustrated them with delightful drawings for his children but, as with most folk tales, the adult reader will also find enjoyment and reward in reading and rereading them. If he is puzzled by inconsistencies, improbabilities, or marvels in the Indian world, he can only be advised to relax and recall the answer given the author by an Indian elder: "Why not? . . . Anyway . . . that's what the old people always said . . . only they don't all tell the same story. Here is one way I heard it."

C. G.

89. *Dance to the Piper*

by AGNES DE MILLE

Although Agnes de Mille (1908-) is an accomplished ballet dancer and pantomimic artist, her contribution to modern dancing lies less in her achievement as a solo performer than in the part she has played in the revolution of musical comedy. Just as the contemporary theater owes the banishment of silliness and triviality from the musical play to such greatly gifted composers and lyricists as Richard Rodgers and Oscar Hammerstein II, it owes to the choreographic daring and invention of Miss de Mille the disappearance of the dull mechanical routines which for so long passed for dancing.

Dance to the Piper, Miss de Mille's informal autobiography, is an account of the unusually hard road she traveled to professional success. As a child, she worshiped Pavlova; despite parental opposition, she was determined to be a ballet dancer. But even when she was old enough to defy her parents' puritanism, Miss de Mille found it almost impossible to make a career in ballet, either in America or Europe. The history of her young womanhood is a record of virtually total failure until chance brought her the opportunity to create the ballet, *Rodeo,* and on the heels of that victory to design the dances for the famous *Oklahoma!*

But the interest of *Dance to the Piper* is not limited to students of dancing or the theater. It has considerable, if accidental, sociological interest as well—and not only because its ironic, self-mocking, passionately dedicated author is so typical of her American generation and cultural class. Daughter of George de Mille and niece of the spectacular Cecil B. de Mille of Hollywood fame, granddaughter of Henry George (see No. 127), the celebrated exponent of the doctrine of the single tax, Agnes de Mille was uniquely situated to experience the chaotic, poignant efforts of many of the cultural pioneers of this century. Her recollections of her strange upbringing and education make a fascinating footnote to the record of confusion which is also the history of so much artistic progress in the past fifty years.

D. T.

90. *Democracy in America*

by ALEXIS DE TOCQUEVILLE

This young French aristocrat's account of democracy in the United States in the time of Andrew Jackson has been called "perhaps the greatest book ever written on one country by the citizen of another." Most Americans would now concede that it must also have been the most prophetic of travelers' commentaries, since Alexis de Tocqueville (1805-1859) anticipated so many of the problems which the young country was to find ahead of it. He and another French youth came to the United States to study prisons. He went back to write two volumes: one a description of the social, legal, and economic workings of the new democratic country; the second a broad philosophic examination of the problems of democracy in general. What he was looking at was then feared and hated by his kind in Europe; indeed, he himself did not like democracy. But he knew it had come to stay.

He anticipated that the executive, the President, would gain in power at the expense of the other "powers" which were balanced by the Constitution. He hoped that this tendency could be checked. The President might be closer to the immediate wishes of the people than Congress or Court, but the wishes of the people might be, at least momentarily, unworthy and a majority could exert the most odious of tyrannies. The protection of liberty, he thought, would lie in the local *administration* of national policies. This protection has diminished in recent years; the stranger to American governmental history can better understand what may seem like a sentimental fight for "states' rights" if he keeps this principle in mind.

De Tocqueville counted also on the extraordinary propensity of the Americans to solve all kinds of problems by volunteer organizations. How this has been maintained, and how it accounts for the strange effect of "overorganization" in our life is described in Bradford Smith's *A Dangerous Freedom* (No. 285). To follow other trends in de Tocqueville's prognosis one can read Frank Thistlethwaite's *The Great Experiment* (No. 303) and the general history by Samuel Eliot Morison and Henry Steele Commager (No. 225). Phillips Bradley's extended introduction is a necessary part of an intelligent reading of the great commentary now; it will keep the reader from supposing that de Tocqueville, even though he was an authentic prophet, could foresee in detail the United States of today.

L. B.

91. Across the Wide Missouri

by BERNARD DEVOTO

By 1848 the United States was in full flood of expansion into the scarcely known lands of the Far West. This movement is the subject of *The Year of Decision: 1846* (No. 93), by Bernard DeVoto (1897-1955), who gives an account in the present volume of the years before the great migrations began, when the Far West was as yet penetrated only by the men of the fur trade, by missionaries, and by a few adventurous travelers, scientists, and artists.

The period of the truly "wild West" did not last long, but long enough to make an undying American legend. The spell of a dangerous, beautiful land, unlike any other, was very strong. It was felt by the "mountain men," the fur trappers, who never realized their hope of wealth but who had no wish ever to change their hard, free lives. It was felt by Captain William Drummond Stewart of the British Army, a man of fortune, later heir to a baronetcy and great estates, who spent five years among the mountain men and never got over his experience. In his Scottish castle he was later attended by one of his Western friends, dressed in kilts, and lived surrounded by Indian weapons and trophies of old hunts. And the spell was manifestly felt by Alfred Jacob Miller, the artist whom Stewart took with him on his travels, to record what was to be seen. (DeVoto reproduces many of Miller's admirable recently discovered water colors.) It was no less felt by the stalwart Marcus Whitman and his beautiful wife Narcissa, missionaries on their way to Oregon who met their deaths at the hands of Indians.

No one has served the memory of the old wild West better than Bernard DeVoto. His feeling for it was as passionate as his knowledge of it was encyclopedic. He can tell us everything we want to know about the mountain men; he understood and admired them without sentimentalizing them. His knowledge of the Indians of the old time is vast—after reading this book, no one can possibly think of Indians in the mass; one will always want to distinguish among the many tribes, knowing that they are all different in appearance and in manners and morals. And no one reading DeVoto's description of the wild joy of a buffalo hunt will fail to grieve that the possibility of such delight is forever gone.

L. T.

92. *The Course of Empire*

by BERNARD DEVOTO

For Bernard DeVoto (1897-1955), the story of geographical exploration was the type case of intellectual discovery. Those courageous men who felt their way into the unknown—led onward by illusion, led astray by ignorance—were to him as valiant heroes in the pursuit of scientific truth as were the discoverers of planets or atomic particles. They replaced myth with fact. They tore aside the veil of false knowledge which had blinded their predecessors; they left behind them knowledge which was firm and reliable, which would not deceive those who followed after, which could be used to build on. But what tantalized DeVoto was the interplay of discovery and delusion. If the discoverers had not been deluded, why would they ever have left home?

The author began this, his grandest and most spacious book, with the intention of recounting the journey (1804-5) of Meriwether Lewis and William Clark, the first two Americans to traverse the continent that would eventually be occupied by the United States. Before he finished his work DeVoto found, as the reader will, that his narrative began with the Moors in the eighth century and encompassed nearly all of the westward adventurers, from the French in the north to the Spaniards in the south. They were linked together for the author by their shared fund of heroism and ignorance, the ordeals they could endure in a common belief that just over the horizon lay one or another of their fabled objectives: the Seven Cities of Cibola, the Welsh Indians, the Northwest Passage, the untapped riches of Cathay. "We ever held it certain," said one of them, "that going toward the sunset we would find what we desired." In destroying such mirages they uncovered for Western man the scarcely less amazing actuality of the American West.

DeVoto's parallel theme is the inalterable impact of geography on the course of events. Since rivers and mountain ranges are where they are, and not where desire put them, some deeds are possible and others are not. The logic of the land mass between the Great Lakes and the Rio Grande held that the national power holding it must extend to the Pacific Ocean. This heartland of America —the great central valley that Lincoln called the "Egypt of the West"—must find its way "to Europe by New York, to South America and Africa by New Orleans, and to Asia by San Francisco. . . . And this is true *wherever* a dividing line or boundary line may be fixed." The three books of DeVoto's great trilogy (the other two are Nos. 91 and 93) can be considered, so he said, as a gloss on this passage from Lincoln's Second Annual Message to Congress.

E. L.

93. The Year of Decision: 1846

by BERNARD DEVOTO

The greatest decision that was made by the United States in 1846 was, as this author of that year's chronicle puts it, to acquire something that "no people had ever had before, an internal, domestic empire." The decision had been a long time in the making. Meriwether Lewis and William Clark had completed in 1805 their famous expedition to the Pacific (No. 92). There had followed an ever-growing stream of emigrants to the West, chiefly to Oregon, which was then occupied jointly by England and the United States. The belief that it was the "manifest destiny" of the United States to expand to the Pacific took hold of the popular mind and became a pressing issue in politics.

The tempo of events was speeded up by the disagreement between the United States and England over the division of the Oregon territory, and by the American belief, well enough founded, that Britain had an eye on California, which belonged to, but was scarcely governed by, Mexico. But the decision to take action was delayed for reasons of internal politics of the gravest nature. New territories meant new states, and with the admission of each new state there would arise the bitter question of whether it would be slave or free. Although the South favored the war with Mexico, the results of that war—the acquisition of California and the opening of the West—shifted the balance of power against her and made secession inevitable. As the author says, "At some time between August and December, 1846, the Civil War had begun."

Bernard DeVoto (1897-1955) was well known as a novelist, critic, and essayist. But his chief interest was the history of the American West, in which he himself was born and for which he had a deep sympathy. Here he has set down the events of a fateful year, the diplomacy, the military movements, the cultural situation that supported the dream of Western empire, and —perhaps most dramatic of all—the actual experiences of the people as they crossed the continent. DeVoto was not a man who pretended to dispassionateness, and this is especially true of him when he wrote about the West. His book is charged with the vivacity of his judgment on the actors in this great national drama, such as his dislike of Frémont, the Byronic explorer and politico; his contempt for Hastings, whose book on the West gave so much fatal misinformation; his delight in Susan Magoffin, the seventeen-year-old bride, whose journal he draws upon; and his admiration for that remarkable soldier and scholar, General Ethan Allen Hitchcock.

L. T.

94. *Intelligence in the Modern World*

by John Dewey
edited by Joseph Ratner

After the death of William James (No. 163) in 1910, John Dewey (1859-1952) was for 40 years the leading American philosopher. His system of ideas was built upon the assumption that the primary concern of philosophy was "to clarify, liberate, and extend the goods which inhere in the naturally generated functions of experience. It has no call to create a world of 'reality' *de novo,* nor to delve into secrets of Being hidden from common sense and science." Dewey's purpose, as a philosopher, was to enable contemporary men to come to grips with the only reality they could know, the modern industrial world transformed as it had been by the findings and applications of science, and to encourage them to modify that world by action informed by common sense.

He followed his own counsel, seeking always to narrow the gap between theory and practice by intelligent making and doing. He advised foreign governments and, at home, involved himself in the activities of the Socialist Party. At critical moments, as in the debate over the application of sanctions against Japan in 1932, he brought the weight of his mind and reputation directly to bear on the formation of public policy. He changed the character of American education by introducing in an experimental Chicago school "progressive methods of instruction" that have, a half century later, become traditional.

This ceaseless engagement in the experience of the society around him was the fullest demonstration Dewey gave of his own philosophy. Man, the measure of all things, possessed in his intelligence a marvelous tool for observation, inquiry, and understanding. In using it he should seek more "to change the world through action" than to change the self, for man already has beliefs about the values for regulating conduct "which scientific inquiry vouchsafes." Dewey elaborates on this proposition in the pages that follow. To some it is an appalling view of life that is presented. However that may be, this book is indispensable source material. In it one may find—clearly reasoned, formally organized, and compellingly stated—a set of attitudes that still reside, unstated and perhaps unrealized, in many of John Dewey's countrymen.

E. E. M.

95. Selected Poems of Emily Dickinson

The power of Emily Dickinson's (1830-1886) poetry has gradually been recognized during the decades since her death in 1886. She lived obscurely in Amherst, Massachusetts; died in the expectation that her poems would be burned; and remained unknown to any public until her sister Lavinia, unable to destroy the manuscripts that survived, took them to a neighbor, Mrs. Todd, who selected enough of them to fill three small volumes which a Boston publisher brought out in 1890, 1891, and 1896. These volumes were successful—it could hardly be otherwise, considering the force that must have been felt on every page—and yet it was not until the second quarter of the twentieth century that the full story of Emily Dickinson was told.

Indeed it is not yet told, for the biography is still obscure in certain places and although the total number of published poems is now greater than 1,700, critics have by no means fathomed all of their meanings and interrelations. Emily Dickinson's reputation continues to grow, not only in the United States but elsewhere in the world. There can be no question of her greatness, but her rank is still to be determined. No competent judge doubts that it will be somewhere near the top in that art which Emily Dickinson practiced with such queer secrecy and passionate devotion for so many lonely years.

Biographers have been busy with the theory that renunciation of some lover was the principal source of her intensity, which often has tragic overtones such as appear in the greatest and most serious music. The evidence as to this lover, however, remains so faint and self-contradictory that an alternative theory now seems justified: Emily Dickinson was born a superb artist, by study made herself an artist still more superb, and ended by leaving behind her a body of work comparable with that of any overwhelming genius. The intellectual and emotional energy in this work is all but unimaginable. It expresses itself, too, with an unflagging wit. There is no poet anywhere like Emily Dickinson.

M. V. D.

96. *Coronado's Children*

by J. Frank Dobie

"Coronado's children" are those innumerable men (and sometimes women) who continue the search in Texas and other southwestern states for fabulous gold, reputed to be waiting under water or dry land until the moment when some intelligent person shall find it. America was first dreamed of as a land of gold—of easy gold, not to be mined but simply to be picked up and packed away, or at the most to be plundered from savage kings who rolled and bathed in it as if it were common stuff. The original Spanish explorers came with nothing less than this as their objective; and, to be sure, the kingdoms of Mexico and Peru yielded up much treasure, just as in the nineteenth century California and Nevada rewarded with gold and silver the first men who arrived over the mountains or around Cape Horn.

But J. Frank Dobie (1888-), a Texan who is fascinated by the living folklore of his section and has made that folklore familiar around the world, is mainly interested in the easy gold which the sixteenth-century Francisco Coronado believed existed not too far away from where he traveled, and which subsequent legions of fanatics have expended their energy in pursuing through passes and streams where someone once saw it or heard about it but had to leave it because on that occasion he could not take it with him.

Perhaps a band of Indians was after his scalp; perhaps he was wounded or ill; perhaps he was weak from hunger and thirst; whatever the circumstance, he had to be content with a glimpse of the ineffable substance and the means he took to make sure that he could find his way back to it again. Only, it was never there; some mistake had been made; it must be over the next hill, or farther down the river; he would have to correct his map, or someone else would after his death. So the stories go.

Mr. Dobie rode far and wide among the ranches and shanties of the Southwest, talking with men who had the faith and were willing to share it with him; or who knew others that had it; or who merely had heard tales. Of such stuff is folklore made, in America or elsewhere, now or long ago.

M. V. D.

97. *Caste and Class in a Southern Town*

by JOHN DOLLARD

In America the social scientist has become a prophet, minor as yet but on his way to majority. But, however hard he may try to be scientific—"objective" is his word—he is still a human being and himself "conditioned," his word again. When therefore he elects to investigate a subject like racial relations and the resultant bias, he is duty-bound to have a look at himself first. He may find that he himself is biased. The author of this book, John Dollard (1900-), a professor of psychology at Yale, found that to be so.

The reader will be obliged to develop a tolerance for the gritty jargon of the social scientist. But he who manages to surmount this barrier and keep a sharp eye about him will find data here on which to begin to form his judgment. As to the data themselves, no fair-minded American, whatever his bias, will demur. As to their selection and arrangement, there may be some question. The data, recorded, tend to lie flat upon the page, undifferentiated as to quality. For example, the chapter titled "The Sexual Gain" takes up in space about a fourteenth of the book's total. In feeling—Southern, and increasingly, Northern—the proportion is in the reverse. All other "gains" are subservient to and dependent upon the white Southerner's determination, whatever its ground, to exclude the Negro or any offspring of the Negro from his caste.

Southern bias, what the Southerner thinks of and about the Negro, and how he feels, is voiced in William Alexander Percy's *Lanterns on the Levee* (No. 245), less explicitly in the writing of his Mississippi neighbors, William Faulkner (No. 108) and Eudora Welty (No. 324). For the Southern Negro, Booker T. Washington, in *Up from Slavery* (No. 320), was an eloquent spokesman of his time; among present-day Northern city-bred Negroes, the most brilliant writer is James Baldwin, author of *Go Tell It on the Mountain* (No. 18).

J. A. R.

98. Lincoln Reconsidered

by DAVID DONALD

Some years ago George Stevens, who then edited *The Saturday Review of Literature,* published a small book about best-sellers entitled *Lincoln's Doctor's Dog.* The title was meant to suggest the infallible formula for literary success: write about a dog, let it belong to a doctor, and have the doctor be Lincoln's. Today the formula might have to be revised as to doctors and for all I know, dogs, but the Lincoln cult continues. Professor Donald, a member of the history department at Columbia University and a specialist on the Civil War and Reconstruction periods, has undertaken to revise the prevailing judgments—not to say the national myths—about Abraham Lincoln (see Nos. 12 and 272).

From Lincoln's personal life to his attitude toward politics, and from his intellectual development to the role of his chief opponents within his own party, Professor Donald covers in remarkably brief compass every important notion that the common reader of the abundant output about Lincoln undoubtedly entertains. And yet it is from that self-same literature—much of it scholarly—that the author draws his corrective arguments, many of them showing that alleged black is white or *vice versa.*

On one point indeed, he is perhaps himself open to amendment, namely, with regard to Lincoln's feelings about dispensing patronage. The President may have occasionally enjoyed his dexterity in achieving his ends, but the proof exists that he hated the drudgery and low cunning of patronage bargains.

What is implied in these trenchant essays is that Americans, like other peoples since the oldest antiquity, have a strong strain of hero worship and a lively myth-making power. It is a noteworthy difference, however, that in the United States the power and the feeling usually exert themselves on national figures once they have passed from the scene. Neither Washington nor Hamilton nor Jefferson nor Franklin nor Lincoln was much of a hero to his people while alive. Party feeling naturally prevents the whole nation from agreeing on one man, but even within his own party the crystallization which made a Gladstone, say, the idol of millions, has rarely appeared in America. We have democratic skepticism and the wide diversity of regions, which split parties, to thank for this.

And that is why, when the myth takes hold and amplifies both virtue and the admiration of virtue, astringents such as Professor Donald's become necessary for the sake of historical truth.

J. B.

99. U.S.A.

by John Dos Passos

This is the most comprehensive panorama of American society ever attempted in fiction. From 1900, just after the Spanish-American War, to the depths of the great Depression in 1935, it ranges transcontinentally, encompassing the lives of many real and fictional people from disparate backgrounds.

Without traditional plot, *U.S.A.* (like the nation whose culture is its real protagonist) seems at first glance chaotic. It is thematic in structure, rather than biographical or dramatic like most novels, and its meaning is conveyed by the complex pattern in which the author has arranged the book's four chief elements: the general social-political scene; the author's own subjective viewpoint; the lives of twelve major fictional characters; and the lives of twenty-five public figures.

For each element John Dos Passos (1896-) employs distinctive techniques. He presents the general historical context in the Newsreels—kaleidoscopic montages of popular songs and snatches from newspapers. He conveys his subjective viewpoint in The Camera Eye—fragmentary stream-of-consciousness sketches which cumulatively reveal the quality of the creative intelligence which has observed and arranged the objective details elsewhere in the book (the lens, or eye, through which actuality has been refracted). For the narratives of his fictional characters he employs a dispassionate case-history technique, relentlessly documentary in tone. Finally, he tells the stories of the public figures in brief, impressionistic biographies. These carefully interrelated elements, in ironic juxtaposition, convey the book's vision of the nation at one of its most troubled moments.

Despite evident links with radical political and artistic movements in Europe, *U.S.A.* is in many ways a very "American" book. Its attempt to comprehend the diversity of the nation by "adding up fractions" relates it firmly to a tradition going back at least to Walt Whitman's *Leaves of Grass* (No. 333). Its concern with the homeless wanderer, whose lonely figure brackets the trilogy and is personified by many of the characters, ties it to Melville's "Ishmael" in *Moby Dick* (No. 211) and to the tales and legends described in Constance Rourke's *American Humor* (No. 268). In its insistence that "mostly U.S.A. is the speech of the people," it becomes a part of the oral tradition which has shaped so much else in American literature.

J. A. K.

100. *Indian Art of the United States*

by Frederic H. Douglas *and* René d'Harnoncourt

In the early days of America's history, European settlers readily adopted in agriculture and wilderness warfare Indian techniques without which many of them might not have survived. The Iroquois Confederation of six separate tribes provided them with a lesson in government as well when, after the revolution against British rule, the erstwhile colonists formed their own peaceful union of thirteen liberated states and agreed upon a federal constitution. And as late as World War II the Signal Corps of the United States Army accepted the advantage given them by Indian soldiers (representative of hundreds of tribes resident within America) who spoke in their own languages messages untranslatable when intercepted by the enemy.

Few white citizens have become conscious, however, of the specific contributions to their culture which are to be found in Indian art. Though the Indians have had in the past little interest in "art for art's sake," they have delighted in creating decorations for their pipes, their weapons, and their tools, and in illustrating their religious myths, many of which prove them a people of fertile and poetic fancy. With their increasing knowledge of materials and methods used by their white neighbors, the Indians have not lost the distinction which previously characterized their arts. This book, based on a representative exhibit presented in 1941 by the Museum of Modern Art in New York City, has done much to prove that white citizens of the United States have for generations been singularly unobservant.

While American tourists have exhibited their sentimental attitudes toward the Indian by purchasing countless cheaply made and tasteless souvenirs in the "Indian Trading Posts" which can be found in nearly all vacation areas of the nation, true Indian art is of a different quality and has exercised a subtle but worthy influence on design and the use of color throughout America. The authors' introduction to this volume is particularly valuable in its insistence that this art, while generally anonymous and stemming from "folk" sources, is not primitive. "Most Indian art," the authors say, "is the result of a long period of development in which capable craftsmen devoted all their inventive skill to perfecting specialized techniques and styles."

C. C.

101. *Sister Carrie*

by THEODORE DREISER

While he was still a boy his family moved to a small drab town in Indiana, and there Theodore Dreiser (1871-1945) saw close up an example of the great American disaster. His father, having given promise of being a success, became instead a failure. At the time there was no middle ground; a man was one or the other, success or failure, and it was personal. If a man was a failure, it was his own fault; he lacked the wit and will to be a success, to make his competitor a failure. The farmer had an excuse, drought or flood, but in the business world there were no acts of God. Every newspaper told the story of success, as did every magazine—one even bore the title. There were other voices speaking for the victims of success, but they were drowned out in the din of praise for the business hero. It would take 40 years and a depression to prove that a man could be a failure by no fault of his own, or a success by no virtue.

But the heroes were men, not women. Woman's place was still in the home, where there was no measurable success, or in—an open confession of failure—the factory or office, or perhaps worse. One of Dreiser's sisters is said to have chosen the worse, and unwittingly given him a model, while his brother Paul changed his name from the hateful German Dreiser to "Dresser" and became a success as a writer of popular songs. Paul had a mistress who was also a success, as madam of a disreputable establishment in Evansville. Paul's mistress was generous, but Theodore never forgot the shame of her bounty. Failure with degradation, success with respectability—he accepted these equations. What made *Sister Carrie* the shocker of its day, postponing the author's success, was that it depicted a woman who was a success, without regard to the respectability of her means. This was un-American.

J. A. R.

102. *Concept of the Corporation*

by Peter F. Drucker

The corporation is the directing agent of the American industrial revolution. Embodying as it does the principle of limited liability, it offers opportunities for calculating and taking risks without which the economy could not develop. Protected from deprivations of liberty or property without due process of law, it enjoys great freedom of movement. Endowed with existence in perpetuity, it provides a firm environment for determining long-range plans and policies. Concentrating as it does the directing authority in the hands of a few responsible officers, it serves as a flexible, efficient administrative instrument to organize and control the tremendous energies at its disposal.

It was not always so. Sixty and 70 years ago the great corporations in this country loomed as clear and present dangers. True, they had organized and developed the sources of material strength in the society, but in so doing they had acquired so much power that they seemed able to act independently in their own special interest without regard to the authority of the state or the public welfare. By an evolutionary process over the past half century, a process shaped in part by legislation and by executive action, restrictions were devised within which the useful actions of the corporation could take place without dislocating the structure of society (see No. 3).

In the course of this development the corporation had to devise means, within itself, to organize and satisfy its constituents; it had to devise means to determine wise plans and policies; it had to figure out ways in which to encourage imagination and maintain energy within its vast system. Corporations, in other words, developed rules, customs, attitudes of mind, and moralities—they became small civilizations. It is with the nature and meaning of these civilizations that Peter F. Drucker (1909-) is concerned. One of his great contributions in this study, based on his own experience with a large American firm, is to assign the corporation its proper place in society. It is more, he indicates, than a place to manufacture things; it is a social institution with all the privileges, obligations, and characteristics this implies.

E. E. M.

103. *America Learns to Play*

by Foster Rhea Dulles

There is some truth to the notion that Americans regard work as play, and go at play rather as if it were work. Certainly our attitudes toward play are full of ambiguities, enough so to provide fertile fields for an economist like Veblen (No. 315) or a sociologist like David Riesman (No. 259). An historian like Walter P. Webb (No. 322) argues that the driving force in our historical development has been "the religion of work," but his argument at least implies that, with the disappearance of the frontier, religion has begun to lose its hold. Foster Rhea Dulles (1900-) seems to offer an inverse parallel, tracing the emergence of the twentieth century's riotous torrent of popular recreation from the rather thin streams which enlivened American life in the seventeenth and eighteenth centuries.

At the moment there is a good deal of evidence that our ways of employing (what a revealing word!) leisure are undergoing rapid change. (Lyman Bryson and David Riesman both imply [Nos. 43 and 258] that the new frontier may be the frontier of leisure itself.) One thinks of men like Irving Langmuir (in No. 340) who, even while he was employed by a hard-headed corporation, said that he never undertook research with a practical goal in mind but only "because I was curious, I guess," and continued it, quite simply, "for the fun of it." Here we have a pure scientist sounding much like an artist, a ski enthusiast, or an amateur musician. Readers of Mr. Dulles' book will want to look also at Ring Lardner's wonderful stories of boxers and ball players (No. 179); Barbara Morgan's *Summer's Children* (No. 222); and perhaps most revealing of all, the enormous section devoted to "Usable Information for Self-Improvement and Recreation" in *The Everyday Reference Library* (No. 68), with its evangelical "pointers" about grooming, vacations, sports and games, handicrafts, and "popular hobbies for beginners."

J. A. K.

104. *Mr. Dooley at His Best*

by FINLEY PETER DUNNE
edited by ELMER ELLIS

The philosopher of Archey Road is less a humorist than an indispensable interpreter of the United States at the turn of the century. The period he covers, however, is a veritable thicket of contradictory appearances, and though Mr. Dooley can be read with full pleasure without notes, any conclusion drawn from his remarks should be tested by reference to direct historical narratives such as Samuel Eliot Morison and Henry Steele Commager's (No. 225) or Frank Thistlethwaite's (No. 303).

For the America that hung poised midway between the Civil War and the first World War can be made to show any aspect one desires. It was the playground of ruthless capitalists and financiers, but also the age of reform and "muckraking"; it was the time of dollar diplomacy and jingoist imperialism —as shown in the Spanish-American War—but also the time when the severest criticism of the national ethos was being written—by Frank Norris, Jack London, and John Jay Chapman, as well as by the older generation: William Dean Howells, Henry James, and Mark Twain himself. It was an era of great capitalist monopolies, but also of trust-busting and public conservation of national resources. In political affairs, Grover Cleveland, William Jennings Bryan, Theodore Roosevelt, and Woodrow Wilson showed that the country was not without thought, integrity, energy, or the powers of eloquence. To outsiders it was still a huge, sprawling, indistinct though noisy entity; yet this was the time when Americans were systematically buying their access to art and culture through the agency of the great collectors, and Andrew Carnegie was taking the lead in redistributing the wealth of learning through his innumerable public libraries.

Mr. Dooley, the Chicago-Irish ward politico, is the philosophic observer of this kaleidoscopic scene. His language shows the detachment of an outsider, but his depth of understanding betrays the earnest concern of a true patriot. He is characteristically American in that he is a newspaperman's creation—an expanded and refined form of the "cracker-barrel philosopher" like Kin Hubbard (No. 170). But he is also characteristic in the fact that while being genuinely an American, he is not "assimilated" in speech, manners, or criteria of judgment.

The literary form of Mr. Dooley's dialogues is worth noting: they are short and tend to be epigrammatic because they have to fit into a newspaper column. F. P. Dunne (1867-1936) was one of the first of the new literary type known as the columnist, and unquestionably he is still the king of them all.

J. B.

105. *The Portable Emerson*

edited by MARK VAN DOREN

In this compact volume Mr. Van Doren has assembled enough of Ralph Waldo Emerson (1803-1882) to give the reader a sense of the living man rather than the would-be prophet-philosopher. Emerson's Transcendentalism and his doctrine of the Oversoul are part of his time and, not having worn well, are now properly the province of students of literature. But there is a great deal of Emerson left, though less now perhaps than was seen by our grandfathers, who could more easily accept his easy optimism and universal cheerfulness.

It was not when Emerson was enunciating vague "truths" but rather when he was observing freshly the life of men around him that he became most electric and persuasive. *That* Emerson is here: in his masterly *English Traits,* which still retains its edge and its gleam of truth; in a few of his abstract essays, pre-eminently those here included; in his center-striking appreciations of some of his contemporaries, notably his two friends, Henry David Thoreau and Thomas Carlyle; in his vast *Journal,* from which a good solid excerpt is here included; and in his letters.

Emerson, though less forthrightly than Henry David Thoreau (see No. 305), stands for certain traits in the American character which, let us say, are now undergoing revision. He believes in the life of the mind: "Life consists in what a man is thinking about all day." He typifies more fully than any of our major writers the traditional American emphasis on the unlimited potentialities of the individual. His democracy is not the old-shoe democracy which cries up mediocrity, but that which assumes that all men are equal in their desire to become better and more highly conscious. At its best his optimism reflects our native vigor and our sense of infinite possibility; at its worst (and it has a worst) it is the ancestor of the cheap inspirationalism which is one of the toxins in our twentieth-century bloodstream. His insistence on the necessity and possibilities of an American—not Europe-imitative—culture was salutary in his day, and retains its point in our own time.

Though others said many of the things Emerson said, they are forgotten. He is still a force because he is an artist, a cunning fashioner of memorable sentences, a master (when he chose to be) of charged, rhythmic, vascular prose. He is witty, though he rarely makes us smile; and, for all his gassy qualities, his prose is wonderfully close to our special native feeling for the English language.

C. F.

106. *The American Treasury, 1455-1955*

edited by Clifton Fadiman
assisted by Charles Van Doren

Somewhere between a book of quotations and an anthology, *The American Treasury, 1455-1955* is an attempt to provide a portrait of America, its spirit, its landscape, its dominant philosophies, and the nature (both serious and comic) of its men and women. It is more than a grab bag of excerpts from the writings, speeches, conversations, slogans, and witticisms that have accumulated to form a spoken and written American literature; it is an orderly assemblage from a vast mass of material of those statements that are most characteristic of the workings of the American mind at its best and sometimes at its worst. It is a portrait with all the wrinkles left in. It includes the petulant words of demagogues along with the professions of faith in liberty and justice of America's greatest statesmen. It juxtaposes the solemn with the frivolous, the serious with the witty, the philosophic with the mindless, the inspirational with the cynical. It omits only the pedantic or tiresome.

The American Treasury can be read from start to finish, as its editors planned it, or it can be used for sampling or for reference; it is excellently indexed by subjects, authors, titles, and familiar words and phrases. It includes passages from every American author of enduring stature and from many whom time had all but buried and who are here resurrected, from farmers and historians, from Presidents and burlesque comedians, advertising copywriters, poets, scientists, song writers, and anonymous sages and wits.

In the introductory essays and in his "general preface," Mr. Fadiman has not only explained the intentions of this volume but has put the selections into perspective for the reader. In his "Envoi" he draws from the 6,000 items a brief portrait of the American as he is revealed in both the statements he has made about himself and those others have made about him. "Wisdom is not our forte," he writes, "nor perfection of utterance. But the Adamic quality of beginningness is."

R. L.

107. *Studs Lonigan*

by James T. Farrell

The period of American life through which the hero of this trilogy drinks and otherwise wastes his way extends from 1916 to the end of the 1920's, which is to say from the middle of Woodrow Wilson's Presidency to the middle of Herbert Hoover's. The first volume, *Young Lonigan,* appeared in 1932, perhaps the darkest year of the great Depression; the second, *The Young Manhood of Studs Lonigan,* in 1934; and the third, *Judgment Day,* in 1935. The reception of the work was instant and immense, and it continues to hold a firm place both as document and as fiction.

James T. Farrell (1904-), discussing his work a few years after its appearance, was frank to say that his hero had interested him as a type no less than as a created individual. Studs, who is barely fifteen when the reader first sees him—and sees, incidentally, into his mind—remains a person about whom one question is always pertinent: How representative is he of his time, place, and class? For his career is deplorable; indeed, it is shocking; and readers have been terrified by the thought that many others like him may exist. Mr. Farrell identifies him as a member of a class whose distinguishing feature is not so much emptiness of pocket as poverty of spirit. Studs, a Chicago boy of Irish-Catholic background, has kept intact so little of that background as to be for all practical purposes a modern city savage. Pathetically well-meaning at moments, and seldom altogether vicious, he nevertheless is ignorant of every sentiment, idea, or scruple which once had helped to build the culture he now repudiates without knowing that he does so.

The trilogy is powerful in its own right as a piece of fiction. It is violent without limit, apparently; yet the limit of art is finally there, so that Studs and his friends—his enemies, too—stand forth as a group capable of moving both horror and compassion. The death of Studs at the end of the third volume is earned as tragedy prescribes: it is painful, it is necessary, and it is somehow good. The entire work had best be taken, perhaps, as fiction rather than history. But this will not mean that it is not true.

M. V. D.

108. *The Portable Faulkner*

edited by MALCOLM COWLEY

Once in a while, on the earth as in the heavens, there is a fit conjunction of stars, when an artist and his proper critic meet. William Faulkner (1897-) is quoted as having said, after reading Malcolm Cowley's "Introduction," that now he knew what he had been doing. Faulkner had not yet received the Nobel prize and besides, he was hard reading and apparently knew nothing about Freud. Nor were there any signposts in Yoknapatawpha County. Mr. Cowley went in alone, and said on his return: "It sometimes seems to me that every house or hovel has been described in one of Faulkner's novels; and that all the people of the imaginary county, black and white, townsmen, farmers, and housewives, have played their parts in one connected story."

But the county is also the Deep South, all of it, as Mr. Cowley says. He does not explicitly say, although he knows as well as Faulkner, that in the Deep South there are two vast families. They are separate, these two, and yet inseparable, neither able for a moment to forget the other. They stand face to face, burning with hate and love. There is a penalty: each must defend its own, every member of the family, however despicable. There is another heavier penalty, paid by the white family. As its aristocracy weakens, giving way to the Snopes branch, there can be no call for help from the other aristocracy, still strong—the Lucas Beauchamps, the Dilseys. The Negro pays a penalty too: separate, suspicious, his first law is to avoid at all costs the other family's law.

Faulkner is like every sentient Southerner. He belongs wholly to neither family, drawn to the Negro by "a certain greatness," to the white by compassion, long memory, and desperate hope.

J. A. R.

109. Show Boat

by Edna Ferber

Of the many novels and stories Edna Ferber (1887-) has produced in the course of an unusually prolific and successful career as a popular writer, none has so tenaciously held the affections of the American public as *Show Boat,* first published in 1926. Miss Ferber's novel about the traveling players on the Mississippi River in the years after the Civil War is still read and fondly remembered, and the famous musical play for which it provided the book continues to be revived for large audiences.

Show Boat falls into two quite distinct sections; in the first, Miss Ferber describes the theater of Magnolia Ravenal's childhood, the old show-boat days on the Mississippi; the second concerns Magnolia's experiences as the wife of a Chicago gambler and the rise of her daughter Kim to stardom on modern Broadway. But undoubtedly it is in Miss Ferber's vividly nostalgic re-creation of the old river life that the fascination of *Show Boat* lies. The familiar color and excitement of New York's Times Square are but poor theater compared to Miss Ferber's glamorous picture of Captain Andy's hard-working, scraggly little troupe making its difficult way up and down the Mississippi, bringing its foolish earnest entertainment to the eager communities along the river's shores.

In no sense an "important" novel, *Show Boat* surely owes much of its success to its happy mixture of the common ingredients of popular fiction—romance, sentimental drama, the illusion without the reality of psychological depth. But apart from this easy appeal, which Miss Ferber's novel shares with any number of novels long since forgotten, its special charm for its American audience of course derives from its historical background. The tradition of the show boats—they had plied the Ohio and the Mississippi as early as 1830—is part of the legend of the American past which includes the rigors of life in the old colonial settlements, the plantation culture of the *ante-bellum* South, the adventure of the new West, the free life of the great Mississippi. Combining several of these legendary elements in a single story, *Show Boat* has itself come to assume something of a legendary place in American fiction.

D. T.

110. *Atoms in the Family*

My Life with Enrico Fermi

by LAURA FERMI

Born in Italy in 1901, Enrico Fermi early revealed the qualities of temperament and intellect which were to make him one of the greatest physicists of our time. While still a boy, he exhibited an uncanny mechanical skill and the ability to absorb the most difficult theoretical knowledge. At an age when other young men were cautiously feeling their way as students of science, Fermi had already established an international reputation for his researches in nuclear physics. From his early experiments at the University of Rome, to his receiving the Nobel prize in 1938, to his world renown as the first man to set up a self-sustaining chain reaction in atomic fission, Fermi walked a firm, sure path to the fulfillment of his genius.

It was the receipt of the Nobel prize that gave Fermi the opportunity he had been awaiting to leave Italy and settle with his family in the United States. Until Fascism had come under the dominance of German Nazism and Mussolini had enacted his racial laws, the Catholic Fermi and his Jewish wife had been able to live their lives untroubled by political considerations. Migration to America crystallized a democratic preference which had hitherto been quiescent. Even before the Fermis had acquired American citizenship, Enrico gladly accepted requisition by the American government into the research program which eventually, and so largely because of his contribution, produced the atomic bomb.

Mrs. Fermi's biography of her husband is not only an intimate account of the personal evolution of a great scientist but also a fascinating introduction to the history of nuclear science in our present century. Especially in the section describing Fermi's activities immediately preceding and during the war can be found an absorbing chapter in the drama of the new relation between science and government which sprang up as a result of atomic research. So far as Fermi's role is concerned, however, the story virtually closes with the end of Mrs. Fermi's book. Apparently in good health in 1953, the date of the last pages of *Atoms in the Family,* Enrico Fermi died in 1954, at the height of his powers and his enthusiasm.

D. T.

111. The Bent Twig

by DOROTHY CANFIELD FISHER

The Midwest public school is a mirror of the community, and in the state university are to be seen the conflicts, tensions, and harmonies within the state. *The Bent Twig* is an accurate, and acid, account of that civilization as it was at the end of the century. Dorothy Canfield Fisher (1879-) was the daughter of a state university president, and from that eminence was all-seeing, through the eyes of her father, who may have been a scholar but must have been a politician. Unlike Sinclair Lewis, Miss Fisher wrote with detachment, being an artist and also a descendant of granite Vermonters. What she saw was rugged individualism giving ground to equally rugged conformity. As long as land was to be had free, the individual could move away from neighbors, but with the closing of the frontier neighbors were there and had to be reckoned with. Since there was and had been no social aristocracy as on the Atlantic seaboard, the leveling tended to be down rather than up, in the university, as a reflection of the state. Status was not inherited, status was defined; and by definition a professor was not interested in music or the growing of vegetables.

In the interval of 50 years there have been changes. Music and the arts generally are now respectable, while intellection has become a goal. Conformity is still the rule, the models now being Harvard or the hybrid Chicago or, looking to Europe, Berlin as it was, not England's Oxford or Cambridge. The social status of students is still determined by the fraternity system, hardly explicable to a foreigner, though *The Bent Twig* gives some clues. But the Midwest is pure American, and as America is an experiment in co-education, the living out of the idea of equality, so the state university remains co-educational. It is a hard schooling, but the Sylvia Marshalls who survive are tough, and not dismayed when they encounter older civilizations.

J. A. R.

112. *The Critical Period of American History, 1783-1789*

by John Fiske

In the critical period described in this book, the several colonies conducted a great experiment in the process of self-government. Their aim was to discover some agency sufficiently strong to maintain order and stability throughout the new nation, yet so limited in its powers that it could not, by its decisions and actions, place the hard-won sovereignty of each colony in jeopardy. The citizens of the country faced for the first time, in these half-dozen years, the antique problem of how to reconcile the opposing and legitimate claims of collective security and individual liberty. Their initial hope was that common courses could be agreed upon in committee and undertaken by voluntary action on the part of the several members. As in so many similar solutions, both before and after, the motive power behind this hope was not so much a faith in the constructive urges of the individual members as a profound distrust of strong central governments insensitive to the particular local requirement.

Out of the confusion and uncertainty of these years came the growing understanding of the nature and meaning of sound government. The results of this experiment were not so much six years of drift and disorganization as the Constitution of the United States under which (with amendments) the country has lived since 1789. What was learned and how it was learned in these years is the theme of this book by John Fiske (1842-1901). The author was only incidentally an historian. He had been one of the primary agencies through which the meaning of Darwinism in its social connotations had been made clear to the country. He was, in part, a sociologist of the persuasion of Auguste Comte. He was, in fact, a magnificent eclectic—clear, eloquent, resourceful. His intent in this book, heavily weighted with Comtean concepts as it is, was to call attention to the fact that the critical period was a necessary stage in the gradual evolution of sound democratic institutions based upon a foundation of power suitably organized and controlled. His book had a tremendous effect in his time—especially on those members of the Republican party who, after 1896, began to increase the concentration of authority in the central government.

E. E. M.

113. *American Building*

by James Marston Fitch

The architecture of America has been the child of necessity and only a cousin of delight. Such authentic style as American architecture has developed has grown out of structural inventiveness to meet the demands of a society at first in danger of its life and later in a hurry to capitalize on its resources. Building has always been more important to Americans than architectural style, the pragmatic approach more important than the aesthetic. By and large the most successful building in America, and also that which has afforded the most permanent delight, has been that which has been dictated by necessity—the earliest "salt box" houses, the barns and mills, and later the factories and bridges and dams and business structures.

James Marston Fitch (1909-) has not written a history of American architecture (though it is here in capsule form) but, as his title indicates, an account of how Americans have built, from the spare dwellings of the earliest settlers to the skyscrapers of the twentieth century. He concerns himself with the ways in which structural and atmospheric problems have been met and solved, with technical innovations and new materials, with city planning, and with the styles that have evolved out of all of these. He is impatient with frivolity, such as the highly ornamented domestic architecture of the middle and late nineteenth century (so entertainingly described by William Dean Howells in *The Rise of Silas Lapham* [No. 155]) and with the revival of styles which has characterized so much of American architecture. (A more sympathetic view will be found in *Art and Life in America* by Oliver W. Larkin [No. 180].) Mr. Fitch's discussion of the evolution of building is interspersed with vignettes of the principal innovators and appraisals of their contributions.

The point of view from which Mr. Fitch writes (which will be found paralleled in some respects in Lewis Mumford's *Roots of Contemporary American Architecture* [No. 228] and John A. Kouwenhoven's *Made in America* [No. 175]) is an increasingly popular one among architectural critics and journalists in America. In the past twenty years they have revolted against the romantic approach of the nineteenth- and early twentieth-century "adapters" of traditional styles from Europe and have adopted, in the best American tradition, a somewhat romantic approach to pragmatism of their own.

R. L.

114. *The Last Tycoon,*
together with
The Great Gatsby

by F. Scott Fitzgerald

The Great Gatsby is the major fable of the Jazz Age. That age began on November 11, 1918, and ended with the disintegration of the stock market in October, 1929. Remaining in the memory of many Americans are representative symptoms of the period; gin made in bathtubs; love, or something supposed to be like it, in a rumble seat; young men jumping into public fountains late at night; and all the rest of it. Beneath the rather garish symptoms was the very real but frequently unconscious anguish of a generation, if not "lost" as Gertrude Stein concluded, at least in active rebellion against the faiths of the fathers. The confused and frenzied activities that took place as young people tried to discover some direction for their new departures offended or annoyed a great many people.

F. Scott Fitzgerald (1896-1940) succeeded with *The Great Gatsby* in making out of the elements of wayward violence a kind of poetry. There was something juvenile in him—as there was in the age—that enabled him to overload such pathos as there may be in the words of popular songs or the fact that summers end. He was also fatally attracted by what he took to be the true romance of great wealth and large, exciting, interminable parties. He could therefore, in a prose that is at times almost magical, lay a gloss or sheen upon what were essentially mundane doings. Because he had a kind of poetic insight he could also go beneath his own surfaces to create a folk hero of the 1920's in Jay Gatsby, who wanted desperately to become an accepted member in a society which he understood only well enough to disrupt.

The Last Tycoon is a later, more adult work. In it Fitzgerald abandoned his concern for the American wealthy on Long Island or the Riviera and tried to find out what life somewhat nearer the center of the American economy was all about. The last tycoon is a genuinely able man in the motion picture industry. Before he could finish his book, Fitzgerald died, but the drift of his intentions is clear enough and on the existing pages there are some remarkable passages dealing not only with the technical problems involved in putting a film play together but, more particularly, with the relation of the art of Hollywood to the life of America. And also in these pages, as in everything Fitzgerald ever wrote, there are moments when things refracted in an extraordinary set of mirrors seem more real and sensible than the things themselves.

E. E. M.

115. *American Painting*

The Light of Distant Skies, 1760-1835

by JAMES THOMAS FLEXNER

The influence of western European painting on the art of America, especially of colonial America and the early days of the Republic, is taken for granted, while the effect that American painters had on the artists of Europe, and especially of England, is rarely considered. In *The Light of Distant Skies,* James T. Flexner (1909-) explores the interchange, of ideas and aesthetic ideals, of concepts of the "grand style," and of techniques, that took place between European painters and the many American artists who traveled to Europe between 1760 and 1830.

By and large the influences were unfortunate in both directions. The vernacular tradition of American painting—crisp, factual, and constantly struggling for verisimilitude—was only superficially influenced by a few European engravings until American artists started to study abroad. But when Benjamin West, the first of the American artists to go to Rome, was infected by the classical theories of Winckelmann, a new element was introduced into American art. West settled in London, where he soon became England's most prominent artist and president of the Royal Academy. A generation of American painters was attracted to West's studio, for he was a kindly man and a gifted teacher, and his ideas of historical painting, which overlay a native respect for fact with a quasi-classical spirit and some baroque theatricality, infected the young painters who so admired him.

The effect on British painting was scarcely happy, and it divorced many young American artists from what was sound in their own tradition and replaced it with a lofty but indigestible notion of the role of the artist. Three of the most gifted—John Trumbull, Washington Allston, and Samuel F. B. Morse—were never again able to reconcile their new ideals of art to their native land. Morse all but gave up painting and became an inventor—most notably of the telegraph (see No. 195). Another artist of the group, Robert Fulton, invented the steamboat. Charles Willson Peale, though he never lost his devotion to the cause of American art, founded America's first museum of natural history.

Along with his discussion of the flow of artistic ideas and the triumphs and frustrations of the artists, Mr. Flexner provides lively, anecdotal biographies of the painters of America's first period of artistic sophistication and more than 100 paintings in illustration. For another point of view on this same period, the reader is referred to Oliver Larkin's *Art and Life in America* (No. 180).

R. L.

116. *William Henry Welch and the Heroic Age of American Medicine*

by SIMON FLEXNER *and* JAMES THOMAS FLEXNER

In the last two decades of the nineteenth century, Americans were working to a scale of heroic proportion. The names of Andrew Carnegie and John D. Rockefeller in industry, Joseph Choate and Elihu Root in the law, and Charles Eliot, William Harper, and Arthur Gilman in education suggest the magnitude of achievement in various fields of American endeavor. The great work of William Henry Welch (1850-1934) fell in this period and, as the Flexners suggest, he built on the grand scale. Like so many of his contemporaries in medicine and other fields of scholarship, he received much of his training in Germany, associating in those student years with men like Robert Koch, von Recklinghausen, and Paul Ehrlich. From them and others he received the knowledge and the technique that enabled him to become a pathologist and bacteriologist of distinction.

Able though he was in his chosen field, it is probable that he made his greatest contribution to the profession through his organizing skill. Before American medicine could free itself of intellectual dependence on Europe or even train practitioners adequately in the steadily advancing field, it was necessary to create sound medical institutions. Dr. Welch was a leading figure in this work. As the first dean at Johns Hopkins, he not only guided the early development of that famous medical school but assisted others—notably William Halsted, Howard Kelly, and Sir William Osler—in establishing standards to which all others in medical education could safely repair.

Later, as adviser to the Carnegie Foundation and the Rockefeller Institute of Medical Research, he exerted all his judgment and energy to extend the development of medical investigation and knowledge throughout the country. Gay and winning as only a man called "Popsy" could be, he was one of the most earnest and constructive men in the American intellectual life of his time. Simon Flexner, himself a pathologist and successful medical administrator, and his son James have conspired to write a book about Dr. Welch that is both a fine study of his mind and heart and a history of the medical school that was, in considerable part, his lengthened shadow.

E. E. M.

117. Paul Revere & the World He Lived In

by Esther Forbes

On the night of April 18, 1775, Paul Revere had himself rowed with muffled oars across the Charles River from Boston to Charlestown. Here he mounted for his famous ride to Lexington. His purpose was to inform the insurgent colonists that the British were marching in force on Lexington and then on nearby Concord to capture a store of arms and supplies hidden in that town. Despite the British patrols sent out to prevent him, Revere reached Lexington in time to deliver his warning. The British regulars were met on the town green by the local Minutemen; a brief skirmish ensued—the first engagement of the American War for Independence. The troops proceeded to Concord without further incident, but on their march back to Boston they were harried and decimated by the embattled farmers.

Paul Revere's ride was not a well-known incident of the Revolution until 1861, when Henry Wadsworth Longfellow published his spirited (but not wholly accurate) poem about it. At once it became, and has remained, one of the most familiar episodes of American history and the symbol of national vigilance and energy in time of crisis.

But the fame of the dramatic ride has had the effect of obscuring elements in the life of Revere that make him worthy of a more general interest than his midnight mission evokes. To be sure, many Americans are aware that he was a master silversmith whose work is cherished by connoisseurs for its simple and noble elegance. But not many know the important part he took in the movement for American independence.

Revere was a leading spirit in the political activities which led to the Revolution. During the War he served, although with ambiguous distinction, as a soldier; he printed paper money for Massachusetts; he constructed a powder mill to make the gunpowder for the Continental Army; he learned the art of founding and made cannon. After the war he became rich and famous as a bell-caster and the discoverer of the art of rolling copper—the copper works he established still continues, one of the major industrial enterprises of New England (see No. 317). He was, in the old-fashioned phrase, a man of parts.

Miss Forbes's vivacious book, in setting forth the achievements of this modest and straightforward man, gives a rich account of the complex life of eighteenth-century Boston, which Revere touched at so many points.

L. T.

118. The Honorable Peter Stirling

by Paul L. Ford

No one would think to call *The Honorable Peter Stirling* an "important" novel. Published in 1894, it is in all too many respects characteristic of the dominant literary taste of the period. It is often sentimental and arch, sometimes facetious. It is carefully protective of the genteel sensibilities of its readers. Its hero is flawless, noble, and lovable. Yet, with all its faults, it is an engaging book that still maintains a charm of freshness and innocence; and it has an intention which is important from the social, if not from the literary, point of view: to enlighten Americans about the true nature of their political institutions.

During the nineteenth century, Americans of the upper and educated classes, especially in the East, had come to think of politics as a "dirty business" with which "no gentleman would soil his hands." They had in mind the gross corruption of which everyone was aware, and also the large part played in political life by the lower classes of American society, including the more or less recent immigrant groups. Paul Leicester Ford (1865-1902) says less in *The Honorable Peter Stirling* about the element of actual corruption than he might have, but he accepts the actualities of a democratic society and tells the truth about realities of political influence and power.

His book appeared at a time when the respectable elements of New York were much exercised over the power of the highly organized political machine of the Democratic party. Their characteristic way of challenging this power was to create Reform parties, to whose idealistic appeals the poor and uneducated voters were unlikely to respond. In contrast to this, Peter Stirling, a "practical idealist"—the phrase is used here perhaps for the first time—lives among the poor, understands their lives, identifies himself with their interests, and thus gains their confidence. With no loss of personal integrity, he accepts organized politics as it is, even to the extent of becoming a "boss" of great power; he is thus able to manipulate the actualities of politics to good ends.

The character of Peter Stirling is said to have been modeled on that of Grover Cleveland, President of the United States from 1885 to 1889 and from 1893 to 1897.

L. T.

119. *U.S.A.: The Permanent Revolution*

by the editors of FORTUNE
in collaboration with RUSSELL W. DAVENPORT

A reader of *U.S.A.: The Permanent Revolution* should observe carefully both the time and place of its original publication. The essays which now form chapters in the book were previously articles in *Fortune,* a very lavish and expensive magazine published by the same organization that produces two of the most popular "mass" periodicals in America. *Fortune,* however, appeals to a more select audience; it is directed to the most prosperous portion of the business community, and its contents (written almost entirely by staff members) are largely devoted to praising business and to educating businessmen. The educational objective of the magazine is fulfilled in the main by articles about the state of the economy in general and of certain sections of it in particular, but *Fortune* also publishes some discussions of broader interest, such as the articles in this book.

This material first came out early in 1951, at a time when it appeared that the Democratic party's twenty-year period of control of the national government was drawing to a close, and that the Republican party, which is the party of the overwhelming majority of the businessmen-readers of *Fortune,* would return to power. With the nomination and first election of General Eisenhower as President later in the year, that expectation was fulfilled, and when his administration was established a large proportion of its important officials were representatives of business.

Apart from its rather elaborate theoretical framework, *U.S.A.: The Permanent Revolution* does two things. First, it warns the business community that the return of the Republicans to power does not mean an end to the social legislation enacted by the Democrats in their twenty years of power; it serves notice on the conservative wing of the Republican party that much of Roosevelt's New Deal and Truman's Fair Deal is here to stay. Second, it proposes a platform acceptable to the liberal Eastern wing of the Republican party, the wing that wanted, and got, Eisenhower as its nominee. Consequently it advocates collaboration with allies in foreign affairs and the "middle of the road" in domestic policy.

The book is a picture of the United States drawn for a very influential portion of the citizenry. It is a good though partial likeness. In some respects, especially foreign policy, events have not come to the full support of the program outlined, but even this discussion is of interest as the kind of appeal on which the Republican party regained the Presidency, though not the lasting control of Congress, in 1952.

P. P.

120. *Why Do People Buy?*

by the editors of FORTUNE

Fortune, which first appeared in January 1930, belongs with *Time* and *Life* to the prosperous group of magazines published by Henry Robinson Luce (1898-). Large, heavy, and expensively printed, it has been from the start a luxury product, intended to convey an aura of wealth and business success. Yet it has occasionally been critical of business. As a member of the family, so to speak, it has been able to tell its readers the things they would not listen to from others. In the years since World War II, especially, it has exercised a surprisingly uninhibited curiosity on a wide range of the American economic experience. One of its editors, William H. Whyte, Jr., has in fact developed a subtle instrument of moral observation by combining *Fortune's* journalism with the tactics and techniques of social science (see No. 251).

It may seem curious to find among *Fortune* articles, for example, such an unsparing analysis as Mr. Whyte's "The Language of Advertising," in which this entire branch of merchandising is told that its methods are both insulting to the customer and ineffective. Elsewhere in the volume, and from its other contributors, are to be found equally skeptical and unexpected views into the world of salesmanship—that precinct of the American business ethic supposedly sacred to the shade of Sinclair Lewis's Babbitt (No. 184) or to the vanishing breed of Arthur Miller's Willy Loman (in No. 78). Yet it appears from *Fortune's* study that "Death of a Salesman" is indeed an appropriate title for the present period, in which promising young men are reluctant to become salesmen and companies must energetically search for the few remaining possessors of the old-time zeal. (Further comments on this change can be found in David Riesman's *Individualism Reconsidered* [No. 258].) To be sure, *Fortune's* aim is better business and its purpose in criticizing is to improve, but in so doing it offers an unexampled vista into the era of consumption, that uncharted realm in which products are easier and sometimes cheaper to manufacture than they are to sell.

E. L.

121. On Being a Real Person

by HARRY EMERSON FOSDICK

For almost a generation, Dr. Harry Emerson Fosdick (1878-) has been the leading voice of Protestant Christianity in the United States. He has not been a theologian in the technical sense but a preacher, heard in a popular New York pulpit and in broadcasts of immense influence. But he has always thought, as he says in this book of good counsel, that he was most concerned with the personal troubles of men and women who sought his help. He tries to do for a mass audience what he tried to do in his own study, to counsel with the aid of all a layman could learn of modern psychology and psychiatry but always in the spirit of a Christian friend.

This is only one of a number of books of practical advice that Dr. Fosdick has written; they have all been popular, as books of this kind so often are in America. This is, in fact, a field crowded with charlatans—like Sinclair Lewis's *Elmer Gantry* (No. 185). An honest writer has to compete with those who recklessly deny the reality of evil, and he has to win the attention of the despairing without offering an easy victory over real trouble. Dr. Fosdick does not offer a religious dogma as a cure for unhappiness, but he asserts his own belief that a theistic view of the universe leads to strength and courage. Life is to be mastered by accepting experience in the faith that we can, when we reach out after truth and goodness, feel ourselves in harmony with ultimate cosmic reality.

His acquaintance with the theories of depth psychology and psychosomatic medicine stand him in good stead in giving substance to what is, after all, an impersonal kind of personal advice. He relies also on the faith, basic in the American dogma, that every human being has the capacity to be, and the duty to be, an individual, fated to suffer unique experiences and to assert his essential self against his fate. He advises us to accept the self we have without regret and do the best we can with it. This is an intelligent and morally responsible version of what strangers have often thought to be typically American, a confidence in the happy ending.

L. B.

122. *The Case for Modern Man*

by Charles Frankel

Since the earliest days of the Republic, geography and history have combined to put the United States squarely in the tradition of historical liberalism, as the word has long been used to designate belief in civil rights, representative institutions, and social progress; and events of the past quarter-century—the depression of the 1930's, the hot war of the 1940's, and the cold war of the 1950's—have had the effect of confirming most Americans in the tradition of modern liberalism, as the word is now used to designate belief in legislation to insure the individual against the social hazards of life, legislation making for greater economic and social equality, legislation to control vested interests for the public good, and internationalism in foreign affairs.

Yet a good deal of the best American political writing since the second World War has been proud to call itself conservative. This fact is less significant than it seems. Part of the new conservative writing is simply a predictable protest of energetic young men against the prevailing public philosophy; much of it is conservative only by comparison and would have seemed radical to a nineteenth-century businessman. Few of the young conservative writers have become apologists for the blatantly reactionary men in political life; in fact their movement is primarily literary—it has produced a hundred stylists for every man of action.

Nevertheless, by 1956, when this book by Charles Frankel (1917-) was published, the need had arisen for a mature and rigorous restatement of the historical argument for liberalism, and his case against its detractors was greeted cordially by those American readers who had begun to fear that liberalism was a sentiment too vague to be intellectually respectable. Mr. Frankel is a philosopher at Columbia University by profession, and his approach to the subject is to analyze four major antiliberal philosophies of history (Jacques Maritain's, Reinhold Niebuhr's, Karl Mannheim's, and Arnold Toynbee's), and to defend liberalism against their attacks. This is the ablest part of his book, though he also offers some excellent correctives to those who have distorted the terms of liberalism in an effort to prove its inadequacy. The concluding chapter, in which Mr. Frankel attempts to suggest a new relation between liberalism and technology, is less successful.

P. P.

123. *Benjamin Franklin's Autobiographical Writings*

edited by CARL VAN DOREN

A bottle of Madeira was uncorked, and "three drowned flies fell into the first glass that was filled. Having heard it remarked that drowned flies were capable of being revived by the rays of the sun, I proposed making the experiment upon these." The experiment was made and two of the flies came alive. Franklin said: "I wish it were possible, from this instance, to invent a method of embalming drowned persons in such a manner that they may be recalled to life at any period, however distant; for having a very ardent desire to see and observe the state of America a hundred years hence, I should prefer to any ordinary death the being immersed in a cask of Madeira wine with a few friends till that time, to be then recalled to life by the solar warmth of my dear country!"

Benjamin Franklin died in 1790. (See Carl Van Doren's biography [No. 313].) If his wish had been fulfilled he would have found something of himself everywhere in 1890. For, in merit and demerit, he was the first "All-American." He and William James, two pragmatists, would have loved each other. Having been the principal inventor among Americans—Jefferson being a close second—he would have felt the "densest happiness" in Edison's laboratory, without astonishment. Mark Twain, 55 years old at the end of Franklin's hundred years, would be close kin. On nearly every page there is evidence: the trick played on a connoisseur of typography; his "Model of a Letter of Recommendation of a person you are unacquainted with"; his inversion of the *lex talionis;* the cardsharper and the Dutchman; his epitaph. And throughout the humor and wit of his language: applicants for commissions who were *"officiers expérimentés, braves* . . . etc., etc., in short, mere Caesars"; his refusal to resign, "being deficient in that Christian virtue of resignation"; prophetic instruction from France for putting on make-up, where "As to rouge, they don't pretend to imitate nature in laying it on."

Hero of the first American success story, the perennial amateur, honest, relying upon common sense, Franklin yet said of himself, "everything of difficult discussion, and that requires close attention of mind and an application of long continuance, grows rather irksome to me."

J. A. R.

124. *From Slavery to Freedom*

A History of American Negroes

by John Hope Franklin

In the Southern states, where metal was precious, there hung by every well and water bucket a dipper made from a long-necked gourd, the drinking gourd. The slaves had a song with the refrain, "Follow the drinking gourd." To the master it was just another slave song, innocent. It was not. The drinking gourd was Ursa Major, the Great Dipper, and the star at the end of the handle was the North Star. The refrain was a direction. "Go North," it said; "in the North is freedom." They went, no one knows how many, traveling the "Underground Railroad" by night. Then, at the end of the Civil War they needed to travel no more. Freedom came to them.

Having breached the first wall, they faced another: ignorance. Few slaves could read, for there had been stringent laws against teaching; but now teachers came down from the North, women for the most part, stubborn descendants of New England Puritans. They were not enough, of course, and, having to make a choice of pupils, chose mostly the young. But the elders wanted to learn too, and along the Carolina coast they would waylay the teacher, "to catch a lesson." They wanted to see on the printed page the words they already knew by ear. For the masters of slaves in the South—the later masters of servants—seemed unaware that the Negro waiting on table or mixing drinks was listening, learning the lesson from those who already enjoyed freedom.

So an opening was made in the second wall, small at first but increasing with the years. Then, with the wall down or crumbling, there came the great debate among Negroes themselves as to what kind of education they should have in freedom. Booker T. Washington (No. 320) gave one answer, that the Negro should "learn by doing," using what he had, hands and good will. The other answer, first voiced by W. E. B. DuBois, is accepted and set forth in *From Slavery to Freedom*. Booker Washington was eventually repudiated because of his outmoded economics, the same charge that was leveled against Gandhi. But more offensive was his acceptance of social separation of the two races, particularly in education. Now that the Supreme Court has decreed that separation on the basis of race in public education is unconstitutional, the last law-built wall has been breached.

J. A. R.

125. The Poems of Robert Frost

The poems of Robert Frost (1875-) enjoy a unique distinction in the United States today: they are both popular and respected. Mr. Frost is successful, that is to say, equally with the discerning and with those who are supposed not to be discerning; though in fact they are, because they are the ones who in the long run determine the reputation of any poet; they are "the world" which criticism merely makes articulate. Criticism may tell them that Mr. Frost's poems are marvelously skillful and incontestably modern, but what they notice is that these poems are interesting in the way all successful poetry is. They are wise, humorous, and humane, and what they say is what everybody knows but until now has assumed to be inexpressible.

It used to be said that Frost was a New England poet; now it is more commonly said that he is simply and greatly a poet. Yet like any true artist of his kind he does have a voice, and it is the voice of New England: reserved, oblique, in love with understatement, cutting on occasion, kind in the end. Also he handles the landscape of his section, particularly that of New Hampshire and Vermont, his favorite states, with such infectious fidelity that he has made readers homesick for a country they never saw. Add to this that his people think and talk for the most part like Yankee farmers, and there would appear to be nothing save New England in him. But that is only where he starts. If the farmer and his wife in "The Death of the Hired Man" are entirely local, the things they manage to say about home will be intelligible—and surprising because so true—to any reader in the world.

These things are said rather than sung. Frost is possessed of lyric power, but his genius is most comfortable in human speech, which he reproduces throughout his work. Like his own oven bird, he knows "in singing not to sing." He is nowhere more modern than in his adherence to this wry and perhaps bitter principle.

M. V. D.

126. *The Great Crash, 1929*

by JOHN KENNETH GALBRAITH

The collapse of the New York stock market in October, 1929, was an event of world importance. Few were aware of this at the moment, and in fact the moment itself took long to pass. "Black Thursday" (October 24), the famous first day of disaster, was followed by days still worse, and then by weeks, by months, and even by years in which the financial gloom grew steadily and incredibly darker. The end of the decline was reached in the summer of 1932; but by that time the great Depression, a more serious phenomenon if its consequences be considered, was well upon its way. Those consequences, direct and indirect, are generally supposed to include the rise of National Socialism in Germany, the consolidation of Communism in Russia, and World War II, to say nothing of developments since.

Professor J. K. Galbraith's (1908-) history of the great crash does not extend to a consideration of its consequences around the world; yet the mercilessly clear view it gives of the moment as it slowly passed permits any number of deductions to be made. The account found here is unique in its detachment and its wit. Its tone, as icy and ironic as that of Tacitus, contains no hint of sympathy for a people capable of so gigantic a folly as the mass speculation of the 1920's. The speculators were fewer than it has been the custom to assume; there may not have been as many as a million of them. But these infected, Galbraith thinks, the entire mind of the time; and the economic brains of the country were incompetent to effect a cure. Indeed they contributed to the disease through an optimism, both early and late, which bore no relation to the facts. The prevailing assurance was that "the economy is fundamentally sound."

Galbraith's hope, and to some extent his belief, is that those words will never be trumpeted again by men who do not know what they mean. His very detachment is finally reassuring. Himself a distinguished economist, he supplies at least one case of intelligence disciplined against the kind of illusion which for a while so deeply damaged America and the world.

M. V. D.

127. *Progress and Poverty*

by Henry George

In the year 1868 a man who lived in California came on a visit to New York City. There he observed a series of "shocking contrasts" between "monstrous wealth and debasing want." He returned home to study just enough economics to enable him to elaborate the theory which, he trusted, would reduce the inequities in American life and release the American energies to build a safer and more humane society. This theory, called the single tax, has become one of the enduring clichés in the intellectual history of the United States.

The line of argument in support of the single tax, as presented in this book, may be quickly stated. Men have as much right to the use of land as they have to breathe the air around them. Therefore, when men pay excessive rent to a private landowner before they can work the land they are being deprived of a natural right. The way to strike off this fetter of economic rent is to require its contribution in the form of a tax to the community which, by its own development, has produced the increase in land value in the first place. With the imposition of this single tax no other regulation of the economic process would be necessary.

For two decades after *Progress and Poverty* was published in 1880, this idea found passionate though limited support in all levels of society. It had the virtues of simplicity; it had, unlike many other nostrums of the time, a discernible rational foundation. Furthermore, in the book it was stated in prose that was beautiful and compelling. Finally, and most important, the single tax was presented by the author as not so much an economic device, interesting in itself, as an instrument to be used in the quest for social justice.

Henry George (1839-1897) burned with savage indignation at the conditions he defined so movingly. He succeeded in evoking this sense of outrage in others. "Ye gods," said one young man after reading *Progress and Poverty*. "If I had the brains, I'd quit this business. I see things here that make my blood boil."

The solution George proposed was, in fact, oversimplified and unacceptable, but nevertheless his book and his presence produced valuable results. He defined essential problems in the growing industrial society; he aroused many members of the society to a genuine concern with these problems. In so doing he helped prepare the public conscience to press for solutions more acceptable than his own.

E. E. M.

128. *Mechanization Takes Command*

by SIEGFRIED GIEDION

American writers often manifest a different attitude toward machinery than that shown by Europeans. They hold it less in awe, they tend to take it for granted, and they are less likely to regard it as innately antipathetic to everything humane. In a sense, as John Kouwenhoven suggests in *Made in America* (No. 175), machinery and democracy have grown up together in America, and intermarried, so that neither can now exist without the other and each is an essential element in the national character. Kouwenhoven, like Pearl Franklin Clark (No. 63), regards the resulting technology as essentially, or at least potentially, beneficent—a view that numerous European writers reject. And yet, paradoxically, many pioneers in the recognition and study of American technology have been European. Perhaps the full extent of mechanization was hidden from the local observer by closeness and familiarity, while it held for an outsider the irresistible charm of the exotic.

The Swiss architectural critic Siegfried Giedion (1888-) was among the pioneers. He had made himself a scholar in an area where American scholarship did not (and largely still does not) exist. He realized the value of irreplaceable records—like the scale models of inventions required by the U.S. Patent Office—at a time when Americans would have thoughtlessly junked them, and indeed nearly did so. And, above all, he was fascinated by the extraordinary mechanical curiosa that his researches revealed. As a result, Mr. Giedion has achieved a history of American mechanization that is unmatched for its scope, its lavishness of detail, and its hints at latent social and aesthetic relationships. Though he valiantly tries to be dispassionate, however, Mr. Giedion is unable to suppress his deeply rooted dislike for the machine; his point of view is "objective" only in being, as he says, that of a doctor toward a disease. The reader should discount accordingly, and should ideally balance his reading with an antidote such as Mr. Kouwenhoven's book (No. 175). If he does so, he will that much better appreciate the fact that Mr. Giedion's concern lest the machine dehumanize Man is, and has long been, shared by many Americans.

E. L.

129. *Vein of Iron*

by Ellen Glasgow

One of the most striking features of modern American literature is the size and quality of the contribution made by writers from the southern part of the United States. Whatever branch of literature one turns to—fiction, poetry, criticism, drama, biography—one finds that much of the best work done in America since the first World War has been written by southerners (see, for example, No. 324).

The reason for this southern preponderance is hard to give, but it is at least tempting to point out a very crude parallel between the recent history of the American South and nineteenth-century Russia, where another great literature was produced. In each instance there were the violent contrasts that enrich and enliven literature; in each there was an old society based on caste being invaded by a new social pattern—in Russia it was an invasion by Western ideas, in the American South by northern urbanization and industrialization. In each instance writers were in a complicated moral position, bound by loyalty to the old order that had produced them, with its semi-religious sanction as Holy Russia or the Lost Cause, yet troubled by the injustices that had made that order possible. Perhaps too in each instance the men and women of remarkable mind and imagination turned to writing because the old order was no longer sufficiently vigorous and the new not yet sufficiently established to absorb their energies.

Ellen Glasgow (1874-1945) is the first of the modern southern novelists. She set out to write a series of novels that would depict her native Virginia not as it had been romanticized but as it really was, and *Vein of Iron* is a good example of the result of her enterprise. In it she portrays the tradition of southern rural Calvinism in decay. She is not a critic of that tradition, but she tries to show how in the years before and after the first World War that tradition ceased to be a satisfying framework for the aspirations and passions of men.

The contemporary American reader is likely to feel that Miss Glasgow achieved less than she set out to do. This feeling arises in part from certain weaknesses intrinsic to her point of view and in part from acquaintance with the greater achievements of her successors.

P. P.

130. *Great Tales of the American West*

edited by Harry E. Maule

The standard "Western," tale or movie, is made of dream stuff. The commuter hastily snatches a copy of his favorite "pulp" magazine and settles down in his club car, to dream. The driver of a diesel cattle truck in Texas climbs down from his cab onto a stool in the wayside diner, and props his favorite against the sugar bowl. He may have read the same story, under a dozen different titles, a dozen times. It makes no difference. "All day long John Muir had been stringing wire for the south pasture." He is John Muir, "a figure to draw the eyes of men as well as women." The waitress slops his coffee. He does not even try to draw her eye. The eye he intends to draw is on the next page, maybe the same page. Or she may be at the end of the parade of sheriff, cattle king, bad man, bad woman, gambler, English lord, bartender. The prudent author has also sprinkled the tale with mountains, deserts, horses —white for heroes, black for villains—cows, impediments all to the action.

Commuter and truck driver alike would read with pleasure most of these *Great Tales of the American West,* but some of the stories would puzzle them —"The Indian Well," for example, in which the action is interior and the author has captured another kind of dream stuff. "To Find a Place" appropriately comes last. In Ordway, manufacturer of cattle, the West of credible fiction comes to an end.

J. A. R.

131. *Form and Function*

by Horatio Greenough
edited by Harold A. Small

In a way it is a very "American" fact that the introduction to this selection of essays, written in the 1840's by the sculptor Horatio Greenough (1805-1852), points up the prophetic, twentieth-century relevance of his ideas by suggesting parallels with the Bauhaus and Le Corbusier. Americans still tend, as they did in Greenough's day, to estimate the value of ideas—especially ideas about art—by their proximity to European standards. It is also suggestive that the author of the introduction, a painter and teacher of painting, admires Greenough's progressive ideas about architecture but dismisses his ideas about painting, based on the same principles, as simply "uninteresting."

Greenough's ideas have been fairly consistently eccentric to the accepted notions of art in America. In his own time his friend Ralph Waldo Emerson found him stimulating, and Henry David Thoreau and Walt Whitman unconsciously shared some of his views, as F. O. Matthiessen generously points out in *American Renaissance* (No. 207). As the first professional American sculptor, Greenough has a modest place in all histories of our art; but not until 1939, when Nancy Wynne and Beaumont Newhall published an article in the *Magazine of Art,* were his aesthetic theories given serious recognition.

Greenough's style, with its curious blend of pulpiteering and colloquialism, is to some a barrier; he was not a polished writer. As he says in the essay on "Relative and Independent Beauty," those to whom he showed his essays were "worried and fretted at the form"; but he correctly felt that there was an organic relation between his thought and his style. "If I seek another form, another dress than that with which my thought was born, shall I not disjoin that which is one? Shall I not disguise what I seek to decorate?" He knew there were places (including literary histories) from which those without dress and ornament were excluded, but he was "too proud to seek admittance in disguise."

By his absolute rejection of absolutes, by his insistence that it is only by the "fruits" of a belief or an act that it can be judged, and by his acceptance of change and development, Greenough unsystematically arrived at perceptions which later found support in the work of William James, Charles Sanders Peirce, and John Dewey. Further echoes will also be found in *Roots of Contemporary American Architecture,* edited by Lewis Mumford (No. 228); Frank Lloyd Wright's *Autobiography* (No. 347); and James M. Fitch's *American Building* (No. 113).

J. A. K.

132. *Inside U.S.A.*

by JOHN GUNTHER

Published in 1947, this enormous one-man survey of the "49 states" (including New York City) and 38 cities is here revised as of 1951. The reader will therefore have to make some allowances for the passage of time. But the hard core of this fascinating book retains its value. If any single volume can tell us, *in concrete detail,* what it means to be an American citizen, this is it.

John Gunther (1901-), who is an expert in continent-swallowing, went everywhere and talked to 900 people, from governors to bellhops. Everywhere he went he asked two main questions: What makes your community distinctive? What *really* runs it? The answers to these queries, properly organized, permit him to call his book "a study of democracy in action." It is not a profound study, not a rigorous one; but it is empirical and it is lively. It manages to give a living sense of American diversity in unity and, at the same time, to locate the levers of power.

It is a complex and at times bewildering mixture of geography, topography, history, reportage, political and social analysis, character-portraiture, biography, speculation, gossip, and wise-cracks. Its emotional tone is as varied, ranging from admiration for the peaks of our physical achievement to cool condemnation of our incredible wastes and follies. But through the entire vast book runs an exultant, but not chauvinist note of faith in American capacities, faith in the country which, whatever its truancies, whatever its "preposterous and flamboyant contradictions," is unique in history in that it was "deliberately founded on a good idea."

Inside U.S.A. is essentially the product of a journalist, but the journalist is a thoughtful one who has read much and thought as deeply about his country as his mode of life has permitted him. The judgments are those of a liberal and humane citizen, aware of the weaknesses in our body politic, and able, by his remorseless probing into the facts, to show us the source of these weaknesses as well as the source of our strengths. In the years that have passed since its first appearance, *Inside U.S.A.* has proved its usefulness, not alone to Americans, but to hundreds of thousands of non-Americans curious to know who runs this extraordinary land, and how, and to what end.

C. F.

133. *The Big Sky*

by A. B. GUTHRIE, JR.

The opening of the West has long been a popular theme in American literature, but of recent historical novels in this field A. B. Guthrie's (1901-) *The Big Sky* has been one of the most widely read and the most memorable. Encompassing the years between 1830 and 1843, Mr. Guthrie's story of the frontier way of life is that of Boone Caudhill, who left Kentucky at seventeen for the great spaces of the mountain country to fulfill a boy's dream of adventure and returned thirteen years later a prematurely old and burned-out man. In the character of Boone is embodied the archetype of the American pioneer—virile, fearless, taciturn, practical, yet possessed of that strong mysticism, that sense of complete identification with the wilderness and an almost religious dedication to it which is found in James Fenimore Cooper's *The Leatherstocking Saga* (No. 67).

Mr. Guthrie, in emphasizing this quality through Boone's obsessive love for the unspoiled, the pristine, the untarnished, has lifted *The Big Sky* out of the realm of adventure fiction and made it a genuinely tragic work. He has succeeded in re-creating the atmosphere of the primitive life of the frontier, with its hardships and its savagery, and in showing what motivated those rough and ruthless men who yearned uneasily for a vast freedom under the measureless vault of the western sky. He has also made a parable in the story of the immoderate pioneers who took their paradise and spoiled it. In evoking the time, and the people, Mr. Guthrie has been faithful to historical detail and has at the same time accomplished an imaginative and often poetic transformation. *The Big Sky,* said Bernard DeVoto, "is an elegy on the passing of the untouched West and on the passing of the breed of men to whom the West meant more than anything else."

C. C.

134. *The Federalist*

by ALEXANDER HAMILTON, JOHN JAY, *and* JAMES MADISON

In May, 1787, a convention of representatives from the several states met in Philadelphia to prepare a frame of government for the United States. In less than five months the convention drew up a Constitution which it then sent for ratification to the various members of the existing confederation. There followed, in each state, a period of remarkable public discussion. Difference of opinion developed over several recommendations in the new instrument of government, but concentrated particularly upon these two related points: the scope of the powers reserved to the states, and the magnitude of the authority granted to the federal government. The debate on these and other issues became so bitter and so prolonged that for a time the ratification of the new Constitution appeared to many unlikely.

The Federalist was a major contribution to this debate. In October, 1787, Alexander Hamilton (see No. 14) sent the first of a series of articles to the *Independent Journal,* a New York newspaper. His object was both to explain and defend the Constitution. During the ensuing months, with the occasional assistance of James Madison and John Jay, he composed 85 of these articles. At least 51 are the work of his hand alone.

There can be little doubt that the publication of these papers, widely read and discussed at the time, contributed materially to the acceptance of the Constitution. Because of this, they possess an inescapable historical significance; but they retain continuing importance in American literature for other reasons. Though conceived to argue a special position and to achieve a practical purpose, they are in tone and argument not so much a political tract as a disquisition on political theory. The product of minds both lucid and experienced, these essays remain one of the best sources of information not only about the intent of the designers of our form of government but also about the nature of the political process in a republic.

E. E. M.

135. This Was America

edited by Oscar Handlin

The opportunity is given in this book for Americans to see themselves as others see them. Similar opportunities in the past have not always been wholly gratifying; one can find throughout the literary landscape outcrops of indignation at Charles Dickens for his reports on what, 100 years ago, he felt and saw here. But, by and large, the impressions of those outside the borders have had a salutary effect, and exposure to these views should prove very useful to those elsewhere in the world who are trying to learn something about this country (see also No. 231).

Oscar Handlin (1915-), the pre-eminent student of the immigrant in this country, has brought together in this book reports from men and women who in the past 200 years have visited these shores. He has had the wisdom to draw these accounts, for the most part, not from people who came simply to observe but from those who came to pursue some particular aim of their own—to buy, to sell, to study, to botanize. Also, these people derived from many different countries and social backgrounds, and in their varied impressions the influence of these differences is clearly discernible.

In view of this variety of points of view, it is interesting to discover how many recurrent themes there are in this book. Apparently the foreign traveler, especially in the nineteenth and twentieth centuries, is perennially fascinated by the restlessness of the country, by how hard American men work, by American machinery, and by what the money earned by men and machines is spent for. Above all other matters of concern, however, are these two: the way of the American male with the American female and the way in which the theorem that all men are created "free and equal" works out in practice.

On these matters, and others, there are many shrewd observations and sensible philosophizings in this book. And yet the most arresting thing may well be the observations on the details of daily life that are so frequently overlooked by those who lead that daily life. There is, for instance, a splendid study of the place, meaning, and procedure of the haircut and, even better, an analysis of chewing gum as a cohesive force. Taken all together in general reflection and in detail, there is a great deal here not only of what America was but what it still seems to others to be.

E. E. M.

136. The Uprooted

by Oscar Handlin

The literature of American immigration is immense because the subject is immense, covering as it ideally does the entire population of the United States, whose oldest families boast of when they first "came over." As most persons now view the matter, however, immigration means a nineteenth-century mass movement from all the parts of Europe; it means the flood of millions who arrived after the country was formed and had taken English for its language; it means "aliens."

The distinction of this book by Professor Oscar Handlin (1915-) is that it treats this horde, of which he considers himself a member, not in terms of the society which had to assimilate it but in terms of itself. There had been memoirs of individual immigrants, but this is a history, written with imagination and warmth, of the whole movement seen as a transplantation, a tearing-up and a rerooting, of ancient human communities so established in their ways that any change at all was painful. By common consent the first chapter is a classic: no other account competes with it in its full, deep, compassionate view of the peasant life which suddenly could be lived no more, at least by those for whom there was no alternative to the "crossing."

The crossing to America, the difficulties in settling there, and the humiliation of being alien—Professor Handlin is eloquent about these too. Making rich use of diaries and interviews, he achieves a composite portrait of Europe replanted; sometimes successfully, so that even the memory of the event deserted later generations, sometimes unsuccessfully, so that those later generations still have the status of minorities, still suffer segregation. The task of the immigrant was to start life again in a context utterly foreign to the habits of his mind and heart. To him the United States was alien; to him it was a strange land; to him its people were unintelligible when they were not hostile. Only the boldest succeeded; and now that immigration has more or less ceased to be, only their descendants can forget.

M. V. D.

137. *The Southpaw*

by MARK HARRIS

Baseball is the American national game. Starting late in winter, sixteen professional teams gather in the warm climates of Florida, Arizona, and California. In early spring the players start training, managers look over new talent, and sportswriters fill the daily newspapers with baseball gossip and publicity. In April, after a round of exhibition games, the President of the United States traditionally throws out the first ball to open the season. Baseball fever rises, and the season is under way not only in such cities as New York, Boston, St. Louis, and Milwaukee, but also in towns and villages where there are no major professional teams. All through the summer a large proportion of Americans are baseball fanatics, or "fans." Cryptic newspaper headlines crowd out more serious items: Giants Beat Cubs, Mantle Homers Twice, Roberts Hurls 1-Hitter. Throughout the country men and boys and even women who have never been inside a baseball park argue about teams and players they have never seen but whose statistics they know by heart. The great names—Christy Mathewson, Grover Cleveland Alexander, Dizzy Dean, Ty Cobb, Babe Ruth, Joe DiMaggio—bring forth admiration, memories, and endless comparisons.

Five months and 154 games after the season begins, one of the eight teams in each of the two major leagues (National and American) stands at the head of its league; these two top teams meet in a crucial 4-out-of-7-game championship contest known as "The World Series." During these exciting days office workers openly listen to the radio, and bars and clubs are crowded with those who have sneaked out to watch television.

The writing about baseball is voluminous, but most of it is specialized and intended for those who know the game well, its players and its jargon. *The Southpaw,* however, is a very readable novel about a left-handed pitcher who tells how he got into big league baseball and describes his first season with the mythical New York Mammoths. Mark Harris (1922-), its author, employs a vernacular style reminiscent of Ring Lardner (Nos. 179 and 278). His novel not only reveals much in its own right about the game of baseball, and what baseball players do, say, feel, and think, but also much about the role of sports in American life and their relevance to the national character.

C. G.

138. *The Oxford Companion to American Literature*

by JAMES D. HART

The Oxford Companion to American Literature is a reference work of peculiar usefulness. It undertakes to give information on virtually every subject related to American literature. Yet, although it is encyclopedic in its range, it is intended, as its name suggests, to be used for convenient rather than for extensive consultation—the information that it imparts on any one subject is of the essential rather than the exhaustive kind. It cannot wholly avoid critical comment, nor does it try to; but criticism is not a chief part of its intention.

The most obvious of the various kinds of entries that the reader might wish to consult are the biographies of American authors. (Brief biographies of authors of other nationalities are given insofar as they have reference to some involvement of the author with American life.) No adequate sense of an actual work of literature can be given by a summary or a description of it, nor does Professor Hart, the author-editor of the volume, suppose that it can; but often it is useful to have information about the general subject of a work one has not yet read, and the volume contains some 900 summaries of American novels, stories, poems, essays, and plays. Certain fictional characters, more or less well known, are identified by reference to the work in which they appear.

In addition to specifically literary matters, the *Companion* takes note of events, movements, and personalities about which a reader might be curious either because they are referred to in literature or because they have an historical importance in the society of which literature is the expression. The reader can quickly discover what a Mugwump was (and is), or a Copperhead, or Tammany Hall, or Jamestown, or the Donner Party; he will be able to acquire at least a sketchy knowledge of the history of the Negro in America, or of the rise of the motion picture; he can gain information about the various Indian tribes and nations; he will find not only the biography of George Washington Cable, the novelist, and of Washington Irving, the essayist and historian, but also that of Washington Allston, the painter, Booker T. Washington, the Negro educator, and George Washington himself, as well as countless political and military figures, explorers, scientists, and philosophers.

L. T.

139. *The Long Ships Passing*

by Walter Havighurst

The Great Lakes, the world's largest body of fresh water and the North American continent's greatest northern waterway, have a history as dramatic as their unique geography. In *The Long Ships Passing,* Walter Havighurst (1901-) has written a processional history which emphasizes their present and future importance.

Mr. Havighurst begins with the tales of Samuel de Champlain's *voyageurs,* the first of whom entered the Straits of Mackinac in 1634 and, assuming that his destination was China, donned an embroidered mandarin robe so that he might fittingly face the merchants and princes of Cathay. Forerunners of the pioneers to come, the French explorers were the first to recognize the potentialities for exploitation of the vast wilderness beyond. After them, following the water route, came the canoes of the Jesuit missionaries, the great brigades of fur traders, and the groups of early settlers. Then began the steady flow of the immigrant boats, discharging streams of Irish, German, and Scandinavian settlers. One of these, pioneer George Stuntz, gazed at the sparsely settled hills and empty waters and prophesied: "This will be the heart of the continent."

And so it became. To the Great Lakes from the Atlantic Ocean via the St. Lawrence River came hundreds of sailing vessels whitening the trade lanes of the mid-nineteenth century. Still later came opulent steamships, and then the long, heavy freighters, "the whalebacks," which today have turned the Lakes into a commercial highway linking the materials (coal and iron ore) that make possible the age of steel. Now that the long-debated St. Lawrence Seaway will soon be completed, sea-going ships will add importance to these inland waters, transforming the Great Lakes into a Mediterranean of the Western Hemisphere and directly affecting the lives of some 50,000,000 people in the United States and Canada.

Mr. Havighurst gives not only the factual statistics of each successive era but also a full measure of legend, scenery, folkway, gossip, and anecdote. He emphasizes the vision inherent in those who made the area the vital center of the nation. "The Lakes," he says, "gave men a sense of the future." And he concludes: "Those shining waters . . . have had power to excite the imagination of America. That imagination sees a new era coming."

C. C.

140. *The Complete Novels and Selected Tales of Nathaniel Hawthorne*

edited by NORMAN HOLMES PEARSON

The reputation of Nathaniel Hawthorne (1804-1864) as a novelist rests upon his one indubitable masterpiece, *The Scarlet Letter* (1850), a somber but exciting narrative of seventeenth-century Puritan Massachusetts. Hawthorne (see No. 314) himself was curiously divided between the modern New Englander he thought he ought to be and the old Puritan he actually was in his imagination. His imagination prevailed in his best works, short or long; the second best were composed out of his conscious wit, a civilized and charming faculty which nevertheless did not reveal him at his greatest depth. Leaving aside *Fanshawe,* a youthful work which may be safely ignored, *The House of the Seven Gables* is notable for its genre painting; *The Blithedale Romance* for its satire upon the current craze for ideal communities; and *The Marble Faun* (known sometimes in Europe as *Transformation*) for its mystical force and its picture of Americans in Rome. These are fine novels, but *The Scarlet Letter* is a great one, and it continues to hold its high place in the fiction of the world.

Hawthorne's short stories—or tales, as he preferred to call them—divide themselves in the same fashion. The best of them are concerned with immemorial moral themes, Puritan in tinge; the next best are sketches or allegories by an artist whose humanely critical touch is still no substitute for the dusky passion that can always be counted on to break through his prose when it is concerned with ultimate matters of the human soul. The division runs through each of the collections from which specimens are given here. "Young Goodman Brown" and "Roger Malvin's Burial" are perfect examples of the greater kind; of the lesser kind, "Sunday at Home" and "The Celestial Railroad." Yet it must be said that in any of his writings Hawthorne exercises a special charm upon his reader. He is somehow always an appealing man, with a power that sometimes seems merely personal, suggesting that this individual who confides in his audience has still further confidences which he will never disclose.

M. V. D.

141. The Selected Writings of Lafcadio Hearn

edited by HENRY GOODMAN

The career of Lafcadio Hearn (1850-1904) is one of the strangest and most appealing in the annals of literature. The son of a Greek mother and an Irish father, he was named after the classical island, Leucadia. He was reared in England, immigrated to the United States, and became one of its rare, *fin-de-siècle* writers, interpreting the new esoteric products of European art in short essays written for New Orleans newspapers. Finally, in 1892, he expressed in action the artistic taste of his generation by transplanting himself to Japan, marrying a Japanese wife, and lecturing to Japanese students on English literature. He thus became the first qualified cultural ambassador of East to West and *vice versa*—at least as far as the English-speaking peoples are concerned.

Never having made a place for himself among the literary men of the Atlantic seaboard, Lafcadio Hearn always lived a laborious existence and therefore produced a very large body of miscellaneous writing, some of it, as might be expected, much inferior to the rest. But when all the necessary pruning has been done, what is left is, quite simply, induplicable.

His best-known works today are those which deal directly with Japan, and of them the last, *Japan: An Attempt at Interpretation,* is to be preferred as less enchanted, more critical, than the earlier descriptions. Reading Hearn on this subject is particularly interesting now, when the second World War has brought many Americans to Japan and created a strong current of American interest in that country. Tourists flock there all year round, and when Japanese movies or artifacts are exhibited in this country they can be sure of wide attention.

For related reasons, Hearn's retold tales, Japanese and Chinese, deserve our regard. But no less interesting are the things he said to the Japanese about standard English authors. Several volumes of Hearn's lectures on the great Romantic and Victorian writers have been reconstructed from notes, and one admires equally the deliberate simplicity of style, the subtlety of cultural "translation," and the critical powers unimpaired by the writer's special task. The remainder of Hearn's output is fairly sampled in this anthology, which should enable any reader to pursue his interest among the abundant stores of Hearn's delicate, sad, and yet solid literary legacy.

J. B.

142. *The Politics of Woodrow Wilson*

edited by AUGUST HECKSCHER

In 1956, the centenary year of Woodrow Wilson's birth, many publications reappraised the work of this man who brought the United States into its first world-wide conflict and who dedicated his last energies to establishing the first League of Nations. The documents presented in Mr. Heckscher's (1913-) anthology deal strictly with Wilson's politics, and one must go elsewhere (for instance, to Josephus Daniels [No. 84]) for an account of the theorist, man of letters, and university president.

From the politics alone, one may easily gather an unfavorable impression of the stiff, moralistic, phrase-making Virginian who obtained the Presidency by a plurality in a three-cornered election and slipped by for a second term on the brink of America's entry into the first World War. That unfavorable impression must be faced, and not dismissed, for it is the characteristic of the man, the essence of his greatness, the very definition of a type of human action. It might be called adversely "the politics of failure," and also, more justly, "the politics of example."

It consists, as these phrases suggest, of attempting to move the world by moral rectitude rather than by the arts of diplomacy. The example is generally "premature," which means that it is badly needed to awaken the people to their errors or opportunities. It is the politics of the prophets. As such it requires the prophetic temperament—unbending, committed to accepting abuse and misunderstanding, and perhaps relishing the thought of being alone right and strong in a world of weaklings and fools.

Wilson had that temperament; it received the Presbyterian ministerial training it deserved; and he went forth, a gay but sober Galahad, in quest of adventure. In the two conspicuous places where he served his country, he failed and was justified in his failure. As president of Princeton University, he fought for intellect and scholarship against very mixed odds, and he was on the point of a possibly forced resignation when he entered politics. The governorship of New Jersey was a mere interlude, and he quickly emerged as the providential man whose phrases and attitudes would moralize the first great cleavage in Western civilization. For a brief moment he moralized the whole world; no one perhaps—not Gandhi or Lenin or Nehru—has held the entire planet expectant and trusting as did Wilson in 1918-1919. He failed again, as he had to. But the memory of this has lain on the world's conscience, and Wilson's memory is therefore green.

J. B.

143. *The Short Stories of Ernest Hemingway*

There are many who feel that, for all the astonishing books he has written, Ernest Hemingway (1898-) has never surpassed his work in the short story. With them he started a new school of writing. But that is unimportant and in some ways unfortunate. What is important is that these are the works of a fine writer, and that most of them are free from the posturing and bellicosity that occasionally mar his longer works.

Some of the tales are so well known that there is little one can say about them. "The Snows of Kilimanjaro," "My Old Man," "The Undefeated," "The Killers," "Fifty Grand"—they are now as much a part of the American heritage as "Rip Van Winkle" or "The Gold Bug." The Hemingway style, in these stories seen at its most transparent, is in a sense equally a part of us. It is not too much to say that singlehanded he remodeled the English sentence, teaching us that it *must* tell the exact truth of a moment, an insight, or an experience.

Now that we are used to Hemingway—to his aggressive masculinity, his profound interest in the killing of men and animals, his absolute economy, his toughness, his emotional concision, his sexual candor, his bitter view of the world, the fortunate persistence in him of a connection with an older, unspoiled, almost frontier America—we can read these stories with an enjoyment that was not possible some years ago. Then he was a man to argue about, to exalt or denigrate. Today all that is over. He is no longer a figure of controversy, but an artist; and the core of his art rests in these tales of the bullfight, the barroom, the African veldt, the Michigan woods, the criminal world, the Paris of yesterday's expatriates, the ski slope, the race track, the prize ring. All do one thing: they make the reader relive the experience the author had in mind. They do this whether you like the stories or not, whether you like Hemingway or not, whether you like this kind of prose or not. His view of human life may seem partial, even totally unacceptable, but it is exposed with such clarity and charged with such impact that it is extremely difficult not to be moved by it.

C. F.

144. *Java Head*

by JOSEPH HERGESHEIMER

Java Head was first published in 1918, three years after Edgar Lee Masters's *Spoon River Anthology* (No. 205), a year before Sherwood Anderson's *Winesburg, Ohio* (No. 11). In 1900 Theodore Dreiser's *Sister Carrie* (No. 101) had been accepted for publication by Doubleday, but, Mrs. Doubleday having read the galleys and received a shock, it was "thrown into the cellar." There it remained off and on for seventeen years, awaiting a bold publisher. The forebears of these writers had turned their backs on Europe, gone to the Middle West, and created something that was their own. The sons also began to create, to forge a new tool, rough at the edges, but of metal that was pure contemporary America.

The writers of and about New England were in sharp contrast. In them and in their writing the new, the contemporary, was interwoven with the old. Edith Wharton's *Ethan Frome* (No. 327) lived in a harsh past and met disaster in trying to escape, while for Eugene O'Neill's gaunt New Englanders (see No. 238) there was no escape, only rebellion. They were writing in the tradition of Nathaniel Hawthorne (No. 140), who saw his people entangled in a religion in which they no longer believed. Others chose as subject those whom Alexander Hamilton had called the "rich and wellborn." *The Ambassadors* (No. 159) of Henry James were not money-makers, they had money.

Java Head, by Joseph Hergesheimer (1880-1954), marks the transition between money-making and money-having. The old grandfather, now land-locked, still sails the seas in imagination, while his son finds it more profitable to sit behind a desk. To Taou Yuen there is "nothing but talk about cargoes and sales and money." For the Salem (Massachusetts) of *Java Head* has little of Hawthorne's grim Salem. That Salem is convulsive, turned inward, witch-haunted. This Salem is haunted by another specter, the loss of trade to its neighbor, Boston, whose clipper ships were outsailing the slow barques.

To this Salem, Gerrit Ammidon brings his Chinese wife, "a Manchu and daughter of a nobleman." China has hitherto meant money and things—silks or teakwood furniture, not living people, a person. The story, from a slow beginning, now picks up speed and moves quickly toward its certain end. Not toward the end of the Ammidons. In time Salem will be deserted for Boston, and the heirloom souvenirs will clutter the drawing rooms on Back Bay, where J. P. Marquand's Apleys (No. 201) sit and sip tea, China tea.

J. A. R.

145. Porgy

by DuBose Heyward

DuBose Heyward (1885-1940), born and reared in Charleston, South Carolina, was a descendant of a signer of the Declaration of Independence, and therefore, as Porgy would have called him, "folks." Being folks, he was free to be at once white and colored, Porgy, Bess—any of the dwellers in Catfish Row. He understood the language of Porgy in the wide sense of the word and spoke it in the narrow, an impossibility to anyone outside the low country. Gullah, the language they speak, is a dialect peculiar to Negroes who live along the Carolina Coast low country. More than any other it retains traces, words and intonations, of African and would be unintelligible to an up-country Negro like Joel Chandler Harris's Uncle Remus (see Nos. 47 and 55).

But beneath the spoken language there was another, of gestures, laughter, the turn of an eye. DuBose Heyward learned this language from the servants, playmates, and neighbors of his childhood, when there was no color bar: for in Charleston there was no segregation, no Negro ghetto such as New York's Harlem. Catfish Row and its like were to be found in the center of a block of ante bellum houses, where slave-owners lived once, their descendants now. But besides proximity there was a stronger tie. William Alexander Percy, in *Lanterns on the Levee* (No. 245), said: "The Southern Negro has the most beautiful manners in the world, and the white, learning from him, I suspect, is a close second."

It is said, and may be true, that no white man can ever understand the Negro. DuBose Heyward came close; Porgy and his Bess were—and in George Gershwin's musical setting are—evidence. Certainly Heyward was the first to write a story that in texture, form, rhythm of speech, and feeling might have been written by James Baldwin (No. 18). He was also the first to record the sense of community among Negroes in the South. Distrustful of the white man's law and its officers, they build an invisible wall around Catfish or any other Row, and within the enclosure must perforce create their own law, their own order. If the burden of freedom becomes at times impossible, Daddy Peter is their spokesman: "I t'ink Gawd onduhstan' de succumstance, an' mek allowance."

J. A. R.

146. *Built in USA*

Post-War Architecture

edited by Henry-Russell Hitchcock *and* Arthur Drexler

During the 1920's and 1930's, when "modern" art was contending for acceptance in the United States, the same battle was being fought on behalf of "modern" architecture—often by the same combatants, with the same tactics, on the same terrain. Frequently the center of the contest was the Museum of Modern Art in New York City, which not only exhibited art but served as a vigorous and effective agency of propaganda. Its exhibits, moreover, led the way in enlarging the definition of "art" to include not merely sculpture and easel painting but also objects of commercial or household use, still and motion photography, and—of course—architecture. The appearance of the Museum's own building is an index of its success: daring and assertive when it was built, in contrast to its city surroundings, by the 1950's it seemed not only acceptable but tame. By the time the Museum came to publish *Built in USA,* in 1953, there could be no doubt from its point of view (in the first words of the preface) that "the battle of modern architecture has long been won."

Built in USA, nonetheless, does not attempt to record the typical buildings of the postwar period. Many of those shown are not even typical of their designers—for example, Frank Lloyd Wright (see his autobiography [No. 347]). Since the Museum of Modern Art now sees its role as that of judge, rather than advocate, the book represents a selection of the structures its editors believe to have the greatest "quality and significance." And yet, perhaps unintentionally, the result is a fair impression of the construction that was typically done at the time: in the variety of purposes—from stadia to music sheds, from schools to Swedenborgian chapels—and in the diversity of effects that are possible even within the limits of the style called "international." There are photographs of buildings (like Lever House) that are almost universally admired, and of others (like the house for Dr. Edith Farnsworth) that have been violently criticized. There are many examples of work by the architects who have come from Europe—Aalto, Gropius, Breuer, Mies van der Rohe, Mendelsohn—to whom we owe much, and also of the less dramatic and conspicuous Americans (like Harwell Hamilton Harris) who exemplify an existing native tradition. Possibly the book is also fair in conveying a sense of the uneasiness latent in victory for "modern" architects. Now that they have won freedom, they are not entirely certain what to do with it.

E. L.

147. Jazz

Its Evolution and Essence

by André Hodeir

Americans have often been tardy in recognizing their own cultural accomplishments, especially in those areas where a characteristic American style was emerging. Robert Frost (No. 125) was first published in England; one of the foremost students of American technology, Siegfried Giedion (No. 128), is Swiss; the stature of Frank Lloyd Wright (No. 347) was first recognized in Holland; and in France were published two of the earliest books about jazz music—Robert Goffin's *Aux frontières du jazz* (1932) and Hugues Panassié's *Le jazz hot* (1934). Both have long since become out of date, but in the judgment of numerous jazz critics they have best been superseded by the book of still another Frenchman—André Hodeir's *Hommes et problèmes du jazz,* here represented in its English translation. Mr. Hodeir's is in any event the first discussion of jazz to be written by a trained musicologist, a winner of first prizes in harmony, fugue, and musical history at the Paris Conservatory of Music.

His book is less an organized treatise than a collection of fragments, articles prepared for the magazine *Jazz-hot* during the period (1947-50) when he was its editor. In them he discusses a series of almost unrelated jazz musicians and questions about their music. What he brings to each chapter is a characteristically French bent for lucidity, for abstraction, for the rationale behind the phenomenon others are so often content to leave as it is. The major figures of jazz have tended to shun definition, because they either were incapable of it or mistrusted the impulse to fix such an emotional nuance as jazz in words. "If you don't know what it is," Thomas "Fats" Waller is supposed to have advised a lady who asked him, "don't mess with it." Perhaps only an observer from abroad, working mainly from phonograph records, could have broken through this traditional reticence and distaste for analysis. Mr. Hodeir's attempts to explain the inexplicable should be read in conjunction with the comments of the musicians themselves (No. 282) and with John Kouwenhoven's treatment of jazz (No. 175) in its relationship to other American "vernacular" arts.

E. L.

148. The True Believer

by Eric Hoffer

Eric Hoffer (1902-) is a self-educated dock worker. But his book would be notable had its author been a don. (Perhaps more so.) Though its style may owe something to H. L. Mencken, and its ideas something to Sorel, Pareto, and Machiavelli, it is essentially a piece of original though not systematic thought, the work of an intuitive psycho-sociologist with a talent for incisive, cold generalization.

Stimulated by the spectacle of the twin triumphs of Communism and Fascism, Mr. Hoffer, undeflected by any personal group-adherences, analyzes the origin, nature, and goals of mass movements, whether past or present, religious, social or political, "good" or "bad." His central conviction is that, from Christianity to Fascism, they are of one family, the unifying trait being that they draw their most energetic adherents from the same types of humanity. These include the poor (though not the creative poor), misfits, the inordinately selfish, the ambitious facing unlimited opportunities, minorities, the bored, and the sinners. In general, mass movements are based on frustration, characterized by fanaticism, and unified by several agents, primarily hatred. The true believer craves "to be rid of an unwanted self."

The contemporary importance of this brief, shattering book lies in Mr. Hoffer's observation that the true believer is everywhere on the march today; that he is shaping things in his own image; and that consequently the rest of us, who do not happen to be dominated by creative frustration, will inherit a world we not only never made, but never wanted.

This central thesis is not in itself absolutely novel, but Mr. Hoffer's reenforcing insights are. The reader will discover them for himself, sometimes with shock, for Mr. Hoffer's clinical attitude is unsparing. This is no book for the tender-minded and it hardly confirms the cheerful view of society that we think of as characteristically American. Indeed the whole book is out of the mainstream of American thought, though it was anticipated in some respects by Mencken and Ambrose Bierce (see No. 34). That makes it all the more salutary.

Mr. Hoffer commands a style of the utmost spareness and force. It has no charm and no beauty, as his ideas have none. It is, like those ideas, pitiless and astringent. A remarkable book, a remarkable man, a triumph of icy reflection.

C. F.

149. The Age of Reform

From Bryan to FDR

by RICHARD HOFSTADTER

In the past 60 years the United States has been in a period of constantly accelerating change. This change has been the product, in principal part, of the steadily expanding industrial energy. Over the past half century this energy has acted to alter profoundly the character of American society. Industrialization has taken multitudes off the land and placed them in the cities, while at the same time it has transformed the life of those who remained on the farms. It has eroded most of the barriers that, however porous they may have been, still served to differentiate the classes in nineteenth-century America. It has shifted much of the significance that previously attached to the several states and concentrated it in the central government.

Some of the modifications in custom or behavior have taken place imperceptibly and unconsciously. Other alterations, especially those in the role of the central government, have been introduced more consciously and painfully. The efforts to accommodate consciously and unconsciously to the new conditions produced by industrial development created what Professor Richard Hofstadter (1916-) calls the Age of Reform. In his analysis of this period he is, fortunately, as much concerned with why people did things as with what they did. He searches for the motivations of those "progressives" who attempted to maintain the old schemes of value within the new and different conditions. He looks behind the variety of solutions originated for the changing problems to discover what the training or status of the originators had to do with the shape of the solutions offered.

This of course is risky business. There is almost as much danger in trying to think intelligently about the past as about the present or future. With certain things—notably his disregard of European and particularly German influences on the thinking of early progressives, or his assumption (even as qualified) of the discontinuity of the New Deal with what went on before—there will not be full satisfaction. But this is a matter of very small concern. This is an illuminating account, solidly supported by immense amounts of information, of the struggles of the country to deal with industrialism. It is written by a man who is willing to have ideas about the past that can be used in considering what to do about the present.

E. E. M.

150. *The American Political Tradition*

And the Men Who Made It

by RICHARD HOFSTADTER

American politics arouses surprising private passions. There were those in 1940 who planned to remove to Canada if "that man in the White House" were re-elected. In 1912 a man turned the picture of Theodore Roosevelt against his parlor wall "forever"; while some years earlier a Democrat in New York took to his bed "all broken up" because he had failed to register and so could not vote against Harrison. In the folklore of almost every family similar anecdotes can be discovered.

These passionate responses are, outside the immediate household, fortunately of small effect and short duration. Men get out of bed and no one really goes to Canada. One of the reasons for this, no doubt, is that, as Professor Richard Hofstadter (1916-) says, despite the local conflicts there is a common ground, a unity of cultural and political tradition where almost all Americans can meet and live together. The way in which this common ground was cultivated and fertilized through the years is the subject of investigation in this remarkable book.

Professor Hofstadter has selected excellent representatives of the dominant ideas in American political life from the founding fathers through the administrations of Franklin D. Roosevelt. Concentrating primarily on what these men did in public life, he has succeeded at one level in giving a general survey of American history. These pages are, in part, that rare thing—a textbook at once reliable, intelligent, and entertaining. But he has not lost sight of the fact that he is dealing with men and ideas as well as acts. There are illuminating personal interpretations here; it would, for instance, be difficult to find elsewhere a more discerning description of Herbert Hoover. Equally fresh and nimble is the way in which Mr. Hofstadter handles the evaluation of the essential sentiments and ideas in our history. It is a fine book, beautifully conceived and stated, that really does make one think in new ways about the American past.

E. E. M.

151. *The Story of American Railroads*

by STEWART H. HOLBROOK

In folklore and finance the American railroad has been *sui generis.* No other institution, at least of the mechanical kind, has nourished so many legends, popular in character and national in scope. The basis for this is doubtless that the railroads built the country; they were necessary to its growth, and they came just when it was ready to grow at a rate hitherto unimagined in human history. And the wizards who could find the money for them were not wanting; nor were they averse to becoming millionaires in the process. The stories about all that are numerous enough, and some of them are unsavory. But the stories of the engines and the cars, and where they went and what men made them move; what dangerous high trestles they crossed; what deadly accidents they met with; what sounds they made in the day, in the night, as they rushed across the land—all this is a still richer body of legend, explored by Stewart Holbrook (1893-) in the belief that some day the whole poetry of steel rails may be a thing of the past, with trucks and planes triumphing in its place.

The first railroads were local to small valleys and limited regions whose inhabitants made sacrifices to build them. Trunk lines and consolidated systems came later, often with the help of funds secured from European investors. But the fascination in both cases was the same, and it took the form of wonder at mighty locomotives whose steam whistles had such a glorious way of reverberating through woods and along lonely mountainsides. It also meant, for boys if not for men, an abject worship of the heroes in the cab, or bending before the firebox, or climbing iron ladders to administer the brakes, or standing between the cars to couple them—the men who were rumored to risk their lives each minute that they did any of these things. The occupation of railroad men became safer as the nineteenth century grew old; yet it remains true, at least in retrospect, that railroading was lovable for the dangers it involved. Mr. Holbrook's book is all retrospect, all affection, and all nostalgia.

M. V. D.

152. *The Autocrat of the Breakfast Table*

by Oliver Wendell Holmes

In American letters there are two Oliver Wendell Holmeses, father (1809-94) and son (1841-1935). The son is the better known today because he was a notable Supreme Court justice and because his correspondence with Sir Frederick Pollock and Harold J. Laski has recently been published, like his chief legal decisions.

But it is permitted to believe that the elder Holmes, a literary physician, will regain his once eminent position. Not, indeed, as a poet, though the anthologies give him a small place, but as the author of *The Autocrat* and other casual essays. The fact that he wrote the first three "psychiatric" novels of the modern age is interesting historically, but will doubtless not save them from oblivion.

The fresh and rare quality of *The Autocrat* is its freedom from a ready-made morality. The elder Holmes lived and practiced medicine in Boston, conversing at the Saturday Club and elsewhere with Ralph Waldo Emerson, Henry Wadsworth Longfellow, James Russell Lowell, Nathaniel Hawthorne, Theodore Parker, and other Transcendentalists, but he was not of their solemn cast of mind. Less "important" from the point of view of handbooks of literature, Holmes may even be called a sentimentalist at times—so may Charles Lamb—but it is the Lamb-like quality that makes the informal essayist, the man to whom surfaces are vividly real and who suppresses rather than expresses the genuine knowledge he has of the world's terrors.

Whatever the secret of compounding, Holmes had the formula, and the characters of his boardinghouse breakfast table are perfectly solid and credible. One may note in passing that it was this good Bostonian who first made fun of that city's pretensions, long before *The Late George Apley* (No. 201) and the novels it has engendered. One should add that *The Autocrat* (this series and two others) appeared in the all-powerful *Atlantic Monthly* (see the Howells reader [No. 155]), and that the opening remark of the book alludes to a gap in the publishing of Holmes by that periodical.

J. B.

153. *George Washington Carver*

by RACKHAM HOLT

A life of George Washington Carver (1864-1943) might have had the title that Booker T. Washington gave to his autobiography, *Up from Slavery* (No. 320), but it would have been misleading. He was born in slavery but was freed too young to carry scars. From that point the ways of the two men diverge for a while, the latter's to take him among people, his own and the alien whites, the former's to the woods and fields. For Carver was a naturalist and an artist by nature, and a scientist by training. His being a Negro he accepted as a fact among other scientific facts, and one not to be overstressed or bewailed. He quietly believed in himself, and by middle age he had given proof of the validity of what he was doing. He had made a name in science, not by gazing at stars and other faraway things, but by having a look at the homely peanut (ground nut)—and not at the peanut alone, but at every living thing that grew at hand. For in his realm he was doing what Booker Washington had urged the whites to do, in his famous speech at Atlanta in 1895: "Cast down your buckets where you are."

Meanwhile the two men's ways had again converged. Carver had been called to Tuskegee to be the head of a science department that did not exist. But there were grass, corn, cattle, pigs, cows, and the peanut. There were also students, and he made them reveal their secret powers to him and to themselves in turn—not only in the classroom, for like all good teachers, he was always teaching everywhere.

Among his own people he could be crabbed and truculent, but to white people he turned a serene face. Jim Crow's claws, as one may read in Woodward's *The Strange Career of Jim Crow* (No. 346), were sinking deeper into the South, or, to change the figure, it was the case of "The Bottom Rail on Top," William Alexander Percy's title for a searing chapter in his *Lanterns on the Levee* (No. 245). Carver spoke to the top rail, or no lower than the middle, not personally offering evidence of what a Negro could do, but impersonally, as an American to fellow countrymen. He knew, as Booker T. Washington knew, that the Negro was on the conscience of every decent Southerner, and time would give it voice. So he endured indignities at the hand of the lower-class whites who are called "rednecks" and "peckerwoods" out of the old belief that such were impotent to do him harm. As to that there was disagreement among his own people; as to him, none.

J. A. R.

154. *Great River*

The Rio Grande in North American History

by Paul Horgan

The third longest of American rivers, the Rio Grande, also ranks with the Mississippi, the Missouri, the Ohio, the Hudson, and the Columbia as one of the most notable in its human associations. Flowing from the Rocky Mountains toward Mexico, and for 1,300 miles the boundary between that country and the state of Texas, it passes through varied territory and has nurtured at least five contrasting cultures. Paul Horgan (1903-), for years a resident of the region it waters and an able novelist who has turned increasingly to history (see No. 278), has told the story of the men and women who have lived beside it. Actually, it is a history of a large portion of the American Southwest, for the Rio Grande and its tributaries touch the soil of Colorado, New Mexico, and Texas, while its peoples have been influenced by the regions now called Arizona, Kansas, and Oklahoma.

Mr. Horgan emphasizes the contrasting cultures of this vast area of sparse rainfall. First came the Indians, of whom the Pueblos were the most colorful and—with their craft skills and ceremonial, rounded plan of life (economic and religious)—the most advanced of North American aborigines. Harassed by the wilder Navajo, Apache, and Comanche Indians, they were conquered in the late 1500's by the Spaniards, and were benignly instructed by priests and shamelessly exploited by officials and settlers. For 200 years the colony was precariously maintained, and even the revolution which brought independence to Mexico in 1821 cruelly preserved the colonial status of the Rio Grande area. How American trappers and traders appeared in Taos and Santa Fe; how others came to Texas as settlers, asserted their independence and surrendered their short-lived republic to become an American state; how the Mexican war of 1846-1848 brought the entire region under American rule; how the Indian tribes were installed on reservations; how the discovery of mineral wealth and the use of modern grazing and farming methods brought the area a greater prosperity—this is told by Mr. Horgan with a wealth of detail and distinction of writing. Like a weaver operating an immense loom, he has skillfully woven the contrasting strands of race, river, land, and war into a colorful tapestry that will bring readers an immediate sense of this region—one of the oldest in the American experience and one of the most fascinating in its cultural character.

F. E. H.

155. Selected Writings of William Dean Howells

edited by HENRY STEELE COMMAGER

It was Howells's misfortune that he was born poor yet won early success as an editor and writer during a period of American life in which he might have been a literary pioneer. The period, the last half of the nineteenth century, saw Walt Whitman (No. 333), Henry James (Nos. 159-61), and Mark Twain (No. 311) all active, and the latter two touched the sprawling growth and crass economic exploitation of the time. Still, there was room for a novelist who could reveal more fully this rapidly growing, materialistic, grotesque, yet fascinating America. Howells perceived the opportunity, but never used it with the full knowledge and searing realism of an Émile Zola or an Arnold Bennett.

Born in 1837, son of a printer in a small Ohio town, Howells never formally acquired more than an elementary school education, but emerged in his early 20's as a widely read, expert, and cultivated writer. A campaign biography of Lincoln won him a consular post in Venice; four years later he returned to America and a place on *The Nation* (New York), then (1866-1881) on the *Atlantic Monthly,* of which by 1871 he was editor-in-chief. In Boston, Howells enjoyed the literary world of James Russell Lowell, Henry Wadsworth Longfellow, and Oliver Wendell Holmes, Sr. (No. 152). Many of his stories and novels, which now appeared in rapid succession, reflect its urbane gentility. Perhaps the wonder is that Howells the creator did not die in the editor and literary mogul; to his credit this did not occur. Instead he explored diligently the America he saw. These *Selected Writings* show him at his best. In both *The Rise of Silas Lapham* and *A Modern Instance* he depicts the crudeness and growing pains of his era; both novels achieve distinction while missing greatness. In *A Boy's Town* he recaptures with suave humor the Middle Western childhood, much of which was to disappear with the automobile and the cinema, and *My Mark Twain* paints a vivid picture of his friend Samuel L. Clemens (No. 311).

Howells had not remained long enough the struggling journalist and enforced participator in life; his acquired gentility shrank from the extreme and limited his high abilities. Yet his work stands out as honest, revealing, and enduring; it comprises the best record we have of an American generation just preceding that which Frank Norris (No. 236) and Theodore Dreiser (No. 101) were to reveal with surer and harsher skill. F. E. H.

156. Where Peoples Meet

by EVERETT CHERRINGTON HUGHES
and HELEN MACGILL HUGHES

No account as brief as the Hugheses' could of course do justice to so complicated a problem as race relations in the United States, let alone place that problem in its world setting. *Where Peoples Meet* is largely confined to the role of ethnic groups in the central occupations of American society—business, industry, and the professions. It necessarily does less justice to those areas where minority ethnic origin counts for little or nothing, such as the arts, the civil service, and so on, and it completely omits sports. An impressive proportion of American national heroes—baseball players, motion-picture and television stars, popular singers, prize fighters, and makers of scientific discoveries—belong to minority ethnic groups.

The book tends to assume that ethnic origin is *the* determinant of status in the United States, though one of the essays in the Appendix—"Dilemmas and Contradictions of Status"—helps to correct that impression. In fact there is a good deal of evidence that what appears to be ethnic prejudice is often actually class prejudice, and as the class status of recent immigrants improves, their ethnic origins tend to be forgotten. In a community where a group of recent immigrants of peasant origin are the objects of prejudice, a man with a title from the same country may be regarded as a suitable husband for the local heiress, and musicians and scholars of the same ethnic origin will be welcome on the local concert stage and university faculty. However, when a marked difference in skin color is involved, the prejudice usually has a truly ethnic or racial basis and will not be greatly altered by shifts in class status.

The book may also leave the impression that there is much greater uniformity of treatment of minority ethnic groups in America than there is. The status of a Jew, for instance, will depend not only on his Jewishness and his own wealth and accomplishments, but also on how long ago his family came to America, where it came from, and where it settled. These circumstances will in turn influence his own attitude toward other ethnic groups. A New York Jew of recent immigration, for instance, will often be an ardent advocate of Negro rights, but a Jew whose family has long been settled in Memphis or Atlanta will usually share the majority opinion of his community on that subject.

P. P.

157. *Picture Maker of the Old West*

William H. Jackson

by CLARENCE S. JACKSON

The drive to record the image of the American West—to make it visually comprehensible—has been something like an obsession. As early as the 1830's, Bodmer and Miller (whose work is reproduced and discussed in DeVoto's *Across the Wide Missouri* [No. 91]) recorded the trans-Mississippi region in water colors and sketches. Many exploring expeditions and government surveys took along "official" artists, and by the 1860's the plains and mountains were apparently swarming with landscape painters. (See "Westward the Course of Landscape," in Larkin's *Art and Life in America* [No. 180].) It was this obsession that shaped the life of William H. Jackson (1843-1942).

As a photographer, Jackson ranks with Mathew Brady as one of America's greatest. Between them they "covered" two of our great nineteenth-century epics: Brady the Civil War, and Jackson the postwar development of the West. Both knew they were recording history, and both kept on under staggering difficulties, at the risk of fortune and life itself.

Though Brady was perhaps the greater photographer, Clarence Jackson's book about his father's work has been selected because of its wide range. Here are sketches Jackson drew as a "bullwhacker" in a wagon train on the North Platte and Stillwater rivers in 1866; photographs of the building of the first transcontinental railroad; photographs of Yellowstone, copies of which were on the desks of every senator and representative in January, 1872, when Congress passed the bill creating our first national park; the first photographs of the cliff dwellings at Mesa Verde; and photographs of Colorado's mountain-goat railways and the cliff-hanging mining towns they served (now the ghost towns of Muriel Wolle's *Bonanza Trail* [No. 345]).

In Jackson's photographs of Yellowstone, Yosemite, and the Wasatch Range there is something of the sense John Muir (see No. 1) later felt in these mountains, that the work of creation is not done, and that "in the midst of this outer steadfastness there is incessant motion and change. . . . Ice changing to water, lakes to meadows, and mountains to plains." But Jackson's West is full of people: construction crews, shopkeepers, explorers, and above all, the Indians. The changes that fascinated him most were those wrought in the West by men.

J. A. K.

158. *Men of Science in America*

by BERNARD JAFFE

The achievements of the United States in large-scale industrialism and technology have been acknowledged all around the world, and from this fame, as well as from the activist spirit of American culture, it has often been inferred, even by Americans, that this country has not made great contributions to the basic sciences on which technology is founded. Bernard Jaffe (1896-) sets out to correct this notion, and his book, because of its polemic purpose and also perhaps because it was written during the second World War, may seem a bit defensive. Mr. Jaffe insists that our scientists must be respected. In this he may be underestimating the judgment of foreign readers who could scarcely know anything about the history of science in the past 200 years without having heard of Franklin, Rumford, Morton, Gibbs, and Morgan.

It is unfortunate that there has been no book of this kind published since 1944, although the newspapers and the magazines have been full of scientific news. Government, industry, and educational institutions have all been busy in this field. But there are many books on special phases. For medicine, there is Helen Clapesattle's *The Doctors Mayo* (No. 62); for the story of a great Negro investigator, Rackham Holt's *George Washington Carver* (No. 153); for the relations between science and industrial progress, Carleton Mabee's *The American Leonardo: The Life of Samuel F. B. Morse* (No. 195).

There is a special value in Mr. Jaffe's book, however, in its excellence as popularization. He makes the scientifically interesting facts in nineteen major careers and a host of lesser ones intelligible to the layman. But he feeds the healthy American appetite for knowledge of scientific advance without palming off wonder stories and mere practical gadgets as the real thing—which makes for public support of scientific progress, and for the spread of the scientific spirit.

L. B.

159. *The Ambassadors*

by HENRY JAMES

Henry James (1843-1916) can be judged only by the sum of his work. But, forced to choose the novel that shows him at the top of his form, one would probably, as he himself did, select *The Ambassadors*—"quite the best, 'all round,' of my productions." (See also Nos. 160 and 161.)

Written toward the beginning of his last period, it has some of the complication and overrefinement of his "mandarin" style, yet not so much as to baffle the conscientious, intelligent reader. It holds in balance most of the Jamesian themes and expresses them in a form perfectly calculated to show them off in all their beauty and intensity. Here, in Lambert Strether's pilgrimage to "save" young Chad Newsome from the presumed corruptions of the villain "Europe," is a story which exhibits James's lifelong preoccupation with the "international theme" and with the contrast between the moral system of his Americans and the facts of life before which that system must give way.

Here, too, is the most moving dramatization of another of his themes—that of the unlived life, the tragedy of the man whose experience is too meager to match the richness of his imagination and intelligence. "Live all you can," says Strether to Bilham. "It's a mistake not to." Here too the reader will find in Strether the ripe demonstration of James's theory of the novel, that the story must evolve out of the consciousness of a single, highly aware person, given to exhaustive discrimination and reflection. The psychological novel of our time finds one of its major sources in Henry James; and that source can be nowhere studied more fruitfully than in *The Ambassadors*.

It shows James at the height of his powers, fully in command of a new, invented style that was on other occasions to betray him into mannerism and needless difficulty. It shows him in control of a collection of fascinating characters, of whom the Countess de Vionnet is perhaps the most appealing. It shows him reflecting with the utmost gravity and cogency on the character of his countrymen—or at least of his upper-class countrymen. In its comparison of European with American modes of sensibility it still, though written more than a half century ago, has much to tell us. In the delicacy and depth of its insights into human beings it betrays no sign whatever of dating. For many readers it will remain one of the dozen or so greatest American novels. Possibly its rank is even higher.

C. F.

160. *The Selected Letters of Henry James*

edited by LEON EDEL

If any one characteristic of the American literary scene can be singled out as dominant in the years since the second World War, it is the decline of ideology. This does not mean that there is no longer a literature of protest and reform; books dealing with certain social problems (especially race relations and civil rights, the insane and other psychological variants) continue to appear in abundance and to show considerable vitality if no great artistic value. Nor does it mean that American literature is no longer interested in ideas; the novel of ideas, for instance, enjoys a vigorous development in the hands of such distinguished practitioners as Lionel Trilling (No. 308) and Robert Penn Warren (No. 319), though these writers use fiction as a way of examining ideas, not as an instrument for promoting a set program. But poetry, criticism, fiction, and to a lesser extent drama (which tends to be rather behind the times in America) have reflected the deep disillusion that confrontation with the ideologies of Fascism and Communism has bred in the American people.

One consequence of the decline of ideology is that American writers of the past, whose primary commitment was to their art rather than to social reform, have enjoyed a tremendous renewal of interest among critics and the more discriminating sort of readers. F. Scott Fitzgerald (No. 114) and Henry James (Nos. 159 and 161) are outstanding examples.

In fact, the revived interest in James is a cultural phenomenon of the first importance. Not only have his novels been brought back into print with enthusiastic introductions by leading critics, but his fugitive essays and travel sketches, his notebooks and letters and family papers, and his plays and memoirs either have been published for the first time or have appeared in new editions. The critical journals are full of essays on James; the first volume of a distinguished biography has appeared. Two of his stories have been successfully dramatized; young writers imitate his inimitable style; and for a time there was even a movement to accord James the tribute no American writer ever gets—to rename a square for him in New York City.

Henry James (1843-1916) will always be the very type of the American dedicated artist, and no single book could better convey the quality of his dedication or of his multifarious personality than this collection of letters which Professor Edel (1907-) has so beautifully selected, edited, and introduced.

P. P.

161. The Short Stories of Henry James

edited by Clifton Fadiman

Henry James (1843-1916) has often been described as "not really American," and many of the circumstances of his life as well as certain qualities in his writing support that view. Yet there is something in his work that unmistakably attests to the land of his birth. It is not in his style, which, especially in its later development, is too personal an idiom to bear the stamp of nationality; if there is such a thing as an "American style" in prose it is to be found in such writers as Mark Twain (No. 311) and Ernest Hemingway (No. 143), writers to whom Henry James stands in about the same relation as Cicero to Al Smith. Nor is the American in James particularly evident in his choice of subject; much as he loved in his novels to play off American characters against an international background (see No. 159), he was really transferring to an enlarged, a hemispheric stage a favorite subject of nineteenth-century English and Continental fiction: the young man or woman from the provinces who seeks his way in the great city.

But James altered this subject by spiritualizing it. The characters he champions do not take to the great stage to get or spend, but to realize their moral being, to have life and to have it more abundantly. It is the sense, playing over all his pages, of life itself as the great golden opportunity that is the American quality in James, as it was the source of his criticism of his native country whenever America seemed to him to betray opportunity for opportunism. James, like the gods, "loved the most living," and he saw that the ultimate tragedy is to have missed one's life.

This great central theme radiates through the stories here collected. Some are tragedies of the unlived life, like "The Beast in the Jungle," "The Jolly Corner," and (it seems to me, though Mr. Fadiman offers a different interpretation in his notes) "The Altar of the Dead"; a variant of the same subject is treated ironically in "The Real Thing." "Louisa Pallant" is the story of a woman who missed her opportunity and tries to make up for it; "The Pupil" and "The Liar," different as they are, both present characters whose golden promise is overcome by the dross about them. The difference between opportunity and opportunism emerges from such stories as "Brooksmith" and "The Birthplace."

P. P.

162. *The Raven*

A Biography of Sam Houston

by MARQUIS JAMES

Historian Henry Steele Commager says of Sam Houston (1793-1863), in his introduction to *The Raven,* that "he serves the history of Texas in the same way that Charlemagne and Alfred and Barbarossa and Valdemar Sejr serve the histories of the nations they helped to make . . . in a sense if he had not existed we should have had to create him." In his own lifetime, Houston was regarded as a semilegendary figure; it was inevitable that posterity would put him into the larger-than-life company of Daniel Boone and Davy Crockett as a New World demigod.

Sam Houston was at once representative and atypical of the American pioneer hero. His 70-year career was compounded of heroism and weakness, chivalry and vice, recklessness and prudence, practicality and dream. Alternately idolized and reviled by his contemporaries, Houston's public history recorded him as frontiersman, hunter, governor of two states, United States Senator, commander-in-chief of an army, twice President of the Republic of Texas. It contrasts grotesquely with the narrative of his personal offenses against the conventions of his day.

Marquis James (1891-1955) was an historian famed for his ability to join the documented lore of formal biography with the seeming trivia that cast significant sidelights on character. The results of this method, both in *The Raven* and in his notable *Andrew Jackson, Portrait of a President,* were recognition of his genuine contributions to history by meticulous scholars and wide popular acceptance by the American reading public. His biography of Houston is no retelling of thrice-told tales, but the synthesis of long and painstaking research. Documenting his narrative from sources both of recorded fact and of legend, he has depicted the man against the background of an era when American history reached one of its most melodramatic crises. Out of the materials of history and hearsay, he has managed—without distortion and without sacrifice of scholarship—to present to his readers a protagonist in surging action upon a panoramic stage, a hero animated by powerful human motives and an almost mystical sense of destiny.

C. C.

163. *Selected Papers on Philosophy*

by WILLIAM JAMES

The name of William James (1842-1910) is associated with Pragmatism, a philosophical movement which flourished during the first two decades of this century. Because James was an American and because Pragmatism is misused to denote the practical life, many have jumped to the conclusion that James's thought is typical of the New Continent—strong on technology and weak in culture.

A reading of the selected essays in this book will begin to show how absurd this misrepresentation is. James's Pragmatism is in the first place not a belief or a doctrine, but a definition and test of truth. The definition states that truth is an activity of the mind before it is a form of words and propositions. How then does the mind work, and how do we test its success or failure in arriving at truth? The answer is: it works towards ends, by the operation of interests, and we judge its success by results in experience. Experience includes, of course, the aesthetic satisfactions of coherence and economy in thought, and any other demands that mind, culture, or tradition may make.

In other words, truth is functional and James is a pioneer philosopher of process. He belongs to the generation of Bergson, Samuel Butler, Nietzsche, Dilthey, and others who rebelled against the mechanistic philosophies of the mid-nineteenth century and showed a way out of simple determinism. The genesis of James's views is shown in his studies and correspondence, as described and quoted in Ralph Barton Perry's *The Thought and Character of William James* (No. 246). The present essays, together with *The Varieties of Religious Experience* (No. 164), will also reveal James as a stylist of the first rank. His blending of subtle inquiry with strong imagination and homely examples is unique among modern philosophers.

J. B.

164. The Varieties of Religious Experience

by WILLIAM JAMES

The Gifford Lectures that William James (1842-1910) was invited to give in 1900 form the substance of his masterpiece, *The Varieties of Religious Experience*. The work is remarkable in this, that for the first time in modern history a scientifically trained philosopher dealt with religious experience on a comparative plan, yet without denying or discrediting the validity of the phenomena he was studying.

James was a moralist and theist in the sense that spirit was to him no illusion; he was also, by his own formula, a radical empiricist, by which he meant that experience was all-inclusive. He found no place for transcendental forms or powers, and finally, he was an anti-dogmatist and anti-absolutist to whom any testimony and any claim represented something to be accounted for, tested, and placed.

This is what he did with the vast literature of religious revelation, mystical experience, and private soul-searching. His work as a psychologist and his familiarity with mental pathology also brought him abundant firsthand evidence. The categories he established have stood the test of time, and the analyses he offered have not been improved upon. With their aid we can at least brush aside the crude physiological explanations of religion that were so long current and are so often revived when new medical or other discoveries tempt their makers to one more reductive account of man's whole being.

The great truth that James pointed out was that the ascertainable concomitants of a religious perception or state of mind do not affect its truth value. That a man is proved to be epileptic does not by itself invalidate his utterances. They must be judged, like other utterances, by their fitness; that is, their concordance with previously known truths and with reproducible experiences—submitted, in short, to the pragmatic test (see James's *Selected Papers on Philosophy* [No. 163]). This point of view has of course become commonplace in the realm of art, where the validity of a report on the moral universe such as Dostoevsky's is not impugned on the ground that he was, precisely, an epileptic.

In James's work the insistence on "Varieties" is consonant with the American ideal of pluralism—an ideal often impaired by the American reality but philosophically required by political federalism, and even more by the natural diversity of regions and constituent cultures on the North American continent. (For the religious manifestation of this pluralism, see also E. S. Bates's *American Faith* [No. 22].)

J. B.

165. Poetry and the Age

by RANDALL JARRELL

Randall Jarrell (1914-) is something of a biological sport in contemporary American literary criticism. The main line of development for the past quarter century has been in the direction of method and theory (see No. 349), and questions of method and theory leave Mr. Jarrell utterly indifferent, except that he is always willing to have some fun at the expense of other critics who take them seriously.

In fact sheer fun is more important in Mr. Jarrell's writing than in the writing of any other American critic of similar stature. His prose is full of invention and playfulness and extravagance. The fine essays on Robert Frost (see No. 125) and Walt Whitman (see No. 333) in this book are perfectly serious critical judgments, but part of Mr. Jarrell's delight in praising these poets undoubtedly arises from the fact that they have been somewhat neglected (and, in the instance of Whitman, even scorned) by the more sobersided, the more theoretical and methodological, of contemporary critics.

But when he addresses himself directly to the critical tradition, as he does in his essay "The Age of Criticism," Mr. Jarrell's indifference to theory and method lead him somewhat astray. The situation described really exists (granting some license to the exuberant wit of the description), but it is only part of the truth. Mr. Jarrell describes certain ridiculous effects of contemporary critical development without doing justice to causes that are not ridiculous.

Since Mr. Jarrell represents no school, no critical formulation, he should perhaps be a frivolous dilettante. But in fact he reveals himself a deeply committed man—committed to literature and to humanity. For all its playfulness, Mr. Jarrell's thought is nearly always in tension between these two poles of his loyalty. He staunchly defends the right of literature to be literature (see "The Obscurity of the Poet"), but he just as staunchly demands that it should somehow get humanity into it.

Beyond these commitments Mr. Jarrell brings to criticism a vast amount of reading of all kinds, a highly personal but highly cultivated taste, and a willingness to come to grips with a poem barehanded. He is one of the most independent, original, and compelling critics writing in America today.

P. P.

166. *The Life and Selected Writings of Thomas Jefferson*

edited by ADRIENNE KOCH *and* WILLIAM PEDEN

Thomas Jefferson (1743-1826) is still the greatest spokesman of American democracy. All through his long and busy life, from his first services to his native Virginia (see No. 199), his drafting of the Declaration of Independence, as diplomat in France, as Secretary of State in George Washington's cabinet, to his election as third President of his new country, he was devoted in public affairs but always eminent among the founding fathers for his eloquent statements of the needs and the basic faith on which democracy was founded.

He was reluctant in action; his letters show his sincere preference for a life of study, art, and experiment. But he was a skillful politician and managed the progress of the party representing the agrarian economy which had to dispossess the commercial economy of the North before a real balance of power could be reached. This often seemed to be a personal battle between himself and Alexander Hamilton (No. 134), who was also in Washington's cabinet. In Jefferson's references to Hamilton it is hard to tell what is the rhetoric of a fighting politician and what is honest distrust. Hamilton stood for finance and industry. Jefferson believed that the liberty of the American people would be lost if they ever built big cities and worked in factories, and he distrusted the centralizing of political power which Hamilton and Adams thought necessary. The intellectual origins of this liberalism are described in Carl Becker's *The Declaration of Independence* (No. 26). The other side of the struggle between two poles of American political thought is romantically given in Gertrude Atherton's *The Conqueror* (No. 14).

It is an irony of history that the modern Democratic party—of Woodrow Wilson, F. D. Roosevelt, and Harry Truman—should have come to rely upon the votes of urban labor, and should be the party which broke the custom of no third term for presidents, which Jefferson wanted to put into law. These modern Democrats have centralized executive power. They have done these things against the protests of the modern Republican party which descends from Hamilton's Federalists. The modern Democrats have claimed that in our modern industrial civilization these changes were needed to secure the purposes of Jefferson, to serve the people and preserve their freedoms.

L. B.

167. *The Country of the Pointed Firs and Other Stories*

by SARAH ORNE JEWETT

The closing years of the nineteenth century were a favorable time in the United States for what came to be known as "local color" fiction. Every section of the country was reported upon in novels and short stories—particularly short stories—which by dialect or otherwise proceeded to render the region's special human character, or if not character, then oddity and flavor. Most of this fiction has ceased to be of general interest; quaint at best, it was not even true to the localities it exploited, for it assumed an absolute difference between those localities and others, and thus produced freaks rather than individuals. But some of it remains classic, and this is notably the case with the stories of Sarah Orne Jewett (1849-1909), whose best-known collection, *The Country of the Pointed Firs,* is still the one source that many Americans possess for such knowledge as they have of the remote State of Maine, the northernmost and easternmost of all those New England states which indeed are a perennially interesting subject in themselves.

Sarah Orne Jewett was native to the section she celebrated, and she celebrated no other; but her devotion to it was delicate and deep enough to penetrate beyond its idiosyncrasies. She was so much in command of those that any reader who by chance is familiar with her chosen people will smile to himself as he hears them talking. Her ultimate devotion, however, was to the human nature she knew how to recognize behind their often hard-bitten exteriors. Her fishermen and farmers, and especially their wives, all have amusing deformities of body or spirit; and all of them without exception are artists in understatement, in the wry, oblique remark whose barb may not be felt until somebody attempts to pull it out; yet sooner or later they reveal themselves as the passionate, kind people their unobtrusive creator knows them to be. Their kindness is matched only by their determination not to show it; their humor only by their pretense that they have none; and their wisdom only by their scorn of such a word.

M. V. D.

168. *Pioneer's Progress*

by Alvin Johnson

Alvin Johnson (1874-) was born in a settler's cabin in Nebraska, of Danish parents who believed in education. So Mr. Johnson learned, in primitive hardships and heavy labor, to fight for his own way. He grew up to be a man of learning and a man of ideas, but he has always also been, as he says, a man who believed that ideas should be put into action. This makes his autobiography the more important because those who might hear of him as economist, journalist, or editor of a great encyclopedia of the social sciences, might never know without this life story that in his time, at the beginning of the twentieth century, the same career could include much more activity —as first director of the New School for Social Research, famous center of liberal studies in New York; as a good soldier on the firing line for the conservation of natural resources, and against racial discriminations; and, above all, as the living force behind the successful movement, after the Fascist eruptions in Europe, to bring persecuted scholars to the United States and set them up in teaching positions.

His own story of his life shows, with flashes of irony and a warm sense of human companionships, how a farm boy in modern America can become classicist, economist, reformer, educator—ending as a sage. It has been said that Alvin Johnson, because of his immense learning, his wit, and never-failing audacity, is the best talker in New York. This book does not prove it, but it indicates some of the reasons for his reputation. It forms an illuminating contrast with the New England restraint of Mary Ellen Chase's story of her teaching career in *A Goodly Fellowship* (No. 59); and it develops themes that are found in Willa Cather's novel of the same pioneer region, *My Ántonia* (No. 53), and in the *Autobiography* (No. 332) of William Allen White.

The political ideas of the western liberals have faded somewhat, as is shown in Richard Hofstadter's *Age of Reform* (No. 149), but the free mind and the free spirit advocated by men of Mr. Johnson's generation, and in him embodied, do not fade.

L. B.

169. Sidney Hillman

Statesman of American Labor

by MATTHEW JOSEPHSON

In the early years of the twentieth century the president of a Pennsylvania coal company gave, in a famous letter, his recommendation for the way in which the country could achieve peace in industry. Laborers, he said, ought to place unfaltering faith in the decisions of the men "to whom God in His infinite wisdom has given the control of the property interests of the country." Things did not work out that way. Leaders of labor today exert their own impressive influence upon social and political as well as industrial decisions. This revolution in the power of the organized workers is one of the transcendent facts of American history in the past half century.

In this plump book, Matthew Josephson (1899-) undertakes to tell the life story of one of the architects of the American labor movement. Sidney Hillman (1887-1946), an immigrant from Russia near the turn of the century, entered the clothing trade shortly after his arrival in this country. An indifferent "pants cutter," he soon revealed great tactical skill in organizing his fellow workers. Beginning in 1914, as the first president of the Amalgamated Clothing Workers, he devoted the early years of his tenure to building up his union. From this secure institutional base in later years he became first a power within the general labor movement and then, in the F. D. Roosevelt administrations, an influential representative of labor on the national scene. Thus in his own biography he represents the various stages of development through which the labor movement itself proceeded.

As with the record of any revolutionary change, the history of this development is both dramatic and complicated. It is distorted by sporadic acts of violence, blurred at times by ideological attachments, confused by struggles from within for internal control, misrepresented from without by those who opposed the new energy. That a complete and dispassionate account of the movement or its leaders could at this time be given is too much to hope; so many facts remained undisclosed, so many prejudices remain. About this book, for instance, there is a religiosity that seems to stem from the author's feeling that he must show how essential truths were revealed to unbelievers by a major prophet. But there is also more here than can easily be found elsewhere about the early institutional history of unions, about the problems and difficulties of union management, and about the vigorous, ambitious men who made the labor union a force in our history. It should be read as one of the first attempts to deal systematically with one of the primary influences on our society.

E. E. M.

170. The Life and Times of Kin Hubbard

by Fred C. Kelly

Kin Hubbard's biographer uses the word genius several times in referring to his subject. This is undoubtedly an exaggeration, unless one puts the word into the context of the common phrase: "X. has a genius for—this or that." Frank McKinney Hubbard (1868-1930) was an eccentric newspaperman who created and obtained wide circulation for the sayings of a countrified character called Abe Martin, many of them printed in this book. One of the very best of Abe Martin's sayings is not in the book and it should be quoted here as an introduction to Hubbard's art: "The first thing to turn green in the spring is the Christmas jewelry."

Now there is some wit here, but it is a mistake to call Hubbard and his American forerunners—Artemus Ward, Josh Billings (see No. 331 for both), "Mr. Dooley" (No. 104)—*humorists.* Their sayings may make one laugh, but those that are not laughable are not failures. For the Kin Hubbards are not clowns but philosophers. In America they are called "cracker-barrel philosophers," in reference to the bygone practice of country men's sitting around the big barrel full of biscuits at the "general store" and passing the evening in observations upon life.

These observations, as Abe Martin's show, are on the whole despondent, mistrustful, sometimes cynical. But they breathe a kind of placidity, not to say resignation; they are valued for their terseness and finality—their art, in short, which surprisingly enough is the ancient Greek art of the apothegm. Not wit or epigram, but perfect wording, as when Aristotle said, "One swallow does not make a summer." It is curious to remember, when one is tempted to generalize about Americans, how often our newspapermen have been cracker-barrel philosophers at the second remove, and to recall Kin Hubbard in particular as the most unstandardized, uncooperative, incorruptible individualist of them all.

J. B.

171. *Miracle at Kitty Hawk*

The Letters of Wilbur and Orville Wright

edited by FRED C. KELLY

Back in April, 1917, Orville Wright (1871-1948) told an interviewer that the airplane, which he and his brother had invented fourteen years earlier, had revolutionized warfare by eliminating the possibility of surprise attacks and would, in the future, exert a far more powerful influence "than leagues to enforce peace . . . in putting an end to wars." Remembering the Battle of Britain and the attack on Pearl Harbor, we know that Orville was wrong. Or was his judgment merely premature? He and his brother were not much given to unfounded assertion.

The letters here gathered reveal the Wrights as they must have seemed to those who knew them: Midwest Americans, with a minimum of formal education and a great deal of dogged patience, who succeeded in spite of official indifference in doing what their "betters" were reluctant to think they could do, and who went on, modestly and without dramatics, to teach mankind how to fly.

Elsewhere the reader will find Orville's own fascinatingly unspectacular account of *How We Invented the Airplane* (No. 348), and in Wilson's *American Science and Invention* (No. 340) there are a number of pictures of the Wrights and their various machines. In Bernard Jaffe's *Men of Science in America* (No. 158) you can read of Samuel Langley, upon whose theoretical studies and unsuccessful experiments the Wrights based their own work. The reader who wishes to know more of Americans as flyers should not miss Charles A. Lindbergh's *The Spirit of St. Louis* (No. 188), or Anne Morrow Lindbergh's *North to the Orient* (No. 187). Fred C. Kelly (1882-), who edited this volume, is also the official biographer of the Wrights and the author of *The Life and Times of Kin Hubbard* (No. 170).

J. A. K.

172. *Profiles in Courage*

by JOHN F. KENNEDY

Someone who has participated in the practice of representative government has an important advantage in defining its character, and Senator John F. Kennedy (1917-) of Massachusetts has brought to *Profiles in Courage* (1955) eight years of experience in both houses of Congress. During a long convalescence from an operation (necessitated by an injury received in World War II, when he commanded a motor torpedo boat), Kennedy sought to find strength in studying the lives of American legislators who in difficult situations showed a notable courage. The result is not only a record of political heroism, but a succession of episodes which show American government at work and reveal its pitfalls and ignoble pressures as well as its more positive character. Senator Kennedy paints not only the background for each successive drama but also a series of portraits not unworthy at their best of Plutarch.

The essence of the book is moral as well as political: what is a representative's duty to his constituents and party on the one hand, and to the whole nation on the other? Senator Kennedy recognizes the need for—and even the courage of—compromise (in Daniel Webster he reveals a statesman execrated by former supporters because he supported a great compromise), but his emphasis is upon independence of judgment in the legislator. One can use John Quincy Adams's statement: "The magistrate is the servant not . . . of the people, but of his God," or that of Lucius Quintus Cincinnatus Lamar, who braved public opinion in his state to promote the unity of North and South: "The liberty of this country and its great interests will never be secure if its public men become menials to do the bidding of their constituents instead of being representatives looking to . . . the interests of the whole country."

Senator Kennedy at 38 did not come to his task as a practiced writer, but he shows high capacity both for the collection and interpretation of facts and for building up the tense situations with which he deals. All his heroes live, whether they are nationally known, or as obscure as Edmund G. Ross, the senator from Kansas who cast the vote, in the teeth of public opinion and party pressure, that blocked the impeachment of President Andrew Johnson in 1868. As a consequence, these pages reveal more effectively than a many-volumed history the character of American democracy and the challenges it offers to the men responsible for its operation.

F. E. H.

173. *Our American Weather*

by George H. T. Kimble

No weather is good, except served on travel folders, but some weather is better than others, and there is no disputing about which. Everyone's bodily thermostat is a law unto itself. The only thing to do about the weather, therefore, is to talk about it.

In America the weather is like the election returns—not only unpredictable but extreme. A newspaper announces in good faith the election of Thomas E. Dewey to the Presidency but actually it is Harry S. Truman who steps into the White House. "Fair and increasingly warmer" is the bland prophecy one reads as the snowflakes begin to fall. This is something that perhaps should not be imputed as a crime to the American people. They are on the whole guiltless of their visitors' blood. Indeed, the overwhelming American hospitality is an effort to make up by kindness and blankets (or, alternatively, electric fans) for the trigger-happiness of nature which, abusing our latitude, turns in an instant from frolic to ferocity.

To understand the causes and consequences of this, month by month, almost day by day, one must read Mr. Kimble's book. He calls it our American weather but takes no responsibility for it. He would be rather inclined to disclaim it, belonging as he does to the most misprized group in America, the weather men. Only baseball umpires have a more tested sense of injustice, but umpires cannot guess the cause of their martyrdom. Mr. Kimble knows: it is the fact that the mountain systems in North America run parallel to the coasts instead of transversely.

There is thus no barrier to arctic winds, so we freeze like voyaging vegetables; and there is an intolerable barrier to Pacific breezes, so we broil like poultry in parts. There is, moreover, in the middle of the country a huge, fearful, flat-bottomed hollow where everything weathersome happens at once. It should be noted that Mr. Kimble discourses of these horrors with a good deal of unaffected insouciance. This is due to the fact that the overnight changes of 40 degrees, the hurricanes and tornadoes and dust storms and ice storms and floods which we record, suffer, and deplore *cannot be counted on.* At this moment the horrid, torrid, humid weather which makes New York City unbearable in summer is nowhere to be felt. It is on its travels, like the Secretary of State. Still, it (and this too) is American weather. Try it.

J. B.

174. *The Columbia Historical Portrait of New York*

by JOHN A. KOUWENHOVEN

A city exists, as John A. Kouwenhoven (1909-) demonstrates in this luxurious volume, in the eyes of its beholders; and New York is as many cities as there are people who have looked at it. He has selected the paintings, photographs, drawings, maps, and prints not, as he points out, merely to tell the chronological story of the development of a metropolis, but to explore what the city has meant to those who lived in it, visited it briefly or, in some cases, knew it only by hearsay. The view is sometimes romantic, sometimes satiric, often affectionate, critical, indignant, and defensive.

This is not strictly a portrait, which by definition is the representation of an individual at one period or moment in his life—or the depiction of character acquired up to that point; this is a pictorial biography with only those facts mentioned which have been interesting enough for roughly ten generations of visually-minded men and women to record. In that sense it is not truly historical. The political and social history of the city is superseded by its visual history. How it looked and looks matters more than why it looked as it did. The result is as much a history of what men wanted to see as of what there was to see, of recorded vision as of recorded fact.

The reader who is not familiar with New York might well start briefly in the final section of this book with the air views of the city as he would see it if he were to fly into modern New York—a vast metropolitan complex spreading over hundreds of square miles, spanning rivers and harbors, hills and palisades, with the pier-fringed island of Manhattan like a centipede at its core. Then let him look at the bare bones of New York as it was first imagined, seen, reported, and mapped by the Dutch at the beginning of the seventeenth century, and follow its visual image through thousands of eyes to the city of today. The origins of the city and its early development the reader will find more fully described in Carl Carmer's *The Hudson* (No. 49); he will find a recent love letter to it in E. B. White's *Here Is New York* (No. 329). But for a fascinating family album of the birth, infancy, and growth of a giant, this remarkable "historical portrait" is unparalleled.

R. L.

175. *Made in America*

by John A. Kouwenhoven

The appearance of *Made in America* in 1948 seemed to indicate that an extended process of reflection and experiment was drawing to a close. Hitherto American popular culture—the arts that Mr. Kouwenhoven calls "vernacular"—had been largely assumed to lack the kind of theoretical foundation that might commend them to academic scholars of "high," or traditional, culture. Actually, *Made in America* has many predecessors; it follows a number of lines laid down, for example, in the works of Lewis Mumford (Nos. 227-9) and of Constance Rourke (Nos. 268-9) or, still further back, in Horatio Greenough's *Form and Function* (No. 131). But the majority of Americans have been too preoccupied with the hazards of constructing a mass culture to justify it in words. Until Mr. Kouwenhoven made the attempt, it is doubtful that many of them could even have tried to identify the principles linking together their architecture, their storytelling, their design of tools and machinery, their journalism, their jazz music, their pictorial techniques, and their system of mass production. Now that he has done it, the job will not have to be done over.

One of Mr. Kouwenhoven's achievements is of special importance, in any case, to readers of this collection. He does away with the view that arts not belonging to "high" culture must necessarily fall into the category of "folk" art, and therefore be quaint or cute. Anyone schooled in the European tradition is likely to consider the "folk" arts to be those practiced by a feudal peasantry—ballads, costumes, household decoration, legends, dances, and so on. These do indeed exist in the United States (see Nos. 38, 189, and 190) but in a somewhat supplementary fashion to Mr. Kouwenhoven's new and more inclusive category: the "vernacular" arts of industrial democracy. The latter are not only of equal "seriousness" to the traditional Western art forms—such as the novel, the easel painting, or the symphony—they are also the true repository of the inner vitality that causes "culture" to exist, and the place for posterity to look for those "classics" that best express the American genius.

E. L.

176. The Desert Year

by JOSEPH WOOD KRUTCH

More of the United States than many strangers might suppose is desert or semidesert. The entire southwestern quarter of it is a land of little rain, and the State of Arizona is a happy hunting ground for those who are in love with the phenomenon of dryness. Of such persons, Joseph Wood Krutch (1893-) in recent years has become the most articulate. But he was helped in doing so by the circumstance that he came to the desert from New England and New York, where there is an abundance of vegetation and where, too, in his own case there had been an abundance of literary and philosophical intercourse. He came, that is, prepared not only to see the contrast but also to think about it with a well-stored mind.

Mr. Krutch's previous work had been done in literary criticism. For years he had been an outstanding reviewer of New York plays; he had published notable volumes concerned altogether with philosophy and art; and his biography of Samuel Johnson had dealt with a man conspicuously addicted to city life. The result is evident in the present book, which is richly allusive and humorous, and ripe with the view its author has of human affairs in their oldest aspect, at the same time that it presents with all seriousness, and indeed with zeal, the case for paucity in water, wealth, and purely civilized society.

For Mr. Krutch the fascination of the desert goes far beyond its power to strike the eye with beauty or to fill the lungs with easily breathable air. Still better than that, it is a world which has studied how to do with few of the necessary goods—so few, in fact, that its survival, not to say its well-being, seems perpetually miraculous. Mr. Krutch studies the miracle both as a naturalist and as a poet; and his final comment on it is that of a philosopher. The background of his thought is the very abundance he abandoned when he went to the Southwest. Abundance is the good most noisily commended in the councils of this century. Suppose, however, that it ceases to exist. Mr. Krutch begins there, and goes on to consider how life may still sustain itself and be perhaps the wiser for the effort.

M. V. D.

177. *The Manner Is Ordinary*

by JOHN LA FARGE, S.J.

Since the breviary, which is read daily by a Roman Catholic priest, is divided into the four seasons, Father John La Farge (1880-) tells the story of his life in four parts, beginning with Winter which is the season of Advent and of youth. His father, an eminent artist who endeavored to restore the ancient art of stained glass, was a friend of Henry and William James and of Henry Adams (see Nos. 2, 159-61, 163-4, and 246). This gives an added interest to the earlier reminiscences, and the later story of a militant priesthood has excitement and distinction.

Father La Farge's early missionary work among the Negroes of Maryland, where he struggled to establish schools and rebuild churches, and to keep within the Church the Negro Catholics of the colonial tradition, gave him a lasting concern for interracial relations. This expressed itself later in a more general fashion in committee work and publications, but he never lost his priestly devotion to the human personalities of his Negro friends.

It was as editor of a Catholic periodical of general national influence, far outside the membership of his Church, that Father La Farge attained his eminence as an advocate of the rights of the underprivileged. As he says, the journal *America* "was designed for those who were interested in the issues and were willing to do at least a little thinking with some possibility of reaching thought-out conclusions." He has never lost his active participation in the social and intellectual movements of his time, secular as well as religious, and his autobiography tells how the devout austerities of a Jesuit's life can allow a gifted man to take a vigorous part in the democratic give-and-take of American public discussion.

Father La Farge's story tells how men of different faiths can work together for good causes, even "lost" causes, in the framework of American political liberty. The experiences of men of good will of other religious opinions, engaged in similar reforms, may be studied in the autobiographies of Lincoln Steffens (No. 289) and William Allen White (No. 332) and in *A Socialist's Faith* by Norman Thomas (No. 304).

L. B.

178. Laughing Boy

by Oliver La Farge

In 1884 Helen Hunt Jackson, by writing a popular novel, *Ramona,* tried to awaken an apathetic nation to the need for drastic reform in the country's dealings with American Indians—a reform that even today has not been fully realized. In 1929, almost half a century later, Oliver La Farge, then a young anthropologist who had just completed studies of the Navajo Indians of Utah, New Mexico, and Arizona, published *Laughing Boy*. Like *Ramona* this was a widely popular love story written out of anger and sorrow over wrongs still unrighted. More modern in style and subject matter than *Ramona, Laughing Boy* differed also in *raison d'être*. Its emphasis was on the romantic aspects of a vanishing race rather than on the emphatic need for a crusade. It pleaded not for the reform of reservation laws but only that modern-day Indians be left alone, divorced from the evil contact of the white man (see also Mari Sandoz, *Crazy Horse* [No. 274]).

In his autobiography, *Raw Material,* Oliver La Farge (1901-), the nephew of Father John La Farge (No. 177), says of *Laughing Boy*: "It was the product of a young man who I have ceased to be . . . I saw our own Indians as inexorably doomed, I saw that they must come increasingly into contact with our so-called civilization, and that (I then thought inevitably) contact meant conflict and disaster." Accordingly, the book is resolved, after the final tragedy, by having the hero Laughing Boy return to what Mr. La Farge later called "my own dreamland, the untouched, undisturbed Navajo country where the white man was not a factor." In succeeding years, Mr. La Farge came to realize that this was not a realistic approach and his later books dealing with Indians (now increasing rather than decreasing in numbers) have taken a more temperate tone, aiming at the ideal of a just and understanding coexistence between the two races.

None of Mr. La Farge's later books, however, has equalled *Laughing Boy* in capturing the public imagination. Had it been written with the zeal of the reformer, it might very well have lost its sustained lyric quality. The moving, inevitably tragic love story of Laughing Boy and the Indian girl ravaged by the white man's malevolent interference is interwoven with the highly evolved moral and religious Indian thinking that springs naturally from the seasons, the elements, the landscape. The inward rhythms and meaning of the Indian world have rarely been recorded in words, save in direct translation or scientific notation. Oliver La Farge, by literally thinking in Indian, has made authentic poetry in the process of transmuting the clear-cut dignity of Indian style and speech.

C. C.

179. The Portable Ring Lardner

edited by GILBERT SELDES

No other writer is the equal of Ringgold Wilmer Lardner (1885-1933) as a mirror of American life in the 1920's. Others captured special aspects of our society in that period—F. Scott Fitzgerald (Nos. 114 and 220) with his stories about the rich and their hangers-on, Ernest Hemingway (No. 143) with his stories about young Americans of the postwar generation in Europe—but Lardner was closer than either to the central developments in American society of the time.

Two phrases serve as a guide both to Lardner's subject and to the society he was writing about: "bush league" and "big league." Both come from baseball; a bush league is an organization of small-town or small-city baseball teams, usually made up of very young players hoping to rise in the sport, with a sprinkling of older players who never made the big leagues or who are past their prime. A big league, or "major league," is an organization of big-city teams, made up of the finest players there are. Their games are followed with avid interest all over the country, and the best of the players are national heroes (see No. 137). To move from a bush league to the big league is to realize the American dream of success, and the terms are very commonly used in a figurative sense outside baseball.

In the 1920's—the decade described by Frederick Lewis Allen in *Only Yesterday* (No. 9)—the United States acquired a sense of itself as a "big league" country such as it had never had before. With the first World War the other nations of the West realized that America was no longer a bush leaguer, that she had the men, the wealth, and the industrial potential of a big leaguer. The flourishing economy of the postwar period also convinced a good many Americans that as individuals they no longer needed to stay in the bush leagues. They moved to the cities in unprecedented numbers, and even when they stayed home they often speculated on the stock market or in land like the "boys in the big time."

Lardner himself was a bush leaguer who made the majors, a small-town Middle Western newspaperman who moved on to Chicago and then New York, where he became a national figure. And his essential subject is this transition—the energy and nerve and shrewdness that made half-literate young people pack up their suitcases and try to escape the bush league, and the emptiness that awaited them when they succeeded. He is their truest and funniest and bitterest chronicler.

P. P.

180. *Art and Life in America*

by OLIVER W. LARKIN

The visual arts in America have never quite made their peace with any tradition, and they have not developed a tradition easily identified as their own. There have, however, been two strains in American painting, sculpture, and architecture which have run alongside one another and which have frequently become intertwined. One of these, the vernacular (as John A. Kouwenhoven calls it in *Made in America* [No. 175]), might be called the arts of use and necessity, the other the refined arts (a better term here, perhaps, than fine arts) whose origins have been primarily in the European tradition. To draw any sharp distinction in early American art between "folk" and "fine" is often next to impossible, though the lines become relatively sharp during the early part of the nineteenth century and remain so.

Oliver W. Larkin (1896-) is concerned with both strains, their interconnections, and their relations to the cultural aspirations of the American people. He sets the visual arts against a backdrop of political and social and literary history, and the waxings and wanings of America's fortunes. The scheme of *Art and Life in America* is an extremely elaborate one, and sometimes confusing. The reader is cautioned to look into Mr. Larkin's introduction, in which it is explained how the book is organized, lest he find himself lost in what appears to be chronological backtracking or leaping ahead. The arts in America do not divide themselves into tidy compartments of time, any more than the internal and foreign influences on them do, and the productive span of many of the artists and architects Mr. Larkin discusses bridges long periods of rapid social and artistic change.

Mr. Larkin, professor of the history of art at Smith College, is a man of catholic tastes and enthusiasms, but his relish for the American arts does not supersede his judgment of them. His volume is the only successful attempt that has been made to tell the story of the visual arts in America in all their aspects, from the beginning of the seventeenth century to the 1950's. For the reader interested in pursuing the American arts in the detail in which they are discussed in other volumes (such as Nos. 24, 61, 113, or 256), *Art and Life in America* will provide a useful and entertaining background against which to project his curiosity.

R. L.

181. The American Impact on Russia—1784-1917

by Max M. Laserson

In the nineteenth century far-sighted Europeans in all branches of culture—de Tocqueville (see No. 90) and Berlioz might be named as examples—predicted that the future lay with the two "new" countries, the United States and Russia. Those who echoed the idea without knowing either doubtless thought only of the rawness and remoteness of each, and none assuredly thought of them as having mutual relations of any importance: they were opposite poles, separated on each side by a continent and an ocean.

Perceiving as we do a quite different image of the reality, we are nonetheless likely to know little about the contacts between the two cultures before the Soviet and the American armies met in mid-Germany a decade ago. Americans do vaguely remember something about "Seward's icebox," namely, Alaska, acquired by the U. S. in 1890, and some recall the exodus of American engineers to the Soviet Union in the late 1920's. But the rest is silent ignorance.

Professor Max Laserson (1887-1951), late of Columbia University, was well equipped to provide in English a continuous historical account of the subject announced by his title. He was a native of Russia, educated in Western Europe, trained in jurisprudence and, at the end of his career, acclimated to English and American academic life. The present book was his last contribution to critical scholarship.

J. B.

182. The Searchers

by Alan Le May

Melodramatic narratives of life on America's vast western plains have been so continuously popular throughout the nation that they have won the generic title—Westerns. Based on true history and widely accepted myth, these works are produced according to a formula so satisfying to the large group of readers who admire them that deviations from it are not lightly approved.

Even the early examples of the western hero—such as Owen Wister's *The Virginian* (No. 342)—are clearly elaborations on an earlier type introduced by the American author, James Fenimore Cooper, in his tales of the woodsman, Leatherstocking (No. 67). Though the cowboy is more romantically accoutered—with his tooled leather boots, jeweled saddle, silver spurs and ten-gallon hat—he is in character a close parallel to Cooper's frontiersman in moccasins and buckskin shirt. Both are skilled in facing the elements, courageous and cunning in opposing savage red men or villainous whites, respectful of women, untutored but wise in experience, fundamentally religious in their response to living among natural phenomena.

The change in American popular taste from walking pioneer to riding cowboy was mirrored in the mid-nineteenth century by paper-covered "dime novels" which in trash-filled pages celebrated protagonists of the Leatherstocking type, then turned to popular idols of the West like Buffalo Bill and Kit Carson. While the "dime novel" gradually disappeared, however, the Western continued in popularity.

Alan Le May's (1899-) *The Searchers* is one of the most deft of recent Westerns. Like others of the genre, it presents one of "nature's gentlemen" as chief figure and allies with him on the "good" side other familiar characters—a brave but inexperienced youth and a simpleton alternately pathetic and funny. Against these the author pits the "bad" people—hostile Indians and renegade whites—and he adds such handicaps as prairie storms and mountain snows. No Western is acceptable without a chase, and the pursuit in *The Searchers,* as the title indicates, is the major action.

By admirable writing, by use of female characters who are credible personalities (a divagation from formula), by convincing revelation of human motives, Mr. Le May has lifted what might have been a run-of-the-mill Western to the level of an entertaining novel.

C. C.

183. *Captain Sam Grant*

by Lloyd Lewis

Every American who knows any history at all knows that the armies of General Ulysses Simpson Grant defeated those of General Robert E. Lee and thus ended the Civil War in 1865. Every such American is likely to know furthermore of the famous surrender at Appomattox, Virginia, when Grant offered Lee a set of terms unprecedented in their magnanimity (see No. 54). Knowledge is less common of either Grant's later career as President or the life that led up to Appomattox, though the terrible character of the war in 1864 is fairly familiar, and not a few persons still read the *Personal Memoirs,* an excellent book in its class, in the writing of which Grant ended his days. Back of 1864, however, lies a story of great interest: back of that year, and of 1863 when Vicksburg fell to Grant's army in the West, and of 1862 when he first became widely known as a soldier who did not know how to incur defeat. Lloyd Lewis's (1891-1949) biography, which but for his death would have run into several volumes, follows the story of its hero from birth to the beginning moments of the war that made him celebrated among the captains of history.

This inarticulate, sensitive, stubborn, and imaginative man is often set down as a failure at everything he tried before 1861. Yet his record in the Mexican War (1846-1848) had been altogether creditable, and at West Point, as a student in the national military academy, he had excelled in English, mathematics, and horsemanship. He never, to be sure, was a success in any of the business enterprises he undertook during certain of his civilian years, and there were always rumors that he drank too much. Nor did a dogged modesty advance him in the ordinary conduct of affairs. But his courtship of Julia Dent, which Lewis tells in greater detail than any other biographer has done, reveals in him a depth and color such as none save a few intimates ever suspected; and indeed the whole of his early life, rendered here with intelligent sympathy, marks him as extraordinary. He deserves his place along with the more romantic and the better-known Lee as an established American hero, not soon to be forgotten.

M. V. D.

184. *Babbitt*

by SINCLAIR LEWIS

In the 1920's everybody knew George F. Babbitt. His voice was loud in the smoking compartment of all the railroad sleeping cars. Almost any day he could be discovered on the site of a choice property in jovial converse with a prospective client. And every single noon he could be found among the hollow men of the Zenith Athletic Club leaning together over the heavy humors of the luncheon table.

Until he appeared on the scene nobody knew quite how to put the American man of business or commerce between the covers of a novel. He usually emerged in fiction as some overpowering and sinister titan of industry; or else as a slightly detached and forlorn figure who made enough money at the paint works or in a publishing house to support a family whose domestic difficulties were the real meat of the story. Such was not the case with George F. Babbitt, whose behavior in and out of the real estate office among his fellow men in a middle western city was the exclusive concern of his creator, Sinclair Lewis (1885-1951).

The rather startling result was that Babbitt turned out, since most Americans are in business or commerce, to be a person almost everybody had at least met somewhere and in whom almost every citizen, jubilantly or reluctantly, discovered something of himself. For many it was a delight to find that in their ordinary, daily lives and philosophizings there was stuff of sufficient interest —and even perhaps of sufficient dignity—to attract the attention of a literary investigator. Others were not quite sure whether they were Babbitt, or whether Babbitt was only the man next door, and they were not quite sure whether they liked either prospect.

The fact is Lewis was not quite sure himself. He wavers in the contemplation of his hero between an observer's sardonic amusement and the annoyed loyalty of a participator. He has been called a brilliant reporter, a shrewd caricaturist, a remarkable mimic—almost everything but a great novelist. Whatever he may have been, he fulfilled in this moment, and at other moments too, the final function of the artist. The data lying around him apparently at random he organized and interpreted in such a way that his readers reached an understanding of a thing present but not previously recognized. That is why, if you look in Webster's New International Dictionary, you will find the word *Babbitt*—"a business or professional man who strictly adheres to the social and ethical standards of his group; used derogatorily."

E. E. M.

185. Elmer Gantry

by SINCLAIR LEWIS

In the opinion of some good judges, *Elmer Gantry* is to be placed side by side with *Babbitt* (No. 184) in Sinclair Lewis's (1885-1951) gallery of modern figures. To those who disagree it might be said that Elmer Gantry and Babbitt are in a class apart through being "culture heroes," if not epic characters. That is, they are larger than life size, in spite of the fact that the technique used for representing them and their surroundings is the novelist's accepted realism.

In any case, it is a mistake to regard Gantry and Babbitt as mere portraits or even as satirical caricatures. Gantry has all the limitations of a narrow upbringing and an extremely modest endowment of brains. It cannot even be said that he is remarkable among men as a great will, for that implies a concentration of desire which is in its way a form of intelligence. But Gantry is instinct with animal magnetism—he is Rabelais's Panurge reincarnated in American dress, and to this he owes his temptations and triumphs.

The power to make others believe in him is something genuine he has innately. He is a hypocrite and a fraud as it were by reflex action, because he has no ideas, moral or religious, and yet has to find some medium of communication with his fellow men flocking around him. With women, sex and its language supply all that is necessary to relate him to them. With others it is sermons and pious cant.

The connection between sex and religion was noted on the American scene as early as Mrs. Trollope's description (see No. 231) of a camp-meeting (1836), and the religious type of magnetic leader has with us been more frequent and more powerful than the political type. This no doubt is because we are a nation founded in religious emigration, and because in our diversified population the language of religion is the most widely intelligible of any. The fact that this has led to other and even greater frauds than Elmer Gantry's does not affect the reality and importance of the religious passion in our national history and culture.

As for Lewis's treatment of it, we observe in this book, as in *Babbitt,* the author's penchant for letting his realism generate extravaganza. His eye is photographic and his ear is an incomparable recorder, but his imagination is forever straying into the landscape of myth. He knew this: once, in the presence of the writer of this note, he was discussing the fact of literary influence, in which he did not at first greatly believe. Finally, he was persuaded: "Yes, I see what you mean; well, the great influence in my work is Sir Thomas Malory."

J. B.

186. TVA

Democracy on the March

by David E. Lilienthal

The Tennessee Valley Authority, created in 1933, promises to be one of the most enduring monuments of Franklin D. Roosevelt's "New Deal." Initially, as an invasion by government of the area previously sacred to private enterprise, it was the subject of partisan debate; but it has since so established itself in public approval as to be almost above party politics. Even those who disapprove in principle of publicly owned electric power systems no longer deny that TVA has proved itself in practice. The people of the Tennessee Valley itself will not hear an ill word spoken of the dams and power plants that have rescued them from a downward spiral of poverty. The example of TVA is an inspiring one, moreover, to the thousands of visitors from abroad who yearly come to inspect the Valley as though it were one of the great tourist attractions of America, more fascinating than Niagara Falls or the Grand Canyon of the Colorado.

Rivers do not abide by state borders. The watershed of the Tennessee River includes sections of the states of Tennessee, North Carolina, Kentucky, Virginia, Mississippi, Georgia, and Alabama; only a power greater than that of state governments could treat the Valley as a single unit, as President Roosevelt believed it should be treated. Only a power so authorized by Congress could make an over-all plan for hydroelectric power development that would also include flood control, land reclamation, the prevention of soil erosion, reforestation, recreation, and the encouragement of diversified industry. Only something like TVA could deal with what David E. Lilienthal (1899-), its chairman from 1941 to 1946, calls the "seamless web" of nature. The region's dilemma was a closed circle: it could not afford to build dams because it was so poor because its land was eroded because it could not afford fertilizers because it lacked electric power because it had no dams. TVA broke the circle, by the means and with the results that Mr. Lilienthal here describes.

Since he wrote his book in 1943, there are now two postscripts to be added to his story: (1) Under the limitations of wartime he could not tell the Valley's best-kept secret, that its abundance of electric power was then being used to stoke the furnaces of Oak Ridge, where uranium was converted into the awesomely explosive material for an atomic bomb. (2) After the war, when

Congress decided that atomic power—like that of the Tennessee River—belonged to the people of the United States and not to the military or to private industry, the Atomic Energy Commission was established. Its first chairman was David Lilienthal.

E. L.

187. North to the Orient

by ANNE MORROW LINDBERGH

It was in the summer of 1931 that a small plane, the *Sirius,* took off from New York on a flight across Canada, Alaska, and Russia to Japan and China, in an attempt to open an air route to the Orient over the great frozen northlands. Such an undertaking was in itself an epochal adventure, but it was made the more exciting by the fact that the pilot of the *Sirius* was Charles A. Lindbergh (1902-), and that the other passenger was Anne Lindbergh (1906-), his gently reared wife and now the plane's radio operator, in charge of the single lifeline between the travelers and civilization.

North to the Orient is Mrs. Lindbergh's account of this journey, written several years later. Although there had been moments when only Colonel Lindbergh's (see No. 188) navigational genius had saved them from disaster, the flight had been beautifully successful. But neither the navigational hazards and accomplishments of the trip nor its contribution to the future of air travel are a major concern of Mrs. Lindbergh's little volume. It is her personal experience of the flight that she wishes to preserve for herself and her readers.

Anne Morrow Lindbergh is a woman of rare courage, but her modest daring is matched only by her delicacy of feeling and her ability to communicate her fine and subtle perceptions. Whether she is recording the emotions of a forced landing in the Japanese seas, or Thanksgiving dinner in the tiny hamlet of Barrow in the midst of the Arctic desolation, or the flooding of the Yangtze River and the starvation which rode in its wake, her account of her adventures is as moving as it is light-fingered. It is a short book that Anne Lindbergh has written, but it is economical only in words. It could not be richer in conveyed impression.

D. T.

188. The Spirit of St. Louis

by CHARLES A. LINDBERGH

Interesting narratives of personal adventure exist by the thousands. Of classics in the field there are few. Here is one.

When, on May 21, 1927, a 25-year-old mail pilot landed at Le Bourget field, outside of Paris, it was apparent that a symbolic event had occurred. Primarily it marked the end of isolation for all countries, but especially the United States. It also emphasized the transference to a new field of certain energies which Americans like to think peculiarly their own—youthful enterprise, pioneering, technological competence, self-reliance. For a few happy weeks Charles Augustus Lindbergh (1902-) seemed to the world to stand for the United States.

His feat, however, would have found its record only in uncertain legends had not Mr. Lindbergh, 25 years later, written this book. It is not an autobiography, but, says the author, a "book about flying, and an aviator's life in the beginning third of the twentieth century." This story of Mr. Lindbergh's early career is perhaps the best existing record of the tryout stage of aviation. Parachute-jumping, circus stunts, early mail-plane flying, "blind" noninstrument piloting, constant emergency landings—these belong to the pioneer history of flight. Lindbergh is the great figure who links aviation's tentative days with its subsequent vast development and its awesome, perhaps catastrophic, future.

His narrative of the flight itself is an astonishing performance. Somehow, perhaps from the example and influence of his wife, Anne (see No. 187), he has learned to write. This is not a dull record, like the Journals of Columbus, but a kind of epic poem, filled with Homeric exultation. It is also part of the exact drama of the machine age, detailed in its technical information, particular in its account of wind and weather, specific in its notation of the relationship of human physiology to sustained, solitary, and sleepless flight. *The Spirit of St. Louis* is at once a landmark in the history of adventure, a classic of human courage and endurance, and part of American literature.

C. F.

189. American Folk Decoration

by JEAN LIPMAN

Jean Lipman (1909-), a successful collector of American folk art, has done students of the nation's social history an important service by writing this volume. In it text and plentiful illustrations are combined to show the quality of decorative works achieved, by untutored and unsophisticated artisans, in rural areas of the northeastern seaboard of the United States (see also *The Index of American Design* [No. 61]). Naturally these craftsmen, some native and others immigrant, depended largely upon three sources of inspiration: (1) memories of European designs, acquired either from experience in their countries of origin or from their elders who brought such memories with them, (2) imitation of the designs of fellow-decorators, and (3) designs emanating from their own creative fancies.

As Mrs. Lipman intimates, this decorating of household and trade objects was usually done either by the owner of the object or by someone he deemed competent, possibly an itinerant artisan. The results are highly colorful and spirited designs. Frequently they indicate a fusing of several influences, including those of foreign origin and those which came from local landscape, community life, and individual imagination.

Mrs. Eve Meulendyke, who has annotated Mrs. Lipman's text with expositions of how the decorations were made and with what materials, has added to modern understanding of the ingenuity, temperament, and artistic intuition of the decorators. The collaborators have acquainted Americans with this important phase of their past so successfully that, largely as a result of their influence, few museums are now without interesting examples of the work of the primitive decorators; and popular interest in these exhibits is constantly increasing.

C. C.

190. Adventures of a Ballad Hunter

by JOHN A. LOMAX

John A. Lomax (1872-1948) was born to listen—and to tell. Like one of the Negro boys who once sang to him, he had "a dancing mind." It knew at once the value in humor and wisdom of a song or a tale or a single monosyllabic riposte. A scholar of colorful and unconventional personality, Lomax had scant patience with pretentious, pompous, or pedantic scholarship. He traveled more dirt roads than paved, visited more cabins than mansions, knew more troubled folk than smug. *Adventures of a Ballad Hunter* is the story of his life as folk song collector and singer, told as simply as a ballad.

The seeker of folk songs must go where they are to be found. "Folklore," says Richard M. Dorson of Michigan State University, "can be procured only by direct contact with informants through fieldwork, or through the most meticulous use of printed sources. The promise held in the word 'folklore' is the revelation of esoteric oral traditions arduously gathered by industrious leg work, to make the contacts, win the confidences, and record the lore." This book is a by-product of just such labor. The words and tunes of canallers, mountain men, cotton pickers, cowpunchers, imprisoned criminals, told Americans what they have been and what they are. And in the telling of how he got them, Lomax revealed himself as an American of ingenuity, humor, independence, candor, dander, and many a unique quality of his own as well.

Though this autobiography, in its occasional assertiveness, does not seem to be that of an overmodest man, the author makes no claim for the results of his labors. Those who know what he has done, however, find them legion. Throughout America, in the history books and historical novels, in the poetry, on the concert stage, in the school song books, on thousands of phonograph records and thousands of radio and television broadcasts, even in the motion pictures, the songs he has found are being returned to the people.

C. C.

191. *The Call of the Wild and Other Stories*

by Jack London

Jack London (1876-1916) occupies a curious position in American letters. One of our most popular authors (he made a fortune out of his work, and spent it lavishly, before he died), and greatly admired abroad, especially in Russia and France, he has not seemed "important" to American critics when compared, for example, to his less popular fellow-naturalist, Frank Norris (No. 236). The explanation may simply be that London is popular with readers, at home and abroad, because he was an engrossing storyteller; that he is admired by some foreign intellectuals because he was a harsh critic of American capitalism; and that he is largely ignored by American intellectuals because his criticism of American life is grounded chiefly in what his own "underdog" emotionalism made of some ill-digested scraps of socialist theory.

Though *The Call of the Wild,* London's most popular book, is a dog story (dogs—literal underdogs—dominate many of his tales), it is also autobiographical, and not merely in the sense that London himself had fought hunger and cold in the Yukon and had known a dog like Buck. Buck, one of the few convincing characters in London's fiction, is essentially the projection of London's own romantic self-image. Snatched from freedom, caged, and put to hard labor by men with clubs, Buck is London, the young tramp who thought of himself as "one of Nietzsche's *blond beasts,*" arrested as a vagrant, thrown into a penitentiary, and put to hard work under the eyes of armed guards. Buck, "surviving triumphantly in a hostile environment," is London's fantasy of his own triumph (from oyster pirate to mansion and yacht) in a world he understands only as "a tooth-and-nail society."

London wallows now and then in humorless primitivism, as in his relish for Buck's lust "to kill with his own teeth and wash his nozzle to the eyes in warm blood," and his prose is sometimes grotesquely bathetic. There's a good deal of muscle-flexing and chest-thumping about it; after all, this was the "strenuous" era of Theodore Roosevelt, as Henry F. Pringle's biography (No. 250) vividly reminds us. But the story, like the short pieces in this volume, is saved from silliness by the vitality of London's interest in a real dog, real landscape, and real events, and by his passionate joy in sheer narrative.

J. A. K.

192. *The Road to Xanadu*

by JOHN LIVINGSTON LOWES

Modern criticism, whether of poetry or of anything else, is much concerned with the process of creation. In other ages criticism had no such concern at all; taking creation for granted, it judged or compared the pieces of literature before it and then rested content. But the typical twentieth-century critic takes nothing for granted, at least in the field where images and symbols operate; for him and his fellows the act of creation is a miracle to explain if they can. And this is no less true in America than elsewhere; indeed, it is sometimes said that American critics are positively obsessed with the problem (see No. 349).

However that may be, one of their scriptures is *The Road to Xanadu.* Its author, John Livingston Lowes (1867-1945), was a professor at Harvard University who in 1919 had made a signal contribution to the understanding of modern verse with a wise book called *Convention and Revolt in Poetry.* He brought his study of the art to a climax in this later examination, still famous and still imitated, of the probable process whereby Samuel Coleridge, a mediocre poet throughout most of his career, twice penetrated to greatness. "The Ancient Mariner" and "Kubla Khan" are so distinctly in a class by themselves among his works that the fact of their distinction has always been noted; but not until Lowes's book, which takes its title from the first line of "Kubla Khan," did anyone attempt to trace the materials of the poems—their images, their suggestions, and in fact their very words—back to their source. The source, as Lowes made clear, was the books Coleridge had been reading before he wrote his masterpieces. He was always a hungry reader, but at this moment in his life he was a powerful one, devouring and digesting at a rate consistent with nothing less than genius. And his particular fare was books of travel: Hakluyt's *Voyages,* the *Travels* of William Bartram, and many others. Like a great detective Lowes hunts down every clue and proves its relevance, and in so doing he comes as near as the mind can come to explaining two extraordinary poems.

M. V. D.

193. *The Future of American Politics*

by SAMUEL LUBELL

The political parties of the United States are perhaps no harder to understand than the political parties of any country in which one does not live. Yet the very names of the two parties, Republican and Democratic, which have been alternately dominant since 1860 may puzzle a foreigner because they sound so much alike: neither sounds conservative, and neither sounds revolutionary. And the fact is that neither party has been altogether one of those things or the other. Neither has represented a class; both have claimed to express the national tradition. Their basic resemblance puzzles even Americans; so that a Presidential election can become an event whose nature few pretend to know until all the returns are in. Only then does speculation commence as to new ideas that have formed in the mind of the electorate. The distinction of this book by Samuel Lubell (1911-) is that it prophesied with unusual accuracy the change represented by Eisenhower's first election in 1952.

Except for a brief period the Republicans had "run the country," as a popular and significant saying goes, between the Civil War and the election of Woodrow Wilson in 1912. After Wilson they were in charge again until the election of Franklin D. Roosevelt in 1932. The twenty years of Roosevelt and his successor Harry S. Truman, since they saw the creation of a welfare state, were supposed by some observers to foreshadow a permanent administration of the country by Democrats. Yet Mr. Lubell, studying the electorate itself rather than the speeches of politicians, not merely detected signs of weakness in the great coalition of forces which Roosevelt had held together; he discovered new alignments in the cities, on the farms, and among the sections, geographical or social, of the nation. His findings are complex, but the political problem he sees ahead is simple enough for anyone to understand. It is the problem of balancing foreign and domestic issues in such a way as to maintain in the government of the United States both strength enough for survival and flexibility enough for freedom and prosperity at home.

M. V. D.

194. Middletown in Transition

by Robert S. Lynd *and* Helen Merrell Lynd

Middletown in Transition (1937) is a classic of American sociological literature, but the reader should bear in mind that in the years since it was written both American sociology and the society it describes have undergone important modifications. If such a book were written today it would rely far less on public and official sources of information, especially newspapers; it would use a more elaborate framework of social classes than the simple two-class system the Lynds generally relied on; it would give more attention to how children are reared (the Lynds limited themselves for the most part to the formal education of children); most important, perhaps, it would be based on more intricate interviewing techniques in an effort to penetrate more deeply into the psychology of the people interviewed and to give more of the quality of their lives.

American society has changed in some respects at least as much as American sociology since the Lynds wrote. For all its length and elaboration of detail, *Middletown in Transition* is essentially an examination of thrift as a social ideal—that is, it is a description (and a castigation) of a society trying to live by an ethics of scarcity in an era of overproduction. To what extent American society in the subsequent twenty years has harmonized its ethical precepts (to be saving and self-reliant, to plan for the future) and its economic needs (large and continuous consumption to keep the factories going) it would be impossible to say. But the nation has pretty largely accepted the assumption that in modern industrialized society the individual can have only a limited liability for his own economic fate, that major dislocations of the economy cannot be corrected by an application of the ethics of scarcity, and that consequently the government must spread some kind of safety net beneath people—though how extensive a net, how far off the ground, and how large its interstices remain subjects of political debate.

The point of view of the Lynds is typical of liberal opinion in the 1930's: their solution to social problems is centralized planning. Contemporary American liberalism is less vociferous on this point; in general it is still ready to use the power of the state to correct injustices, but it takes a slightly more benevolent view of local initiative and is concerned lest the power of the state become destructive of civil liberties.

P. P.

195. The American Leonardo

The Life of Samuel F. B. Morse

by CARLETON MABEE

If *The American Leonardo* today seems a pretentious title, in the America of the mid-nineteenth century it would have seemed only just. Samuel F. B. Morse (1791-1872), known now mainly as the inventor of the telegraph (see No. 340), already enjoyed a reputation in the United States, at the time when his invention was revealed, as one of the young nation's most gifted painters, as president of the National Academy of Design, and as an important figure in politics. Later he was to help promote the transatlantic cable.

Carleton Mabee (1914-) has procured much new material to supplement the story of Morse as told by previous writers. Although he came to his task as a young writer, Mr. Mabee wrote with a skill which won him the Pulitzer Prize and made a contribution to our sense of the period in which Morse lived. Morse was born during George Washington's first administration, was trained as a painter by the Americans Benjamin West and Washington Allston in England (see No. 115), and painted the Marquis de Lafayette. He was a friend not only of the aging French general but of James Fenimore Cooper, the novelist, and of William Cullen Bryant, the poet. Morse's father was an able clergyman, a true Puritan in doctrine, and although the son developed a freer mind and a warm, outgoing personality, he could at times be a severe moralist and was always at home in controversy.

His America was not kind to artists. Morse was himself a victim of its immaturity (although he had periods of prosperity, he was often in desperate financial straits and often could not maintain a home for his own children). He strove heroically to dignify his profession, and his efforts toward this end were perhaps as great a contribution as his painting, which holds a place today beside the work of John Trumbull, Gilbert Charles Stuart, and Charles Willson Peale. But the land was kinder to inventors, and Morse's energy and organizing ability enabled him to earn wealth and reputation in his second profession which eclipsed those he won in his first. Mr. Mabee has told the entire story with a liveliness and skill which, if they show his hero to have been less the resourceful inventor than contemporaries like Eli Whitney, reveal him as a complex and colorful character who made a dual contribution during a formative period of his nation's life.

F. E. H.

196. *A Short Walk from the Station*

by PHYLLIS MCGINLEY

For more than twenty years the pages of *The New Yorker* (see Nos. 233-4) have carried the light verse of Phyllis McGinley (1905-). But, as her steady readers know, her work is in a class apart by virtue of two qualities that she almost invariably unites: exquisite polish and accurate social observation. With her, light verse is not mere verbal play or frothy entertainment but the gay expression of genuine thought and feeling.

The title of the present collection is made clear in the introduction, which, being an essay on American suburban life, discloses the setting in which Phyllis McGinley's satire works. The reader who lives in the hinterland or in a large city may too readily classify suburbanites as all of one stamp, dull characters worn smooth by domestic gentility and the routine of "commuting" to their work in the big city; or, alternately, as sober businessmen by day who turn into disgusting playboys at night in the country club. Miss McGinley's verse shows that their foibles are not so easily predicted and dismissed, and that if one visited the ancient suburb of Larchmont where she herself lives, one would be surprised, perhaps bewildered, to discover the full diversity of humankind. One could certainly not have foreseen the presence of a feminine Horace in the midst of junior executives and advertising copy writers, nor have been ready to catch the delicate inflections of a voice that sings:

> This is the house that I knew by heart.
> Everything here seemed sound, immortal.
> When did this delicate ruin start?
> How did the moth come?
>
> Naked by daylight, the paint is airing
> Its rags and tatters. There's dust on the mantel.
> And who is that gray-haired stranger staring
> Out of my mirror?

J. B.

197. *The Web of Government*

by ROBERT M. MACIVER

In one sense this is a brief historical survey of the field of political theory. Most of the great names are here—Aristotle, Ulpian, Bodin, Mill, Hobbes, and the rest. In another sense it is a statement of the author's own beliefs about the origins and purpose of government. And, finally, it is a well-argued brief in support of his conviction that a government based on the ways of democracy is the most appropriate agency to organize and direct the activities of modern society.

Professor MacIver (1882-) begins with a consideration of man's nature and of his needs as a political animal for some kind of social organization which, like all organization, must rest upon some central authority. In developing his account of the evolution of government from the beginnings within the family to the present prevailing forms, he says little to which one may take exception and little that is new, but he includes—on such matters as sovereignty, the relation of man to authority, the exercise of power—not only the thoughts of the familiar political theorists but also the findings of the contemporary social scientists, and he sets forth the information at his disposal clearly.

His most interesting and immediately useful observations are those on democracy—that form of government which, one tends to forget, "is never completely achieved." Some sensible things are said about the difficulties attendant upon any attempt to thrust democracy upon peoples who are unfamiliar with its methodology and also about the special conditions within which democracy can safely develop. Some interesting things are proposed, too, about the relationship between democracy and cultural and economic advance.

The core of the argument in this book is that, given the modern situation in which society is based upon a constantly changing technology, democracy is the most suitable form of government. The diversity and mobility of contemporary life, the "incessant formation and re-formation of groups," ease of communication, the differing means of exerting control over the many forms of power—these and other factors, Professor MacIver effectively argues, "dispose men everywhere to demand a voice in the determination of their affairs at every level. . . ." There is in this conclusion, as in the whole book, little to quarrel with and a good deal—gravely stated—that can be usefully taken into account in trying to provide a stable social organization for societies founded on the shifting energies of technology.

E. E. M.

198. Collected Poems, 1917-1952

by Archibald MacLeish

Born in the American Middle West, educated in New England, an enlisted private in World War I who became a captain, a resident for a time of the American literary colony in Paris, Archibald MacLeish (1892-) worked through a period of influence by Ezra Pound and T. S. Eliot (Nos. 208 and 336) to a style and attitude of his own. His early work revealed, especially in his lyrics, a freshness of form, a surge of feeling, and a distinction of phrasing that gave him increasing reputation.

In 1928, when he was 36, he began work on an epic of the Spanish conquest of Mexico which appeared as *Conquistador* (1932). Following the actual route of the invaders and studying records of their incursion, he selected the prose account of Bernal Diaz del Castillo, one of Cortez's companions, as his basic source. He used Diaz as narrator, and recaptured the color and drama of Mexico as it burst upon the wondering eyes of the Spaniards. MacLeish wrote the entire poem in a variant of *terza rima,* substituting assonance for rhyme. Employed with bold craftsmanship, this stanza gives the work an artistic unity which is lacking, for example, in Stephen Vincent Benét's *John Brown's Body* (No. 29).

Conquistador brought MacLeish a widening reputation and the Pulitzer Prize for poetry in 1933. Although he has written much about America, this narrative of a neighbor land remains the most ambitious and the best-known of his longer poems, and may prove to be the most enduring.

In such works as *America Was Promises* (1939), *Actfive* (1948), and *The Trojan Horse* (1952), MacLeish shows a revealing awareness of the problems of his own time. The latter two, with *The Fall of the City* (1937), a radio verse play not in this volume, offer a memorable interpretation of the vacillation, credulity, submissiveness, and stubborn spiritual heroism of mankind during the second quarter of the twentieth century.

F. E. H.

199. Jefferson the Virginian

by DUMAS MALONE

In every crisis America has turned again to Jefferson, as guide and prophet. On the eve of emancipation for the Negroes Lincoln said, "All honor to Jefferson—to the man, who in the concrete pressure of a struggle for national independence by a single people, had the coolness, forecast, and sagacity to introduce into a merely revolutionary document an abstract truth, applicable to all men and all times, and so to embalm it there that today and in all coming days it shall be a rebuke and a stumbling-block to the very harbingers of reappearing tyranny and oppression."

Jefferson's words, addressed by a single people to a single king, were, "We hold these truths to be self-evident, that all men are created equal, that they are endowed by their Creator with certain unalienable Rights, that among these are Life, Liberty and the pursuit of Happiness. . . ." So a new nation came into being—nothing new in that, it had happened before. What was new, and made the United States unique, was that its foundation rested upon an abstract truth. The people approved and applauded Jefferson's words, and have been approving and applauding ever since, and trying to find out what they mean.

Jefferson knew. He knew that, in the exuberant moment of signing the Declaration of Independence (No. 26), its signers did not really believe what they were signing. Men of property for the most part, they would have preferred to assert their rights in the then familiar words of John Locke: "life, liberty, and estate." But, on that happy day, they signed up for happiness. Nor were they all of them firm in their belief in the right to life, for others, and liberty was for those who were already free. Not for slaves, certainly not. And as to the abstract truth "that all men are created equal," nobody believed that. Jefferson knew this, too. How a Virginia country gentleman, lawmaker, musician, architect, scientist came to be the voice of his country, and in time the voice of all humanity, Dumas Malone (1892-) has set forth here in affectionate detail.

J. A. R.

200. *U.S. Camera 1957*

edited by TOM MALONEY

For 22 years this Annual has reflected changing taste and changing emphasis in American photography. It is, as the editor almost truculently insists in his introduction to the section on news photographs, "a working photographer's annual." Throughout the volume the emphasis is on photographic equipment and technique, on the pictures themselves rather than on aesthetic theory about them.

Perhaps the most interesting section, from this point of view, is that which offers selections from a "Creative Photography" exhibit held at a southern university. Text and pictures alike demonstrate the continuing self-consciousness about photography's role as an art; both alike suggest that the creative visual image in photography is the direct product of what the camera records "under certain conditions of light and psychological circumstance," without any "hand-manipulation" of the print to alter what lens and film have caught. It is significant, too, that so many of the photographs in all sections of this sampling of a year's work are primarily concerned with what Philippe Halsman calls "capturing the essence of a human being," rather than with using a human subject "as a component in an artistic arrangement." In this sense, as also in its inclusion of work by photographers of many nations, the Annual is less provincial than its title suggests.

It is nevertheless true that photography has had a special role in American life ever since the painter-inventor Samuel F. B. Morse brought Daguerre's invention to this country (see No. 195). In our literature there has been a strong current, allied to the reporting of which Richard Henry Dana's masterpiece, *Two Years Before the Mast* (No. 83), was an early classic, in which facts speak for themselves and in which the emphasis therefore falls on presenting fact with photographic realism. Walt Whitman liked to claim that in *Leaves of Grass* (No. 333) "everything is literally photographed." In our own time the poet-biographer Carl Sandburg has asserted (and demonstrated in his biography of Lincoln [No. 272]) that he prefers "a good photograph that has not been monkeyed with" to an interpretive study whether in pigment or words; and the novelist, John Dos Passos, in his panoramic *U.S.A.* (No. 99) conceives his role to be that of "The Camera Eye." So too in American painting, fidelity to visible fact has been a more pervasive influence than in European art. Many of our painters, from Morse to Thomas Eakins to Charles Sheeler, have been photographers as well.

J. A. K.

201. *The Late George Apley*

by JOHN P. MARQUAND

Although the United States is by European and Asiatic standards a "young" nation, it has evolved certain types, now geographical, now occupational, as objects of satire: the inbred Southern aristocrat, the business tycoon, the state-proud Texan, the Bostonian of wealth and family. Born in Delaware, John P. Marquand (1893-) went to school in Newburyport, Massachusetts, and at Harvard College, and worked for several years on the most dignified of Boston newspapers, the now defunct *Transcript*. He was therefore well prepared to satirize the old Puritan families of that city, who had prospered as merchants, bankers, and textile-mill owners, sent their sons to Harvard, and developed an exclusive aristocracy where "the Lowells speak only to Cabots, and the Cabots speak only to God."

When *The Late George Apley* appeared in 1937, it won instant recognition (with the Pulitzer Prize for fiction in 1938) and was in part a literary sensation because Mr. Marquand had been known for a dozen years as a successful writer of serials for popular magazines. Here his technique was different; he chose as the narrator of Apley's story one of the hero's close friends, a pretentious professional writer who had penned biographies of proper Bostonians. As the novel reveals, Apley had rebelled in his youth against the complacent world in which he had been reared, but had yielded to the influence of parents and friends and become increasingly a loyal if at times wistful member of his class. Mr. Marquand, like Sinclair Lewis (Nos. 184-5), is a satirist who cannot wholly separate himself from his subject. He has improved upon a tale that might merely have been one of struggle and adjustment by revealing the virtues, as well as the narrowness and absurdities, of the Boston aristocracy.

The Late George Apley appeared at a time when American readers had been completely weaned away from the literary conventions which realists like Theodore Dreiser (No. 101), Lewis, and Sherwood Anderson (No. 11) attacked. Mr. Marquand's book singled out a small cult whose ironic exposure the public fully enjoyed; but his story remains memorable for its penetrating and amusing detail, and for the subtlety and skill with which its theme is developed.

F. E. H.

202. *Point of No Return*

by JOHN P. MARQUAND

John P. Marquand (1893-) belongs in that all-too-small company of American novelists who direct their work to a large general public but who at the same time command the notice and regard of serious critics. An acute and witty social observer, he is the author of a series of engaging novels of contemporary American society, most of them set in New England and concerned, more or less satirically, with the peculiarly compelling effects of the traditional culture of this section of the United States upon its present-day heirs.

In *Point of No Return,* which is less well known than Mr. Marquand's earlier *The Late George Apley* (No. 201) but which has won the most critical approval of any of his books, the satiric element is suppressed in favor of a greater complexity of social understanding. Here, too, Mr. Marquand deals with New England and with the inability of anyone bred in the conventions of a puritan society to free himself from the mandates of duty and principle. But *Point of No Return* adds a new imaginative dimension to Mr. Marquand's other New England stories by being located not in Boston, that familiar stronghold of ritualism and propriety, but in a small town called Clyde, where the puritanical restraints upon the free life of the individual are reinforced by the usual pryings and gossipings of any small town; and even Clyde turns out to be a symbolic representation of the universal restrictions which society imposes upon a free spirit. When Mr. Marquand's unheroic young hero leaves New England for New York City and employment in a conservative bank, he not only carries within him the paralyzing inhibitions handed down to him by generations of New England forebears; he also enters an environment as rigorous and codified as any he knew at home. What Mr. Marquand would seem to be saying is that wherever a man goes, he meets his fate; the exercise of free choice is only an illusion.

But even if this is the new perception Mr. Marquand wishes to communicate in *Point of No Return,* he does not permit its suggestion of grimness to cast any but the most passing shadow over the pages of his novel. Like all of Mr. Marquand's books, *Point of No Return* is first and always skillful, intelligent entertainment and remarkable social reporting.

D. T.

203. *The Limits of Foreign Policy*

by CHARLES BURTON MARSHALL

The Limits of Foreign Policy is not only a general inquiry into the nature of foreign policy and a remarkably succinct re-examination of many of the crucial decisions in American foreign policy in the first half of the twentieth century; it is also a kind of character sketch of the American people in their relation to the international problems and responsibilities that they have had to face in the years since the second World War.

Charles Burton Marshall (1908-) speaks from a wide background as a student and planner of foreign policy; but, almost equally important, he also speaks as a man who has talked about the subject to audiences all over the United States. From their response and from specific questions asked at the end of his lectures, he has learned a good deal about the weak points in the American citizen's efforts to think about foreign policy, and in his book he skillfully exposes certain major paradoxes he has encountered.

One paradox—noted also by Gabriel A. Almond (No. 10)—is the all-or-nothing attitude Americans are likely to take, believing either that their country should withdraw altogether from international affairs or that it should intervene to the hilt and straighten things out once and for all. They are likely to think either that foreign policy can accomplish nothing or that its opportunities for accomplishment are unlimited. The central argument of Mr. Marshall's book, as his title indicates, is that the truth lies between these two extremes and that, since America can no longer abstain from participation in international politics, it must not fly to the other extreme and believe that its participation can accomplish everything. Although Americans are generally regarded as enamored of process, they have great difficulty in thinking of foreign policy as a process, an unending series of adaptations and accommodations, and they do not judge generously those diplomats who fail, as all diplomats must, to produce clear-cut, final solutions.

Related to the first paradox is the second: though Americans have great respect for law, as befits a people living under the oldest written constitution still in effect, they tend to be suspicious of the instruments through which law operates—government and its inevitable concomitant, politics. So they tend to think of foreign policy in terms of legal systems—international constitutions, courts of arbitration, and the like—rather than in terms of negotiations underwritten by power.

P. P.

204. *The Dance*

by JOHN MARTIN

John Martin (1893-), dance critic of *The New York Times,* is generally considered the leading American expert in his field. In this volume he tells in brief compass the story of the dance, calling to his aid a well-chosen collection of photographs, many of them lovely. To some the ballet may seem a highly artificial form; but, as Mr. Martin makes clear, its movements, however stylized, are—like a worried man's pacing of the floor—natural rhythmic expressions of inner motivations. In this sense all dancing—folk, ballroom, ballet, expressive dance of the post-Isadora Duncan school, or softshoe—is one. The problem is to feel sympathetically in one's own body what the dancer is trying to convey, and to perceive the form which the dancer's emotion must inevitably create.

Mr. Martin first considers the dance as a basic natural gesture; then folk and social dancing, which do not presuppose an audience; then the dance as spectacle, a phenomenon traced from the French court ballet of the sixteenth century through Noverre, Fokine, the Ballet Russe, Pavlova, Nijinsky, Diaghileff, Massine, and the non-Russian era of our own time, with the United States and England emerging as developers of the classic tradition and as successful experimenters in new forms; then "dance as a means of communication," from Isadora Duncan to Katherine Dunham and Pearl Primus; and finally "dance in the technological era," offering a brief survey of how such dancers as Gene Kelly and Fred Astaire have adapted their art to the demands of the motion picture camera.

Published in 1946, this book was not able to cover the influence of television on theatrical ballet. The ten years that followed it have witnessed an extraordinary revival of American interest in folk dancing and, more particularly, in the ballet. The latter is ceasing to be the property of a select, "arty" group and is beginning to rival the theater in the affections of the intelligent public. For these new balletomanes Mr. Martin's book will prove more than useful, both for its historical information and its interpretation of the classic and modern artists. It is written with a minimum of jargon and is quite devoid of the insider's snobbery that disfigures the work of some dance critics.

C. F.

205. *Spoon River Anthology*

by EDGAR LEE MASTERS

Edgar Lee Masters (1869-1947) is a man of a single book, though he wrote many. He was born in Kansas, and grew up and was educated in Illinois. In his young manhood he made law his profession and literature his avocation. But in 1915 the course of his life was changed by the success of *Spoon River Anthology*. This volume, thought by some to be scandalous, had an explosive effect. Masters became famous, gave up the practice of law in Chicago, removed to New York, and devoted himself to literature. He published voluminously, but none of his books repeated the success of *Spoon River Anthology*. His last years were made painful by illness and poverty as well as by disappointed hope.

But *Spoon River Anthology* is a work that will endure. The convention of the free-verse poems which make up the volume is derived from that of the Greek Anthology—a person who has died addresses a curious and sympathetic stranger who is standing at his grave and imparts the circumstances of his death and the irony or pathos of his fate. The dead of Spoon River tell the truth that they concealed when they were living persons, and the effect of their disclosures is to destroy the legend of the respectability of the Midwestern small town. Most of the speakers tell of the bitterness and frustration of their lives, although a few, like Lucinda Matlock, the old pioneer woman, or Ann Rutledge, Abraham Lincoln's legendary lost love, or Fiddler Jones, the musical farmer, can speak of fulfillment or joy.

The effect of *Spoon River Anthology* upon American literature has been notable. It was one of the first successful attempts to deal realistically yet sympathetically with the life of the American small town, particularly the small town of the Middle West. For American literature of the two decades following its publication it established the canon of the small town's vices (pettiness, intolerance, acquisitiveness) and of the virtues which are slighted or overcome by the rigors of its life (gentleness, disinterestedness, the love of art); Sherwood Anderson (No. 11), for example, is Masters's direct literary descendant. But the influence of *Spoon River Anthology* will be found to be pervasive throughout the literature that makes American rural life its subject.

L. T.

206. *A Dictionary of Americanisms on Historical Principles*

edited by MITFORD M. MATHEWS

No sooner had the English language been carried to America than it began to differentiate itself from the English of England. Dialect forms that in England had a subordinate place became dominant in the colonies, while words and syntactical constructions and pronunciations that were later forgotten in England were maintained in the New World. A major influence on transplanted English was the vocabulary of other languages. The English colonists learned the names for many new things from the Indians; and, as English spread, it picked up words and idioms from the Spanish, the German, the Dutch, the French, and the Scandinavian tongues, all of which were spoken in one section or another. The rhythm and intonation of speech changed; local dialects developed; and, in the metaphors of its slang, or in its picturesque or humorous phrase-making, the American form of the language showed itself to be very different in spirit from the native English.

By the time of the founding of the young republic the differences between the two forms of the language were already sufficiently great to lead some to prophesy that eventually they would become two separate languages. That American English had indeed become a new language was asserted by H. L. Mencken (1880-1956) in the title of his famous work, *The American Language* (No. 213). The predictions of extremists have not come to pass and are not likely to. Speakers of English English and of American English have no difficulty in understanding one another, and modern means of spoken communication permit the two forms to come closer together in reciprocal influence. Yet the differences between the two forms are considerable, and the extent of their differences in point of vocabulary alone may be quantitatively judged (almost weighed!) by *The Dictionary of Americanisms.*

The editor of the *Dictionary,* Dr. Mitford M. Mathews (1891-), was for nineteen years a collaborator of the great British lexicographer, Sir William Craigie, one of the editors of the *Oxford English Dictionary,* who came to America in 1925 to work on the *Dictionary of American English.* The 50,000 entries in Dr. Mathews's new *Dictionary* record and explain, with examples dating from their earliest appearance in print, words that have come into English first in the United States, established English words that have acquired a particular American meaning, phrases first used in America, American nicknames and slang. It is a work that may be not only consulted with profit but read with pleasure in the course of discovering how flexible and variously inventive a language can be.

L. T.

207. *American Renaissance*

by F. O. Matthiessen

Exactly one hundred years after Ralph Waldo Emerson (No. 105) published the first volume of his *Essays,* that is to say in 1941, a modern critic still felt him to be the mainspring of the great literary movement which distinguished the America of his time. F. O. Matthiessen (1902-1950), a professor at Harvard University, was not the only citizen of the present century to see in the decade or two before the Civil War an exceptional flowering of the national genius. Another historian has called it just that; and still another has named it "the golden day." No such commentator fails to be impressed by the powerful influence of Emerson upon both the thought and the expression of his long generation. *American Renaissance,* making full use of critical and historical methods which did not exist in the nineteenth century, explores this influence to its innermost recesses.

But the influence of Emerson was negative as well as positive; he stimulated resistance no less than he inspired agreement. Matthiessen traces agreement in Henry David Thoreau (No. 305) and Walt Whitman (No. 333) at the same time that he finds deep differences in Nathaniel Hawthorne (No. 140) and Herman Melville (Nos. 211-12). The first pair resemble Emerson in style; the second pair depart from him in thought. The style of Emerson was visionary and prophetic; in its own day it was even said to be angelic. It proceeded from an assumption that the knowledge of words is somehow the same thing as the knowledge of objects, and that both kinds of knowledge come easily to him who keeps his mind open to a universe ready to address it. Thoreau and Whitman in their various ways believed this too, and prophesied accordingly. But Hawthorne and Melville, however much they respected Emerson, painted darker pictures than the ones which shine forth from his rapturous pages. They had what he lacked, a sense of tragedy and evil. Matthiessen, in a book which requires to be read with the greatest care, follows out all the subtle lines of relationship that spin a sort of spider web among the minds of these five masters.

M. V. D.

208. *The Oxford Book of American Verse*

compiled by F. O. MATTHIESSEN

American poetry is of course a branch of English poetry, and this is the best reason that for a long time it did not show any startling originality of form, idiom, or outlook. The most cultivated part of the "new" population lived on the Atlantic seaboard and there was no interruption of communication between it and the mother country, even after the political separation.

At the same time, there was not that immediacy of response to moods and events which makes the poets of one age and one place share certain common preconceptions and even show a family likeness. A gap of anywhere from fifteen to fifty years is discernible in the attitudes of poets separated by the Atlantic, though once it is bridged for any generation, the current flows as if no interruption existed. Thus William Cullen Bryant writes "Thanatopsis" at seventeen as if Wordsworth held the pen, but he does it fourteen years after "Tintern Abbey."

The more original voices, being for various social reasons isolated, are quite unmistakable but often incomplete. From Ralph Waldo Emerson and Edgar Allan Poe to Emily Dickinson and Walt Whitman, one feels large powers lacking the benefit of daily attrition with other poets—the attrition that hardens and polishes. This state of affairs ceases to exist in the modern period, when the effect of a reversal of influence begins to be felt. Poe takes effect on Baudelaire and through him on the French Symbolists, after which French influence working on Ezra Pound and through him on T. S. Eliot (as well as modern Englishmen) inaugurates the international era in which contacts are rapid and repercussions unpredictable.

But this schematic view of a literary development is not necessary for an enjoyment of the present anthology. Its compiler, the late Professor Matthiessen (1902-1950) of Harvard, was eminently qualified to make a choice that should be classic without being conventional. His acute sensibility, coupled with his wide knowledge and scrupulous scholarship, permitted him to bring together a selection which—subject to the limitations of any anthology—may be said to be at once an Oxford Book and a Golden Treasury of American Poetry.

J. B.

209. *The Social Problems of an Industrial Civilization*

by ELTON MAYO

The word "pedestrian" turns up frequently in this little book. Elton Mayo (1880-1949), the most unpedestrian of men, used it to suggest how tired he had become of the full-blown epithets—the "dark, satanic mills" and all the rest—that had been flung at industrial civilization since the eighteenth century. His governing desire was to understand the society in which he found himself; such understanding could be attained, he believed, only by patient, pedestrian observation and analysis of what actually took place in industrial situations.

To this end he organized a series of experiments designed to produce evidence about the behavior of men at work under modern industrial conditions. The most celebrated of his inquiries, briefly described in this book, took place at the Hawthorne plant of the Western Electric Company. The conclusion Mayo reached after his years of investigation was that "the rapid development of science and industry put an end to the individual's feeling of identification with his group, of satisfaction in his work." The line of his argument was this: Men tend to build up a scheme of values, a culture, around what they do. In the past the way men did things changed so slowly that it was possible to construct upon this activity a relatively permanent cultural scheme, what Mayo called an established society. Within this settled civilization, with its sense of continuity in human affairs, the individual had a chance to find personal security and satisfaction. Science altered all this. By its ceaseless advance it produced constant modification in technology and these modifications in methods of manufacture introduced constant changes in the schemes men live by.

Therefore, if men are to take satisfaction in what they do, means must be discovered to shift from the established society of the past to the adaptive society of the future. What the precise nature of this adaptive society will ultimately be is less clear, in this book, than is the author's concern to define the real nature of the industrial process on which the future society must rest. His purpose is to call attention to the world we live in, to clear the air of prejudice, sentimental attachments, and misconception. In this unpretentious and little-known volume he goes some way toward the achievement of his object. He does so with skill and wit, and also rather more by intuitive understandings than by the pedestrian analysis he urges in others. E. E. M.

210. *And Keep Your Powder Dry*

by MARGARET MEAD

And Keep Your Powder Dry is a sketch of the American character executed in the technique of the cultural anthropologist, rather broadly applied. The portrait that results does not contain many surprises: like others who have tried to catch the likeness of the American, Dr. Margaret Mead (1901-) portrays him as a man on the move and on the make, competitive, believing in effort and progress, leaning on the future. But her method in arriving at these conclusions is less conventional.

Traditionally the discussion of national character has been primarily the province of the historian (an excellent example of the historian's approach is D. W. Brogan's *The American Character* [No. 40]). Since historians are usually adult males writing about the achievements of their own kind, they have tended to see national character as adult male behavior. But cultural anthropology is, among other things, an acknowledgment of the contribution to society made by women; it attempts to get at underlying habits of family life by which the behavior of adult males is shaped and their achievements are supported. Where, for instance, the historian Brogan bases his prediction of how American soldiers will fight in the future on his study of how they have fought in the past, Dr. Mead bases her treatment of the same subject on the attitudes toward fighting inculcated in little American boys by their mothers. Where historians have found the conditions of the American character in the frontier or democracy or the Spirit of 1776, Dr. Mead finds them in sibling rivalry, the adoption fantasy, and the hypocritical role of parents. No contradiction is necessarily involved; cultural anthropology offers an explanation of how the large concepts of the historian get built into the character of the small member of society.

The reader of Dr. Mead's book should bear in mind two major reservations. First, it was written when the depression of the 1930's was the last great experience of the American people. Since then we have gone through a decade and a half of prosperity, and one need not agree with extreme right-wing critics who say that Americans have lost their competitiveness or their belief in effort and progress to grant that prosperity and other social changes have wrought some alteration. And second, the reader should remember that Dr. Mead's sketch is highly generalized and schematic. It is related to the American character as a very small map is related to the large and living landscape.

P. P.

211. *Moby Dick*

by HERMAN MELVILLE

Moby Dick is one of the masterpieces not only of American literature but of world literature, yet for a long time it was a book scarcely known by Americans, let alone by the world. Its author was by no means an obscure person—Herman Melville (1819-1891) was a well-known writer for some years before the publication of *Moby Dick*, his greatest work. Though he was descended from prominent Dutch and English families long established in New York, the financial ruin and death of his father put Melville to the necessity of giving up his schooling at an early age and going to work. He followed the sea for some years, and his experiences were the basis of *Typee* (see No. 212), *Omoo, Mardi,* and *White-Jacket*. These books, all remarkable, won him a solid reputation with the contemporary public. But with the publication of *Moby Dick* in 1851 Melville lost his literary following, for the book was extravagantly disliked, apparently for the very qualities of eloquence and high, free imagination which make it now so greatly admired.

Melville wrote and published much that was very fine in his later years, but in his lifetime he never regained his old repute and he lived and died in obscurity. It was not until the appearance of Raymond Weaver's *Herman Melville, Mariner and Mystic* in 1921 that critics and scholars came to know him for what he was, a man of genius.

Moby Dick is a story of adventure, and it should be read as one—an awareness of its complex and profound meanings should not be allowed to obscure the pleasure of its sheer excitement of quest and chase, of dangers confronted. It is also natural history, a first-rate account of the habits of whales. And it is a superb description of the whaling industry, once so important in the economy of New England. But undoubtedly its greatness derives from its symbolic representation of man's existence. The symbolism of the book has been read in numerous ways—one critic has discerned seven levels or layers of possible interpretation—and there is surely no single right way to read it. Most critics agree that Moby Dick, the terrible and unconquerable white whale, represents the evil of the universe. But whether Captain Ahab's fanatic desire to destroy the monster is to be praised or blamed, or both, has been a matter for debate, and each reader will, and should, settle the question in his own manner.

L. T.

212. *Selected Writings of Herman Melville*

The career of Herman Melville (1819-1891) is one of the strangest in literature, and perhaps the most fitful. Beginning at 25 he wrote and published, at the dizzy rate of one a year, six long books—the last of which, *Moby Dick* (No. 211), was the longest and best, and indeed his masterpiece—and then for the remaining years of his life, though he was by no means silent, he scattered his force in the desultory production of poems and stories whose worth was various and whose unity has never become apparent.

The present selection samples him early and late, from *Typee,* the first of his books and the one by which most readers knew him in his time, to "Billy Budd, Foretopman," a remarkable allegory which he left in manuscript. *Typee,* an ideal report of Melville's own visit as a seaman to the Pacific islands, enchanted a generation with its picture of the Golden Age come true again in the flesh, and outraged the missionaries who failed to find themselves flattered on any page. "Billy Budd," the work of an old man still in possession of tempestuous powers, remains one of the most interesting tales ever to probe the recesses of man's morality. Between these two narratives lie the long books of Melville's first flowering, and after them the miscellaneous shorter tales which tend to bewilder by their radical variety.

The mind of Melville, never at rest, plowed through metaphysics and theology in search of symbols with which to express its tormented vision of the world. Or else it played, as on occasion it could, over surfaces of life as commonplace as that of "Bartleby," whose utterly undistinguished hero, a scrivener in a New York counting room, grows by his very silence into a mysterious figure representative of more than meets the eye. "The Encantadas" and "Benito Cereno" are on the other hand complex and brilliant in their colors, as certain other pieces shine with a wit, sometimes satirical, sometimes savage, enlisted in the service of social criticism. Melville is the hardest of all American authors to sum up. *Moby Dick* is his masterpiece, but here is his further range.

M. V. D.

213. *The American Language*

by H. L. Mencken

Henry Louis Mencken (1880-1956), the militant derider of the American "booboisie," is also the man who devoted the last 40 years of his life to cataloguing—so to speak—the language of his despised compatriots. The truth is that he did not despise them; he was impatient and angry with them as one is with members of one's family; and the few that he thoroughly hated and contemned, he would have hated and contemned regardless of their nationality (see for example some of his statements in *The American Treasury* [No. 106]).

What attracted Mencken to the study of the new language was its vastness, variety, heedlessness of tradition, picturesqueness, genius, and folly. Not trained as a linguist, Mencken could chiefly list and classify, and this he did with such persistent zest that the one volume first brought out in 1919 was by 1948 expanded into three, each much larger than the original. The accuracy and semantic intelligence of Mencken's work can be measured by the gratitude expressed in the latest scholarly publication on the same theme, Mitford Mathews's *A Dictionary of Americanisms on Historical Principles* (No. 206).

The reader of Mencken will probably be struck first by the sardonic note that emerges from time to time as he describes the views, acts, customs, or speech of his fellow-citizens. Then will come the reflection that whatever be the crudity thus ridiculed, Mencken does not wish for its expected opposite—refinement or academic discipline. The strictures of foreign critics of the language, he repels with vehement scorn. Finally, the reader will discover, and doubtless be surprised by, the extent to which Americanisms are simply old English speech or borrowings from foreign sources. This does not mean that the vein of native invention is a myth, but only that it has been flanked by the usual elements of old memory and fresh adaptation. What is clearly a great invention here is Mencken's own style and his original conception of the language in which he wrote.

J. B.

214. *The Human Mind*

by KARL MENNINGER

Sigmund Freud could never bring himself to like the United States or to expect much of its culture. It is therefore something of an irony that the Freudian psychology should have established itself more firmly in America than in any other country in the world. It is a yet more dramatic irony that psychoanalytic therapy, which is usually associated with the sophistication of metropolitan cities, should have as one of its chief centers in America the famous Menninger Clinic at Topeka, in the heart of agricultural Kansas.

The Menninger brothers, Karl (1893-) and William (1899-), are known as the chief American propagandists for mental health and for psychotherapy on Freudian principles, and their influence as practitioners, teachers, writers, and administrators has been decisive in the remarkable development of psychotherapy in America. Dr. Charles Menninger, their father, was an eagerly questing personality, a prairie boy who struggled against great odds for an education, trying his hand at law and teaching and eventually turning to medicine. A visit to the famous Mayo Clinic in Minnesota (see No. 62) gave the elder Menninger the vision of an institution of a similar kind in Kansas. Under the direction of his sons, the Clinic that bears the family name is one of the largest in the world, and the Menninger Foundation is one of the greatest and most authoritative institutes for psychiatric research and training.

Dr. Karl Menninger's *The Human Mind* has been a classic of scientific popularization since it was published in 1929. It is in all respects faithful to the view of the mind which Freud expounded, but it sets forth Freud's very complex and difficult theory of the unconscious dynamics of the mind with so remarkable a simplicity that at least the essential principles may be readily understood by any reader. It is written for the layman, including the physician who has not had special training in psychiatry, and it is often assigned to medical students as their introduction to the study of the afflictions of the mind. Its tone of warm friendliness (which in America is likely to be thought of as a trait of the Middle West), its insistence on the frequency, even the usualness—one almost says the normality—of mental abnormality have done much to diminish the ignorant horror of mental illness and to lead to a sensible and hopeful attitude toward therapy.

L. T.

215. Collected Sonnets of Edna St. Vincent Millay

The sonnets of Edna St. Vincent Millay (1892-1950), like her poems generally, enjoyed success with a wide audience during the quarter century following 1917, and their success was never the result of technical innovations or of surprises in style. Their felicity, to be sure, was new and surprising as felicity may always be; but her derivation was plainly from the older English poets—from Shakespeare most of all—and from the Greek and Roman lyric poets whose mythology she had made natural to her thinking. What did seem novel was her frankness in discussing love. Here she was taken as speaking, or singing, for a generation emancipated from its aunts and uncles, not to say its mothers and fathers, and from the comfortable sentiments of fidelity which it attributed to them. She addressed her poems to many lovers, not one, and she made it clear that all of them were but incidents in a career of her own choice and direction.

Not that Edna Millay had no other theme than this, though she pursued it to the end. She had her intellectual concerns as well, and finally a set of social ones. Her popularity, which survived her death in 1950 and continues firm, may still be based in large part upon the early poems, but it did not fail to follow her into the moral and political fields where at last she was at home. Her final sonnets, grimly enough, were an "Epitaph for the Race of Man." As sonnets they surpass in complexity the first ones she wrote, without however burrowing into congestion or obscurity. At all stages she cultivated a purity of line which meant for her an unflagging attention to melody as well as to the perfect articulation of her thought. And she was thoughtful. She was witty, too, and not without an irony that struck suddenly, exerting all the more force because it issued from the sweet voice she had made so familiar. She excelled herself in the sonnets here collected. She never abandoned the form; rather, she studied its infinite resources and put into it all she possessed of feeling and idea.

M. V. D.

216. *Jonathan Edwards*

by PERRY MILLER

Theology has long since ceased to be a popular subject, whether in America or elsewhere. And this is particularly true of Puritan theology, which Jonathan Edwards (1703-58), a Massachusetts divine, exemplified at the height of its power and beauty. For then it was a subject of deep public concern, and there was no indifference in his audience to prevent Edwards from expressing his full genius. He was a genius in philosophy, in psychology, and in art; few Americans, and few men anywhere, have been his equals in either literary or intellectual skill.

But historical imagination is needed by one who would measure his achievement now. The controversies to which he gave his strength, and in a sense his life, are difficult to see in their contemporary bearings, not to speak of such bearings as they may still have in a world that appears to have left Edwards so far behind. Perry Miller (1905-), to whom these controversies are not dead, places them no less in modern thought, which he considers the poorer for its ignorance of their meaning, than in the thought of men who could say "justification," "Arminian," and "free will" as if they were words to shake the world.

The story of Edwards, however, is more than the story of his mind, though that is where he chiefly lived. He was an embattled preacher, contesting not merely with rival theologians but with members of his congregation in Northampton, Massachusetts, who found him to be of sterner stuff than they could bear, and who finally cast him out. The giant who argued so mightily with the best intellects of New England and of Europe was no match in personal strategy for certain merchants of his town. It is a tragic story, yet in its working out the whole rich nature of the man would seem to have been revealed. He was marvelously subtle, sensitive, and acute, and the powers of his mind were immense; but he was overbearing too, and his sense of society deserted him at least once too often. The sermons, the autobiographies, the histories, the treatises that he left are nevertheless his proper monument, and it is mainly this which Professor Miller with great learning and sympathy surveys.

M. V. D.

217. *Men in Business*

Essays on the History of Entrepreneurship

edited by William Miller

The popular image of the American businessman is an extraordinarily blurred one, considering what an ubiquitous fellow he is. In fiction he frequently appears, often as the representative American. Henry James's *The Ambassadors* (No. 159), William Dean Howells's *The Rise of Silas Lapham* (No. 155), Abraham Cahan's *The Rise of David Levinsky* (No. 48), Sinclair Lewis's *Babbitt* (No. 184), and F. Scott Fitzgerald's *The Great Gatsby* and *The Last Tycoon* (No. 114) all deal with businessmen as representative figures; but the reader will learn more from them about America's ambiguous attitudes toward business than about the men who run American business. James, for instance, is not at all interested in Strether's business as such, but only as the source of the wealth which frees him to go abroad where he can become "interesting" in James's sense. Cahan and Lewis know a good deal about the business of their heroes, but they know it only in order to despise it. Howells and Fitzgerald are less interested in business than in the conflict which business success brings on between the values of business and those of "culture."

One has the same problem with the few available autobiographies of American businessmen, for in them (as in Andrew Carnegie's [No. 50]) the authors are more concerned with their roles as public figures or benefactors of learning and the arts than with their business activities. Indeed, our business leaders are generally disposed to belittle in public their entrepreneurial functions and to call attention, instead, to their after-hours role as sponsors or disciples of culture. (See for example the report of their comments during the Corning Conference—itself an example of industry taking its cultural responsibilities seriously—in *Creating an Industrial Civilization* [No. 288].) The essays in the present volume are therefore doubly interesting and significant as being among the first serious attempts to study objectively the role of the businessman *as* businessman, and to see him in the context of the general social environment, its laws and prejudices, institutions and habits.

J. A. K.

218. *The Martial Spirit*

by WALTER MILLIS

The Spanish-American War extended for the length of a single spring (in 1898) and ended in a victory that was, by modern standards, virtually bloodless. For so short and simple a conflict it produced some amazing results. Elbert Hubbard was inspired by it to write *A Message to Garcia,* the most widely read parable in American history. The fame Theodore Roosevelt acquired at San Juan Hill eventually secured him the Presidency of the United States (see No. 250). The nation was appalled for weeks by the news that our troops had been fed "embalmed beef," a phrase that still remains an epithet in the national vocabulary. And finally, at the peace, we received an imperial domain.

In spite of all the attendant excitement and rewards, Americans have always been more than a little uneasy about this war. In part this is because of what we got out of it and, in part, because of how we got into it. The empire, with its connotation of old-world attitudes and solutions, was disturbing. There were some who were quite prepared to take up the "white man's burden," but there were others who felt, with Senator Hoar of Massachusetts, that the devil had taken us up on a high hill. As a whole, the community remained more troubled than pleased over the obligations assumed after 1898. Some discomfort was also felt when the history of the events leading up to the war was subjected to cooler appraisal than had been possible in 1897 and 1898. It became clearer as time went on that along with the desire to give aid and comfort to the Cubans had been mixed other less attractive motives. No student has subjected this period to closer investigation than Walter Millis (1898-), or written about his findings in more skillful fashion. This book, when published in 1931, not only assisted in setting a doubtful historical record straighter but helped to confirm many, disillusioned with the world after the Treaty of Versailles, in their opinion that no war can be justified.

E. E. M.

219. *Gone With the Wind*

by MARGARET MITCHELL

Margaret Mitchell (1909-49) was a one-book writer. There were thousands like her in the South, each with a book inside. Every sensitive girl and boy of her generation had a treasure house of transmitted memory. The Yankees had no need to remember. They had defeated—no, overwhelmed—the South and had gone on about their business. But the vanquished do not forget. They remember, and their descendants, having had poured into their ears and souls the tale of misery and glory, also remember. But Margaret Mitchell was different from the rest. She wrote the book, and no Southerner, old or young, can think of anything that is missing.

Scarlett O'Hara, the heroine, if that is the proper word, was by definition a young Southern lady. She was in fact nothing of the kind. She was never young, born old; she was no lady, and not Southern. She happened to have been born at Tara in up-country Georgia, of a mother who was "a Coast"—meaning Gulf Coast—"aristocrat of French descent" and an Irish father. She might just as well have been born of a Danish skivvy and English lord, and in Cairo (either one, Illinois or Egypt) or in Singapore. The completely ruthless woman has no origin. She is suddenly there.

There must be a man, a match or nearly—not a mate, whatever she may think. She may destroy him, as William Faulkner's Miss Emily destroyed hers, Regina in *The Little Foxes* of Lillian Hellman (*Sixteen Famous American Plays* [No. 284]), or Theodore Dreiser's Sister Carrie (No. 101) her several, but for a diapason of irony he should be her equal, ruthless as she. Rhett Butler was that. (Rhett, an old honorable Charleston name; Butler, name of a Yankee general still execrated in New Orleans.)

But they are not mere figures. Margaret Mitchell created her people in the round. They live and move, and they talk as they did really talk, all of them; for she, like Dickens, never skimped, every character getting her full loving attention, from the incomparable Prissy to the bumbling aunt. She was also a good storyteller. From the first page, while the twins may dawdle, she does not. The story moves, up to the advent of Sherman, the Yankee general who shocked delicate sensibilities by saying, "War is hell," and proved it by burning Atlanta, and from there down home to Tara once again, Scarlett leading, chin up.

J. A. R.

220. *The Far Side of Paradise*

A Biography of F. Scott Fitzgerald

by Arthur Mizener

With the appearance of F. Scott Fitzgerald's unfinished last novel, *The Last Tycoon* (No. 114), and the publication of a volume of letters and other Fitzgerald documents edited by Edmund Wilson, a literary reputation which for long had taken second place to a personal legend finally established itself in American critical judgment. But if there is now no doubt that Fitzgerald was more than the flamboyant playboy of the 1920's, that he was in fact one of the most dedicated writers of this century, the story of his tragic self-destructive life still has the power to grip the imagination even of readers unacquainted with his literary achievement.

It is this life story that Professor Mizener (1907-) deals with in *The Far Side of Paradise,* a book whose title makes ironic play with the novel which first brought Fitzgerald to fame, *This Side of Paradise*. The gods who attended Fitzgerald at birth must themselves have been ironists to have endowed him with such an abundance of gifts—talent, good looks, extraordinary charm—plus conscience of a kind which was bound to bring him acute suffering. The struggle between Fitzgerald's artistic instinct for order and his always-increasing inability to find either place or peace in the chaos of possibility presented by the prosperity of the 1920's is more than an individual tragedy. It is also the peculiar tragedy of American society during a period when its growth was unsupported by adequate faith in either its sources or its direction. Yet Professor Mizener understands how important it is to recognize that Fitzgerald, so archetypically the child of his undisciplined times, firmly and with the sternest literary discipline took his conscious stand in the great Romantic tradition.

D. T.

221. *Collected Poems*

by MARIANNE MOORE

Marianne Moore (1887-) is a poet who is in love with prose. It is a habit of hers to quote in her poems phrases or sentences which, for one reason or another, have taken her fancy: these quotations are almost always from prose works. It is the cadences of the speaking voice rather than the cadences of the singing voice that her lines seek to achieve; there is perhaps not a single lyric passage in all her work. This, of course, says nothing about the intensity of her poems. It only suggests the means by which she achieves the intensity.

The speaking voice which Miss Moore wishes to suggest is that of a person whose intelligence is equal to his feeling, and who is concerned to use words with precision lest his feeling be corrupted by mere approximateness. Like many another modern poet, Miss Moore fears the habit of "poetic" thought. She speaks of true poets (taking the phrase from an essay by William Butler Yeats) as "literalists of the imagination"; she goes even further and says that they are "pedantic literalists." The true poet, she means, sets more store by the fact as it really is than by his impulse to say something about the fact.

T. S. Eliot, writing about Miss Moore's poetry, has said that the poet carries on a struggle for the "maintenance of a living language, for the maintenance of its strength, its subtlety, for the preservation of quality of feeling which must be kept up in every generation." And he goes on: "Miss Moore is, I believe, one of those few who have done the language some service in my lifetime."

Miss Moore's feeling for the accuracy of prose is of a piece with her characteristic choice of subjects. She has a consuming interest in objects which are remarkable for their elegance of precision and efficiency; she especially likes them if they are odd or rare. Most often it is animals that engage her curiosity (see, for example, "The Jerboa," "The Pangolin," "The Wood Weasel") but often it is a contrivance made by man ("Four Quartz Crystal Clocks," "A Carriage from Sweden"). By their speed, or grace, or accuracy, or by their oddity or uniqueness, these things propose to the mind that observes them the qualities which mind should have.

To a first reader of Miss Moore's poems, it will be useful to know that in some of them the title is to be read as the first words of the poem.

L. T.

222. *Summer's Children*

by Barbara Morgan

The picture-book genre, in which text and photographs combine in "meanings" neither alone could convey, finds one of its loveliest and most satisfying examples in the present volume. With a minimum of text—snatches of song, bits of the children's conversation, brief descriptive or explanatory phrases—and with evocative and dramatic photographs, Mrs. Barbara Morgan (1900-) has set a high standard of what picture-books can be.

Such books began to appear in the early 1930's, at about the time that the photo-journalism exemplified by *Life* and *Look* began to develop. Yet picture-books in the modern sense are related also to the equally ill-named "comics" and to the movies and television. Like all of these related forms they are apparently symptomatic of a twentieth-century preoccupation with pictorial as opposed to purely verbal values in communication—a preoccupation variously interpreted as a heightening of visual awareness or as a deplorable evidence of declining literacy. In any event, there is nothing new about the American's fascination with seeing. A century ago Ralph Waldo Emerson remarked that "Our age is ocular"; Walt Whitman insisted upon "pictures, pictures," in his poems; Nathaniel Hawthorne chose a daguerreotypist as the representative American artist in *The House of the Seven Gables* (No. 140).

In a sense, as the introduction to *Summer's Children* says, this is a book about childhood. It is also a book about an important development in American education: the summer camp, whose history is briefly told and evaluated in Helen Haskell's prefatory essay. More significantly still, it is a book about the contemporary feeling, expressed in so many ways, that our civilization needs rebalancing. As Mrs. Morgan puts it, "We do not want to be engulfed by a one-sided technology. We want a way of life which is of itself whole." The book will be most revealing to those who think of it in connection with the contemporary revival of interest in Henry David Thoreau's *Walden* (in No. 305), with the scholarly romanticism of Joseph Wood Krutch's *The Desert Year* (No. 176), or with the cautious optimism of William R. Van Dersal's *The American Land* (No. 312).

J. A. K.

223. *Admiral of the Ocean Sea*

A Life of Christopher Columbus

by SAMUEL ELIOT MORISON

Since Columbus was the discoverer of America it is fitting that the discoverer of Columbus should be an American. Samuel Eliot Morison (1887-) is just that, a discoverer, for when he set sail the map of Columbus's history was as distorted as the map the future Admiral had shown the Spanish queen. On that map the earth was six-sevenths land, and the Atlantic was a narrow ocean over which in a few days—*paucis diebus*—one would land on the island of Japan, which was 1,500 miles east of China. The map of history was as queer. Maps, rather, for on some of them the real discoverer was not Columbus at all, on others he was a skillful liar. The scholar sails perilous seas, and there may be a Carib at every landing.

But the author is, unlike other historians of Columbus, also an admiral (see No. 224). It makes a difference. As a sailor he has retraced the voyages and re-created for himself the experience of Columbus. Also, as a good sailor, he likes to know where he is at all times, and takes no small chances. As a result, he knows more about Columbus and his times than anyone has ever known, including Columbus.

Columbus did not know that, but for the birds, he would have landed on Cape Canaveral, the site today of Patrick Air Force Base. Nor could he know that his discovery of San Salvador was not only "a clean break with past experience," but a prophecy of the creation of a new nation. The pious reader of the Bible does not know what the Queen of Sheba had to do with the discovery of America. The tobacconist does not know that there is more than one way to smoke a cigar. Nor does the young girl swinging in a hammock know who invented that admirable device.

But scholarship, even when salted with seamanship, does not make palatable fare. It takes art to do that, the art of telling a story, of taking the reader into the feeling of a moment: the moment of laughter, the sailors doubling up at the predicament of a Very Reverend Lord Bishop; or of painful foreknowledge, shame, when the innocent Indians troop down to shore. And though "Never again may mortal men hope to recapture the amazement, the wonder, the delight of those October days in 1492," still, it's a near miss.

J. A. R.

224. *The Struggle for Guadalcanal*

by SAMUEL ELIOT MORISON

The island of Guadalcanal was only one of the many bits of land in the vast Pacific over which the Americans and Japanese fought bloodily in World War II. Other shore battles were as vicious, or more so; other naval engagements as decisive. But the name of Guadalcanal nonetheless occupies a special place in the public imagination—both because it was a turning-point, like the battle of El Alamein, and because it was there that the American soldier first met his Japanese opponent in the warfare of tropical jungles at which the latter believed himself—with good reason—to be supreme. Moreover, in men and vessels this was one of the costliest naval battles (or, rather, group of battles) in history. "You may search the seven seas in vain," writes Admiral Morison, "for an ocean graveyard with the bones of so many ships and sailors as that body of water between Guadalcanal, Savo and Florida Islands which our bluejackets named Ironbottom Sound."

For six months the land, sea, and sky forces of the two nations contended for possession of this 90-mile oblong of mountains, mud, and mosquitoes. Guadalcanal saw six major naval engagements, dozens of ground actions, and air combat that was virtually continuous—yet all were a part of essentially the same story. Rarely is it possible to convey so clearly, in a single narrative, the interdependence that "modern" warfare demands of the army, navy, and air arm. For ultimate control of a patch of water, a company of Marines clung bitterly to an inland ridge; for a land victory weeks in the future, pilots nursed their battered planes aloft against all odds; and for possession of an airfield, warships miles distant pounded at one another in a darkness fitfully lit by searchlights, gunfire, and flaming wreckage. Any one of the three armed services could have thrown away the victory; none alone could have secured it.

Samuel Eliot Morison (1887-) recounts *The Struggle for Guadalcanal* from mainly, though not exclusively, the Navy's point of view. He is a native of New England, cradle of the maritime tradition to which both he and the sailors he affectionately writes about respond. In civil life a distinguished historian (No. 225), with a knowledge and love of the sea (No. 223), he was asked by the late President Roosevelt to undertake the official History of

United States Naval Operations in World War II, of which this work is Volume V. Its publication scarcely a half-dozen years after the fact reflects a more general trend—to commit quickly to paper, as objectively and readably as possible, the significant events of the recent past. But of all the "war" histories which have resulted, Admiral Morison's is by common consent the most successful and, of all his volumes, this one is best able to stand alone.

E. L.

225. *The Growth of the American Republic*

by Samuel Eliot Morison *and* Henry Steele Commager

The question of where to begin a history of the United States is never easy to answer; the true beginnings of the country are in Europe, and so antedate its existence. Professors Samuel Eliot Morison (1887-) and Henry Steele Commager (1902-), of Harvard and Columbia Universities respectively, have in successive editions of the present work pushed its boundaries both forward and backward: in the one case to keep up with new events, and in the other case to enrich that perspective of the past without which any history tends to be meaningless. They went back finally to the coming of the first men to America—not Europeans, of course, but migrants from Siberia; though the second chapter took them swiftly on to the situation of Europe at the end of the fifteenth century when America was discovered by those peoples who gave it its present civilization. Perhaps this popular and respected history is nowhere more interesting than at the point where it describes the "decadence" of 1492. Europe felt then that it was finished; the powerful movements of the Middle Ages had spent their force, and there was thought to be no future for mankind. But Columbus sailed west and discovered a new hemisphere; and Western life, if only by an extension of its scope, began again.

If the authors pursue a single theme through the many pages that follow it has to do with this departure which America represented in the affairs of an old world. For it has continued, in the mind of that world if not in its own, to mean many things and to inspire many hopes. The part of it dealt with here has meant more steadily than anything else democracy. It is democracy that the United States has in the long run made its chief effort to understand and maintain. So the authors believe, and the whole of their eloquent work attests this faith. Their narratives of the separation from England, the construction of a government, the ordeal of that government in the Civil War, and its further ordeals in the world wars of the twentieth century, not to speak of all the intervening domestic crises, are informed by one conception: democracy on trial—and, hopefully, surviving.

M. V. D.

226. *Encyclopedia of American History*

edited by Richard B. Morris

Readers of American books will often find this thoroughly indexed encyclopedia useful, for its maps and biographies as well as for its compressed narratives and explanations of historical events. There are references in many books in this collection to people, places, and dates which seemed self-explanatory to the author but which may be quite unknown to readers abroad and to many Americans too—particularly if the book was written some time ago or assumes a specially well-informed audience. "He was the Mark Hanna of the campaign," "fifty-four forty or fight," "a Mann Act romance," "the Palmer Raids"—these and countless other references can be clarified by turning to this volume.

Part I is a basic political and military chronology, from the age of discovery to the first election of President Eisenhower in 1952. Part II contains topical chronologies, dealing with national expansion, the Constitution and the Supreme Court, various aspects of the nation's economy (agriculture, industry, finance, labor, and so on), science and invention, religion, education, literature, the arts, and other aspects of social and cultural history. Part III contains brief biographies of 300 Americans, with date references which will guide the reader to pertinent sections of the chronologies.

For a full narrative and interpretive history, the reader is referred to Samuel Eliot Morison and Henry Steele Commager's serviceable *The Growth of the American Republic* (No. 225), and for an English view, Frank Thistlethwaite's *The Great Experiment* (No. 303). Three other reference books which will be helpful to the reader are *The Oxford Companion to American Literature* (No. 138), which identifies authors, titles, characters in fiction and drama, literary movements, etc.; *A Dictionary of Americanisms on Historical Principles* (No. 206), which defines words and illustrates usages which differ from those in British English; and *Collier's World Atlas and Gazetteer* (No. 64).

J. A. K.

227. *The Brown Decades*

by Lewis Mumford

For 30 years after the Civil War—a story that begins in Claude G. Bowers's *The Tragic Era* (No. 39)—the surface of the United States presented an unpleasing spectacle. In politics the nation exposed its exhausted conscience through such sterile or corrupt maneuvering as the Tweed Ring or the Crédit Mobilier. In industry and finance pilferers like Jay Gould and James Fisk made their precarious fortunes out of the misfortunes of others, while the ruthless organizers of the great industrial combinations crowded their small competitors off the scene. A ground swell of unrest revealed itself in shocking moments at the Haymarket riots in Chicago and the Homestead strike in Pittsburgh. To many it appeared that the country had given itself over to the simple plunder of the material and human resources with which it had been so generously endowed.

Surveying this unpromising landscape, major creative talents like Henry James (Nos. 159-61) fled to the sanctuary of Europe as from some blasted heath. For a long time it was believed that all the other talents had followed them or been buried forever in the hurly-burly of American life during the period. Lewis Mumford (1895-) does much to dispel this assumption. He reveals in this book that behind the repellent brown façade large amounts of energy and imagination were at work trying to give shape and meaning to native materials. Men like Frederick Law Olmsted set themselves the task of organizing the landscape in attractive form; men like Louis H. Sullivan, H. H. Richardson, and John W. Root were slowly evolving a design for buildings appropriate for the actual life that went on within them; painters like Thomas Eakins and Winslow Homer began to search for authentic interpretations of authentic native activities.

Those who went away to write or paint made themselves valuable by presenting soundly conceived criticisms of the aimlessness and barbarism they found in American life; those who remained to make their tentative statements about what could be done here became invaluable. The men Mr. Mumford describes in this book in fact laid the foundations upon which their successors, in continued search for a satisfying culture to fit American conditions, could safely build. Their contribution is more suggestively stated here because Mr. Mumford is not only himself passionately committed to the search, but is willing to take more intellectual chances than those whose views have been ground down in the cautious mills of American scholarship.

E. E. M.

228. *Roots of Contemporary American Architecture*

edited by LEWIS MUMFORD

It has become in recent years something close to an obsession with students of American civilization to attempt to sort out and define those aspects of our culture which can be said to be essentially American. This attempt at self-identification is chauvinist at its worst, but at its best, as it is in *Roots of Contemporary American Architecture,* it is a healthy way of explaining the American to himself without isolating him. The long traditions of his arts come essentially from Western Europe, and this he takes for granted; in architecture especially he has periodically tried to recapture these traditions through the revival of European styles. But he is less aware that his own invention, his own particular relationships with his environment, his own special attitudes toward useful objects have produced a genuine *style* quite different from anything he brought with him to this continent or borrowed from Europe later on. (See Kouwenhoven's *Made in America* [No. 175].)

The emergence of this awareness of an American style (that is, a fitting visual expression of national character) appeared in writing about design before it appeared in new forms of architecture, and it is in these writings that Mr. Lewis Mumford (1895-) searches in this volume for the roots of our present architecture. He finds it first in the concern of the nineteenth-century sculptor, Horatio Greenough (1805-1892), who was delighted with the grace and economical design of clipper ships and who in his writings "laid the groundwork for a new aesthetic doctrine, a doctrine capable of dealing with the new forces and values that science and mechanization were producing" (see also No. 131). He finds it in the writings of an expatriate art critic and collector, James Jackson Jarves (1818-1888), who was impatient with America for its subservience to European artistic ideas. He finds it in the writings of architects, like Louis Henri Sullivan (No. 298) and Frank Lloyd Wright (No. 347), and in the essays of Henry David Thoreau (No. 305). He finds it in architectural critics and historians, in the proponents of the arts-and-crafts movement, and in those who saw a revelation of structural possibilities in such innovations as the Bessemer steel process and the Brooklyn Bridge. Out of these Mr. Mumford has compiled not only an anthology of American writing about architecture but a source book of great variety and intense interest for those who are concerned with the problem of why Americans build as they do.

R. L.

229. *Sticks and Stones*

by LEWIS MUMFORD

Nowhere in his book does Lewis Mumford (1895-) quote the jingle, known to almost every reader as a child, which gives his title its particular meaning to Americans: "Sticks and stones may break my bones, but names can never hurt me." What Mr. Mumford is saying is that architecture, wood and masonry, had so far (1924) had greater impact on the American culture than appeared in words, least of all in words that could correspondingly affect its future constructions. He was a pioneer in the treatment of architecture as visual evidence of, and an organic element in, the innermost convictions of American communities. His is the satisfaction of knowing "that scholarly buildings are now being built, in distant historic territory, over the buried ashes of a hasty campfire I once lighted, near a spring from whose waters I was the first explorer to drink."

Americans are fortunate in their architects, more fortunate, indeed, than Mr. Mumford knew. As he says in his preface to the 1954 edition, he did not then appreciate the continuity which led from H. H. Richardson to Louis Sullivan (see No. 298) to Frank Lloyd Wright (see No. 347), a deficiency that he sought to repair in *The Brown Decades* (No. 227). These three men have steadily risen in critical regard, not least by Mr. Mumford's efforts, to the point where they may now be said to claim the rank of master builder on any scale, American or other. Concern with city planning, moreover, has become so widely shared that it is now a profession, and university degrees are granted in the subject matter that Mr. Mumford—a free-lance thinker who had not then attained to academic respectability—brought to the forefront of our general concern.

It will be noted that Mr. Mumford, even in this early work, has no great sympathy for cities. Later, under the influence of Patrick Geddes, he was to move even further toward a distrust of modernity and mechanization similar to that of Siegfried Giedion (see No. 128). It is an understandable attitude, but atypically American. The reader might especially note that it is not the attitude of the architects—even of Sullivan and Wright—whose achievement Mr. Mumford so movingly records.

E. L.

230. *An American Dilemma*

by GUNNAR MYRDAL

The "dilemma" described by Gunnar Myrdal (1898-) arises from a conflict between practice and principle: our actual treatment of Negro citizens as opposed to the set of egalitarian beliefs, embodied in government and law, which Dr. Myrdal calls the "American creed." The resulting "race problem" is unique, since ours is the only modern industrial society both (1) to have within its borders in important numbers a population of a different color, greatly in need of educational and economic advancement; and (2) to have adopted political and legal tenets long since which make inevitable, though no less arduous, that population's rise to equality of rights and opportunities. The fact that America has been the arena, partly by choice, for conflicts most Western nations have yet to experience is in good part the reason why it "feels itself," as Dr. Myrdal says, "to be humanity in miniature"—and why the "dilemma," though it is "America's greatest failure," is also its "incomparably great opportunity for the future."

Dr. Myrdal's book is the product of a six-year study, financed by Carnegie Corporation, in which nearly 150 people of both races were employed. Because the subject is so charged with emotion, the sponsors of the study had been especially desirous to secure, as director, someone from a foreign country which had high scholarly standards but no history of racial or colonial conflict. After making many inquiries, the Corporation selected Gunnar Myrdal, a Swedish social economist who was then a professor at the University of Stockholm, an economic advisor to the Swedish government, and a member of the Swedish Senate. In the years since *An American Dilemma* was published (1944), he has been executive secretary of the United Nations Economic Commission for Europe, and he is now (1957) making a study of economic development in Southeast Asia.

It is popularly assumed, particularly in the American South, that *An American Dilemma* has played an important part in the progressively favorable treatment of the Negro by courts, notably the Supreme Court in its decision to abolish segregation in the state-supported schools. This drastic change in folkways is resisted by many Southerners, who are therefore highly critical of Dr. Myrdal. The reader who wishes to compare his book to others in this collection might turn to John Dollard's *Caste and Class in a Southern Town* (No. 97), John Hope Franklin's *From Slavery to Freedom* (No. 124), or C. Vann Woodward's *The Strange Career of Jim Crow* (No. 346).

E. L.

231. *America Through British Eyes*

edited by ALLAN NEVINS

It sometimes seems to the citizen of the United States that he lives in the most constantly rediscovered nation in the world. For two centuries visitors have arrived, many of them from England, to look about them—often with astonishment—at the customs and manners of Americans, and to return home to publish their observations. Some of this comment has been extremely perceptive and reliable, though by no means wholly complimentary; some has been amused, affable, and tolerant; some has been snide and some downright malicious and inaccurate.

It has often surprised visitors from abroad how seriously Americans take the comments made about them and how sensitive they seem to be to any sort of criticism. But Americans have been eager to establish themselves as important in the eyes of the rest of the world at the same time that they have not wanted to seem to be subservient to Europe, especially, for their standards of behavior. Culturally young America was a child of Europe, but the nation was engaged in an effort to prove a political experiment that it felt was far superior to any Europe had tried. In recent years Americans have become far less defensive, though many of the same criticisms that are leveled against their manners and customs now are almost precisely those that stung them when Mrs. Frances Trollope in the 1830's or Charles Dickens in the 1840's committed them to paper. Materialism, worship of the dollar, inability to enjoy leisure, these have been (and still are) recurrent themes in the writings of observers of America. But they are by no means the only themes. Ingenuity, inventiveness, hospitality, egalitarianism, and humor are just as recurrent.

America Through British Eyes is a just and entertaining portrait of America, for it looks with all sorts of eyes at all sorts of aspects of the United States. It is, of course, uneven; some of the observers wrote with far greater skill and precision or charm than others. The best known to Americans are Mrs. Trollope, Dickens, and Frederick Marryat; but the reader of today will find persistent truths about America in the excerpts from men like John Bernard, Alexander Mackay, and Lord Tweedsmuir. For other nineteenth-century observations the reader is referred to *Democracy in America* by Alexis de Tocqueville (No. 90), for a recent account to D. W. Brogan's *The American Character* (No. 40), and for reports of various visitors to Oscar Handlin's *This Was America* (No. 135). R. L.

232. *Ford*

The Times, the Man, the Company

by Allan Nevins, *with* Frank E. Hill

There were kings before Agamemnon, as Allan Nevins (1890-) remarks, and there was mass production before Henry Ford. Whichever of its constituent principles you choose—the assembly line, interchangeable parts, repetitive skills, mechanical handling of materials—each had been discovered long before Ford applied it to his epoch-making automobile. Roger Burlingame, in *Backgrounds of Power* (No. 45), gives examples as ancient as the Arsenal of medieval Venice; and John Kouwenhoven, in *Made in America* (No. 175), draws upon early American innovations that neither Ford nor his retrospective ghost writers seem to have heard of. There is some doubt whether Ford himself was actually responsible for the first, true continuously moving assembly line, set up in his own Highland Park plant in 1912-13. Certainly, as Nevins makes amply clear, there were other men in the Ford Motor Company (for example, James Couzens) who were as essential to its success. But always, and throughout, there was Henry Ford: the one man demoniacally possessed by the simple, incredible fantasy—a cheap car for the masses—that set all else in motion.

This rustic tinkerer, who could not (or would not) read a blueprint, created an industry and became unimaginably rich, the "last billionaire." So doing, he permanently reshaped his own society and initiated what has been called the Second Industrial Revolution—the principle of lowering prices and raising wages that has become accepted business doctrine in America but is still anathema in Europe and incomprehensible to most European capitalists. How Ford came to do these things, out of his own background and the existing knowledge of automotive manufacture at the time, is the story that Professor Nevins tells. He takes it, in this volume, up to the peak of Ford's triumph, the creation of the Model T and the adoption of the five-dollar-a-day minimum wage in 1914. Dark days lay ahead, in which Ford was to grow more and more to resemble the unhappy figure caricatured in John Dos Passos's *U.S.A.* (No. 99). For that sad second chapter, in which Ford—like a true hero of tragedy—was destroyed by his own success, the reader must turn to Roger Burlingame's all-too-brief biography (No. 46).

E. L.

233. *55 Short Stories from The New Yorker*

Selected from the stories published in *The New Yorker* during the decade of the 1940's, these tales offer a fair illustration of that remarkable magazine's standards and prepossessions. Almost without exception they are well written, low-toned, rather casually shoulder-shrugging about life, sharp-eyed and contemptuous of the canons of the "well-made" story. They trail off rather than end; but, if one is tempted to make fun of their party-line pattern, one might recollect that it is Chekhov's pattern too. While the characters are in most cases drawn from the big-city gentility, those stories that deal with more highly charged people and situations are often the most effective, and the book is particularly rich in "offbeat" and fantastic stories that carry perfectly the dry sherry tone of *The New Yorker* at its most "new-yorkerish." The generally high quality of the collection is shown by the fact that many stories, anthologized again and again, have achieved a quasi-classic status: "The Enormous Radio," "The Catbird Seat," "Act of Faith," "The Lottery" (see also Nos. 47, 55 and 306).

New Yorker fiction occupies a middle ground between the machine-made entertainments of the big commercial magazines and the somewhat overwrought art of the little noncommercial ones. Reading it in large doses (which is not the way to read short stories) one begins to recognize a certain repeated tonality, despite the seeming variety of theme and background. On the other hand, put to the question, it would be hard for one to name any American periodical which in recent years has published more intelligent, if not always moving, fiction. The authors' names alone are a guarantee of quality and workmanship. Any anthology that includes James Thurber, Irwin Shaw, Hortense Calisher, E. B. White, J. D. Salinger, Mary McCarthy, John O'Hara, Jean Stafford, Oliver and Christopher La Farge, A. J. Liebling, Jessamyn West, Brendan Gill, S. N. Behrman, and Marjorie Kinnan Rawlings is bound to be a show-window of some of the best short fiction written by Americans in our time.

C. F.

234. *The New Yorker Twenty-Fifth Anniversary Album, 1925-1950*

The reader who is not thoroughly familiar with the American scene and with the New York scene in particular will find many, but by no means all, of the cartoons in this album mysterious or entirely meaningless. *The New Yorker* is, and has been since it was first published in 1925, a local weekly magazine for the edification and amusement of New Yorkers, wherever located. Its circulation has become national (and even international), but it is edited with almost militant provincialism for residents of the metropolis. There have been many attempts to imitate it but none has been commercially or editorially successful. It is a magazine of humor, criticism, social comment, fiction (see No. 233), and reportage (which the editors of *The New Yorker* call "fact pieces"). It is published for the presumably urbane and sophisticated reader but not for the highbrow. Its literary contributors are as distinguished a lot of writers as those of any American periodical and its cartoonists, to which this album is devoted, have set a standard of draftsmanship and humor that no other American magazine achieves.

Most of the topical cartoons of the 1920's and 1930's will make better sense to the reader who has explored the pictures and text of Agnes Rogers and Frederick Lewis Allen's *I Remember Distinctly* (No. 263); most of the others are the common coin of humor and fantasy and satire that is negotiable anywhere. In general the *New Yorker* cartoon is not typical of American visual humor, which is broad and often violent; these cartoons are for the most part underplayed and their flavor is rather more literary and verbal than strictly visual. They are in that sense "gag" cartoons that would be meaningless without text. A few of the artists, notably Saul Steinberg (No. 293), George Price, William Steig, and O. Soglow are true visual humorists. A few others are purely literary—James Thurber (No. 306), Mary Petty, Clarence Day (No. 87). Most of the others fall somewhere between, and they provide evidence in their satire of the American's delight in gadgetry, good works, bigness, earnestness, and our own special kinds of flummery. The result is an oblique insight into the contemporary American character and scene.

R. L.

235. *Memoirs of a Superfluous Man*

by Albert Jay Nock

The thing that made Albert Jay Nock (1873-1945) superfluous, he says, was his decision that "economism"—railroads, steel mills, foundries—was not enough. It could build a rich society, one through which there was a wide diffusion of material things, but it could never create "a lovely world, a world of depth and savor and the attraction loveliness wields." Such a lovely world Nock was well equipped to enjoy and adorn. He had a fine mind, well trained and packed, by a stern and thorough education, with an immense amount of information. Besides this he was a man of both perception and taste.

These assets he found he could not employ, with satisfaction to himself and others, in the America of the twentieth century. Unable, as he preferred, to remove himself to the France of 1810-1885, he did the next best thing and, like others of his disenchanted countrymen, he sought the seclusion granted by contemporary Europe. While there he succeeded in detaching himself almost completely from action on the contemporary scene. But he retained a wonderfully acute eye for the current American enterprises and he continued to speculate on the meaning and direction of the modern cultural arrangements. The sum of these speculations he puts down in this book. With urbanity and a sense of irony that in itself puts him beyond the American pale, he broods about what he takes to be our failures in the arts, in education, in the relations between men and women, in our social arrangements, and in the state itself. There is much in what he says in this delightful book on which we may also brood.

Nock is of the company of Shaw and Butler and Swift and Voltaire; but he is on the fringes of this circle, sharing with them the turn of mind but not their rather hard-bitten self-assurance. There is in fact more of wistfulness than anything else in his title. Like others in our history who have sought his solution, he was never quite clear whether he had abdicated or been thrown out. So he never could quite believe that reflections such as his are always indispensable for the health of an unreflective society.

E. E. M.

236. *McTeague*

by FRANK NORRIS

At one time Frank Norris (1870-1902) was regarded as the great emancipator of American fiction, the writer who freed our novel from the narrow limitations of gentility so that it could deal with the raw experience of American life. Now, on the contrary, his work strikes many readers as excessively literary, in the unfavorable sense that it is highly derivative from other novelists (the French naturalists) and marred by rather flimsy journalistic writing and theatrics. Even the "raw experience" which once seemed so fresh and vigorous is at least in part derivative; for instance, Norris's use of miserliness as a central motif in *McTeague* probably owes more to French fiction than to American life.

But essentially both views of Norris are correct: he was both an imitator and a pioneer. In introducing French naturalism to America he (along with certain contemporaries) established an attitude in American fiction which to this day continues to be widely held among writers and widely admired by the popular audience for fiction. In some quarters it is even still regarded as new and daring. It is an attitude which exalts subject matter over art and regards life as more real the closer man comes to the level of the brute.

Naturalism has had a great appeal in America because it enables the writer and his reader to conform to the ideal of manliness evolved by the social and industrial frontier, but it has often been destructive of talent because it has denied the writer the right to use his own most vital experience; it has made him assume a tough swagger that has not often been really his. The split between writer and subject is already apparent in Norris. He came of a prosperous and cultivated family who wanted him to become a painter; he seems to have been the first important American novelist who took college courses in writing to learn how to be a novelist. In short, his approach to his work was self-conscious and academic; he wrote as an outsider, a reporter, and he (along with Stephen Crane [No. 75] and others) established the connection between the newspapers and the novel which is still a marked characteristic of much American fiction.

P. P.

237. *Appointment in Samarra*

by JOHN O'HARA

John O'Hara (1905-) has made himself a student of the sordid and the unattractive in our society. He has concerned himself with the fortunes of night-club singers who think of women as "mice"; he has analyzed the dry rot that eats away at the oldest pillars of society in middle-sized Pennsylvania towns; he has peered at the sleazy doings of the fairly rich along the Long Island coast. From his descriptions of these phenomena he has drained away all grace and any sense of shock or even distaste. He appears to report in dry, clinical prose precisely what he has seen with his searching eye and heard with an ear that is unerring.

The results are not always happy. Sometimes his little pieces seem meaningless, as unrewarding as snatches of conversation at a public bar. Sometimes his larger novels fall apart into the little pieces from which they have been put together. This is not the case with *Appointment in Samarra,* which has both shape and point. It is a dreary enough tale. Julian English is a wealthy young man who drinks too much. With little to do he quarrels incessantly but without much obvious provocation with his wife, his friends, and any casual person accident brings in his way. Appalled after one great public brawl, he takes his own life. This sombre anecdote is set forth with all the detachment and economy of means O'Hara has learned to employ so skillfully.

But in this instance he has managed to invest this particular episode with general implications. Julian English is a decent young man deprived by a peculiar set of conditions—wealth, upbringing, the spirit of the times—from discovering any direction or purpose in life, either the life around him or his own. In these circumstances he could pass the time only by seeking sensation and could establish the relationship with his surroundings that all individuals must try to make only by threats of violence against others. Since this is an unsatisfying solution, it brought him finally to the act of violence against himself.

Because Julian English was one of a considerable company of young men who, in their time and place, came home from college without finding much to do but wear away the day in pointless action, his particular calamity lingers in the memory. It is probable that John O'Hara would find it as distasteful to be accused of pointing a moral as of unnecessarily adorning a tale, but there was, in 1934, at least an object lesson submerged in this book and it may still be there.

E. E. M.

238. *Nine Plays*

by EUGENE O'NEILL

Almost since the beginning of his career in 1914, Eugene O'Neill (1888-1953) has been the most impressive personality in the American theater. It is often said, and with sufficient justice, that he alone is responsible for the development of an American drama of true seriousness and sincerity.

O'Neill was born to the theater. His father, James O'Neill, a Shakespearean actor of genuine gifts, was best known for his role as the hero of *The Count of Monte Cristo,* which he played for many years. And however far the son advanced beyond the intellectual content of the old stage, he never lost touch with its primitive effectiveness; the force of his best plays owes much to his feeling for bold theatricality and melodrama.

After spending a year at Princeton University, O'Neill lived a random and adventurous life which included prospecting for gold in Honduras and shipping as a fo'c'sle hand on cargo boats. In 1912 his health broke down and he turned to writing. He spent a year at the famous "47 Workshop" of Professor George Pierce Baker of Harvard University, where he learned something of the craft of the playwright, and then became associated with the Provincetown Players, one of the first, and probably the most important, of the new little theater groups. In 1920 *Beyond the Horizon* (No. 253) won the Pulitzer Prize, and his reputation was established as the leading playwright of America. His fame spread to Europe, where it became perhaps even greater than in America, and in 1936 he was awarded the Nobel Prize.

The early critical view of O'Neill held him to be a writer of great emotional power but of no ideas. But O'Neill himself has said—Joseph Wood Krutch quotes the remark in the introduction to the present volume—that he was not at all interested in the relation between man and man but only in "the relation between man and God," and that may serve as the beginning of our understanding that from his earliest days O'Neill was preoccupied by speculation about man's fate in a seemingly hostile universe. He is not a "philosopher," his thought is often naive, the language in which he expresses it is almost always awkward and heavy. But the persistence of his concern with the problem of man's loneliness and pain accounts for much of the genuine power of his work.

L. T.

239. *Anything Can Happen*

by George Papashvily *and* Helen Waite Papashvily

America being what it is, a country to which people come, it is natural for us to have developed a special subsection of literature: the literature of Americanization. Most of the notable books of this order are today unreadable. They were written by good, earnest, intelligent immigrants who just didn't happen to be natural writers. But George Papashvily (1898-) is a natural writer and a natural humorist. His book is short, minor, unimposing, and delightful. What gives it quality is not the wonder and greatness of the land Giorgi, an emigrant from Russian Georgia, discovered; but Giorgi himself, generous-hearted, ebullient, sly-humored, philosophical, and clamorously patriotic.

Giorgi Papashvily was a sword-maker by trade. The demand for swords was not as great here as it was in his wild and beautiful native land, but Giorgi was the kind to get along regardless. This book is the record, told in an amusing, slightly fractured English, of his love affair with our country, of his fantastic adventures as dishwasher, garage mechanic, kitchen aid, tourist, inventor, and farmer. Everywhere he seems to have run into Georgians as well as Americans; and everywhere he carried with him his bright humor, his Georgian energy, his love of food and fun and jokes, and a curious, moving tenderness of heart.

The Easter Day beach party which ends the book sums things up nicely. Giorgi's friend Challico proposes a toast to Home: "Lotsa other kinds of people we are here, too. Georgians, Russians, Greek, Latvian, Irish—regular League a Nations. I drink for all those Homes too, and it gives me hope when I see us sitting so peaceful together, maybe whole world gonna learn how to do it, too. After all it's only enjoyable way for to live. So—for Home." To which Giorgi replies: "I drink with pleasure. For Home. Its floor is the earth; its roof is the sky."

C. F.

240. *The Oregon Trail*

by FRANCIS PARKMAN

Over a century ago Francis Parkman (1823-93) set out for the wild Indian country of the Pawnees and Sioux. Leaving St. Louis in April, 1846, Parkman and his cousin went by boat to Westport (the present Kansas City, Missouri), where they obtained an experienced "mountain man" as guide. Proceeding in a northwesterly direction, they reached the Platte River and journeyed upstream in two months' time to Fort Laramie, on the eastern edge of what is now the state of Wyoming. Parkman had come "into the country chiefly with the view of observing Indian character," and the main part of *The Oregon Trail* is concerned with his experiences among the Indians near Fort Laramie. As Mark Van Doren points out in his introduction, Parkman followed his purpose of living among the Sioux (whom he called Dakotas) and becoming, "as it were, one of them." Not only did he join a village, he shared their quarrels and their feasts of dog meat; he tramped, rode, and hunted buffalo with them; and he even prepared to join them in a war of retaliation.

Throughout his six months' trip he kept a journal of his experiences. Poor eyesight troubled him on his return, but he dictated an account which retains both the authenticity of his notebooks and the lively quality of a firsthand narration. The resulting book, Parkman's first, which has been reprinted continually for over a century, is one of the best reports of American expansion in the eventful year of 1846. It is often pointed out that he missed much of the import of the "year of decision," the significance of which is vividly explored by Bernard DeVoto (No. 93). Nevertheless Parkman, who later emerged as a great historian (see No. 241), was aware "that a time would come when those plains would be a grazing country, the buffalo give place to tame cattle, farm houses be scattered along the watercourses, and wolves, bears and Indians be numbered among the things that were."

While enriching American literature with the most lifelike Indians it was to know for many years to come and thus supplanting the romantic concept of the Noble Savage (see James Fenimore Cooper's *Leatherstocking Saga* [No. 67]), Parkman also gives us glimpses of the westward movement and the trailblazers who opened a continental empire in those early and exciting years. *The Oregon Trail* is above all a great tale of adventure told freshly, sensitively, and with a vigor that re-creates this segment of the American past.

C. G.

241. *The Parkman Reader*

edited by SAMUEL ELIOT MORISON

One of the great pageants of our history—indeed, of all history—is the exploration and conquest of the northern and western parts of this continent. It is a pageant of vivid contrasts and magnificent proportions reaching from the unknown, untenanted wilderness to the sophistications of the court in Paris. In the development of this great domain most of the motives, most of the physical and intellectual skills, most of the aspirations, and all the endurance human beings possess were called into play.

The pre-eminent recorder of this great pageant was Francis Parkman (1823-93). He read the available documents; he followed the *coureur de bois* through the forests and down the watercourses; 200 years after the event he imagined himself with all the others in New France. The result, as his editor says, is that the murmur of the forests is in his prose. Also there is the bravery, the sordidness, the vision and the heartbreak on which empires are built. And also something more. Parkman is one of the few historians who can directly communicate a sense of space and also, in somewhat lesser degree, of time. These factors of time and space are two of the principal elements at work in the evolution of this imperial venture, and Parkman conveys their workings with consummate skill.

The whole account is set forth on a scale commensurate with the achievement it describes. From its multitudinous volumes Samuel Eliot Morison has selected material for this single book. He has sensibly taken pieces that are, in themselves, self-contained episodes, and he has had the wisdom to choose things which taken together will reveal the history of New France in its full range. Finally, in prose that rivals that of his author, the editor has supplied in his introduction an affectionate glimpse of Francis Parkman (see also No. 240).

E. E. M.

242. *The Colonial Mind, 1620-1800*

by Vernon Louis Parrington

The colonial mind was a loose federation of ideas and attitudes brought together in America in the early days. Some of these ideas were obtained at second hand—brought from England or borrowed from the Continent —and some were devised on this soil to meet local or novel contingencies. It is with the collision, interaction, and modification of these ideas and attitudes over a century and a half that Vernon L. Parrington (1871-1929) was primarily concerned.

This is the first volume (1927) of three that Professor Parrington devoted to tracing what he called the "main currents of American thought" from the beginning to the twentieth century. Much of his evidence he obtained from poems, songs, and such fiction as was written in the first days. But, profoundly influenced by the French critic Taine, he was anxious to liberate the history of literature from the confinement of purely aesthetic judgments. Thus he drew evidence for his narrative from contemporary philosophy, political and economic theory, sermons, newspapers and broadsides. The result of his tireless investigation appears, in these pages, as a kind of relief map of the intellectual terrain of the colonies and the Republic in its first decade.

It is a map drawn to the author's own scale. He had strong views on what was high and what was low and what was inconsequential. For instance, as a son of the middle border in Kansas, Parrington finds both Puritans and Puritan theology unattractive. He watches Alexander Hamilton with suspicion and Thomas Jefferson with admiration (see also No. 14). In the recurring conflicts of the colonial period one finds him always supporting free thought against doctrine, the individual against constituted authority, the rights of man against the rights of property. He was, in his own word, a liberal, and his liberal interpretation of our early history is an impressive achievement. There is a great deal of information here, set forth in rather stately prose. Above all, there is a passionate explanation of that Jeffersonian scheme of things which has contributed so much to our history.

E. E. M.

243. *Genesis of a Music*

by Harry Partch

Anyone with but a listener's interest in music can read, without difficulty and with much profit, the first 63 pages of this book. What he will find there is an original view of the classical and modern music he knows, coupled with the intimations of a wholly new genre which has already produced some remarkable works. The remainder of the book is for technicians from a variety of disciplines—the physics of sound, the theory of music, instrument making, and composition. The author, who is also the composer of the remarkable works referred to, combines in himself the knowledge of the remaining subjects, to which he adds an uncommon familiarity with the literature and history of the musical art.

His innovation as a musician is, in brief, to make music on a new scale of 43 degrees. It is a scale of just, not tempered, intervals; its divisions are "natural" in that they are dictated by the overtone series; and its great flexibility means that it is in closer rapport than any other system with the inflections of the human voice. For these reasons its creator considers it a fusion of science and humanism par excellence. To the skepticism with which any large departure from venerated means is bound to be greeted, Harry Partch (1901-) offers the comforting answer that he will accept nothing as proof of his ideas except musical works that shall persuade by themselves. And such works, according to a growing body of appreciators, Mr. Partch has produced, notably his "Babylon," "Barstow," "U.S. Highball," and his latest, the full-sized drama, *Oedipus*.

In other words, one need not agree with the composer's division of music into Abstract and Corporeal, or with his animus against the massive expressions of classical music, to enjoy his Monophonic, which is to say, individualistic, muse. Musical originality has spontaneously appeared in the United States before, as with Charles Ives (No. 71), and need be no cause for dismay. One must see Mr. Partch's work as a vigorous attempt to escape from the impasse of the major-minor mode plus enharmony, and at the same time to resist the mechanical influences that threaten to sterilize the modern artist. What he has to say about Paul Hindemith, Arnold Schoenberg, Henry Cowell, and jazz will interest students of twentieth-century music while disclosing his unique and provocative position as theorist and composer.

J. B.

244. *Philosophical Writings of Peirce*

edited by JUSTUS BUCHLER

Charles Sanders Peirce (1839-1914) has always been a difficult philosopher, mostly because his profoundly original ideas were unsystematically expressed in scattered essays. Professor Buchler has done an admirable job of piecing together the essential ideas, so as to make Peirce accessible to the general reader. While the layman may have been unaware that Peirce existed, the professional scholars of the United States and Europe have been slowly building his reputation to something like its just proportions. Pragmatism, usually thought of as the typical "American" philosophy, was developed by William James (Nos. 163-4), John Dewey (No. 94), and others, and they gave credit to Peirce for the name as well as for the original ideas. Pragmatism as they taught it, however, was part of a later-nineteenth-century trend toward anti-intellectualism, and Peirce's disciples were in fact distorting his classical position. Peirce bequeathed the word "pragmatism" to James, renaming his own doctrine Pragmaticism, which he thought might be a term "ugly enough to be safe from kidnappers."

The usual criticism aimed at the Pragmatists is that they had no standards for truth other than practical material results. Whether or not this is true of James and Dewey can be decided by studying their works. It misses Peirce. The principle of Pragmaticism is to determine the *meaning* of a statement by its consequences; Peirce did not believe that he was offering a new method for testing truth. James seemed—to some of those who listened to his popular lectures and read his brilliantly persuasive books—to think that truth could be coerced by the Will-to-Believe and tested by personal usefulness. On this Peirce remarked, "What is utility if it is confined to a single person? Truth is public."

There was, however, a generous friendship between the two men. Peirce knew that James would be listened to, while he would have to wait, as indeed he has had to do, for half a century. Of James he wrote, "Who, for example, could be of a nature so different from him as I? He is so concrete, so living: I a mere table of contents, so abstract, a very snarl of twine." With Professor Buchler's help we can unsnarl a little of that precious twine and get some notion of the reasons for thinking Peirce one of the greatest of American philosophers.

L. B.

245. *Lanterns on the Levee*

by William Alexander Percy

"In the South our anxiety is not to find new ideas, but to bring to realization old ones which have been proved by years of anguish—a far more difficult undertaking." That, "in the South" omitted, is the creed of the conservative anywhere. But in the South anxiety, and the word is carefully chosen, has a peculiar quality. It is the heritage of what was called by earlier Southerners the "peculiar institution"—slavery. Booker T. Washington said in his autobiography (No. 320): "I pity from the bottom of my heart any nation or body of people that is so unfortunate as to get entangled in the net of slavery." Slavery, the peculiar institution, was abolished by legal fiat, but the net remains and all are entangled in it, every Southerner. There has been an easing here and there; words have changed, and descendants of the master who owned a slave now hire a hand, who has the privilege of moving from one part of the net to another. "Cook," once a slave word, now means Thursdays off, or any other time.

The Northerners—"Yankees" down South—having set the Negro not free but adrift, returned to their enjoyment of unqualified freedom. So they thought; but they were, and are, in the net too. At first, when the cords began to pinch, they blamed the butt-headed prejudiced Southern whites. Then, being men of good will, and also up-to-date, they sought unbiased opinion from scholars. One, William Alexander Percy's (1885-1942) "learned gentleman from Yale," found out painfully that even he was biased, in the net, and had the pluck to say so (see No. 97).

Not that *Lanterns on the Levee* is all about the net. It is about a kind of man and a kind of life that will not be again. It is about a poet at school, in college, in war; about people, all sorts; about managing a plantation, and about "Fode." Percy's experience was not "given convulsive life by his emotions," as Malcolm Cowley says of William Faulkner's (No. 108). He is spiritually closer kin to Eudora Welty, another neighbor (No. 324). The three, and one of them winner of a Nobel Prize, were born and reared in Mississippi, statistically the most illiterate state in the Union.

J. A. R.

246. *The Thought and Character of William James*

by Ralph Barton Perry

For understanding the genesis of James's thought (see Nos. 163-4) and enjoying the lively play of his mind and pen, this abridged intellectual biography is recommended. The original is a two-volume work of 1,600 pages, published in 1935 and reduced by its author, Ralph Barton Perry (1876-1957), to the present compass in 1942.

Though born in New York City, William James (1842-1910) belonged to that New England intellectual society which throughout the nineteenth century was the principal gateway into the United States for world currents of thought. The James family traveled widely and frequently in Europe, and from an early age the brothers William and Henry (Nos. 159-61) were trilingual—French, German, and English thought were at their command. William's preparation for philosophy was through the study of literature, painting, pure science, medicine, and psychology. His work in the last marked an epoch in the science and endowed American literature with a masterpiece, the two-volume *Principles,* published in 1890.

All his life, as the present book shows, James was in intimate correspondence with the leading European philosophers, from Bradley, Mach, and Lotze to Renouvier, Bergson, and Papini. Whether they were philosophical allies or enemies, he won their esteem and affection and became what Whitehead was later to call him, "that adorable genius, William James."

J. B.

247. *Wild America*

by Roger Tory Peterson *and* James Fisher

In April, 1953, Roger Tory Peterson (1908-), American ornithologist, author, and artist, met his British friend James Fisher (1912-), a naturalist and an authority on sea birds, in Newfoundland. Their rendezvous was the beginning of a strenuous 100-day, 30,000-mile field trip, a naturalist's grand tour of the North American continent. By plane and by automobile, the two men journeyed down the east coast to the Florida Keys and the Dry Tortugas, across the Gulf States to Mexico, thence to the Grand Canyon, the Salton Sea, and the Coronado Islands, and up the Pacific coast as far as the seal islands of the Bering Sea.

For both men their pilgrimage proved exhilarating. Between them, they observed some 600 different species of avifauna, many of them rarities. But their wandering on the perimeter of North America gave them more than an opportunity to immerse themselves in their favorite studies. To the European, it was a journey of exploration and of wonder. To the American it was a rediscovery of his own country. To both, it was an emphatic affirmation of the "spiritual necessity of wilderness values," a necessity that Americans have recognized by setting aside 21,000,000 acres administered by the National Park Service. It was certain of these acres—the National Parks, the Fish and Wildlife Refuges, the National Nature Monuments, the Audubon Bird Sanctuaries, all revealing the beauty and immensity of the country—that the Englishman found astonishing and overwhelming. "We would give our souls to have some of them on our side of the Atlantic," he says. "You cannot realize until you are as crowded as we are how important wilderness values are."

Here, in *Wild America,* is an image of the nation not generally exported in movies and reading material, an image that has nothing to do with big business, production know-how, or high-pressure economy. (For some earlier efforts to sustain this image, see the books of John Muir and Henry David Thoreau [Nos. 1 and 305].) It is earnestly to be hoped that the non-American reader, when he reaches the close of this narrative, will find it difficult to disagree with James Fisher's retrospective view of Americans: "They show us too little of their earthly paradise, and publicize too little their determination to share it with wild nature. Never have I seen such wonders or met landlords so worthy of their land. They have had, and still have, the power to ravage it; and instead have made it a garden."

C. C.

248. *The Complete Tales and Poems of Edgar Allan Poe*

The place of Edgar Allan Poe (1809-1849) in the pantheon of American letters is secure but uncertain. In the formal histories of literature Poe is always taken to be a figure of the first importance. And there can be no doubt that his stories and poems are part of the early literary experience of every American, and not merely by school prescription. Yet few Americans, when they reach maturity, are inclined to read Poe with pleasure or any sense of personal involvement. They are likely to be amazed and amused by the high admiration in which the French have held him ever since he came into their ken: in France he is established as one of the great seminal figures of modern literature. The American reader, while willing to concede the genius of the man and the daring of the genius, is probably more aware of Poe's faults than of his achievements, and is put off by the strain of provincialism and pretentiousness in Poe's criticism, by an element of what some critics have not hesitated to call vulgarity in his verse and prose fiction.

But it is possible to admit Poe's faults to the full and yet to understand his unique achievement. Perhaps no one has done this with such subtle discrimination as D. H. Lawrence in the essay on Poe which makes one of the finest chapters of his *Studies in Classic American Literature* (in No. 337). Lawrence could mock Poe's mechanical elaborations of style and yet perceive that the stories go very deep in what they imply of the excesses and deficiencies of the modern consciousness. The horror that is characteristic of Poe's stories is not gratuitous; it is not contrived to the end of mere sensationalism. It is appropriate to what the stories deal with, the extravagances of the soul—its destructiveness and self-destructiveness, its arrogant search for knowledge of what cannot be known, its cruelty that springs from loneliness and self-hatred, the willed completeness of its isolation.

L. T.

249. *Flowering Judas and Other Stories*

by KATHERINE ANNE PORTER

Katherine Anne Porter (1894-) occupies a position all her own among contemporary American short-story writers, yet it is not easy to say where her uniqueness lies. She is identified with the Southern literary renaissance, but a large part of her work is not set in the South. She is, in fact, a very cosmopolitan writer who has spent many years not only outside the South but also outside the United States, in Europe and Mexico, though her roots go back to the section of Texas dominated by Southern manners. And before her special quality is ascribed to her Southern origin, it must be remembered that several of Miss Porter's most distinguished contemporaries in the field of the short story are also from the South—William Faulkner (No. 108), Eudora Welty (No. 324) and many less well known.

Again it might be thought that Miss Porter's contribution to the short story has been her utter freedom from formulas, from conventional ideas about plot and character. But in fact she has been only one of a number of writers who have refreshed the short-story form by disburdening it of received ideas about what it should be, though few have been as scrupulous as she in seeing that each story has its own structure, suited to its own needs. Still again, Miss Porter's interest in the psychic borders of life, in behavior just beyond the edge of reason's control, might be considered her peculiar merit, if it were not for the fact that this interest is shared by many contemporary writers of fiction.

Perhaps the best way to discover what is unusual about Miss Porter is to read one of her stories. "He" is the best to start with. It is set in the South, the South of the tenant farmer, but it might be set in any place where people are poor and love their children and are subject to disaster. It is simple in structure, covering the years swiftly but catching their spirit in a few wonderfully telling scenes. The characteristic interest in the psychic border appears in the mother's concern for her feeble-minded son, who seems to be beyond the reach of human love but in the final heartbreaking moment reveals that he is not. "He" shows why Miss Porter is entitled to her high position among American short-story writers.

P. P.

250. *Theodore Roosevelt*

by HENRY F. PRINGLE

There are so many different Theodore Roosevelts (1858-1919) that it is difficult, perhaps impossible, to bring them all within the pages of one book. There is the historian who wrote one of the enduring studies of our early western history; there is the explorer who followed the course of the River of Doubt; there is the naturalist who produced a minor classic on western deer; there is the ranchman raising cows in the Bad Lands of Dakota Territory. There is the ornithologist, the literary critic, the soldier, the essayist, the lay preacher, and the small boy (see also No. 265).

Not long ago it appeared possible that some of these Roosevelts would be remembered longer than the President of the United States (1901-1909). There was a feeling abroad that although Theodore Roosevelt had said a great deal and called a great many people by unpleasant names and had laid claim to a great number of accomplishments, he had not, in fact, done very much as the Chief Executive. In recent days this view has changed. It can now be seen that he was the first President to deal imaginatively with what may be called the modern conditions of our national life. He defined, as no President before him had done, the implications of the industrial developments of the time and he did what he could to contain the thrusts of industrial energy that were shaking our society. He also did all in his power to bring the country out of its insular position and into the community of nations.

Henry F. Pringle (1897-) has put most of the cast of Roosevelt characters into his book. For 200 pages he writes one of the most illuminating and engaging biographies that have ever been written in this country. But when he takes leave of the cowboy, the Police Commissioner, and the Rough Rider to deal with the President his instinct for the diverting detail betrays him from time to time. He cannot quite go to the trouble to follow carefully and in detail the serious business that was going forward. Thus Roosevelt does not grow as large in this book as he actually did in office. Nonetheless Mr. Pringle has provided the most engaging and instructive account of the work of Theodore Roosevelt, in and out of office, that is now available.

E. E. M.

251. *Prize Articles 1954*

edited by LLEWELLYN MILLER

The American magazine article is an instrument of many uses. It can serve, like the first entry in this volume, to encourage community self-improvement. It can enlighten and educate, like the last entry. It can convey the opinions that one waits to hear from a returning world-traveler, like the twice unsuccessful but much respected Democratic candidate for the Presidency, Adlai E. Stevenson. It can penetrate the privacy of a famous person, such as William Faulkner (see also No. 108), in embarrassing depth and detail. It can, in the hands of a skilled professional like William H. Whyte, Jr. (see also No. 120), become the medium of stinging moral and social criticism. In the hands of a master journalist, such as John Bartlow Martin, it can employ the bald rehearsal of fact to move the reader, profoundly and emotionally, on a subject of acute and general public interest.

Great American magazines—like *The New Yorker* (see Nos. 233-4), *Life* (see No. 19), or the *Saturday Evening Post* (see No. 278)—have personalities that partly color whatever they do, so that no anthology from a single publication can fairly represent them all. In 1954, however, the Benjamin Franklin Awards were created in the effort to establish for magazine journalism an equivalent of what the Pulitzer Prize has come to mean in newspaper journalism; and this is the first annual volume of its winning articles. They manage to cover the field without unduly glorifying what is at best an ephemeral art, and also to offer a representative sample of the reading matter Americans might expect to find in their periodicals at a given moment during the 1950's. The problem of developing underdeveloped areas, or of the privileged American abroad, for example, cannot be fully perceived apart from the violent self-criticism implicit in Ray Bradbury's short story, "Sun and Shadow."

E. L.

252. *From Immigrant to Inventor*

by MICHAEL PUPIN

The career of Michael Pupin (1858-1935) must have seemed a reassuring omen for the times, in the early 1920's, when his earnest and cheerful autobiography first was published. From a Serbian immigrant boy, with five cents in his pocket, he had risen to be a distinguished scientist and inventor—an eloquent witness to the American success story. Even if Professor Pupin had not sought out this role, by the manner in which he wrote, readers would nonetheless have attributed to his book much of their own self-satisfaction in belonging to so open and rewarding a society. Today it is less easy to regard him in the relatively naive frame of reference in which he regarded himself, and *From Immigrant to Inventor* has a slightly different interest for our times than for its author's.

For the day came when Pupin felt qualified to take a step beyond becoming an American, "to apply for citizenship in that great state called science." The driving ambition that carried him through long hours of labor and study was also a drive toward knowledge; and the qualities in him that sociologists would now call "upward mobile"—and that enabled him to slough off provincial mannerisms—were also those of a willing and plastic mind. Pupin took nearly everything at face value (note his reference to that "ideal type of a genuine American," Warren G. Harding) and wealth and station never lost their fascination for him. But it is one of the charms of his book—as it reputedly was of the halcyon prewar period in which he flourished—that rising in the world of men and rising in one's knowledge of the natural world should have seemed so completely blurred together in Pupin's mind. Though his inventions have turned out to be less memorable than those of his magnificent pupil, Edwin H. Armstrong, Pupin's evocative description of how and why he made himself into a full-fledged scientist is what the contemporary reader of *From Immigrant to Inventor* is most likely to admire.

E. L.

253. *Representative American Plays*

From 1767 to the Present Day

edited by ARTHUR HOBSON QUINN

Professor Quinn's collection, equipped with scholarly notes, lists of *dramatis personae,* and bibliographies, is standard in its slightly musty field. It would be foolish to argue that every one of these plays, until we come to our own day, is pleasurably readable, except for the historian, the scholar, and the antiquary. But as a concrete record of "the development of our native drama from its beginning to the present day" it has high value; and there is a certain nostalgic satisfaction in savoring the quaintness of the older plays.

Professor Quinn's opening selection is Thomas Godfrey's bit of fake-Shakespearean bombast, "The Prince of Parthia," produced in 1767, the first play written by an American to be performed on this continent by professional actors. His concluding play is "South Pacific" (1949), a far cry from "The Prince of Parthia." In between are 29 plays, fifteen from the nineteenth century, fourteen from our own. Included are such interesting curiosities as "Charles the Second," written by Washington Irving in collaboration with John Howard Payne; Joseph Jefferson's famous acting version of "Rip Van Winkle"; William Gillette's "Secret Service"; the Belasco-Long "Madame Butterfly"; and Dion Boucicault's "The Octoroon" (1859), successful in its day with its portrayal of a conflict and a problem that have persisted to our own time. The pre-moderns—Clyde Fitch, Langdon Mitchell, Augustus Thomas, William Vaughan Moody, Percy Mackaye, and Edward Sheldon—supply characteristic samples of their best work. Of the moderns, along with Richard Rodgers and Oscar Hammerstein II, the creators of "South Pacific," Rachel Crothers, Eugene O'Neill, Lulu Vollmer, Sidney Howard, Philip Barry, Maxwell Anderson, and William Wister Haines ("Command Decision," 1947) are represented: a selection that leans a bit to the arbitrary in one or two cases.

Even more than novels, the reading of plays allows us to sense the change and development of the national idiom. Except for the blank-verse dramas, each of these specimens is written in a prose more or less reflecting the tone of conversation of its day—so that one can trace the fascinating evolution of actable speech over the past 150 years.

C. F.

254. *I Came Out of the Eighteenth Century*

by JOHN ANDREW RICE

Somewhere in this absorbing autobiography, Mr. Rice (1888-) says that all conversation in the South is personal, that to a Southerner ideas come "wrapped up in people." Perhaps the reason is that, as he also says, Southern society is matriarchal. At any rate, the statement suggests a good deal of the flavor of his book. For this account of a Southerner's childhood and education is a conversational book, and very personal; and though it deals trenchantly with ideas, it never deals with them abstractly—as though they could be disembodied (which they can't)—but always "wrapped up in people."

And what wonderful people they are! Uncle Ellie, known to the voters as "Cotton Ed" Smith, who "might have been a great man, if he had only repudiated something," but became instead a U. S. Senator by flattering and cajoling those whom he despised. Uncle Coke, the "glandular Christian," and his wife Aunt Kate, who had no respect for the church but made the best of her husband's being a bishop and, while he was being good, saw to it "that goodness did not go unrewarded." Sawney and John Webb, the brothers whose unconventional school in Bell Buckle, Tennessee, turned out more Rhodes scholars than any other in the land. The book is full of portraits, some mere sketches, others rich in detail, all incisive and compassionate.

But the book is not "about" these people. It is about the "old South"—not only the technicolor South of *Gone With the Wind* (No. 219) but the puritan South which seldom gets into novels or movies—among whose decaying remnants Mr. Rice was brought up. It is about the conflicts between the eighteenth-century values of that South and those of the "new" South. It is about freedom, equality, violence, and love. The people one comes to know in its pages, the decaying gentry, the poor white trash, the plantation Negroes and the city Negroes, the ministers, politicians, teachers, and townfolk, are the living tissue of the political, economic, and social problems discussed in such books as W. J. Cash's *The Mind of the South* (No. 51), John Dollard's *Caste and Class in a Southern Town* (No. 97), and C. Vann Woodward's *The Strange Career of Jim Crow* (No. 346).

But it would be a mistake to think of Mr. Rice's book as a substitute for a sociological field trip. That would be to miss its individual savor—a savor which can be suggested, perhaps, by saying that it is written as Swift might have written had he had the gift of loving those whom he had reason to despise.

J. A. K.

255. *American Romantic Painting*

by Edgar P. Richardson

Although Edgar P. Richardson (1902-) as an accomplished museum director of catholic tastes, believes that "periods exist only in books" and so refuses to tell us what he means by "Romantic," his brief essay is a sufficient introduction to his large subject. The painters of America during the first half of the nineteenth century were vivified by the charged atmosphere which made that period one of the most varied and productive in Western art and thought.

In the United States, pictorial Romanticism had rich opportunities for the pursuit of its chief interests and the exercise of its chief virtues. The concern with man and nature, the imagination of grandeur and despair, found free room in the wild vistas and trackless wastes, and fit subjects in the primitive or modern wanderers over these fresh scenes. Thought was never far behind observation, and at its best it gave unforgettable images of aspiration, melancholy, and factuality. Where all was strange and new, technical prowess could also justify itself, and the innovations in color of Washington Allston, or those in form of Thomas Eakins, retain their value even if they were ignored by public and professionals alike.

The illustrations in this book are all black and white, but they are often evocative enough to arouse an abiding interest in the work of a galaxy of admirable painters.

J. B.

256. *Painting in America*

by Edgar P. Richardson

The earliest visual records of America were not, as one would now hope, accurate statements of observed fact, but romantic impressions stated in currently fashionable European styles. It was the New World as the European wanted to imagine it rather than an unexplored continent as its discoverers found it. The development of painting in America for several centuries was the distant echo of European painting, whose stylistic changes reached the American shores (mostly as engravings) and traveled inland; nearly always they were considerably altered by the voyage. Not until the late eighteenth century did American artists travel to Europe and absorb at first hand, and contribute to, the current styles of Italy and England (as James T. Flexner has described in his *American Painting* [No. 115]). The American tradition of direct and simple visual statement, developed largely in portraiture, was overlaid, on the return of the American artists from abroad, by a "grand manner" primarily concerned with romantic interpretation of historical subjects. It was not until the first quarter of the nineteenth century that a sophisticated American landscape and genre art developed. It retained the best of the unsentimental directness of statement of the folk (or vernacular) painters coupled with far more expert techniques of composition and brushwork.

Edgar P. Richardson (1902-) traces in great detail the development of painting from its very first interpretations of America to the art of today, relating it continuously to parallel developments in Europe. He has provided brief biographical sketches of the most important artists and has reproduced works of a great many of America's best known painters. This is an extremely methodical, carefully and clearly organized, somewhat encyclopedic history of painting in America; and it has an excellent bibliography. Some of the illustrations have unfortunately been cropped without indication that they have been, and so are misleading. For a more sympathetic treatment of painting since 1900 the reader is referred to John I. H. Baur's *New Art in America* (No. 23), and for a more general study of the American arts to *Art and Life in America* by Oliver Larkin (No. 180).

R. L.

257. *The Trees*

by CONRAD RICHTER

The American westward trek began toward the close of the eighteenth century, when early pioneers made their way into the trackless forests of the old Northwest Territory—the land west of the Allegheny Mountains, today the southeastern section of Ohio. These migrants and their battle against the opposing sea of trees take on epic proportions in *The Trees,* published in 1940. Though it stands alone, this was the first book of a trilogy, tracing the growth of a pioneer settlement through the story of Sayward Luckett, who came to the forest from Pennsylvania with her family as a young girl and lived to see the lonely clearing evolve into a farming community (in *The Fields*) and thence into a thriving city (in *The Town*).

The Trees is an accurate literary restoration—in terms of atmosphere, character, incident, and language—of the frontier way of life. The forest itself is the central character, its elemental force surrounding and saturating every activity of the settlers. The people of the story—some of whom choose to live by the forest, others to subdue it—include the brave as well as the weak. All are driven by inarticulate dreams and passions, and a few like Sayward possess heroic strengths of flesh, spirit, and vision.

With unobtrusive scholarship, Conrad Richter portrays the life of frontier families, describing their houses, food, clothing, tools; their rude attempts at doctoring; their songs and children's games; their marriage customs; their relationships to Indians, fur traders, and one another. The special flavor of the book, however, is discovered in its style, at once poetic and colloquial. It is based on the simple, pungent language of the people of the time, "approximating," the author says, "the stores of early living speech compiled . . . from books, letters, and personal records of colonial days." It is a speech vivid in imagery, resembling that of mountain people in the American South today who have retained a vernacular once generally spoken. With this spare, lyric language, Conrad Richter has fused the forest and its mood with the struggles of early American pioneers against nature, man, and beast.

C. C.

258. *Individualism Reconsidered and Other Essays*

by David Riesman

David Riesman (1909-) is one of America's leading interpreters of her own culture, as *The Lonely Crowd* (No. 259) suffices to demonstrate. But he is also an historian of ideas and a critic of modernism as these manifest themselves outside the boundaries of the United States. The present volume collects his chief writings in a fifteen-year period, and those who want to withhold judgment on the American subjects that Mr. Riesman treats will nonetheless be captivated—by his thesis in the first place, and by his extended treatment of Freud in the second.

The thesis is not pushed in every essay; indeed it is only in the introduction that it finds anything like formal expression. Yet every essay brings its weight of evidence pro and con, for Mr. Riesman is as impartial toward himself as toward the facts, knowing as he does that a vast multiplex society does not move all in one direction, much less signify only one thing. What the thesis states is in fact this very observation and conviction in explicit form: modern life is not a cage for the imprisonment of modern man. There are loopholes. And here appears the relevance of Freud: a naturalist and a determinist and a depth-analyst, Freud is nevertheless a believer in mind and the will. He exaggerates some of the things in his doctrine that compel man. But this may be a defect due to his time and place. Fundamentally, he liberates us by defining the immovable limits and irresistible forces.

And that is what Mr. Riesman himself does in his analysis of Society. He shows that even where the current of fashion, the weight of stupidity and indifference, the commercial manipulation of weakness, the stampede of folly and fear are strongest, the result is not a solid mass of undifferentiated human beings packed like sardines in the airtight box of anonymous conformity. There is on the contrary variation and the possibility of self-assertion. The possibility—not, automatically, the desire. If the desire when present is to find its reward, there must be the wit and will to "take" the unchangeable conditions in an original way, there must be an "autonomous personality," one that is ridden neither by a rigid imperative nor by the soft compulsion of the mass. In short, the mass man is not a fated inescapable result. Individualism, reconsidered, is a continuing fact of experience. J. B.

259. *The Lonely Crowd*

by David Riesman

Few modern works of social science have aroused so wide an interest as David Riesman's (1909-) study of the changing American character, *The Lonely Crowd*. Published in 1950 by a university press, it soon transcended the limited audience for which it was intended. When the book was brought out in a paper-bound edition, it sold so widely that it became a prodigy of the publishing world. The terminology of the work, especially the phrases "inner directed" and "other directed," have become part of the American vocabulary.

The Lonely Crowd presents the hypothesis that there has been a significant change in the character and ideals of the American people over the past few decades. This change is described as a movement from "inner direction" to "other direction." It is not possible in this space to do justice to the meaning of the two concepts. In general it may be said that the trend away from inner direction toward other direction implies that the ambitious, competitive character, highly individualistic and making great demands on itself (and others), is becoming less typical of American culture, yielding to a less assertive and more conciliatory character, attuned to the requirements of the group either in cooperation or in conformity, taking its direction from the ideals and demands of others.

Mr. Riesman wishes not to be partisan with either form of "direction," although he is aware that most of his readers will find that inner direction as he describes it is more attractive than other direction. He accepts neither as an ideal form of motivation and offers as an escape from both the difficult ideal of *autonomy*. But as an objective observer of American life (see also No. 258), he can note the advantages as well as the dangers of the new tendency. He sees the diminution of inner direction as implying a lessening of individualism, personal self-definition, energy, and sheer interestingness. But he is no less aware that the increase of other direction implies a lessening of raw competitiveness and an increase of cooperativeness and of friendliness, if not of friendship.

L. T.

260. *Oil! Titan of the Southwest*

by CARL COKE RISTER

Industrial and technical history, long neglected by scholars, has recently received some of the attention it deserves. Books by responsible historians, dealing with the development of specific industries, have been published with some frequency. Not that there is any revival of the nineteenth-century glorification of business heroes; the *Age of Reform* (No. 149), as Richard Hofstadter calls the period from William Jennings Bryan to Franklin D. Roosevelt, effectively undermined any such euphoric relish for uninhibited self-help and bland self-interest. But the old notion that history consists of politics and war has been dispelled, and there is an increasing awareness of the significance of technology and industry in modern civilization as well as an increasing respect for the imagination, courage, and skill which find expression in such areas.

A number of the best of the recent industrial histories have, like this one, been made possible by grants from corporations whose officers find that the tax laws and their own genuine curiosity about the historic significance of what they have been up to combine to justify allocation of the funds to independent scholarly research. Industries with an eye to their public relations have long hired writers to grind out "histories" of their enterprises; but the new method, as illustrated by Professor Rister's book, is different in both aim and result.

This particular example of the new industrial histories was selected both because of its intrinsic competence and because the search for and development of oil resources is so important to the free world. Scientific prospecting, the complex organization of production and distribution, and the evolution of "reasonably circumspect" corporate ethics (in the interest of conservation and under the shaping influence of state and federal law) are increasingly meaningful in a world whose oil requirements by the year 2000 will, according to the available estimates, be four times larger than today. Places like Spindletop, Smackover, and Desdemona will have their parallels all over the earth, and men like Al and Curt Hamill, "Dad" Joiner, and Burt Hull will be recognized as at least as important as John D. Rockefeller, one of the financial titans of the oil business, who is relegated in Professor Rister's book to a footnote.

J. A. K.

261. *Rabble in Arms*

by Kenneth Roberts

The historical novels of Kenneth Roberts (1885-) are based on prodigious research and produced by a mind extraordinarily gifted in creating imaginative and convincing narrative. Few American writers of fiction set against a background of authentic records have achieved this author's eminence as an artist or popularity as a storyteller.

Rabble in Arms (the title stems from a contemptuous remark of British General John Burgoyne about General Washington's forces in the early days of the American Revolution) shows these qualities in Mr. Roberts and adds to them one other—a resolute and uncompromising independence of judgment. Despite the general favor that his novels have won, many of his readers have found him far too sympathetic to the American Tory. His championing of Benedict Arnold, who is the real hero of *Rabble in Arms,* was bound (as the author knew) to have unfavorable repercussions, even though the book treats an early stage of General Arnold's career, three years before he tried to sell West Point to the British and so earned his title as the arch-traitor of American history.

Rabble in Arms is chiefly concerned with an action in which Arnold much distinguished himself, the Battle of Saratoga (1777). A heroic attack, led by Arnold and costing him a leg, brought about the decisive defeat of the British forces (under General Burgoyne) which had invaded New York State from Canada. Burgoyne's capitulation removed the threat that the Colonies might be cut in half and did much to insure their alliance with France in the following year. It should be added that some historians disagree with Mr. Roberts on the stupidity, ineptness, and lack of courage that he ascribes to other American generals, depicting them as dull foils to the flashing blade that was Benedict Arnold.

C. C.

262. *Tilbury Town*

by EDWIN ARLINGTON ROBINSON

Shortly after the turn of the century Edwin Arlington Robinson (1869-1935), descendant of an old New England family, seemed to have slight hope—despite the publication of two short volumes of verse—of winning recognition as an eminent American poet. He had left Harvard College after two years, and was working in New York as a subway construction checker. When his second volume came to the attention of President Theodore Roosevelt, who promptly hailed him as a genius (see No. 265), the outlook for this shy, struggling writer seemed if anything worse. Critics reproved the nation's chief executive, and Robinson exclaimed, "I shall never live it down!" However, through the President he moved from the subway to a desk in the Customs House, and continued to write. With *Captain Craig* (1902), *The Town Down the River* (1910), and *The Man Against the Sky* (1916) he won wide reputation, partly because the American poetry "renaissance" of 1913 had provided readers who could appreciate his realistic, finely wrought work. Robinson had really been ahead of his time. While his reading had been classical and conventional—he later listed Wordsworth and Kipling (!) as early influences, and knew George Crabbe—he had already in *Tilbury Town* (Gardiner, Maine) sketched a background for his characters and observations which mildly anticipated Edgar Lee Masters's *Spoon River Anthology* (No. 205), a realistic portrait of a Middle Western town whose free-verse lyrics set the nation talking in 1915. Robinson, writing in conventional rhyme and blank verse, had exposed in a more decorous fashion the hypocrisies of a small community, and championed individuals of whom it disapproved. *Tilbury Town* represents him well, although it contains none of his longer poems, one of which, *Tristram,* was eventually chosen by a book club and won him a flutter of larger fame. The short poems are actually his best. Like Robert Frost's (No. 125), they are true New England; like Frost's they have an idiomatic ease and fine sense of humor. But Robinson attempts to be the more universal poet, seeking to observe and assay the whole of life. He is philosophical, in a casual way even scholarly; his adaptations from Greek drama are distinguished. He has an elusive, at times teasing quality; he prefers to imply rather than to proclaim. This quality narrows his potential circle of readers, but those who give his work the close attention it deserves are likely to be rewarded, by both the content and the art of what is said.

F. E. H.

263. *I Remember Distinctly*

compiled by Agnes Rogers
text by Frederick Lewis Allen

Between the end of the first World War in 1918 and the day the Japanese bombed Pearl Harbor in December, 1941 (the period covered by *I Remember Distinctly*), the United States lived through a period of roaring prosperity followed by almost a full decade of deep depression. The 1920's were a time of hero-worship and frivolity, and of the "noble experiment" that bred the gangsters of Prohibition. It was the "jazz age," but it was also a time of industrial expansion, of rapid growth of suburban communities (made possible by the inexpensive automobile), and of almost unlimited optimism. It was the era of which F. Scott Fitzgerald writes in *The Great Gatsby* (No. 114) and which John O'Hara describes in *Appointment in Samarra* (No. 237), a decade of lax morality, extravagance, and empty values. It was also an age of new heroes—of movie actors and athletes and fliers (Charles A. Lindbergh, *The Spirit of St. Louis* [No. 188]), and of the decline of "society" (Dixon Wecter, *The Saga of American Society* [No. 323]).

The stock market débâcle of 1929, described by J. K. Galbraith in *The Great Crash: 1929* (No. 126), turned optimism into panic, a panic followed by gloom. Banks failed, life savings were wiped out, bankruptcies were commonplace. Unemployment and dislocation grew to alarming proportions (see *The Grapes of Wrath,* by John Steinbeck [No. 292]). In 1932 the voters turned the Republicans out of office and elected Franklin D. Roosevelt, the Democratic party's candidate, to the Presidency. There ensued a period of economic experimentation and business and social legislation, some of which is described by Mrs. Roosevelt in *This I Remember* (No. 264) and by Robert E. Sherwood in *Roosevelt and Hopkins* (No. 283). The arts flourished under a program of public works; the labor movement solidified its gains and established itself as a powerful political force. As war clouds gathered over Europe the American economy began to gain momentum once more and the fear of poverty was replaced by the fear of war.

Frederick Lewis Allen (1890-1954) and Agnes Rogers (1893-) (Mrs. Allen), by means of news photographs, headlines, advertisements, cartoons, and an anecdotal text, have re-created the sharp individual flavors of two greatly contrasting decades, themselves full of contrasts. Mr. Allen wrote more extensively of the 1920's in *Only Yesterday* (No. 9) and put the two decades in a longer perspective in *The Big Change* (No. 8).

R. L.

264. *This I Remember*

by Eleanor Roosevelt

The wife of the President of the United States is often referred to as the First Lady. Certain informal privileges are hers, and a certain public interest attaches to her actions and opinions, throughout her husband's tenure of office; but as a rule the wives of Presidents have returned, upon leaving the White House, to a relatively quiet obscurity. Mrs. Franklin D. Roosevelt (1884-) was an exceptional First Lady in more than one respect, and in nothing so much as the position she has come to occupy since her husband's death in 1945. It was during these years, in fact, that her countrymen truly learned to recognize Mrs. Roosevelt's full measure as an individual of extraordinary graciousness and good sense. While U. S. delegate to the United Nations from 1945 to 1953, she earned in her own right the invented but unchallenged, and far from empty, title of First Lady of the Free World.

This volume of her reminiscences covers the period, from the early 1920's to the mid-1940's, in which Franklin Roosevelt recovered from a crippling attack of polio to become, successively, governor of New York State and President for four terms. It is, without primarily intending to be, a revealing supplement to such historical accounts of these times as Robert E. Sherwood's *Roosevelt and Hopkins* (No. 283), but it is even more revealing as an account of how Eleanor Roosevelt grew, gradually and in part unconsciously, into her unique role. She too was a Roosevelt, the niece of President Theodore (see No. 265). By temperament incapable of inactivity, she used her opportunities for travel and widespread human contact to become her immobilized husband's eyes and ears, and to develop in herself such potentialities for public life as she had not realized she possessed. Throughout the book she also remains the wife and mother, writing with candor but never without tact of her sometimes difficult relationships to children, to mother-in-law, and not least to the President himself, whose stature she can the better portray for knowing his weaknesses. Then he was gone, and she was—in her closing sentence—on her own, the unsuspected years of her own achievement lying ahead.

E. L.

265. *Theodore Roosevelt's Letters to His Children*

No doubt the letters in this volume would not have found their way into print had they not been written by a President of the United States. But, unlike the poetry of Frederick the Great or the musical compositions of Benjamin Franklin, they lay a claim on the reader's attention by their own intrinsic merit, quite apart from the eminence, in other fields, of their creator, Theodore Roosevelt (1858-1919).

These letters can be read in so many different ways. They indicate, for one thing, the incredible range of interest that was the author's dominant intellectual characteristic (see No. 250). Writing to a fourteen-year-old son, Roosevelt deals on two succeeding pages with the conduct of a Hessian at Leipsic, the poetry of E. A. Robinson, the advantages of a live pig as a birthday present, the condition of the slums in New York, the reason for reading novels, and the state of the snapdragons in the garden.

Again, these letters may be read as a period piece; a source book on the life and times of a large, reasonably well-to-do American family at the turn of the century. Like other families, the Roosevelts occasionally ate too much ice cream and chocolate sauce, got poor marks at school, read aloud before the fire, went for picnics on the river bank, fell off ponies, wondered what they would do when they left college, and argued with their parents about the modern novel. It is true the situation was not typical; the tennis partner usually turned out to be a cabinet member, or the man who was "It" in a game of hide-and-go-seek was the French Ambassador. But the distinguishing characteristic appears, in these pages, to be not so much an array of great names and famous men as the handling of an atmosphere—these people seem always out of doors and in the sunlight.

The most interesting way to read the letters, however, is the way in which their author wanted them read. Near the end of his life he said he would rather have this book published than anything ever written about him. Certainly there is a great deal of Theodore Roosevelt here, and what is not is not essential. The reason he was a good soldier, a superb politician, a fine President was that whether in a conference with seventeen governors or in a pillow fight with a six-year-old child he was always himself—lost to everything but the immediate event.

E. E. M.

266. *The Education of Hyman Kaplan*

by LEONARD Q. ROSS

The American "melting pot" no longer bubbles as vigorously as it did in the nineteenth century and in the early years of the twentieth, when immigration brought many millions of men and women from all parts of the world to become American citizens. In recent years, as they have tried to throw off their isolationism and to combat discrimination, Americans have become rather self-conscious about humor inspired by racial or national characteristics. But for many years the new arrival and his attempts to learn the ways of the New World—to Americanize himself and put on, like an ill-fitting suit, new customs and manners—has been an unfailing butt for good-tempered humor. Hyman Kaplan, infallibly optimistic, frighteningly ingenious, and determined to "improve" himself in night school, is both the despair and fascination of his teacher, Mr. "Pockheel," the earnest, all-forgiving pedagogue.

Behind the humor of *The Education of Hyman Kaplan* there lies, as it so often does in American dialect humor, the seemingly simple but acute observation of the naive individual. Kaplan, like Mr. Dooley (No. 104), provides a singularly sharp mirror for Americans (especially New Yorkers) of their most cherished ideals and cherished clichés. But Mr. Kaplan, whose language and outlook is that of the New York Yiddish-speaking community, also has some of the characteristics of the literary "noble savage," kindly, moral, courageous, and treated by his author with both respect and humor, like the Negro Jim in *Huckleberry Finn* (No. 311) and Queequeg, the South Sea Islander, in *Moby Dick* (No. 211). Furthermore, it is characteristic of the uneducated (or unassimilated) bumpkin of American humor to confound by his native wit and intelligence the more sophisticated men and women who cross his path.

Hyman Kaplan, murderer of the English language, pits his wit against his teacher and his classmates in a series of short stories. They can be read quite independently of each other and are, indeed, more enjoyable if not read all at one sitting. Kaplan has close relatives in the cartoons of Hoff (see *The New Yorker Twenty-Fifth Anniversary Album* [No. 234]) and in Milt Gross's *Nize Baby,* parts of which are included in Nos. 55 and 331. Leonard Q. Ross is the pseudonym of Leo C. Rosten (1908-).

R. L.

267. *Hollywood*

by Leo C. Rosten

The Hollywood of 1941 was just at the close of its gilded age. It was still a place where the stars of the entertainment world were gathered in splendor, and *Hollywood* gives us an idea of both the real money that purchased the splendor and the false glitter that it bought. The personalities have changed since then and the movies no longer dominate Western man's recreational phantasies as they once did; but that section of Los Angeles is still the center of the modern worship of entertainment celebrities and also, unfortunately, a symbol in some quarters of America itself.

Dr. Leo C. Rosten (1908-), with the aid of a crew of technicians, set out to measure the phantasy, cast up the accounts, and number the headaches. Some of the methods of the investigating anthropologist were used to locate and describe *genus hollywoodiensis* and the result shows that the movie capital, as a center not only of American but also of Western culture, originates almost nothing but imitates and exaggerates everything. This is true of money, morals, and moods.

The reader is not struck with envy. One is inclined to think of these shining creatures as human sacrifices to the love the rest of us have for obvious romance, for sensation, and for vicarious sin. These studies and ample statistics show us also that there is, surrounding the 200 men, women, and children who make up the Hollywood élite (measure: $75,000 or more a year from current earnings), a quiet, steadily laboring, respectable population. These thousands more may feel a little superior to all other carpenters, lawyers, charwomen, hack writers, extra actors, engineers, sweepers, porters, bookkeepers, and policemen because they are at least in the outside rim of the bright lights, but they live quite ordinary lives.

No country boy or girl would be tempted by reading Dr. Rosten to run away to try his luck in Hollywood. And no sober American could be reassured by this report or be persuaded that these people under these conditions should decide what "pictures" of his country should go abroad. The book may help to explain to a friendly stranger why the gulf exists between movies and life.

L. B.

268. *American Humor*

by Constance Rourke

Published originally in 1931, this brief, compact book has in the course of the years emerged as a classic. Do not look to it for any abstract theories of humor, or for any extended consideration of individual humorists, or for jokes and laughter. Here is a serious study, not so much of our comic literature, as of those elements in the national character and those crucial events in the national history that have made that literature possible and given it its special native tone and color. Constance Rourke (1885-1941) was, among other things, a distinguished folklorist; and her theses are rooted in the conviction that the American humorous imagination flows out of the people, out of popular slants, prejudices, ways of talking, ways of feeling (see also No. 269).

Certain early-American "characters" provide the foundation: pre-eminently the Yankee peddler, the ebullient backwoodsman, and the Negro. Later certain urban types come into play: the Irishman, the Jew. But Miss Rourke's notion of humor is wide and philosophic. "Professional" humorists do not interest her greatly although she gives them ample consideration. For her, Henry James and Emily Dickinson are artists in comedy, as indeed they are; and so, in different ways, are Sinclair Lewis and Edwin Arlington Robinson —and Abraham Lincoln. Our greatest literary figures of the nineteenth century drew on the humorous vision of their countrymen and reflected it, often in strange guises: Emerson, Thoreau, Whitman, Hawthorne, Melville, even Poe.

As Miss Rourke approaches our own time her touch becomes less sure. She seems to be less interested in her subject as the influence of the folk imagination begins to dwindle with the rise of industrialism and the town. This book is read most usefully when its subtitle—"A Study of the National Character"—rather than its title is kept in mind. It is truly an essay, often a brilliant one, never a superficial one, on the American character as it shows itself in our comic mythology.

C. F.

269. *The Roots of American Culture and Other Essays*

by CONSTANCE ROURKE

Constance Rourke (1885-1941), whose death removed a historian of unique dedication and distinction, was haunted by the belief that the arts of any country owe their ultimate power to elements in the folk mind of that country, and by the desire to establish in the United States a sense of what popular tradition, if only it were understood to exist, might contribute to American literature, painting, architecture, music, and design. As Van Wyck Brooks points out in his preface to this posthumous collection of her essays, Constance Rourke had first of all to prove that a popular tradition did exist; for this was doubted, and American artists for the most part looked to Europe for their models. The proof required research among materials by no means easy to salvage from the past. But Miss Rourke put all of her strength into this research, and emerged with remarkable findings. Her book *American Humor* (No. 268) went both wider and deeper into its subject than any book had gone before; for it found connections between the humor of the people and that of such austere artists as Ralph Waldo Emerson (No. 105), Nathaniel Hawthorne (No. 140), and Henry James (Nos. 159-61); which is to say, it located in those authors the source of their final power, it showed how they had become what all artists desire to seem and indeed to be, namely, natural.

The six books published by Miss Rourke before her death, like the essays here collected, were in her mind only a token of the great comprehensive work on the subject which she planned. Her hope was to build a solid bridge between the people and the artist, a bridge over which thoughts, feelings, symbols, and ideas could meet each other as they crossed. Toward this end she labored to remind sophisticated Americans of such exciting episodes in their country's past as the growth and decline of the Shaker community. The Shakers were nothing less than a community of artists, first in the business of living and then in the making of houses, furniture, and tools. But like others of their kind, they had been forgotten. Miss Rourke's effort, here as elsewhere, was to repair a ravaged national memory.

M. V. D.

270. *Life in the Far West*

by George Frederick Ruxton

The "mountain men" of the Rockies who succeeded James Fenimore Cooper's Leatherstocking (No. 67) and his heirs as the heroes of Western adventure novels were discovered for fiction, not by an American writer, but by an Englishman. *Life in the Far West,* originally published as a serial in *Blackwood's Magazine* in 1848, was written by a 28-year-old former lieutenant of Her Majesty's 89th Regiment.

Bernard DeVoto once described Ruxton as one of those young English gentlemen "who provided the absent-mindedness in which the British Empire was acquired." Courageous and self-reliant, he had a happy talent for adventuring in regions of acute interest to the Empire. He fought in Spain for Queen Isabella II, whose cause Britain espoused; when serving with the 89th in western Canada, he resigned to roam through the Far West from Oregon to Mexico in the years when England was very much interested in Oregon and in limiting American expansion into Mexican territory. He also explored parts of the southwest coast of Africa which England soon after occupied.

His appetite for adventurous travel was unbounded, but he was happiest in the West. Just before leaving London on his last trip to America (he died in St. Louis, Missouri, in 1848) he wrote to a friend, in the mountain man's idiom which his tale fastened upon subsequent Western fiction, that "human nature can't go on feeding on civilized fixings in this big village; and this child has felt like going west for many a month, being 'half froze for buffler-meat and mountain doin's.'"

Ruxton's story is not history, but he justly affirmed that it was "no fiction." The characters were real people, and he insisted that he had not invented a single incident, though he admitted that he had "no doubt jumbled the *dramatis personae* . . . and may have committed anachronisms." The result is a unique picture of men and events which America's own writers for a hundred years either ignored or grossly romanticized and perverted. (See the chapter on "The Mountain Man as Western Hero" in Henry Nash Smith's *Virgin Land* [No. 287].) Not until A. B. Guthrie published *The Big Sky* (No. 133) in 1947 did an American novelist seriously attempt to understand the mountain men as human beings whose lust for self-sufficient freedom and detachment from the past made them revert toward barbarism, but at the same time made them into trail blazers of civilization.

J. A. K.

271. *Boss Rule*

by J. T. SALTER

City politics in the United States can be as much of a mystery at home as it doubtless is abroad. There are legends of powerful, secret leaders who walk like jungle cats in the alleyways, and pounce upon and devour their prey at will, just as there are legends of numberless, faceless fauna—little functionaries, pale people of the side streets—who conspire to worship and obey that will. Beyond this mythology few citizens go in their thought of municipal government, which most of them dismiss more or less cheerfully as corrupt at the same time that they think it might be fascinating. The mythology does make sense; the cities have been run in some such way; but those who know the details insist that they are less sinister than is customarily believed (see also No. 118).

J. T. Salter (1898-), a professor of political science at the University of Wisconsin, came all the way to Philadelphia in the early 1930's in order to study at close range one of the most sensational systems extant; he interviewed the functionaries; and he emerged with the picture here set forth—not of predatory but of eleemosynary politicians, not of thugs but of philanthropists. To be sure, they did their people favors in return for votes; but they did them favors, and these favors were something to which as citizens they were entitled, except that the formal government of Philadelphia was not up to the responsibility of administering them as rights. In reality they are rights, and Professor Salter looks forward to the time when politics will not pervert them. That time has partially arrived since he wrote his book; public welfare is beginning to replace private or party benefits.

Yet his history, since it is written with the author's eye so directly upon the object, will retain its validity long after the change to which it looks forward. The interviews with division leaders have the interest that all faithful reporting has, even of days before the Flood.

M. V. D.

272. *Abraham Lincoln*

The Prairie Years

by CARL SANDBURG

Abraham Lincoln was destined to become one of the two or three most famous Presidents the United States has thus far had. But such a destiny was doubted by many Americans, even in the North which elected him, when he took office in 1861. He was little known in the nation as a whole. He was thought by some to be an Abolitionist—one, that is, whose desire was to put an immediate end to slavery on the continent—in spite of the fact that he disclaimed the label. He was thought to be a crude country lawyer, a backwoods humorist and philosopher, when in fact he was a man of rich intellectual and moral distinction. He was thought to be a common man, and he was most uncommon. He was thought to be a fanatic who might wreck the institutions of the country, and he remained to prove himself an executive remarkable for his cool, far-seeing patience. The next four years would demonstrate all this. Yet further decades of study were necessary before a full picture of the man emerged. And it was not until 1926 that an American poet, Carl Sandburg of Illinois (1878-), published the sort of account that the American people needed in 1861 but did not have.

Mr. Sandburg's account was based on more than a reading of the numerous documents time had made available. It was fortified by conversations with old men and women who had known Lincoln in his native state of Illinois; and it was colored by a loving imagination. For Lincoln was a singularly lovable person, with a temperament so complex that imagination is necessary for its understanding. His humor, his integrity, his realism, his tenderness, his strength, his acumen, his cunning—these do not easily compose themselves into a portrait. (See, for his own writings, No. 12.) But Mr. Sandburg's portrait is successful, and by common consent it stands as the most truthful one in existence, even though it is softened here and there by touches of sentiment which are not appropriate, since Lincoln was never sentimental. The parentage, the birth, the childhood, the education, the marriage, the legal and political experience, and finally the election to high office are here set down to stay.

M. V. D.

273. *The People, Yes*

by CARL SANDBURG

In the 1830's de Tocqueville prophesied that democracy's poets—unable to celebrate individuals, since the principle of equality would render them "all insignificant and very much alike"—would inevitably write of "the destinies of mankind—man himself . . . with his passions, his doubts, his rare prosperities and inconceivable wretchedness." In 1936, a century later, two books appeared which gave substance to the prophecy: John Dos Passos's *U.S.A.* (No. 99), in which society itself is the "hero," and, broader yet in scope, *The People, Yes* by Carl Sandburg (1878-).

Both books presented difficulties for readers. *U.S.A.* was not a novel by familiar standards, and Mr. Sandburg's "populist epic" was so unconventional that even a sympathetic critic complained that hardly a fifth of the volume was poetry in any sense of the term. A recent history of American poetry suggests that Sandburg merely heaped together "half humorously" the kind of data you could find in an almanac.

The difficulty was, in part, that by 1936 Mr. Sandburg's poetic reputation was in partial eclipse. The rough vigor and haunting (if enigmatic) mysticism which had seemed such an arresting mixture when his *Chicago Poems* (1916) and *Cornhuskers* (1918) appeared, seemed naive to a generation which preferred the poetry of dextrous wit and sumptuous emotional geometry. (A number of Mr. Sandburg's early poems are in Nos. 208 and 336; see also Randall Jarrell, *Poetry and the Age* [No. 165].)

But in part the difficulty was that, unlike his poetic contemporaries, Carl Sandburg was interested less in the currents of international literary fashion than in what might be called folk life and folk history. He has collected and sung folk songs in almost every state in the Union, and research for his epic biography of Lincoln (No. 272) has steeped him in American history. He has worked at almost as many jobs as are mentioned in John Dos Passos's panorama: theatrical scene-shifter, truck-handler in a brick yard, Kansas harvest hand, hotel dishwasher, salesman, soldier, department store advertising manager, Social-Democratic organizer in Wisconsin, and Chicago newspaperman. It is in "the speech of the people," which he knows so well, and which permeates the 107 deceptively casual sections of his major poem, that Mr. Sandburg finds a clue to mankind's fateful and eternal brotherhood.

J. A. K.

274. *Crazy Horse*

by Mari Sandoz

Mari Sandoz (1900-) was born and reared on the last frontier, western Nebraska, where a neighbor who lived ten miles away was too close for comfort. In another story, *Old Jules* (No. 275), she has told of her wild father, a white man to whom the white man's civilization was as distasteful as it was to the Indians. He needed room, as they did, to be alone and to make friends by choice. Among his friends were Indians, themselves remnants of another way of life, who told him the sorry tale of their treatment by the white city-man and his policeman, the soldier. While other young Americans were reading James Fenimore Cooper's *Leatherstocking Saga* (No. 67) and learning to play Indian, Mari Sandoz was playing with Indians, the children of her father's friends. From them and from her father she learned to hear names—No Water, Man Afraid, Iron Hand—not with condescension at their quaintness, but as a New Yorker heard Jones or Smith.

Old Jules's daughter did not forget. She became a student at the University of Nebraska, and in time a careful scholar, learning about the Indians in a scholar's way; but she has always remembered Indians as people, and it was out of this memory that she wrote the story of *Crazy Horse*. Historians may quarrel with her conclusion that it was Crazy Horse rather than Sitting Bull who defeated Custer, but to others this is a mere brush stroke in the portrait of a man. The book is long, and must be, for it takes time for the reader to learn how it feels to be an Indian. It also takes time to acquire something of Mari Sandoz's double vision, to see the strength of a people and a people's weakness. The Indian's ethical reach was too short, and even so wise a man as Crazy Horse was slow to learn that, facing the white man, all Indians should be one.

In the end he did learn, but the white man remained a puzzle to him. The expression of his dismay has the quality of prophecy. "I am no white man," he said. "They are the only people who make rules for others and say: 'If you stay on one side of this line it is peace but if you go on the other side I will kill you all.'"

J. A. R.

275. *Old Jules*

by Mari Sandoz

The American "Western" is an art form which has been brought to high excellence in the standard cowboy and trapper tales and in some movies, as, for a classic example, "High Noon." It has produced the chief myth in our folklore and even colors our serious historical writing. It is the romance of the great migrations across 3,000 miles of forests, mountains, and plains. The migrations are made the central theme of Frank Thistlethwaite's *The Great Experiment* (No. 303). Novels that tell parts of the story, without disguising evasions, are exemplified in Willa Cather's *My Ántonia* (No. 53), Alan Le May's *The Searchers* (No. 182), and A. B. Guthrie's *The Big Sky* (No. 133). In Mari Sandoz's biography of her father we get still closer to the struggle to subdue a continent to peaceful human purpose.

Jules Sandoz (1859-1928) was born to an easy urban life in Switzerland, but his courage and his energy in the struggle which toughened his body and his spirit made him a successful pioneer. Success in that calling, however, does not mean security, or quiet, or comfort; those goods are for the softer generations who come after. The successful pioneer is the one who follows his dream to the end of his life without letting the fierce opposition of nature break his heart.

Mari Sandoz (1900-) was always afraid of her father; she was born to live in the softer generation. She saw what the Nebraska sandhills did to women and she gives us touching hints of how the three of Jules's wives who tackled the natural enemies with him on this fighting salient of civilization accepted the brutality but never lost their own dream, which was not land or wealth, or even comfort, but a better life for their children.

Old Jules had a love of beauty beneath his harshness; he showed it in making the sandhills grow flowers. But he showed in his 44 years of daily warfare, never beaten but never victorious, no other gentleness. Even his daughter found it hard to love him. But his kind were the shock troops. The debt to them cannot be paid by their heirs of today; it need not be forgotten.

L. B.

276. *The Last Puritan*

by George Santayana

It was at the age of 73 that George Santayana (1863-1952), the world-famous philosopher, published his first and only work of fiction. Had the author of *The Last Puritan* achieved no other intellectual distinction in his long lifetime, he would surely claim a permanent place in American literary history for this single remarkable performance, a novel as subtle and witty as it is profound and commanding.

Of Spanish Catholic birth, Santayana was brought as a boy of nine to live among his American Protestant relations in Boston and stayed on at Harvard, first as student, then as teacher, until 1912, when he returned to Europe to follow an independent philosophical career. From the conflict between his Latin origins and the stern self-denying culture in which he came to manhood stems the material of *The Last Puritan,* embodied in the contrasting portraits of Oliver Alden, the tragic hero of the novel, and his Italian cousin, Mario. The child of inherited wealth and social position, endowed with all the gifts of a good life except the capacity for guiltless enjoyment, Oliver is Santayana's brilliant representation of the old Boston aristocracy for whom, even in a present generation, the mandates of conscience and duty so effectually stifle the principle of pleasure. The dashing and volatile Mario, counterpoint to Oliver's negation of vital experience, is the statement of Santayana's own preference for the instinctual as against the Protestant-rationalistic view of man and society.

But the fact that *The Last Puritan* can be read as a fictional demonstration of the penalties that accrue in the life of the individual who chooses reason before nature, and thus as a kind of large imaginative footnote to Santayana's formal philosophical work (see No. 277), must not be taken to imply any triumph of pedantry over charm in Santayana's novel. The ideas which inform the story of Oliver Alden are inferential rather than overt, communicated entirely through the vivid development of character. One need have no knowledge or even interest in Santayana the philosopher to be captivated by Santayana the novelist.

D. T.

277. *The Life of Reason*

by George Santayana

The Life of Reason first appeared in five small volumes in 1905-6 when Santayana was 42 years old. It was his first comprehensive work, the first soundings of his deeply troubled spirit, and his teacher and friend William James (Nos. 163-4, 246), who loved and admired him without sharing any of his views, called it "the perfection of rottenness." On his side Santayana came to believe that *The Life of Reason* owed much too much to James's unwanted but powerful influence; in the light of Santayana's later evolution the work was too full of "dogmatisms and pragmatisms." Accordingly, a few years before his death at the age of 89 he planned its revision, which was carried out by his friend and companion, Daniel Cory.

The differences between the first and the present version are interesting but they do not affect the central character of the work, any more than Santayana's later doctrine of essences changes the figure which he cuts in the world of modern thought. He is the Ambiguous Man par excellence—not that his utterance is not always perfectly clear, but that its clarity shows a mind forever eager to be two things at once. This might be deemed a common enough dialectic since Hegel, if it were not that Santayana does not want movement but static repose. *The Life of Reason* is designed to reassure the traveler about the outcome of the journey before it is begun. And yet the philosopher is forced to admit that things grow, develop, change, and twist unexpectedly, and that reason is a name given in retrospect to fortunate conjectures.

Santayana's own life, as he himself repeatedly said, is a clue to his position. He was descended from a Spanish family and transplanted, through his mother's earlier marriage to an American, to Boston. In both continents he was well cared for but poorly loved, and he grew up with fear and disdain in his soul. Hence his desires, which he always tried to correct by a superior intelligence that never yielded weakly to an almost pathological sensitivity: he claimed to be a Catholic but called all beliefs myths; he was proud to be known as a Fascist, but threw overboard the *mystique* and passion of Fascism; he preferred the name of materialist, but the pure deliverances of science and naturalism seemed to him incomplete and indeed childish. He wanted art, reason, spirit to grow out of matter, but not "pragmatically"—rather, necessarily, as by a divine order.

The result is a beautiful structure of ideas, couched in superb—sometimes all-too-fine—prose, and sustaining the morale of a very representative "modern," which is to say, a man of the old world forced against his will to acknowledge the existence of the new.

J. B.

278. *The Saturday Evening Post Treasury*

edited by Roger Butterfield

In the matter of taste, America is a classless society. No person or group, whatever the elevation of brow, has the final say as to what is good or bad. The play "Abie's Irish Rose" was damned by every critic, and ran for innumerable nights. The expensive definitive edition of Henry James's works could shortly be had for a few cents on the dollar, and later became a collector's item. *Uncle Tom's Cabin* (No. 297) was being read everywhere —except of course in the South—while Herman Melville's *Moby Dick* (No. 211) was not. Jazz (see No. 282), beginning in the dives of New Orleans, wound up in Carnegie Hall—a, if not the, sanctum of music. The mobiles of Alexander Calder were funny (see No. 299) until they began to twirl in the Museum of Modern Art.

So it is with food also. Until fairly recently, every town of any size had its grocery store for the rich, stores for the poor, stores for the in-betweens. But now the supermarket has put them all under one roof, and there is something for every customer. The housewife or husband pushes a cart along the aisles and makes a free choice, from caviar to corn meal.

George Horace Lorimer (1867-1936), who had once been a wholesale grocer, anticipated the retail trade by some 50 years. He took over the editorship of a small magazine of tenuous history—Benjamin Franklin would be astonished at his credit line—and created a supermarket for readers, something for every taste, in the *Saturday Evening Post.*

Not in every issue, however. In the course of a year the constant reader may hope to find at least one, perhaps more than one, unforgettable story or article, such as F. Scott Fitzgerald's "Babylon Revisited" or Gene Howe's account of his father. But when he opens his weekly copy he will constantly expect to find most of the contents forgettable. They are meant to be; the *Post* is what is called a mass medium; the editors know their business. They also know a good thing when they see it. The evidence is here. Also here is the fluctuating taste-line of the American reader of the past 50 years: what he hoped, was ready to believe, found amusing, approved. Taste in heroes has changed, from Armour to Judge Medina. Taste in sentimentality has remained fairly constant, while taste in humor is for more tartness, and satire has become almost a staple.

J. A. R.

279. *Literary America*

A Chronicle of American Writers from 1607-1952

by David E. Scherman *and* Rosemarie Redlich

Two flourishing and relatively modern American interests have combined to produce *Literary America.* The first is our passion for the photograph; the second our recent awareness that we are old enough to have a cultural past. From their merger has come this handsome text-and-picture book.

While the mainspring of the authors' efforts is their affection for America's literary past and present, they have avoided the conventional emphasis on "shrines" and vital statistics. Thus there are no portraits of the authors themselves, very few of their birthplaces, home-towns, or burial places. Many of the photographs are "mood-pictures" intended to match in feeling the emotional core of the writers' work. Many record places they wrote about or merely suggest the general topographical background of their works.

The book starts with Captain John Smith (1580-1631). It ends with Eudora Welty (1909-) (see No. 324). In between are most of the well-known names, together with some not usually included in the orthodox literary canon, such as Davy Crockett and Augustus Longstreet. Figures like Lincoln and Jefferson, perhaps not ordinarily thought of as writers, are quite properly represented. Minor figures of the past—Samuel Sewall, Philip Freneau, George Washington Cable, Joaquin Miller, Edward Eggleston (and even Zane Grey)—are given respectful treatment; and a major stress is laid on recent and contemporary writers, including several whose literary value is arguable.

The value of this camera-eye view of the American literary heritage lies in its double stimulus. On the one hand it supplies a set of concrete, beautiful, or troubling images to which we can attach our formless affection for the vast and various American land. On the other hand it reveals to us, in an easily digested form, the richness of our literature, its slow growth from our Puritan beginnings to the era of William Faulkner and Ernest Hemingway. We are now old enough to cultivate our past, to claim, as do other countries, a fairly long and clearly identifiable cultural tradition.

C. F.

280. *The Age of Jackson*

by Arthur M. Schlesinger, Jr.

There are, perhaps, two or three incidents from the American past that virtually every American has heard of. One took place at the reception for Andrew Jackson on the day, March 4, 1829, when he became President of the United States. Huge, disheveled men in muddy boots stamped through the White House upsetting chairs, destroying property, ignoring protocol. One detached observer heard the sound of tearing skirts, smelled whisky in the air. Another was reminded of northern barbarians flooding into Rome.

Those unmannered men surging through the Executive Mansion were the West entering our history as a ponderable force. About the time Andrew Jackson was elected President the center of interest and energy had begun to swing slowly away from the coastline and toward the interior lands. In the West there was a buoyant urge for change, for home-grown remedies, for the expression of individual needs. The eastern shore represented a scheme of things more settled, more touched with Europe's influence, more highly organized and differentiated. The friction between these opposing views was revealed, as the rival attitudes rubbed against each other in Jackson's time, in many ways—as an opposition between worker and employer, between trade and self-sufficient agriculture, between hard currency and fiat money, between the rights of property and human rights.

The President was a strong man with strong views on these matters. He tried, by every means at his disposal, to enable the society to take into account the claims of the new regions and the needs of the ordinary man in every region. Since strong, adroit men opposed him, it was a turbulent time. No one has described this time more interestingly than Professor Schlesinger (1917-). He brings to his subject something of the President's love of contention, something too of his distaste for economics; and, like the President, he is fully committed to the energies and values the Jackson administration sought to conserve. Written in the year the New Deal ended, this book was as much a tract for our times as illuminating history.

E. E. M.

281. *A History of American Philosophy*

by HERBERT W. SCHNEIDER

As it is true in American poetry, music, and the plastic arts today, so it is true in philosophy that the country has entered the stream of international thought. There is no withdrawing from the fact, for it is a world phenomenon, and unless world communications break down, there are not likely in the future to be any local traditions anywhere capable of being written about as national styles.

This is what gives Professor Schneider's book, though written in 1946, its markedly retrospective look. Not that he is dealing with a provincial movement of purely historical interest; but he is dealing with the American branch, so to speak, of the Western Philosophic Trust. At almost every point from colonial pietism to late nineteenth-century academic idealism, the currents of deliberate thought in the United States have their headwaters elsewhere; which shows at least that here was no stagnant pool but part of the general system in motion. In other words, to the extent that one denies the originality of the main traditions one must affirm their lively participation in the Atlantic community of thought.

But again as in the other arts, America did produce in philosophy some figures of unique complexion and interest: Jonathan Edwards (see No. 216), Ralph Waldo Emerson (see No. 105), C. S. Peirce (see No. 244), and William James (see Nos. 163-4 and 246) are philosophers by birthright sooner than by profession. They are by any standards geniuses, great men and great writers, and if they have not in the vague public eye the same towering stature as their European congeners, that is a peculiarity of their culture. America in their day already lacked what all the world today is learning to do without: a stage for the display of individual achievement.

Professor Schneider (1892-) of Columbia University is especially adept at showing what the culture took from the American philosophers, great and small, and what it did with what it took. The amount of assimilation was remarkable, suggesting a new kind of believer, who acts rather than doctrinizes. In the history of American philosophy one may see most steadily, though not invariably, the literal existentialism of thought which finds its fulfillment where the propounder hoped but did not expect to see it—in behavior.

J. B.

282. *Hear Me Talkin' to Ya*

edited by NAT SHAPIRO *and* NAT HENTOFF

American jazz is both a music and a legend, and both are evanescent. Though much of the music has been recorded phonographically, the best—according to legend—has often been lost; and we will never really know what extreme of emotion made one listener (so they say) throw a chair at Bix Beiderbecke, or how many more than 200 consecutive improvisations (all different) Louis Armstrong once played on the tune "Sweet Sue," or what the almost-mythical cornet-player Buddy Bolden actually sounded like when he "called the children home" with his horn. And the legend, especially those parts of it which are true, is essential to the music; for jazz, like other folk art, is so deeply embedded in its origins as to be inexplicable without—and sometimes indistinguishable from—its background.

The problem of deciding how much of the legend is based on fact resists the routine scholarly tools. Jazz arose from low life, which does not habitually document itself, so that we are dependent on the untutored memory of participants. While an extraordinary number of them have survived into our own times, they have not always had the incentive to put down on paper what they knew. Even where they did have, memory is fallible and one man's may contradict another's. Moreover, the musicians are clannish, unconventional in their customs, and accustomed to express themselves in slang expressions whose meanings frequently change. The student of jazz needs a wide experience before he can recognize every nuance in the simplest of his materials. (For a musicologist's view of jazz, see André Hodeir [No. 147].)

Readers who come unprepared to *Hear Me Talkin' to Ya* should therefore expect to be puzzled at many points. The authors, two professional critics of jazz, have chosen to tell its story entirely in the words of musicians—without apology, without explanatory notes or sources, without express judgments as to reliability. It is a method which largely conceals the artfulness that has gone into it; like the makers of a "documentary" movie, the editors have exercised great skill in superimposing varied images, each torn fresh from experience and still quick with vitality, in such a way as to balance each against the rest. They have thus provided the most "objective" picture we have of the world from which jazz came—with all its tensions and contradictions, its vices and sorrows, and its moments of tarnished but shining grandeur.

E. L.

283. *Roosevelt and Hopkins*

by Robert E. Sherwood

The White House is the domicile of lonely men, and every man who has lived there has sought means to beguile his loneliness. There have been court jesters who played the mandolin or told funny stories. There have been confidants—men like Archie Butt who just listened to the President talk. There have been poker parties on Saturday night with "the boys." Innocent diversions such as these have been looked upon with sympathy by a society that itself is always hoping to find someone to talk to or someone who will turn out to be the life of the party.

Now and then these relationships go beyond sociability and—as in the case of Woodrow Wilson and Colonel House (see No. 84)—become involved in the formation of public policy. When this happens, because the extent of the influence of the relationship is incalculable and beyond procedural limitation, there is public concern. Such were the implications of the friendship between Franklin D. Roosevelt and Harry Hopkins (1890-1946). Here was a chronic invalid, as thin as Cassius, this pink who came out of the parlor and into a White House bedroom to live. What hold did this gray-faced eminence have on the President and through him on the country?

No one will ever be able to unravel all the intricate connections that held these two complicated personalities together. But Harry Hopkins, when the dross of such personal ambition as he may have possessed was washed away, became, with the aid of Roosevelt, a great public servant. A crisp and hard-boiled administrator, he used his eccentric position to cut through or bypass obstacles placed in the way by failures of political nerve or the inertia of bureaus. As a personal ambassador of the President, he strengthened the bonds of material aid and personal affection that held this country to England throughout the war. And, after the war began for this country, he became the agency to whom many frustrated officials turned to get the right things done at the right time and in the right place.

Robert Sherwood (1896-1955), who helped the President write his speeches, gives in this book a description of some of the contributions made by Roosevelt and Hopkins individually and together. He was, as a playwright (see No. 284), more familiar with the nature of men than with great affairs; but he was close enough to the source of power to learn a good deal, and his book emerges as a revealing account of how and why many things were done in the years from 1940 to 1945.

E. E. M.

284. *Sixteen Famous American Plays*

edited by BENNETT A. CERF *and* VAN H. CARTMELL

Are modern plays readable? Can they, in addition to being long-run stage successes, tell the quiet, reflective reader anything memorable about life and, for our purposes, American life? This excellent anthology throws light on these questions and answers both with a reasonably vigorous affirmative.

Sidney Howard's "They Knew What They Wanted," which opens the collection, was first produced in 1924; Howard Lindsay and Russel Crouse's "Life with Father," which closes it, in 1939. A good argument can be made for the thesis that this decade and a half was a kind of Golden Age in the American theater. It produced one masterpiece, Thornton Wilder's "Our Town"; a beloved classic of comedy, "Life with Father"; a moving morality play, "Green Pastures"; and first-rate examples of work by such brilliant dramatists as Sidney Howard, S. N. Behrman, Eugene O'Neill, Robert E. Sherwood, Sidney Kingsley, Lillian Hellman, and George Kaufman and Moss Hart. The vitality of the period is demonstrated by the fact that the majority of these sixteen plays have been successfully revived on the stage or have been adapted to other media, such as the movies, musical comedy, radio, and television. These are not dead plays; they are part of a living theater.

It is useless to pretend that more than three or four will be permanently readable, but that is the fate of all but the greatest plays. We are strongest in comedy. (Eugene O'Neill [No. 238] may be our finest dramatist; he is not our most representative.) The plays are not, for the most part, experimental—Mr. Saroyan is an ad libber rather than an experimenter. Only two ("Ah, Wilderness!", "Our Town") have values that we may properly call universal. The others bear emphatic witness to the variety and restlessness of the American scene; to the fresh strains of comedy and religious sentiment brought in by minority groups such as the Jews and the Negroes; to our genius for dramatizing our own foibles; and to the strong native strain of idealism which shows itself in such apparently divergent works as "The Little Foxes" and "Our Town."

C. F.

285. *A Dangerous Freedom*

by Bradford Smith

In *A Dangerous Freedom* Bradford Smith (1919-) attacks the myth that "the United States is a capitalist-materialist-individualist culture in which the individual, through the mechanism of a free economy, devotes himself to the piling up of material goods and comforts as his sole end and aim in life." What this myth neglects, he says, is a vast buffer zone between the individual and the impersonal political and economic mechanisms—a buffer zone created by an endless variety of voluntary organizations. By exercising their "dangerous freedom" to form associations independent of the state, Americans have been able to express their social concern, their generosity and good will, their gregariousness and faith in teamwork in a way that minimizes compulsion, standardization, and bureaucracy.

Smith's book is itself symptomatic of an important trend in contemporary America. Thirty years ago such a book could not have attracted serious readers. Then H. L. Mencken regularly referred to the clubs organized for community service as collections of fools, and novelists like Sinclair Lewis (Nos. 184-5) savagely caricatured small-town societies for mutual improvement. Fortunately the voluntary organizations survived their critics of the 1920's, as they survived the opinion, common in the 1930's, that they should surrender many of their functions to centralized and official agencies of the state. They continue to make an enormous contribution to American life, both by what they accomplish and by giving people a sense of belonging to and shaping their own society.

Yet *A Dangerous Freedom* is a rather extreme example of the recent tendency to find in the once-despised traditional American culture of farm and small town a source of all social virtues. It is not that Mr. Smith exaggerates the importance of the organizations he discusses—in fact, any American reader can think of other worthy groups he leaves out. But Mr. Smith largely omits the dark and difficult aspects of his subject. There have been a good many unhealthy voluntary organizations like the Ku Klux Klan; some organizations, such as labor unions, are now not so purely voluntary as Mr. Smith's account seems to indicate; and the long struggle in recent years over allegedly subversive organizations (see also No. 56) shows that the status of some voluntary associations is still in dispute.

P. P.

286. *Musical Comedy in America*

by CECIL SMITH

Americans are very likely to think that the musical comedy is an indigenous American art form and that through its invention they have contributed something rather special to the world's pleasures. Though this is true in part, the musical comedy is compounded of so many elements—comic opera, vaudeville, burlesque, farce, pageantry, and so on—and takes so many forms that, if America has a claim, it is not for the invention of an art form but for a process of distillation. No one quite knows what distinguishes musical comedy from other kinds of musical theatrical performance. The form is constantly changing. Is Gilbert & Sullivan, for example, "musical comedy"? No, the American will say, it is light opera, but he will be hard put to it to say why he makes the distinction. Cecil Smith (1906-1956) defines it as follows: ". . . musical comedy may be distinguished from such other forms of entertainment as comic opera and burlesque by its direct and essentially unstylized appropriation of vernacular types of song, dance, and subject matter; and it may be distinguished from its chief source of inspiration, the variety show, by its employment of a plot and, at least in some slight degree, of consistent characterization."

This is by no means a definition that limits the scope of his book. Smith considers historically the popular musical theater in America (as opposed to the serious musical theater, the opera) from its inception in the 1860's to the near present—from *The Black Crook* to *South Pacific* (see No. 253). He reviews the minstrel show, a great American favorite in the nineteenth century, the now almost defunct low comedy *cum* music *cum* strip tease called the burlesque, the musical extravaganzas, the elaborate revues based on the Folies Bergère, the "intimate reviews" which were mainly parodies, and the modern musical comedy with its shred of plot, its usually expensive production, its "song hits," and its ballets (called "dance numbers"). The heroes and heroines of this account are the "great names" of the musical theater—composers, directors, actors, singers, comedians, producers, dancers, and writers—of whom many were imported from Europe with reputations already established and many others grew to fame in America. Whether or not it is indigenous to America, of all forms of "live" theatrical performance today there is no question that the musical comedy in its many guises is the most popular with Americans.

R. L.

287. *Virgin Land*

by Henry Nash Smith

The United States became a great industrial nation—exploiting its natural resources, building machines and factories, and creating a vast transportation network—all in a sort of agrarian daydream. This book is an analysis of the myths and symbols around which that daydream was woven, and of the hold they have had upon the imaginations of the novelists, poets, and historians who have given expression to our self-image.

From the times of Thomas Jefferson to our own, the West has nourished an agrarian philosophy and myth which purports "to set forth the character and the destinies of the nation." Admirable as many aspects of the philosophy and myth have doubtless been, both encouraged men either to ignore the industrial revolution altogether or to regard it, in the author's words, as "an unfortunate and anomalous violation of the natural order of things." Just as Jefferson in the eighteenth century clung to his faith that the small landholder and husbandman were the basis of American democracy, Henry Ford in the twentieth, while carrying industrialism to one of its greatest climaxes, devoutly adhered, outside the factory, to the values and prejudices of the rural village and farm. The assembly line which Ford perfected may be as indigenous to our civilization as the square dances he helped to revive, but the agrarian daydream didn't permit either Ford or the rest of us to acknowledge that fact.

Professor Henry Nash Smith (1906-) explores the development of the myth from the theories expounded in eighteenth-century England and France to its classic formulation in the 1890's by the historian Frederick Jackson Turner (whose work is also discussed and expanded in W. P. Webb's *The Great Frontier* [No. 322]). Even more importantly, he traces the growth and modification of the myth in the imaginative literature and popular fiction which has crystallized it in the popular mind.

At the same time, Professor Smith analyzes the ways in which the materials out of which the myth was made were warped in the process of fitting them into the literary forms which were available to American writers. His chapter on James Fenimore Cooper's Leatherstocking (No. 67), for example, brilliantly describes the incompatibility of Cooper's real theme and the form of the sentimental novel as taken over by Cooper from his English contemporaries. And throughout the book Professor Smith has illuminating things to say about the extent to which the myth has shaped, and been shaped by, intellectual and literary conventions.

J. A. K.

288. *Creating an Industrial Civilization*

edited by EUGENE STALEY

An account of a conference on social problems, attended by disputatious men and women of many different backgrounds and interests, and reported by several observers, can scarcely make a single impression on the reader. The effect of unresolved variety is increased when the reports are interspersed with excerpts from stenotyped records of the actual conversations. All this is true of this book about the Corning Conference edited by Dr. Eugene Staley; and yet there is a strong impression to be gained from it, namely that men and women speaking for labor and management, education, science, religion, government and different nationalities, may agree in general on the aims of an industrial society and yet argue with good will and mutual benefit over the means of realizing them.

The conference was called in May, 1951, by the Corning Glass Company, manufacturers, at Corning, New York, in celebration of the company's centennial; and the American Council of Learned Societies joined in its sponsorship. It had, of course, no legislative or commercial purpose. There were among the delegates some differences in diagnosing our present discontents, for example as to the degree of success with which American resources for the good life are now being used. What is leisure for, anyhow? And who shall decide what to do with it? Is it possible for workers standing at assembly lines to get satisfaction out of their work? The three days of talk were mainly devoted to these two themes, derived from four background papers which had covered Work, Leisure, Community, and Confidence.

Nowhere in these deliberations was there any sign of surrender to the tyranny of machines. One labor delegate said: "Human beings are fighting back!" And a psychologist rejected the original statement of the conference theme, which was "Living in an Industrial Civilization," in favor of the title of the book, "*Creating* an Industrial Civilization." To the extent that agreement came out of all the discussions here reported, it was focussed on militancy and hope.

L. B.

289. *The Autobiography of Lincoln Steffens*

Among American autobiographies those of Benjamin Franklin (see No. 123) and Henry Adams are pre-eminent; on a lower level the name of Lincoln Steffens (1866-1936) deserves a similar place. In accomplishment he ranks well below the other two; but as an observer he is their equal, and his account touches most closely our own industrial age.

Born in California, Steffens from boyhood manifested a probing curiosity about the meanings of life. The son of a well-to-do merchant, he studied at the University of California and, after graduation, for three years in France and Germany, choosing ethics as his subject. He concluded that although his professors were learned, they could lead him but a short distance toward the understanding he craved, and he returned to the United States believing that he would be able to answer his own crowding questions better through working and living than from a scholar's study. He turned to journalism, and showed high skill as an interviewer and writer; then shifted to the magazine field, and became associated with writers like Ida M. Tarbell and Ray Stannard Baker, who were probing the abuses of business and politics then rampant in American life. With them he became a "muckraker."

Steffens chose politics as his field and, invading a number of cities and states, he exposed with startling skill the corruption existing behind the façade of representative government. His magazine articles reappeared in such books as *The Shame of the Cities* (1904) and exerted a wide influence. Steffens found the reformers often impractical, the bosses realistic. He came to feel that the opportunities for profit permitted by a careless citizenry were the cause of the evils he found. When asked once where "graft" began, he went back to Adam, who blamed Eve, who said, "No, no . . . it was the serpent." Said Steffens: "Now I come and I am trying to show you that it was, and is, the apple." When accused of being an anarchist, he retorted that he was worse—a believer in the principles of Christianity. Later he became fascinated with the Communist experiment in Russia, although as an extreme individualist he would probably in time have rejected it. While persistently seeking the truth, Steffens was a popular writer rather than a searching theorist like Thorstein Veblen (No. 315). His account of his experiences with American business, politics, labor, and government from 1895 through to the 1920's is unsurpassed for its liveliness, shrewdness, and revealing clarity.

F. E. H.

290. *Mormon Country*

by WALLACE STEGNER

In 1847, the members of the Church of Jesus Christ of the Latter-day Saints, founded in western New York State by Joseph Smith in 1830, had been so driven from place to place and so persecuted that Brigham Young (who had succeeded Smith as their president) decided they should leave their winter quarters, at Council Bluffs, Iowa, and seek a region which other Americans would not covet. Accordingly, he led an advance party west to the valley of Great Salt Lake in Utah. "This is the place," he said, and the next morning his followers were planting crops on the valley floor.

The Mormons, as these people were usually called (because of their acceptance of The Book of Mormon as a truly ancient manuscript-history of the Western Hemisphere), had come to the bowl-like depression, surrounded by high mountains, which holds the big blue lake. After the remaining members of the sect had arrived, Young began sending them out to establish farms and towns. They settled in the deserts, rocky canyons, and treeless barrens of a strangely beautiful land where high winds had sculptured the red sandstone rocks into grotesque statuary. Here they plowed, irrigated, and planted, learning an agriculture that was to conquer all obstacles and bring prosperity. Today the apparently unproductive earth has proved rich in both crops and metals.

Mormon Country, by Wallace Stegner (1909-), is a sensitive and authoritative essay. No adequate history of the Mormons and their land empire could be compressed into so few words, but the author has chosen the most significant facts about Utah and its environs to give his readers both history and atmosphere. Because of their intelligence, their pioneering spirit, and their strong belief that Joseph Smith was a true prophet of the Lord, the Mormons —now numbering nearly 2,000,000 United States citizens (besides thousands in foreign countries throughout the world)—are a unique people. "Peculiar" is their own descriptive word for themselves.

The Mormons have qualities not observed among Americans who live in other sections of the United States and who subscribe to other religious creeds. Theirs is a separate chapter in the history of the American West. In contrast to the riotous and amoral communities of frontier days, the Mormon settlements were quiet, religious, hard-working, and thrifty. Mr. Stegner, who has lived fifteen years of his life among Mormons, describes their differences from their fellow-Americans with sensitivity and perception.

C. C.

291. *Selected Writings of Gertrude Stein*

edited by CARL VAN VECHTEN

To the general reader Gertrude Stein (1874-1946) is known for two things: one, a line of perhaps verse—"A rose is a rose is a rose"—the other, for having put upon Ernest Hemingway and his age-fellows the tag, Lost Generation. Among critics and scholars she was a center of controversy, and loved it. Being early convinced that she, like her later friend Picasso, was a genius, she set out to win acceptance. The battle lines formed and there was no neutrality.

She was an American twice removed, by derivation from a minority, by choice expatriate. In her student days her teacher was William James, author of the disturbing *Varieties of Religious Experience* (No. 164). With the bright new weapon of psychology, she aimed at a different target, literary piety. From her experiment in automatic writing she learned that most language, written or spoken, was, if not quite automatic, certainly stereotyped, a conclusion since verified by students of linguistics. From this beginning came her experiment of breaking up language in order to recover meaning, to recapture the experience out of which language had been born.

She has recorded that when she met Picasso she at once recognized a fellow genius. There is no question of their likeness. Both were attempting to break up, smash old forms and create new. In "Melanctha" she has not yet quite found her medium. It is, as Carl Van Vechten says, "imbued with the influence of Cézanne." In other words, she is here halfway between the old writing and the new, in her manipulation of language new, in feeling old.

"The Making of Americans" is interminable, literally. Miss Stein gave up after having written how many thousand words? and it has never been successfully denied that no reader has ever read it to the end. The "Autobiography" is different. It is communication, and got a hearing for the "Lectures" and "Four Saints." Then, after some ten years, in writing "Wars I Have Seen," it was as if she had again heard Melanctha's Jeff saying, "What could he ever know, who had to find his way with just thinking?" Meanwhile she had long been an oracle to the young writers who sat at her slipper-shod feet.

J. A. R.

292. *The Grapes of Wrath*

by JOHN STEINBECK

In the almost two decades since its first publication (1939) *The Grapes of Wrath* has emerged as a kind of *Uncle Tom's Cabin* (No. 297) of the Depression. Constantly reprinted, made into a successful motion picture, it has reached the hearts and minds of millions of Americans. The attention paid to improving conditions in the Dust Bowl of the Southwest is in large part the consequence of this compassionate novel. In two respects it is distinguished sharply from the "proletarian fiction" of its decade. First, the author's cause is not that of a party, but of people; second, these people live. *The Grapes of Wrath* is squarely in the tradition of the humanitarian novel and has certain qualities that may remind the reader of *Les Misérables* or *Oliver Twist.*

Yet it is intensely American. Its characters, the dispossessed and disinherited small farmers and sharecroppers of Oklahoma and Arkansas, are completely untouched by non-native influences. They are of old American stock, these Joads, God-fearing, simple, pathetic in their hopefulness, inspiring in their self-reliance. They are the kind of folks who once created the country west of the Appalachians. But in a fiercely competitive culture their virtues are given no chance of expression. Lured to California by false hopes, they are exploited, reduced to virtual peonage. The respectable America of the west coast tolerates them only as serfs, not as citizens.

John Steinbeck (1902-) draws a picture that is powerful, generally moving, occasionally (as in the much-debated final scene) theatrical. There can be no question of his deep sincerity; or of his equally deep knowledge of the folk myths, folk talk, folk obscenities of the strange migrant culture he describes; or of his feeling for the land, whether it be California's lush valleys or Arkansas's devastated bowl of dust. Pity and indignation have merged to create a book that still has power, though the conditions it describes no longer obtain, to stir us to a more thoughtful patriotism.

C. F.

293. *The Passport*

by SAUL STEINBERG

America's most original and gifted contemporary visual satirist, Saul Steinberg (1914-), became an American citizen in the 1940's. He was born in Rumania, studied architecture in Milan and, as he was anti-Fascist, found it expedient to come to the Western Hemisphere (first to Haiti and Santo Domingo). He arrived in New York in 1942. The next year he joined the United States Navy, was soon transferred to the Office of Strategic Services, and served in the Orient (where he taught guerrilla fighters how to blow up bridges), in Italy, India, and North Africa. He lives in New York, travels extensively, and draws everything. His work appears frequently in *The New Yorker* magazine (see No. 234), and his drawings are in many museums and private collections.

Mr. Steinberg does not like to be called a cartoonist; he is a serious artist, an extraordinarily facile draftsman with a biting, elliptical, and deceptively simple but extremely decorative style. He sees everything, as he once said, with a line around it, and everything is worth drawing. He is a visual wit, and many of his drawings are visual puns—plays on line. His humor does not depend, as does that of many cartoonists, on "gags"; he thinks with his eyes. The quarry of his satire is almost exclusively pretension—in architecture, in dress, in officialdom, in ostentation of every sort. His parodies of official documents, of group photographs, of mustachioed generals, fake cowboys, tycoons, false-fronted buildings, automobiles, skyscrapers, and frilled and furred women are at once pitiless and amused. He is a moralist but not a reformer, a critic but not a crusader, and his vision of America is less the record of a country (though there is a deadly accuracy to his satire) than a concept of human fallibility stated in local terms.

R. L.

294. *The Builders of the Bridge*

The Story of John Roebling and His Son

by D. B. Steinman

The Brooklyn Bridge, built in 1869-1883 across New York's East River to link Manhattan Island with Brooklyn, is not only one of the nineteenth century's greatest engineering triumphs but also one of its artistic masterpieces. In the tension between the massive repose of its granite towers and the supple lightness of its steel cables and roadway, the architecture of the past meets the architecture of the future (as Lewis Mumford says in *The Brown Decades* [No. 227]) in a climactic moment of transition.

Significantly, the men who designed and built the bridge were not architects but engineers, who thought only in terms of "how the thing was going to work and how to make it last." The professional architects of that time were, by contrast, primarily concerned with surface ornament and styles. It was the engineers who made the great nineteenth-century advances in construction and demonstrated in practice the validity of the very "modern" architectural theories which had been vigorously, sometimes tartly, expressed in the 1840's by Horatio Greenough (No. 131).

But the Roeblings' masterpiece is more than a great work of engineering and architecture; it has become a symbol through which painters and poets have sought to project their visions of America. To it Hart Crane dedicated his epic poem, *The Bridge* (1930), most of which is included in *The Oxford Book of American Verse* (No. 208). One of the many paintings inspired by the bridge is Joseph Stella's, reproduced in *The Columbia Historical Portrait of New York* (No. 174).

The Roeblings' story is told here by one of the great bridge engineers of the twentieth century, David B. Steinman (1886-), born in the shadow of the Brooklyn Bridge just three years after it had been completed. To its inspiration he credits his own rise from a poor boy to the height of his profession; to honor its builders he took five years out of his professional life to write this biography of the father, John A. Roebling (1806-69), who rose from a poor immigrant to be the founder of a great industry and who gave his life to the bridge he had dreamed, and the son, Washington, who sacrificed his health and all his dynamic energies to complete the monumental work his father had begun.

J. A. K.

295. *The Collected Poems of Wallace Stevens*

Is the work of a businessman incompatible with that of a poet? Wallace Stevens (1879-1955) did not think so; to the end of his life he was the successful officer of an insurance company, meanwhile distilling from his whole experience these strange revelations of sensibility. Many readers find him almost impossible to understand at first acquaintance. They are assured by critics, other poets, and a body of devoted readers which has grown steadily for a generation that his meanings are worth digging for.

The obscurities in Stevens, however, if it is fair to call them that, are not caused by the literary and historical allusions which sometimes burden the writings of T. S. Eliot or Ezra Pound (see Nos. 208 and 336). Those two poets (American-born but choosing to be Europeans) sometimes seem to be testing a reader's erudition rather than his responsiveness. The difficulty for a new reader of Stevens is rather that the poet evades the obvious meanings of what he has to say. Since every work of art has layers of more and more recondite significance, Stevens decided that he could leave out the structure of event or logic on which his essences depend, and give us the essences pure. The effect, once achieved, is communication of a special intensity.

If the fact that the poet was also a businessman had any effect at all upon the subject matter of these poems, it may be in the frequent hints of a background of cultivation and commonplace luxury. This poet is not roaming the world, except in his imagination. He finds cosmic significance enough in the comforts of home or as much of the exotic as is available to a businessman on a vacation cruise. In this, in spite of his strange images, he is like some Dutch painters who saw the problems of man's fate in the sunlight and shadow on ordinary things.

It is the business of a poet not to be "national" in any obvious way but to help make national tradition in new forms. So Wallace Stevens was a deviant, as Edgar Allan Poe (No. 248) and Walt Whitman (No. 333), in such widely different ways, were also deviants. It remains to be seen how much of his unique quality will come to be known as "American."

L. B.

296. U.S. 40

by GEORGE R. STEWART

Though there are parkways, turnpikes, and thruways (so spelled) which carry an increasing share of American motor traffic, numbered routes still dominate travel by automobile and truck. Of these, U.S. 40—one of the eight main highways which span the continent—provides a national cross-section in both space and time. Geographically it runs through the center of the country, traversing parts of fourteen states, eight of our largest cities, and hundreds of towns and villages. It crosses the Atlantic coastal plain, the Appalachians, the prairies and great plains, the Rockies, the great basin, the Sierra Nevada, and the coast range. It passes through the corn belt, the wheat belt, and the cattle kingdom; through grasslands, forests, and desert. Chronologically it spans the nation's history. George Washington as a young man laid out part of it; part of it was the first national road, authorized during Thomas Jefferson's administration; and long stretches of it follow the Boonslick Trail, Zane's Trace, the California Trail, and other roads along which the nation moved westward to the Pacific.

This book about U.S. 40 is an attempt, then, to present a cross-section not only of the nation as it was when the author drove across it in 1949 and again in 1950, but also of the history which underlies and shapes the present reality. Like several other books in this collection it is an experiment in the new "picture-book" form, combining photographs and text in an integrated design (see Barbara Morgan's *Summer's Children* [No. 222]). The author's chosen photographs are deliberately documentary rather than impressionistic, and the accompanying text serves the double function of conveying what cannot be shown in pictures and of calling attention to precisely what the pictures do reveal.

Before publishing *U.S. 40,* George Stewart (1895-) had written two best-selling novels, *Storm* (1941) and *Fire* (1948), both of which displayed an extraordinary gift for developing the dramatic significance of technical data and masses of concrete factual information. His notes for both those novels included hundreds of photographs of objects, processes, and places with which his stories were concerned—an experience which must have taught him a great deal about what can be derived from a picture apart from its over-all aesthetic effect.

J. A. K.

297. *Uncle Tom's Cabin*

by Harriet Beecher Stowe

"So you're the little woman who wrote the book that made this great war!" It is with these words that Abraham Lincoln greeted Harriet Beecher Stowe (1811-1896) when she was introduced to him in 1862, the second year of the Civil War. The compliment to the author's powers is not so extravagant as it now might seem: perhaps no other single book has ever so directly influenced the course of history as *Uncle Tom's Cabin*. In America, in the first year after its publication, it sold 300,000 copies—it is not possible to compute the number of copies that were subsequently printed, in all languages all over the world—and the effect that it had on American anti-slavery sentiment was enormous. It overrode considerations of national policy and brought the issue of morality and humaneness squarely to the fore.

In the year after its publication, *Uncle Tom's Cabin* was dramatized, with unheard-of success. It was played all over the North by troupes of every kind. Its popularity continued for decades, and the "Tom Show," as it was called, became proverbial for its melodrama, sentimentality, and bad, extravagant acting. It is perhaps in the light of its stage presentations that the novel is chiefly remembered. This is unjust, for actually the novel is by no means bad. Mrs. Stowe was no genius, but she had a very competent talent and she could tell a good straightforward story. Indignant as she is at the institution of slavery, she tries to be fair to the South—though no Southern reader is likely to think she has succeeded. Of Uncle Tom's several masters, only Legree is represented as actually brutal, and Mrs. Stowe is at pains to say that the cruelty lies in the system and not in the plantation owners. She was an intelligent woman and there is intelligence in her novel.

As for the book's creative power, it must at least be said that no other work has contributed so many legendary figures to American lore, even though some of them are referred to with irony: Eliza crossing the ice to escape the bloodhounds is the type of persecuted innocence, as Little Eva is the type of saccharine self-conscious childish virtue; whatever has no ascertainable origins can be counted on to bring a reference to Topsy, who "never was born" and just "growed"; Simon Legree is the name for any cruel superior; and among Negroes Uncle Tom is—rather unfairly—the name for a Negro who ingratiates himself with the whites by his pious sentiments.

L. T.

298. *The Autobiography of an Idea*

by Louis H. Sullivan

Of the three great names of American architecture—H. H. Richardson, Louis H. Sullivan, and Frank Lloyd Wright—the one most tragically and paradoxically fixed in a high place is that of Louis Henri Sullivan (1856-1924). For a time he was an unchallenged leader of his profession, yet he died in penniless obscurity. He was a master and devotee of ornament, yet his principle that "form follows function" has been used by his successors to excuse an almost complete absence of ornament. He was an originator in designing "skyscrapers" that made the most of steel-frame construction, yet his pioneering path has not been followed by others in any number nor have his major buildings been treated with the respect they deserve. (Other examples of his work are in Nos. 113 and 227.) Sullivan was by all accounts a difficult man to get on with—"You have a God-given eye," his grandfather told him, "and a dull heart"—and he remains difficult to explain, a genius who seems *sui generis* in all respects but one: his determination to produce a style of design, devoid of imitation and falsity, that would be generic to his native land (see also Nos. 131 and 228).

Out of foliate and fibrous patterns from the natural world, plus an inborn sense of somewhat mystical geometry, Sullivan created his new "order" in architecture. But, like the mythology that the English poet William Blake invented under similar pressures, it led nowhere. Sullivan dominated Chicago in the heyday of its adventurous construction, but the World's Fair of 1893—followed by a stock-market panic and depression—ended his pre-eminence. The Fair, the "white city by the lake," persuaded a majority of Midwestern Americans that an imported, eclectic "classicism" was the standard of perfection. What Sullivan called "the feudal idea," and hated, came between the public and his own passionate dream of an indigenous and "democratic" architecture, condemning him to failure and reserving the ultimate success for his pupil and protégé, Frank Lloyd Wright (see No. 347).

In later years, cut off from his natural medium of expression, Sullivan turned to writing in the hope of somehow conveying his own "idea" before it was lost. The first bound copy of his autobiography was brought to him, in a small hotel room in Chicago's South Side, two days before he died.

E. L.

299. *Alexander Calder*

by James Johnson Sweeney

Like a good many other American artists who are now in the forefront of creative innovation, Alexander Calder (1898-) had his awakening in Paris. The modern movement that had been born in Paris during the first decade of the century was still sending out new branches, and in 1925, just a year before Mr. Calder's arrival, the great Exposition of Decorative Arts had shown what the "international style" meant in furniture, glass, tapestries, and other objects intended not for the museum but for the house and the office.

Alexander Calder carried away with him an idea admirably suited to his strong constructive instincts, and he has made it his own by playing changes upon it with a virtuosity unparalleled in modern American sculpture. That idea was the mobile; the use, namely, of modern materials in attenuated shapes that act as lines defining broader and more complex spaces than did traditional sculpture. Some of Mr. Calder's mobiles have "subjects" or starting points, but their interest lies in the multiplicity of aspects that they offer to the view, whether in stillness or in motion. In this regard they may be likened to a mountain—to the skeleton of a mountain, rather—which invisible forces might have set astir.

Sometimes Mr. Calder's mobiles are motor-driven; at other times they are firmly moored and become stabiles. But in any case they have the role of occupying and dividing space in such a way that the beholder sees endless vistas of forms—as in the Cubist painting and sculpture from which Mr. Calder derives, but still more liberated from representation and solidity. His sculpture is aerial and dynamic in the literal sense of the words.

James Johnson Sweeney (1900-), an authority on James Joyce and T. S. Eliot, and formerly a curator of the Museum of Modern Art, now directs the Guggenheim Museum of nonrepresentative art. His sympathy with modernism as well as his great learning make him the ideal introducer of Mr. Calder, through words and pictures, to a public which still contains a large number of the unsuspecting blind: though they brush by all the elements of modern art in their daily routine, they seem still to be petrified when a Calder, a Marcel Duchamp, or a Henry Moore organizes these elements for them in powerful and imaginative creations.

J. B.

300. *Crime and the Community*

by FRANK TANNENBAUM

Crime in any society, says Professor Tannenbaum (1893-), is a function of the whole of that society; or, to put it bluntly, crime in America is the crime which American society deserves and even desires, so that nothing short of a total change in this society will totally alter the amount and kind of crime it has. Drives against criminals, moral outcries, and legal reforms will by themselves avail little or nothing, just as improvement of prison and parole systems will still miss the mark. (See, however, John Bartlow Martin's description of the genesis of a prison riot in *Prize Articles 1954* [No. 251] for how badly such reforms are needed.) Professor Tannenbaum says these things with compassion and yet with firmness; nor in the end does he venture to suggest how the society he considers might totally change itself. He is interested in what he finds to be the facts, and he sticks to them faithfully throughout his long investigation of a subject which many would prefer to ignore. As facts they are singularly eloquent; they have impressed those in America who ought to be impressed; and they will enlighten people in other countries who do not know what to think, say, about gangs and gangsters and the cities that do not suppress them.

Professor Tannenbaum explains the gang—itself a little society within a great one—in terms of a national history whose final maturing chapter remains to be written. A tradition of unrest, unsettlement, and violence still provides the possibility that men and boys will organize themselves against the law and look upon themselves as free competitors with its power. The American criminal is usually indebted to such an organization for his motives and his techniques. And even the organization is indebted to a society which not only tolerates but uses it for special purposes, not invariably corrupt, though sometimes they are so, undreamed of by the average peaceful citizen. It is here that Professor Tannenbaum makes his most disturbing contribution. Politics and crime have an extraordinary relation in the cities of America. Both are organized, and too often both are cynical. And the community in which this is possible continues to exist.

M. V. D.

301. *Alice Adams*

by BOOTH TARKINGTON

If it is useful to compare a competent and representative novel with a great one, we might say that Tarkington's *Alice Adams* is an American *Madame Bovary*. The comparison shows the differences between the American fiction of a generation ago and the French tradition, the differences between a realistic civilization and a puritanical one. Novels now being written in the United States, such as James T. Farrell's *Studs Lonigan* (No. 107) or John O'Hara's *Appointment in Samarra* (No. 237), represent a successful defiance of the puritan tradition. Booth Tarkington (1869-1946) was a puritan but he was also a realist. The phases of life he chose to depict are set forth honestly in a fine lucid style.

Alice Adams herself is innocent and in the end triumphant. She lives in narrow circumstances, among commonplace and insensitive people. She dreams of escaping from meanness into provincial social glory. Her posturings and coquetries are those of a young girl, not an experienced woman; her dreams are vague and also innocent. But her spirit is just as bruised by reality as was the more determined, more sensual, and more complicated spirit of Emma Bovary in a provincial town in France.

The happy ending might be put down to the old, bad American habit of bringing all real problems to an unreal solution except that it is happy only because Alice grows up. Even in France in Flaubert's time there must have been silly women who grew up and came to terms with life. The time of the story of Alice, in the swift changes in American life, is marked by the nature of the fate she dreaded—which was to go to work. The happy ending comes when she walks up the dingy steps of the business college to learn stenography and sees that "the steps at the top were gay with sunshine." This meant for Alice triumph over her phantasies and her pride. Times have so changed that, in present-day America, going to work would seem another romance to a girl like Alice. Her test of character would come, however, sooner or later, and Tarkington has made a touching story of how the test must be met by the young in a society mobile and socially tolerant but inhabited, like all other societies, by the foolish, the cruel, and the proud.

L. B.

302. *Center Ring*

by Robert Lewis Taylor

Since colonial days, the circus has been part of American life. Though not indigenous to the United States, the circus of vast size and mobility was distinctively American. Where the British circus is a caravan, the continental circus a music hall fitted with a single-ring arena, the Middle Eastern circus a side show, the American—as perfected by the Ringling Brothers and Barnum & Bailey (see No. 103)—was an enormous, nomadic, three-ring composite. Billed since impresario P. T. Barnum's days (1810-1891) as "The Greatest Show on Earth," it was a spectacular form of entertainment, offering multiple exhibitions in gigantic tents, and moving performers, staff, working crew, animals, and paraphernalia on its own railway cars.

Center Ring, by Robert Lewis Taylor (1912-), is not a formal history of the big circus, but it does give, through profiles of important persons of the contemporary circus, a feeling of the traditions and flavor existing in an institution that employed about 250 performers of 27 nationalities. Mr. Taylor has been a circus "aficionado" since he sneaked under the tent flaps as a small boy, and a tinge of boyish delight remains in his sophisticated reporting. He traces the careers of such circus personalities as John Ringling North (whose rise to managerial power is termed "a triumph of hoopla over decorum"); press agent Roland Butler ("a confidence man at heart"); personnel director and former clown Pat Valdo; the late Lillian Leitzel and her aerialist partner and husband, Alfred Codona; the great clown Emmet Kelly; the superb trapeze artists known as The Flying Concellos; and Gargantua, the world's best known and possibly unhappiest gorilla.

Mr. Taylor's book was completed just before the suspension of outdoor, "Big Top" circus operations in 1956. In his Introduction he mentions dwindling profits, high cost of operation, and lack of facilities in crowded cities, but a more searching look would reveal that the circus, perhaps fighting the competition of television, had been losing its old dignity and gradually becoming a slick extravaganza, overdecorated with such artificialities as tinted sawdust. Whatever the reasons, the circus as Mr. Taylor had known it was vanishing; his book at least serves to document its more memorable aspects.

C. C.

303. *The Great Experiment*

by Frank Thistlethwaite

A book written to provide the British undergraduate with what he needs to know about American history might have been expected to seem strange to an American reader. Frank Thistlethwaite (1915-), however, who teaches at Cambridge University, writes very much like an American professor —though better than most of them—and differs only in being more gentle with our faults and less boastful about our virtues. His errors of fact are minute and inconsequential.

The knowledge of the country on which this history is based is not entirely derived from its substantial documentation. The author has studied and taught in the United States enough to catch the spiritual accent of our lives. He uses a principle of organization in his story, not unknown to natives, but not used by others with so much effect. He describes the origins and growth of a "mobile" society. He says in explaining his purpose, "The American variant of Western society is a new thing."

The first migrations across the Atlantic, and then the pouring in of great numbers of European pioneers who overflowed further and further westward, kept the pot boiling until immigration was checked. At that point, Mr. Thistlethwaite says, America became nationalistic in a new way and its problems were changed. The second World War projected the American struggle with the difficulties of democracy and power on the world stage. The mobile society has become a mighty factor in world politics.

This brief but substantial history serves as introduction to such a comprehensive work as Samuel Eliot Morison and Henry Steele Commager's *The Growth of the American Republic* (No. 225). The drama of immigrant life is depicted in Mary Antin's *The Promised Land* (No. 13) and in Oscar Handlin's *The Uprooted* (No. 136). Bernard DeVoto's trilogy, beginning with *Across the Wide Missouri* (No. 91), describes the western expansion, and Mari Sandoz's *Old Jules* (No. 275) gives a vivid, true account of the struggles of the settlers of the West with natural odds, as it lasted even into the twentieth century. These books are a few of those that give color and detail to "the great experiment," indicating both the difficulties and the energies that will decide its success. Frank Thistlethwaite is one informed and thoughtful observer who thinks that "the most ambitious ideal ever to command the allegiance of a great nation" still has a chance.

L. B.

304. *A Socialist's Faith*

by NORMAN THOMAS

It is a socialist leader who writes, "By any simple interpretation of the Marxist formula the United States . . . should have had long ere this a very strong socialist movement. . . . Actually, in no advanced Western nation is organized socialism so weak." Norman Thomas (1884-) has been six times the Presidential nominee of the American Socialist party and he has been the leader of the "weak" movement for a lifetime. In his political autobiography and declaration of principles he tells why he continues in his faith in spite of never attaining political success.

In one sense, the socialist movement in the United States has been successful. One after another, changes advocated by the socialists—measures for social welfare or the restraint of capitalist management—have been incorporated into the platforms of both major parties and legislated into effect. Norman Thomas, who began as a clergyman and had to break with his church because of his pacificism in 1917, has been breaking with orthodoxies all his life, and has watched the progress of his ideas into new orthodoxies.

America has avoided Socialism, Thomas says, not by falling into either Fascism or Communism (both of which he has fought against) but by the prosperity of capitalism, which has been aided by the continental scope of the economy and by a constitutional system which makes splinter parties futile in the struggle for power.

No political party, under any of the leaders who have been his contemporaries, has achieved as much for social justice as Mr. Thomas has thought possible. He admired the political skill of Franklin D. Roosevelt but says that "by his peace policies or lack of them he made the going for democratic socialism or any constructive substitute unnecessarily difficult throughout the world." But Mr. Thomas does not think the leaders of other countries have done much better, for he is as much opposed to the domination of the state over the individual as any nineteenth-century liberal.

In his apologia, Norman Thomas explains why the movement he has led has had a pragmatic rather than a formal success; he reveals in the process how a man can become a national citizen, admired and trusted by all kinds of Americans, without ever lessening his radical criticism of national faults.

L. B.

305. *The Works of Thoreau*

edited by HENRY S. CANBY

Henry David Thoreau's reputation is not so much growing as hardening. It is possible that he will outlast all other American writers of the past 150 years. He attracts strongly, is quoted constantly, has nothing about him of the "recommended" classic. He and his major works, especially *Walden,* become more and more central as the years go by.

The reason for this is rather an odd one. He is a great stylist, possibly the greatest commander of the *sentence* in English prose. He is a first-rate nature-writer (though not a first-rate scientist). But these do not deeply touch the meaning of his flintlike durability. What makes him of passionate interest to us is that he is opposed—not obliquely, not implicitly, not partially—but head-on opposed to most of what we now believe. The most eloquent attack on mid-twentieth-century American life was made by a man born in 1817 whose greatest book was published in 1854 and who died in 1862.

This man did not have time to waste in making money. He distrusted the state; indeed his essay on *Civil Disobedience* profoundly influenced Tolstoi and Gandhi, and so world history. He cared little for comfort or for things, for profit-making or profit-taking. He rejected industrialism and technology years before they had even come to their first flowering. He had no religion unless it was nonconformism. "Progress" he derided; social-mindedness and do-goodism no less, despite his defense of John Brown. He stood for himself and he abhorred systems of interdependence and mutual aid. The life of activity and accumulation meant nothing to him; he lived a life of thought and observation. He distrusted the city and felt that man's first duty was to seek out his proper relation to nature. He preached one non-twentieth-century word: Simplify.

Thoreau is alive because he makes us question ourselves and the life we have made for ourselves. He is not doctrinaire or reformist or propagandist. He is a great artist in words; and so makes us eager to follow him even in his indictment of our dearest aims. That is why he seems so contemporary.

C. F.

306. *The Thurber Carnival*

by JAMES THURBER

The secret life of James Thurber (1894-)—which he is at some pains to reveal in this collection of his essays, stories, fables, and drawings—is a continual state of war with no armistice in sight. He depicts himself as a mild and docile man haunted by the fear of suffocation, inwardly in conflict with domesticity and the powerful female, trapped by convention, and forever seeking escape. He is on the side of men who daydream their way out of bondage into heroism, out of the humdrum into adventure. There is something of Walter Mitty (of his famous "The Secret Life of Walter Mitty," here included) in nearly all of Mr. Thurber's stories and in many of his drawings as well—a reality heightened in fantasy but never disassociated from the commonplace, and a kind of progression from the usual to the fantastic (and often hilarious) in perfectly logical steps. He is a satirist and parodist of remarkable economy and precision, and his style is deceptively casual and relaxed, almost as though he were surprised himself to be stating such large observations in so simple a frame.

Mr. Thurber's reputation as a storyteller and humorist, of which he is surely one of the most accomplished now writing in English, is very closely associated with *The New Yorker,* to which he has been a regular contributor for as long as the magazine has existed (see Nos. 233-4). *The Thurber Carnival* is a selection which he has made himself from a number of earlier collections of his short pieces. His reputation as a cartoonist is based almost not at all on his drawings but on the captions, which are literary rather than visual humor. He has had few imitators as a cartoonist (no one who could draw would imitate him) though he has had a far-reaching effect on the "gag" cartoon as an instrument of fey social satire. He has also had few literary imitators (no one who can write *could* imitate him). He is one of the few humorists of the twentieth century whose reputation is already secure, and is likely to become securer.

R. L.

307. *Yankee Lawyer*

The Autobiography of Ephraim Tutt

by ARTHUR TRAIN

Since Americans first recognized traits typical of an area or group among themselves, the nation's writers have attempted to present them in literary works. Royall Tyler's inclusion of Jonathan in his play, *The Contrast,* produced in 1787 (see No. 253), was certainly in the pattern if it did not set it. The honest, unlettered, self-respecting Yankee, comic in his misconceptions but wise and virtuous beyond what might have been expected from his background, was the first of a long parade of such figures on the American stage. Certainly a logical parallel to him is James Fenimore Cooper's old scout, Leatherstocking (see No. 67), whose adventures have influenced writers in many countries.

The most recent of such widely loved character-creations has been Arthur Train's Ephraim Tutt, sometimes called "the best known lawyer in America." Train (1875-1945), himself a lawyer, brought to his work such ingenuity of plot, such authentic background, and such convincing corroborative detail, that many of his readers believed Tutt to be a real person and accepted *Yankee Lawyer* as an authentic record (see also No. 278). One disillusioned reader was so enraged at discovering that Tutt was a product of a writer's fancy that he sued Arthur Train in the courts of law for practicing a deception on the public by offering for sale a book of which the contents were not as stated in its title.

The people of many nationalities have been fascinated by fictional characters who have depended upon their wits to defeat less admirable persons who have sought to take unfair advantage of the helpless. Ephraim Tutt may therefore be regarded as a creation with universal appeal, though he is at the same time a summing-up of many qualities which Americans like to regard as distinctively their own.

C. C.

308. *The Liberal Imagination*

by LIONEL TRILLING

No other book of literary criticism published since the second World War has found so large an audience in America as *The Liberal Imagination*. The success of the book in no small part results from the qualities Lionel Trilling (1905-) shares with any fine critic—his acute and generous intelligence, his extensive reading, his power of analysis, his admirable style.

But in part, too, the success of the book results from its attempt to find a way out of a peculiar impasse American criticism had reached by the time of the war. The preceding years had been unusually rich in the development of criticism, but the development had proceeded in two directions diametrically opposed. Headed in one direction were the ideological critics, arguing that the function of literature is to dramatize certain ideas so that they will prevail in history. (The literary historian Vernon Louis Parrington [No. 242], discussed in Mr. Trilling's first essay, is an example.) Headed in the opposite direction was, and continues to be, the group called the New Critics, who argue that a literary work is autonomous. They do not judge a work by the ideas it contains but by its specifically literary qualities; since what they find valuable in the work is timeless, they tend to regard history as irrelevant to criticism; although many of them have been deeply interested in politics and society, they deny that the object of literature is social action. (Among critics Mr. Trilling mentions, Allen Tate, Cleanth Brooks, Robert Penn Warren, and Austin Warren are closely identified with the New Criticism and are represented in Morton Zabel's *Literary Opinion in America* [No. 349].)

Mr. Trilling is an eclectic critic in a good sense. He rejects the ideology of the ideological critics, and with it their easy optimism, their limited view of human possibility (especially the possibility of evil), and their simple notion of the relation between art and action. In taste and technique and literary sophistication he is much closer to the New Critics, but he thinks they isolate the literary work too much; he agrees that it is autonomous, but he insists that its autonomy is *conditioned,* and the conditions he is particularly concerned to defend are history and ideas.

In recent years American literary criticism has often been a kind of metaphor of political and social thought. Mr. Trilling has made that metaphor more explicit, and his book has deeply influenced the thinking of many readers not primarily interested in literature.

P. P.

309. *The Middle of the Journey*

by Lionel Trilling

The years of the Depression in the United States were characterized by a sudden addiction of the intellectuals to Marxism. Whereas previously the nation had been criticized in the name of art and general culture, now it was indicted further in the name of social injustice and unworkable anarchy. The two movements embraced the same facts in successive views that gave expression to a common idealism. And Russia was of course the Mecca of the new faith.

As this mood of the early 1930's had to weather the shocks of the Russian purges, the pact with Nazi Germany, and the contradictions of the unpredictable Moscow line, the conspiratorial character of modern Communism was disclosed and innumerable individual disillusions and disasters followed. *The Middle of the Journey* depicts a representative instance, rooted in closely observed reality but in no sense to be taken as autobiography. The somewhat passive hero is a device for witnessing the deconversion of the famous Communist "courier" Gifford Maxim in contrast with the muddled, well-meaning "liberalism" of the Croom couple. These last, incidentally, were not patterned after any namable people, and if in retrospect they look like portraits of persons made notorious in a famous trial, this only shows the perceptiveness of a writer who compounded a vivid reality out of a diffuse phenomenon.

Lionel Trilling (1905-), though best known as America's leading literary critic in the generation following Edmund Wilson's (Nos. 337-8), has published other fiction besides this one novel. All of his work is marked by intensity of thought expressed in the calmest prose. He conveys animation by wit and unexpected comparisons, rather than by any violence of vocabulary. Because his chief critical works have been about Matthew Arnold and E. M. Forster he has been taken for a disciple of either or both, but this facile conclusion is false. He has written no less notably and profoundly about Keats, and the likeness of mind and style is far closer there, despite the difference of genres.

J. B.

310. *Year of Decisions*

by HARRY S. TRUMAN

The career of Harry S. Truman (1884-) will always be debated by students of democratic government, because it is in a sense a test case of that kind of government. After a long and for the most part unremarkable career, much of it in the humbler political ranks, Mr. Truman suddenly found himself the head of one of the most powerful nations of the world at a time of unsurpassed criticalness. The death of Franklin D. Roosevelt early in his fourth term left on the shoulders of his successor the responsibility for concluding the second World War and conducting the highly delicate negotiations of the peace. To some, Mr. Truman's performance in these immense tasks proves that he was simply the ward-heeler who held the lucky lottery ticket—a disaster in leadership such as the democratic system invites; to others his performance demonstrates that democracy has some kind of built-in mystique whereby those who are called to power by the people, however limited in nature, are elevated and made worthy of leadership.

But the reader of these memoirs is likely to conclude that both views are wrong and that the truth does not lie somewhere in between. To be sure, Mr. Truman came to the Presidency with no recondite gifts; he had no native ability that most men do not have in some measure. But he was extraordinarily endowed with ordinary powers, and he had combined those powers in a personality of unusual effectiveness. By the time he became President he knew something about the problems of agriculture from a decade of work on his father's farm; he had learned about the problems of the small businessman by failing in business himself; he had acquired a lifelong interest in (and enthusiasm for) military and defense problems from his service in the first World War. But most important, he had educated himself in the processes of democratic government by wide reading in history and through an impressive variety of practical political experience.

The publication of *Year of Decisions* in 1955 stirred up some very lively controversies. At least six men who figure prominently in its pages (headed by General Douglas MacArthur and former Secretary of State James Byrnes) have challenged the accuracy of the former President's account. Characteristically, Mr. Truman has retracted nothing.

P. P.

311. *The Family Mark Twain*

Mark Twain (Samuel L. Clemens, 1835-1910), summing up much of our nineteenth century, shows no sign of being neglected by the twentieth. His Huck Finn and Tom Sawyer and Mississippi River have become symbols of the youth on which we look back so wistfully, to a time simpler, perhaps more poetical, than our own. Mark Twain's own frontier experiences, which gave us so much of his early work, typified our pre-Civil War period, free-swinging, optimistic, future-facing. His later life, like his later work, reflects an America in which the individualistic gusto of the pioneer has given way to a less happy industrialism. "The Man Who Corrupted Hadleyburg" shows us a Mark Twain afflicted with the doubts and self-distrust of an America that had too abruptly left its innocent youth behind.

Twain is far more than a mirror, however. He is a source. The wonderful prose of *Huckleberry Finn* and the first part of *Life on the Mississippi* announced to the world the existence of a magnificent American vernacular, with its own rhythms and tonalities, quite unaffected by European models. Intellectually, too, Mark Twain emphasized, often with naïveté, his alienation from European tradition. His *Connecticut Yankee* is an affirmation of the Yankee virtues of common sense, cleanliness, and inventiveness as opposed to the presumed obscurantism of the Middle Ages.

Though Twain is thought of primarily as a humorist, as time goes on we laugh less and less at his jokes. *Huckleberry Finn* is no longer a diverting story of the adventures of two boys; it has deepened in our minds until it has become the nearest thing we have to a national epic. It is central, like its own Mississippi; and, though it is loved by generation after generation of American boys, it is read also by the mature as a great revelation of fundamental strains in our character. In his own hatred of sham, his special frontier dead-pan humor, his intellectual limitations, his prudery, his independence of judgment, his egalitarianism, his energy, his combination of apparent optimism and underlying uneasiness, Mark Twain was also about as typical a great American as his century produced.

C. F.

312. *The American Land*

by William R. Van Dersal

It is surprising that as late as 1943, when *The American Land* was published, no one had written such a primer of the simple facts of American forestry and agriculture. Mr. Van Dersal's study made no claim to comprehensiveness, and during the past decade such advances have been made in improving soils and soil fertility that his volume seems even more elementary than he planned. Nevertheless *The American Land* is a basic survey of the development of America's leading crops. It differentiates between the indigenous and the imported, summarizes the history of each, and speculates on the future of all.

Despite the strenuous efforts of soil experts, Americans have not yet learned how to protect all their lands from their sometime enemies—the winds and the waters. Erosion continues in certain areas where topsoil is blown from fertile surfaces, where floods wash rich earth away, where forests are leveled without regard for the resulting failure of the earth to maintain cohesiveness. The American lumber merchants and planters were, in early days, so ignorant or so careless that they were wildly spendthrift of the country's seemingly limitless resources. But in these days of strip cropping and contour cultivating, of terracing and of covering with residue mulches, the land is returning to stability and fertility.

Experimental stations and the agriculture and forestry departments of American universities continually make valuable discoveries. The corn belt, thanks to new hybridizations that have created hardier plants, is moving its northern boundary toward Canada. A section of Florida has been found receptive to the lichee, a Chinese fruit previously thought impossible to grow in America. Such facts have appeared in American technical journals, but there is need for a new edition of *The American Land,* incorporating a summary of recent advances and adding a discussion of problems created by overproduction. For, when foreign markets can profitably buy the surpluses of American crops, much of the hunger in the world will no longer exist.

C. C.

313. *Benjamin Franklin*

by CARL VAN DOREN

Published in 1938, this became at once and has remained the standard biography of one of the greatest of Americans. It is ample, leisurely, perfectly researched, and as full of common sense as was its subject. It rescues Franklin from the "dry prim people" who "seem to regard him as a treasure shut up in a savings bank to which they have the lawful key." It also disposes of the notion, still obtaining in some quarters, that Franklin was a glorified industrious apprentice—a notion he himself fostered with *Poor Richard's Almanack* and his *Autobiography* (see No. 123). In its author's proud but not boastful words, his book gives Franklin back "in his grand dimensions, to his nation and the world."

The benign burgher's 84 years summed up much of the eighteenth century and all of what is important in our national beginnings. He is our nearest approach to the Leonardo or Goethe type, a man of well-nigh universal interests, memorable in a dozen fields, including trade, journalism, statesmanship, politics, diplomacy, city management, science and invention, literature, social intercourse. Dr. Van Doren (1888-1950), whose own style is Franklinian in its restraint and clarity, reminds us that Franklin was also a remarkable stylist, a crack writer in a century that produced crack writers effortlessly.

He reminds us too that the real Franklin included a man given not merely to social pleasure but to venery and the delights of lewd talk. And, although much of the book is properly devoted to Franklin's vast services to the colonies and to the new nation, there is plenty of time and room left in which to point out a hundred generally unfamiliar facets of his personality. Not many of us know that he was a pioneer in the diagnosis of lead poisoning, in phonetic reform, in the study of the Gulf Stream and the common cold; or that he taught himself four languages, reformed the Post Office, wrote charming love letters, foresaw the future of the United States, suggested the merits of crop insurance, published and probably drew the first American cartoon, and devised a flexible catheter.

We learn all this and a great deal more in this sound biography. More than any other single factor, it is probably responsible for the renewed interest in Franklin and in the changed estimate of his now irrefutable greatness.

C. F.

314. *Nathaniel Hawthorne*

by MARK VAN DOREN

Mark Van Doren (1894-) has established a solid reputation in many fields—pre-eminently in poetry, but also in education, scholarship, journalism, and criticism. It is probable that this brief but full life of Hawthorne represents him at his critical best. Hawthorne is a subject well suited to his own temper, in which passion and reflectiveness are mingled.

The external events of the life of the author of *The Scarlet Letter* (No. 140) are not exciting: a delicate, almost invalid Salem childhood; an unimpressive college career at Bowdoin, where he became fast friends with Franklin Pierce, who was to attain to an undistinguished Presidency; a secluded young manhood in his native town, still murmurous and shadowed with the Puritan past that was to become the leading motive of Hawthorne's imaginative life; the early sketches and stories, at first rather unregarded by the public and the critics; the beginnings of literary fame; the idyllic courtship of and marriage in 1842 to Sophia Peabody, one of three remarkable sisters; the appointment in 1839 to a minor job in the Boston Custom House; the brief stay at Brook Farm, later to bear fruit in *The Blithedale Romance;* the fertile, happy years in Concord; the critical year of 1850 which saw the triumphant publication of his masterpiece; friendships with Ralph Waldo Emerson and Herman Melville; the consulship at Liverpool and the stay in Rome, a consequence of which was *The Marble Faun;* the return to America, the slow decline, the quiet death in 1864.

The problem of relating these events, which are history, to the spiritual geography of Hawthorne's brooding mind, and this in turn to the works, great or unsuccessful, that flowed from it, is solved by Mr. Van Doren with deceptive ease. He loves Hawthorne but is not blind to his weaknesses, to the insufficient vitality that Hawthorne himself so frequently mocked, to his tendency to harp on a few strings and to surrender too easily to the temptations of easy allegory. This grave and affectionate study somehow manages to assess all the familiar elements of Hawthorne's art—his preoccupation with guilt, his obsession with allegory, his use of moral symbolism, the influence of his Puritan background—with both originality and exactness. "His one deathless virtue," says Mr. Van Doren, "is that rare thing in any literature, an utterly serious imagination."

C. F.

315. *The Theory of the Leisure Class*

by THORSTEIN VEBLEN

In current discussions of American leisure (for example, David Riesman's [in No. 258]) the word "Veblenian" is often used to denote an attitude—ascetic, sparse, Puritan, functional, production-minded—that almost seems antipathetic to the idea of leisure. It is indeed ironic that our understanding of work and play today should owe so much to this mocking and forbiddingly austere son of the Scandinavian-American Midwest, who had such little use for luxury and frivolity. Thorstein Veblen (1857-1929) was an economist teaching at the University of Chicago when this, his first, book was published (1899). Later, in his other works, he was to elaborate on his contempt for "pecuniary" culture and his preference for replacing it with a technocracy in which production and distribution would be controlled by soviets of engineers. Nonetheless, *The Theory of the Leisure Class* remains —and justly—his best-known work.

Veblen wanted both to shock his readers and to impress them with the weight of his own learning. Thus there is a certain clutter of obsolete (and somewhat ridiculous) scholarship in his pages which the modern reader must be prepared to brush aside. What remain are the copious Veblenian virtues of sharp observation and exquisite irony, and an indictment of the late-nineteenth-century industrial "aristocracy" so scathing that the American upper class, in a sense, has never quite recovered from it. A phrase of Veblen's like "conspicuous consumption" has achieved a currency that reflects the tacit adoption of his standards, on such a scale that the twentieth-century rich have had to adopt (as he shrewdly foresaw) the practice of "*in*conspicuous consumption."

This is not to say that "emulation" or "vicarious waste" or "trained incapacity" do not continue, or that Veblen's observations are not relevant to the present American preoccupation with leisure (see Nos. 103 and 288). He may not have foreseen a society in which the vast majority would have to acquire the skills in leisure consumption that he himself so conspicuously lacked, yet he anticipated many terms of the dilemma with sympathetic awareness. There was (as David Riesman has remarked) a warm "feminine," as well as a cold "masculine," side to Veblen. When he speaks of women's unique capacity to deplore waste or war and to see the futility of the predatory masculine culture, Veblen is still an effective critic of America and the voice of our enduring dissatisfactions with a Puritanical society. It is the "warm" Veblen who speaks to us now, and echoes in Mr. Riesman's own *The Lonely Crowd* (No. 259).

E. L.

316. *The Man on the Assembly Line*

by Charles R. Walker *and* Robert H. Guest

The assembly line is, to many, the dominant symbol of modern industrial America. Some see it as a symbol of man's ingenuity and technology's bounty; others as a symbol of man's subjection to the machine (as in the classic wrench-and-bolt fantasy of Charlie Chaplin's movie, "Modern Times"). Yet, until recently, little reliable information about its development or its consequences has been available. Many Americans, as well as many people in other lands, have based firm theories about its merits or its horrors upon inadequate knowledge.

Elsewhere in this collection the reader will find the fruits of recent research on the history of the assembly line, notably in Roger Burlingame's *Backgrounds of Power* (No. 45), Siegfried Giedion's *Mechanization Takes Command* (No. 128), and Allan Nevins and Frank E. Hill's *Ford* (No. 232). But what of the line's effects upon those whose jobs are shaped by it? So new is our interest in the human and social implications of modern technology (see Elton Mayo's pioneering study [No. 209]), and so long have we been willing to judge it by standards formed in the context of older productive systems, that when representative American and foreign scholars, businessmen, labor leaders, and technical experts met at Corning, New York, as recently as 1951, to consider the problems of living in an industrial civilization, no data were available on how assembly-line workers really feel about their jobs (see *Creating an Industrial Civilization* [No. 288]).

The present study, published a year after the Corning conference, is the first of its kind. Its authors are careful to remind us that it is a study of 180 individuals in a specific plant, not a definitive study of assembly-line workers as such. Furthermore, 90 per cent of the men involved were new to the line, having worked previously in very different jobs, and their reactions are therefore those of people who have made the transition from jobs typical of earlier types of production, not those of men to the mass-production manner born.

Bearing these limits in mind, the reader will find here fascinating data on the human consequences of assembly-line techniques. And he may also discover implications which will illuminate the analyses of American culture in such books as David Riesman's *The Lonely Crowd* (No. 259) and Lyman Bryson's *The Next America* (No. 43).

J. A. K.

317. Shaping America's Products

by Don Wallance

Before the advent of mass production, the design of consumer goods could reasonably be left to the individual craftsman. Where each object was different, at the whim of its maker, shape and color did not have to be precisely defined. In fact, the style that John Kouwenhoven calls the "vernacular" (see No. 175) was in good part the outcome of numberless individual technicians exercising their empirical knowledge of the processes through which products are made and employed. At first, with the triumph of industrialism, the same "engineering" standards prevailed; products were designed mainly for their convenience of manufacture, or not designed at all. Later, when it became apparent that fashion and aesthetics were of interest to the customer—and of relative unimportance to the engineer—there took place that shift in emphasis from technology to style which shaped in such measure the tragedy of Henry Ford (see No. 46) and brought into existence a new profession—that of the industrial designer.

The author of *Shaping America's Products* is himself a member of this new profession (he includes a sample of his own stainless-steel tableware). Concerned by the fact that design achievements in industrial society are so often anonymous or undocumented, he set out to study (with the aid of the American Craftsmen's Council and the Walker Art Center) a series of "case histories" in contemporary design—how did the product come to look as it does, who worked on it, what considerations moved him? Don Wallance is especially concerned to show the interweaving of forces—technical, commercial, artistic—that enters into "good" design. He offers examples of such design out of his own conviction that America's most significant contribution to the twentieth century is "the widespread distribution of material goods" and that the "forms of everyday objects are a key to the character of a democratic industrial culture."

E. L.

318. *Democracy in Jonesville*

by W. Lloyd Warner *and Associates*

Modern America is addicted to examining itself for signs that it has or has not changed. It usually has, or so somebody says; and it listens with eagerness to all of the details, even when they are uncomplimentary. The authors of the present study find that a typical town in the Middle West has changed for the worse with respect to the principle of equality which once inspired its settlers. Jonesville, North Prairie (actually Morris, Illinois), now has classes. There are four or five, depending on how one counts the members of the highest class; if this class includes both the Old Families and the New People with money, then that makes one; and beneath it come those who are just above the common people, the common people themselves, and those who live in shanties on the other side of the canal.

The Old Families and the Shanty People are the only ones who never worry about their status: in the one case because they can never cease to be what they are and in the other case because they have nothing to lose. So it is throughout the world, and so it has always been; but in America the discovery comes slowly and with pain. The residents of Jonesville whom the authors interviewed were unanimous in their adherence to the principle of equality, yet none of them denied that the society of the town had stratified with time. The authors believe that at the least these people benefit by remembering Thomas Jefferson and Abraham Lincoln, both of whom declared that all men are created equal.

A generation of social scientists has been busy with such researches as this one. In 1929 Robert and Helen Lynd anatomized Muncie, Indiana, in *Middletown,* later in *Middletown in Transition* (No. 194); and there is no end to the special studies that have been made of places, occupations, institutions, and the like. No one pretends that the whole truth can be in any such work; but whatever can be measured is set down frankly; and on the whole the nation continues to accept the portrait for which it has sat.

M. V. D.

319. *All the King's Men*

by ROBERT PENN WARREN

In Louisiana, Huey Long (1893-1935), who is the Willie Stark of *All the King's Men,* traveled a political road, new to that state, with the dizzying speed of the language of the first chapter. Until he began his career, selling pots and pans to talk-hungry housewives and learning the uses of a brassy manner, the state had been controlled from New Orleans, where corruption was as indigenous as the anopheles mosquito. The political machine, small, compact, hereditary, had been since the post–Civil War Reconstruction spreading poison as impartially as the mosquito spread malaria. Nor did the machine, any more than the mosquito, make any return for its privileges, or even bother to make promises. Huey Long, from up in the poor-white country, made promises. He promised new roads, schools, bridges, a university that would outmatch New Orleans' Tulane, where he had been subjected to indignities. He promised to destroy the New Orleans machine, and anything else that stood in his way.

He kept his promises. If in the course he approached absolute power, at least he was a man of his word, something new in the state. Then he began to reach beyond state lines, his "Share-the-wealth" clubs a feeler, with their motto, "Every man a king." When national leaders of the Democratic party heard his harsh raspy voice on the radio they began to shiver. With reason, for he might at last have gone to the White House, if he had not made the one inexcusable Southern mistake. "Tar-brush"—meaning Negro blood—was a lethal word, as he had a moment to learn when the young man stepped from behind a pillar in the State House, gun in hand.

He was the latest of a line of Southern demagogues that began with Tillman in South Carolina and Tom Watson in Georgia and continued into Alabama and Mississippi (see the chapter entitled "The Bottom Rail on Top" in *Lanterns on the Levee* [No. 245]) with Vardaman and Bilbo, who was affectionately called the "slick little bastard." But the figure of the spider's web in Cass Mastern's story has, in addition to its general, a specific application. When Huey Long began to peddle his wares, Louisiana State University at Baton Rouge was insignificant. It became, at his hand, the best university that money could buy. It had the best buildings, best football team, best coaches, and also professors. Robert Penn Warren (1905-   ) was at that time a professor there.

J. A. R.

320. *Up from Slavery*

by Booker T. Washington

The slave child sat on the dirt floor and, eyes shut, held out the tin plate for the Sunday treat, molasses brought from the "big house" by his mother. In time he would not need to keep his eyes shut in the hope that this day the helping would be bigger. In time his plate would be full, and his cup, as he sat at table in the White House, guest of the President of his country. It was his country. He was as American as Thomas Jefferson, or George Washington, whose name he took, having no surname of his own. He was also as tough. He had to be, to lead his people, as they had led theirs, into freedom.

But first he must learn the uses and adversities of freedom, the long hard journey to Hampton Institute and the long pull to get an education there. His telling has the quality of immediate experience, from his sleeping underneath the raised sidewalk to the day he founded another college for his people at Tuskegee, where a hen house became a classroom and a symbol. The students were from farms, and for farmers book-learning took second place. Skill with the hands came first. Economic equality must be won, proved. Political equality could wait. This pleased responsible listeners, North and South, and applause was loud when he said at Atlanta in 1895: "In all things that are purely social we can be as separate as the fingers, yet one as the hand in all things essential to human progress."

But there were other voices. There were white Southerners who had a new kind of leader too, who approached the Negro, rope in hand. They, this "alien breed of Anglo-Saxon," eagerly followed the Southern demagogue portrayed by William Alexander Percy in *Lanterns on the Levee* (No. 245). Nor did all Negroes approve the prescription of Booker Washington (1856-1915). Some, alert, intellectual, could find no place for themselves in a philosophy of "learning by doing." Berlin or Harvard University were the proper models, not Hampton. They did not agree that Negroes should stay out of cities. They repudiated Washington's speech of 1895, which they called the "Atlanta Compromise," and ultimately Washington himself, for reasons fully reported in John Hope Franklin's *From Slavery to Freedom* (No. 124).

J. A. R.

321. *Victor Herbert*

by EDWARD N. WATERS

In any backward glance at the characteristic products of the two decades that flanked the opening of this century, the operetta deserves an important place; and although the genre has been diluted into musical comedy (see No. 286), its masterpieces in the stricter form are as good as they ever were. Indeed, some of the managers of grand opera today survive only by the judicious injection of operetta into their repertory. The life of Victor Herbert (1859-1924) is accordingly of permanent interest for this external reason, quite as if it were not interesting in itself as a saga of human effort and achievement.

Like so many others here described, Herbert is an American by adoption. Born in Dublin, the grandson of Samuel Lover the novelist, Herbert might have had an international career as a virtuoso on the 'cello. But he felt the stirrings of genius to create, and without pretense or false modesty he succeeded as an undoubted master in a secondary genre.

Mr. Waters (1906-), who is assistant chief of the music division in the Library of Congress, was well equipped to write this first scholarly biography of the composer of *The Red Mill, Naughty Marietta,* and countless other scores. He is a musicologist of repute and an authority on Liszt. At times one might wish that the biographer restrained, not his enthusiasm, but his bubbling expression of it. Yet the facts are sufficiently arousing and incredible (as in the story of every embattled artist) to justify Mr. Waters's exclamation points. For in addition to composing, conducting, and managing his own enterprises, Victor Herbert divided his energies among a host of musical activities, not the least of which was the establishment of musical copyright against legal, political, and social odds. Today the American Society of Composers, Authors and Publishers stands as a monument to his farsighted generosity and resourceful doggedness.

J. B.

322. *The Great Frontier*

by WALTER PRESCOTT WEBB

In 1893, a 32-year-old historian read a short paper to a meeting of the American Historical Association and, with that single act, revolutionized the study of American history. Frederick Jackson Turner's (1861-1932) "The Significance of the Frontier in American History" became the guiding document of a generation of scholars and Turner's influence so pervaded the national mind that his ideas are now commonplace to many who never have heard his name. Those ideas center on the proposition that, in his words, "The existence of an area of free land, its continuous recession, and the advance of American settlement westward, explain American development." The most significant American area in Turner's view was therefore the West, and the year 1890, by which time the country had so filled up with people that the frontier had disappeared, was the end of a great historic era.

Turner's thesis was intended to combat the two dominant orthodoxies of his time, which held that America could be explained in terms of the slavery question or of transplanted Anglo-Saxon institutions. Unhappily, it too became an orthodoxy in turn, and a new generation of historians then arose to challenge Turner for his sins of omission and other sins committed in his name (see the last chapter of Henry Nash Smith's *Virgin Land* [No. 287]). But Walter Prescott Webb (1888-), an historian who grew up in the frontier environment, responded differently. Instead of repudiating Turner's thesis, he has enlarged upon it. Instead of treating the frontier as a purely American phenomenon, Professor Webb treats it as an essential element in the creation of modern Europe—the Metropolis, as he calls it, which found its own frontier in the near-empty land of the four continents that the great discoverers opened up for exploitation in the fifteenth century. Professor Webb sees the characteristic European ideas of individualism and progress as dependent on this great frontier, and the centuries that have been dominated by Western Europe are to him a "four-hundred-year boom" now coming to a close.

Perhaps Professor Webb can be criticized, as Turner was, for being too concerned with land and capital, and for failing to take account of the multiplying factors of power and productivity introduced by industrial technology. His skepticism about the possibility of replacing "fossil" fuels with atomic ones seems unjustified already, only five years after his book appeared. Even so, he argues an able case and his eye is clear even when his mood is that of nostalgia for the land of bright promise he will never know again —a tone set by the Grandfather he quotes from Steinbeck's *The Red Pony* (see No. 47): "Westering has died out of the people. Westering isn't a hunger any more. It's all done."

E. L.

323. *The Saga of American Society*

by DIXON WECTER

By "society" Dixon Wecter (1906-50) meant the polite society of the upper classes and not, as most informed American readers would think if the book were published today, "society at large." The word society is now little used in America to mean a social élite. As Professor Wecter points out in his first chapter, which was written prior to 1937, the prominence of "society" was declining even then in the face of Hollywood's carefully nurtured and press-agented brand of "high life." The public is no longer bemused as it once was by society entertainments and marriages and divorces. That is not to say that Americans are not concerned with social aspirations; it is merely that in recent years these aspirations have taken a somewhat different form from that which Wecter describes.

There have been, as he recounts, almost continual efforts to establish some sort of permanent social élite—first a landed aristocracy of planters and patroons, later of New England merchants, and in the second half of the nineteenth century, during America's vast industrial expansion, of financiers. But American society has always been fluid, and one's rise in it has had less to do with birth than with the attainment of distinction in business or the professions or, sometimes, in politics. America's social paddocks have been more successful at keeping "thoroughbreds" in than in keeping out those who were determined and urbane enough to climb their fences. If first-generation wealth has not always been a passport to society (as it was not in the case of Silas Lapham and his wife [see No. 155]) its scions have had little trouble attaining social position.

With a richness of entertaining anecdote, comments on many socially and politically prominent Americans, notes on the eagerness with which Americans have bought books of etiquette and manuals of polite behavior and established exclusive clubs, Wecter traces the attempts of a young nation to behave like something it was not. The strength of the democratic tradition, while it permits the establishment of social élites, never allows them (as Wecter demonstrates) to persist as monoliths or to attain control over other Americans.

R. L.

324. *Selected Stories of Eudora Welty*

Drop an abstract idea into a conversation in the Deep South and watch it sink unnoticed—or, if noticed, with embarrassment for the stranger's ignorance, until the talk begins to flow again, all about people. Mississippi is in the Deep South and Eudora Welty (1909-) lives in Mississippi.

She is a listener. She hears every sound, for she has a keen ear, particularly for what is not said. She has a keen eye, for the gesture, sudden movement, and the movement that never moves. In the story "Memory" there are a man, two women, two boys together on a beach. "There had been no words spoken among these people, but I began to comprehend a progression, a circle of answers, which they were flinging toward one another in their own way in the confusion of vulgarity and hatred which twined among them all like a wreath of steam rising from the wet sand."

She is, however, almost color-blind. The South is a closely woven texture, and a neighbor of hers, William Alexander Percy, saw the warp and woof as distinctly black and white, as one may read in *Lanterns on the Levee* (No. 245). She sees instead gray. There is Powerhouse. "You can't tell what he is. 'Niggerman?'" And Livvie, and Jenny in "At the Landing," could swap skins.

Another neighbor inscribed on a map of his mythical Yoknapatawpha County, "William Faulkner, sole owner and proprietor" (see No. 108). Eudora Welty has no county. She has places: a beauty parlor, railway stations, farmhouses, bathing beach, dance hall, post office. She has towns: Ellisville, Natchez, The Landing, Farr's Gin, Victory, Midnight.

These are stage settings, to some writers mere necessities, but the reader of these stories senses at once a subtle connection, communication, between actor and surroundings, between Leota and her beauty parlor, Livvie and the lonely cabin near the Old Natchez Trail (see No. 279). For Mississippi, by statistics illiterate, is in fact preliterate, and still enjoys every means of communication known to man, from Neanderthal up. Eudora Welty is a magician. She puts it into words.

J. A. R.

325. *The Grandmothers*

by Glenway Wescott

When *The Grandmothers* appeared in 1927 intelligent Americans, with World War I in the near past, were seeking a fuller understanding of national growth and character. In a world sense, who were they? What was important in their past? What were the chief experiences that had built them? Glenway Wescott's (1901-) novel was one answer to such questions. Born on "a poor Wisconsin farm," studying at the University of Chicago and spending several years in Europe, he had both an intensive knowledge of an American region and the training and experience to see it in perspective. He undertook to depict a Middle Western farm family, and the picture he painted reached back and out: in time, to the pioneer settlement of the 1830's, through the Civil War and the Spanish-American War; in place, eastward, west, and southwest.

Mr. Wescott's narrator is a member of the family—a sensitive, observing young man who sees much and is told much by others; and in writing his account of the group Mr. Wescott shows an insight not unworthy of Proust, although his is a faster pace. Preceded by an impressive forerunner, *The Apple of the Eye* (1926), *The Grandmothers* was an extraordinary accomplishment for a young man, Wescott being only 28 when the book won the Harper Prize for Literature and raced through some twenty printings in its first year. It told Americans everywhere much about themselves, in writing distinguished enough to arrest their attention. While other American novelists had dealt with their country's past, Mr. Wescott gave it fresh and more personal meanings.

He himself later stated that as a writer he had been influenced by Henry James, by D. H. Lawrence, and by other English authors. However, he seems also to have absorbed much from American contemporaries like Sherwood Anderson, episodes in *The Grandmothers* showing similarities to stories in *Winesburg, Ohio* (No. 11). Appearing a year later than Ernest Hemingway's *The Sun Also Rises,* and two years before Thomas Wolfe's *Look Homeward, Angel* (No. 344) and William Faulkner's *As I Lay Dying,* Mr. Wescott's novel seemed of comparable promise with these books. Although such a promise was never fulfilled, *The Grandmothers* has lost little with time, and will give readers abroad a revealing interpretation of American character as seen in a widely varying but typical group of men and women.

F. E. H.

326. *The Friendly Persuasion*

by JESSAMYN WEST

The nostalgic novel of rural manners that traces the fortunes of a family through several generations (often from the middle of the last century to the beginnings of this one) is a fairly common twentieth-century American literary form. Miss West in *The Friendly Persuasion* (like Glenway Wescott in *The Grandmothers* [No. 325]) sets her story in a Midwestern farming community whose first settlers have hewn rich, tillable land out of primeval forest in which, until they came, Indians lived and hunted. The family that Miss West describes, in what is more nearly a series of short stories than a formal novel, are Friends (that is, Quakers) who have settled on the banks of the Muscatatuck River in Indiana. They are Christian pacifists who look upon all forms of ostentation as works of the Devil, their churches are called "meeting houses," and their religious gatherings are often held in complete silence unless a member of the group is "moved" to speak; they have no clergy.

The central characters of *The Friendly Persuasion* are Jess Birdwell and his wife Eliza, who is a Quaker "preacher" (one often moved to speak). They are prosperous, hard-working farmers, whose life is filled with enjoyment of their children and neighbors and the wonders of the countryside. Miss West, who was herself brought up as a Quaker, writes about the details of their lives with a humor that is always respectful, and she tells of the conflicts between their humanity and their religious principles, of the growing up and away of their children, of their pleasures and tragedies with a delight and appreciation that are loving but never sentimental.

Through the novel runs a theme of constant change, of increasingly civilized countryside and the growing prosperity of the farmer's life from log cabin to substantial homestead. The Birdwells are removed from but not unaware of the expansion westward. Their life brushes but does not meet headlong the terrors of the Civil War, and it encounters the wonders of science and the delight of gadgetry when finally their house is illuminated with gas. Hard-headed, God-fearing, and friendly both by conviction and from natural kindliness, the Birdwells exemplify the militantly democratic manners of America's Middle West.

R. L.

327. *Ethan Frome*

by Edith Wharton

In his introduction to the present edition of *Ethan Frome* the late Bernard DeVoto brilliantly analyzes what is wrong with the book, and most of his criticisms remain unanswerable. But it should be remembered that DeVoto's introduction appeared in 1938, the year after Mrs. Wharton died. Authors' reputations are often at their lowest just after their deaths, and in Mrs. Wharton's instance other circumstances contributed to her eclipse. For one thing, the work of her last years was not up to her best; more important, she was identified with the rich and snobbish society of old New York, and most of her stories (though not *Ethan Frome*) deal with the lives of the rich and/or well born. Therefore the younger readers and writers and critics of the 1930's, distressed by the economic depression at home and the rise of Fascism abroad, and often convinced that literature should deal with social reform, had little patience with her work. (The great popular American hero of the 1930's, Franklin D. Roosevelt, represented a background very much like Mrs. Wharton's, but he made rather different use of it: Mrs. Wharton withdrew to live abroad, whereas Roosevelt identified himself with popular movements.)

Today Mrs. Wharton's reputation stands much higher than it did. She is the subject of considerable critical discussion, and scholars await the opening of her personal papers, scheduled by her will to take place 25 years after her death. Possibly the fuller biography that will be possible then will show that Mr. DeVoto was too hasty in dismissing as purely external her knowledge of the kind of life she portrays in *Ethan Frome*. It is true that she knew little of the life of the poor from the inside, but there are reasons to suppose that she knew more of the patient endurance of intolerable situations than was once thought.

It is not speculation about Mrs. Wharton's private life, however, that has restored her to favor. Rather it is a revived interest in the novel of manners and in the technique of fiction as an art in itself, quite independent of any social purpose it supports. The writer whose reputation has profited most from this reversal of critical taste is of course Henry James (Nos. 159-61), but his great friend Edith Wharton has been borne upward by the same wave, if not quite on its crest.

P. P.

328. *Selected Chapters from the Autobiography of Andrew D. White*

In the middle years of the nineteenth century, American university education became acutely aware of its deficiencies and undertook to meet the demands of the age by means of revision, reform, and expansion. One of the leaders of the new movement, challenging comparison with Charles W. Eliot of Harvard University and Daniel Coit Gilman of Johns Hopkins, was Andrew D. White (1832-1918), the organizer and first president of Cornell University.

White was the son of an established family in the northern part of the state of New York. He early showed an inclination to scholarship and the intellectual life, and no part of his attractive autobiography is more charming than his account of his early schooling in communities where learning was respected and the means of acquiring it were usually scant but sometimes good. After a year spent at a small country college where the instruction was as bad as the discipline, he went to Yale. This was a better experience, but still inadequate for an eager and serious mind, for the method of teaching was chiefly formal and almost always dull. In the tradition of American scholarship of the early nineteenth century, White spent several years of study in Germany and other European countries. Upon his return he accepted the chair of history at the newly founded University of Michigan. It was here that he conceived his ideal of popular higher education. He was able to realize it when, having left the University of Michigan and having been elected to the legislature of the state of New York, he had for a colleague the remarkable financier and philanthropist, Ezra Cornell.

With Cornell, White planned a university to be established in the beautiful town of Ithaca. Cornell endowed it generously, White served as its first president, and the two men worked harmoniously to organize it and to bring it through its first difficult years. It opened its doors to students in 1868 and under White's guidance Cornell University expanded and flourished to become one of the leading universities of the United States. The first president's account of its growth is of high interest, both as the record of an important cultural phenomenon and as the romantic story of great difficulties overcome.

Although passionately devoted to the University, White did not allow it to dominate his life. He was prominent in public affairs and served on important government commissions and as Minister to Germany and Russia and Ambassador to Germany. As a scholar he is best remembered for his *History of the Warfare of Science with Theology in Christendom.*

L. T.

329. *Here Is New York*

by E. B. WHITE

If any classic defense is possible of that overpowering monstrosity, New York City, this is it. E. B. White's sharp and tender, ruminative essay was written, quite properly, in a hotel room in mid-town; and, though it cites no more than a baby's handful of statistics and adduces few "facts," it manages to come close to the heart of its subject. Though Mr. White passionately loves his city his emotion is tempered in the cooling bath of common sense. No rhapsodies; no Whitmanesque celebrations; no awe of the city's mere largeness, perhaps its dullest characteristic. (Houston will be larger some day; Los Angeles will be larger.)

Wisely, he does not describe Gotham. Instead he tries like a chemist to isolate those essences that place it apart from all of the great cities of the world. Of these quiddities the very first is that for which it is loved by some, hated by others: its curious ability to let its citizens alone. The essay's opening sentence is: "On any person who desires such queer prizes, New York will bestow the gift of loneliness and the gift of privacy." But, though the city's immensities hold out solitude, they also offer participation, the participation of the village, for "the city is literally a composite of tens of thousands of tiny neighborhood units." (In other words New York City is most attractive when it is being least like New York City.)

E. B. White (1899-) is concerned with the New Yorks of the commuters, the natives, and the settlers—but mainly with the latter, for the settlers give the city its passion. With an economy notable even for him (see Nos. 330-1), Mr. White re-expresses this passion. Whether he describes that awe with which the young beginning settler looks upon the city's great; whether his compassionate eyes regard the low-toned love-making in a nearby restaurant booth, or the curious serenities of the city on a summer Saturday afternoon—whatever he sees he places before us quietly and clearly. His modulated sentences have in them both the whir of the wings of poetry and the plain honest accent of twentieth-century American speech.

Into these few lucid pages is condensed what tens of millions have vaguely felt about their town (see also No. 174). *Here Is New York* will have a long life because it contains so much of what oft was thought but ne'er so well expressed.

C. F.

330. *One Man's Meat*

by E. B. White

At the moment E. B. White (1899-) is probably our finest essayist and our most delicate and thoughtful humorist. His work will take its place in the classic tradition that has its spring in Montaigne and has been developed by such writers as Charles Lamb, William Hazlitt, and Henry David Thoreau. Especially marked is the influence of Thoreau (No. 305), whose acute perception of the natural world and whose doctrine of simplicity he modifies to accord with the pressures of mid-twentieth-century America.

For all his seeming whimsicality of temper, Mr. White is a realist. That is to say, he owns the poetical eye that sees through things to the truths that lie behind appearances. The sweet and bitter of his careful prose well out of an awareness of the unreality of so much that we take for granted. He is aware of the substitutes for things, the substitutes for human beings that make up so much of our daily life. He is an original writer in that his mind naturally works from origins. His most casual remarks (most of them are casual; he has no full-dress manner) derive from a sense not only of what man is but of what he started from. They are almost always based, though rarely explicitly, on an original—that is, fundamental—proposition which men when they are being reasonable accept as true.

The 55 essays that make up *One Man's Meat* are representative of Mr. White's talents and his interests. They were written for *Harper's* magazine "from a salt water farm in Maine" while the author was "engaged in trivial, peaceable pursuits, knowing all the time that the world hadn't arranged any true peace or granted anyone the privilege of indulging himself for long in trivialities." Their essence lies in Mr. White's ability to write of the small and large at the same time, even in the same sentence. Thus the subject may be a raccoon hunt or a lambing or a park for caravans; but it is also freedom and democracy and the American notion of individuality. Mr. White's influence has been unobtrusive but definite. A journalist, essayist, and poet, he has drawn thousands of readers toward the humane and civilized.

C. F.

331. *A Subtreasury of American Humor*

edited by E. B. White *and* Katharine S. White

The editor says in his preface that he hopes the book he and his wife have compiled is not what Mark Twain once found such a collection to be, namely, "a cemetery." Mark Twain was referring to the familiar fact that fashions in humor die fast; forever in this field, he said, means 30 years. The people of the United States have had their humor from the first; or, if Benjamin Franklin be excepted, from early in the nineteenth century. Franklin's eighteenth-century wit is still superb, but it is not quite the thing recognized today as humor.

E. B. White (1899-), one of its finest modern practitioners (see No. 330), has difficulty defining it, nor does he care very much to do so. He leaves the subject where it has always lain, near the bottom of the human mind, down near the soul, the nerves, the digestion, and whatever is the seat of laughter, silent or otherwise. It was the nineteenth century that created humor in America; and if the twentieth century continues it, as manifestly it does, the same reason must be operating, though it might take a surgeon to locate that reason. It probably has to do with the double life every American lives: his public one, which requires him to be like all the people around him, and his private one, which is buried so deep that even he does not know when it will rise and astonish him with an utterly inappropriate thought. All human beings function thus, but in America, the theory goes, they do it in extremes.

The Whites have long been associated with *The New Yorker* (see Nos. 233-4), she as an editor and he as star contributor, and this brilliant magazine is liberally represented in their compilation. But their search through the literature of American humor, old and new, has gone farther than that; and since their taste is unexceptionable, it can safely be said that no better introduction to the subject exists, either for a native or for a foreign reader. The latter, lost among many strange names, might look first at Mark Twain, Ring Lardner, James Thurber, George Ade, Don Marquis, Finley Peter Dunne, Robert Benchley, Franklin P. Adams, S. J. Perelman, Clarence Day, and E. B. White.

M. V. D.

332. *The Autobiography of William Allen White*

If there really is, or ever has been, an American Dream, William Allen White (1868-1944) is somewhere in it. His father was a half-trained, itinerant medical man and unsuccessful storekeeper; his mother had been a schoolteacher in Illinois. They had been brought together when the "doctor" wrote the teacher he wished to make her acquaintance with the object of "Matrimony." Acquaintance was established and the object achieved. Thus William Allen White started out in life the only child in a poor family; a fat boy in a small town on a Western plain. Since education was about the only tool of improvement and advancement he could be given in these circumstances, he was urged by his father first to explore the world of books and then to attend the state university. From the university he went to a newspaper as a reporter, and then in 1895, on borrowed money, he bought the Emporia (Kansas) *Gazette*. When he rode into the small town to become an editor, he was in his late twenties. He had one dollar in his pocket and in his heart "a sense that I had the world by the tail with a down hill pull."

Not long afterward he put into the *Gazette* an editorial called "What's the Matter with Kansas!" These 1,500 words written in two hours in an election year placed him in the middle of American life, where he remained for 50 years. In that half century he wrote some delightful, widely read books and came to know well almost everybody who contributed to the arts and letters of this country. In time, also, mayors, governors, Senators, and Presidents sought his aid and counsel. In 1912 he stood with Theodore Roosevelt "at Armageddon" and helped to found a new political party. Later he traveled to Versailles; and in his last years he did everything he could, during the 1930's, to bring America out of the chrysalis of isolation. By the time he died he was called a sage.

Actually he was called the Sage of Emporia. Though he became a name he preferred a local habitation; he sat there in the center of the country at his roll-top desk, checking the copy on church sociables and town fires for the next edition and passing the time of day with his neighbors through the office window. His hold was that while he acquired national influence and worldly wisdom he never lost faith in the meaning of the life on Main Street. This faith—simply and at times sentimentally stated—shines through the illuminating accounts of American customs and politics that fill this book.

E. E. M.

333. *Leaves of Grass and Selected Prose*

by WALT WHITMAN

If America has a national poet, he is Walt Whitman (1819-1892). It is not certain that the acquisition of this status is the most fortunate thing that could have happened to Whitman. It has led many readers—many American readers—to believe that they know all that he has to say and to think of him as a mere propagandist for a national geography, habits, and institutions which they are quite willing to take for granted. The misconception is a profound one.

The reader who comes to Whitman for the first time must have one thing firmly in mind—that, no matter what Whitman himself may say to the contrary, he is first of all, and last of all, a poet. From this it follows that we cannot take any of his utterances with an entire literalness. By America he does indeed mean an actual America—or, as more than one critic has pointed out, he means an America that was already in the past, the America of before the Civil War—but he also means something for which America stands in his mind as a symbol. It is his way of speaking about freedom, expansiveness, newness, and possibility, about the multiplicity and contradictions of life, about the totality of the universe seen in mystic vision.

As a poet, Whitman is primarily concerned with language, with the precise and conscientious use of language. He seems to deny this, both implicitly, by his grandiloquence as well as by his slang and colloquialism, and explicitly, by speaking of his "barbaric yawp." But we need not be deceived—he is one of the most subtle and delicate of poets as well as one of the grandest; and he can be ironic and humorous as well as solemn. The verse form that he created is, at its best, a triumph of revolutionary invention. It is, of course, not to be thought of as an escape from the difficulties of traditional metrical verse; indeed, cadenced verse is more difficult to use successfully than metrical verse. The effect upon the best modern poetry of Whitman's verse, as of his language, cannot be overestimated.

The power and charm of Whitman are perhaps most immediately apparent in two poems, "When Lilacs Last in the Dooryard Bloom'd," the great elegy for Lincoln, and "Out of the Cradle Endlessly Rocking." The reader to whom Whitman is new might well turn to these poems first. (They gain much by being read aloud.)

L. T.

334. *Street Corner Society*

by William Foote Whyte

In 1936 William Foote Whyte (1914-) was a Junior Fellow at Harvard University with the prospect of spending three years at any kind of intellectual enterprise that attracted him. He undertook to make a study of an Italian slum district of nearby Boston. He lived in the district for almost the entire term of his fellowship, learned Italian, and was received into the life of the community. As time passed, he began to understand that his original plan of describing the whole community was too extensive to be successfully carried out. He therefore decided to confine his research to the groups or gangs which were the recognized form of social organization of the boys and young men of the district.

The book which Mr. Whyte wrote on the basis of his experience in "Cornerville" has become one of the classics of American sociology. It is not a technical book—what must first strike any reader is its human warmth. The young men with whom young Mr. Whyte spent his time knew what his purpose was, and they were interested in it and approved of it. Their awareness of his superior education and social status, and their knowledge of his intention of writing a book about them, did not put them under constraint. They accepted him as one of themselves. One of their number, older than the rest, the remarkable man who appears under the name of Doc, thought of himself as Mr. Whyte's collaborator in the project, as indeed he was.

Mr. Whyte explores with sympathy and subtlety many aspects of the social relations of the young men. Any reader, American or not, will find of special interest the treatment of the question of American social mobility, the account of how some of the young men undertake to make their way in the larger world outside the Italian community, and of what are the avenues, and the barriers, to this adventure. But Mr. Whyte's own chief interest is in the nature of the organization of the gang itself, the loyalties and commitments involved, the qualities that make for leadership in the group, the manner in which personal influence is exerted. It is this emphasis that leads him to his enlightening sections on rackets, the police, municipal politics, and the chain of political influence (see also No. 271), an investigation which makes one of the best available treatises on "practical politics"—which is to say, on politics.

L. T.

335. *Heaven's My Destination*

by THORNTON WILDER

The Depression of the 1930's produced no odder novel than this one, a picaresque narrative about a young American who got into trouble solely because he was good. It was an odd novel for Thornton Wilder (1897-) to write, too, because it is not couched in the careful classic prose of his other and more famous narratives, but in a plain American vernacular that owes a good deal to Sinclair Lewis. It is a funny book and remains funny no matter what interpretation one cares to place on the story.

George Brush, aged 23, is working his way through Texas selling textbooks. In no time at all a thoroughly un-Wilderian succession of experiences befalls him, involving a holdup, a haymow seduction, jailing, several fist-fights, some drunken revelry, and an interlude in a brothel.

George is a kind of Middle Western Don Quixote crossed with an Oxford Grouper. Or perhaps he is what St. Francis would have been like in the America of the Depression. He contrives to make shaking hands a moral occupation; he doesn't believe in either the theory of interest or that of evolution; and in his insistence on the virtues of voluntary poverty and nonresistance, he is a veritable Mahatma Propagandhi.

The humor of the book, continuous and sometimes hilarious, flows from the logic of George's character in relation to the logic of his environment. St. Francis was not funny, because his world was willing to back up his idea of sainthood. George is funny—and, alas, unsuccessful—because his world is quite unrelated to sainthood. It cannot recognize the logic of virtuous action.

There are at least two Thornton Wilders, it would seem. The first is exquisite, learned, and philosophical; the second is freewheeling, satirical, with a turn for farce and extravagance. The second Wilder produced some of the later plays (see No. 31) and first announced itself in this delightful short novel of moral adventure and comic incident.

C. F.

336. *A Little Treasury of American Poetry*

edited by OSCAR WILLIAMS

To select the best in the American poetic output of the past 150 years is a task that would be performed differently by any of a dozen qualified editors. The *Little Treasury* is rather markedly a book of personal choices. From William Cullen Bryant into the early 1900's its selections are fairly catholic, with adequate representation for Ralph Waldo Emerson (see also No. 105), Edgar Allan Poe (No. 248), Walt Whitman (No. 333), and Emily Dickinson (No. 95). No one will quarrel violently with the editor for his avowed neglect of John Greenleaf Whittier, James Russell Lowell, and Henry Wadsworth Longfellow, although the last at his best might deserve more than one selection in an anthology which presents ten of the vital but uneven poems of the novelist Herman Melville.

Into the early years of the present century American poets—except for Whitman, Dickinson, and the short-lived Stephen Crane—had been conventional in form and to a large extent in theme (or original subject matter, as in Longfellow's and Whittier's narratives, had been dealt with in a conventional manner). But the poetry "renaissance" of the early 1900's, often associated with the appearance of the magazine *Poetry* in 1913, lifted the entire level of poetic effort, bringing to notice writers like Ezra Pound, E. A. Robinson, Robert Frost, Vachel Lindsay, Wallace Stevens, Carl Sandburg, Edgar Lee Masters, "H. D." (Hilda Doolittle), and T. S. Eliot. Others soon followed: Edna St. Vincent Millay, Robinson Jeffers, Archibald MacLeish, Stephen Vincent Benét, and Hart Crane among them.

The *Little Treasury* perhaps does more than justice in space to such poets as Pound, Stevens, Crane, Marianne Moore, and William Carlos Williams, all experimental in form and often obscure in meaning, but a reader new to American poetry would never guess from its selections the stature of Archibald MacLeish (No. 198) or Carl Sandburg (No. 273), given seven and five pages respectively, when the solemn but stammering Samuel Greenberg receives five, and the interesting but lesser John Peale Bishop fifteen. (For a different selection see F. O. Matthiessen's *Oxford Book of American Verse* [No. 208].) In the recent period of poetic activity Mr. Williams necessarily lacks perspective for his task, and it is perhaps not too important that at least half of his authors and selections could be matched with others whom many critics would regard as equal or superior. For the reader who knows little of American poetry, the anthology will offer an adequate introduction, characterized by a strong preference for the experimental which, if a bias must exist, is a healthy one.

F. E. H.

337. *The Shock of Recognition*

edited by EDMUND WILSON

American writers, like artists of any kind in any country, have had a good deal to say about one another. "For genius," remarked Herman Melville in a sentence from which Edmund Wilson (1895-) takes his title, "all over the world stands hand in hand, and one shock of recognition runs the whole circle round." Mr. Wilson's book is not a collection of pieces by professional critics; rather, it listens in on the talk of certain creators concerning other creators whom they liked or disliked—in most cases, liked, for the breath of such men is seldom wasted on failure. Mark Twain had no use for James Fenimore Cooper, but Henry James knew how deeply he was indebted to Nathaniel Hawthorne and his early book on Hawthorne is perhaps the masterpiece of this anthology. It is more than a critical essay, though it is certainly that; it is the musing of one professional about his next of artistic kin. The talk of artists is always interesting when it is specific and unembarrassed, and when it takes craft into account. So for the most part Mr. Wilson's authors do; and Mr. Wilson does not claim too much when he says that their combined efforts add up to a living history of American literature.

Famous names are paired here, and famous influences are explored. As James acknowledged his debt to Hawthorne, so T. S. Eliot has acknowledged his to James. And Ralph Waldo Emerson took the occasion of Henry David Thoreau's untimely death to compose one of the most charming biographical sketches on record. Melville's friendship for Hawthorne was clearly warmer than Hawthorne's for him—not that Hawthorne liked Melville less, but that he loved silence more—yet Melville's review of *Mosses from an Old Manse* was generous to a fault. William Dean Howells on Mark Twain, George Santayana on William James and Josiah Royce, and Emerson and Walt Whitman on each other—the list is long and the feast is rich. Nor is Edgar Allan Poe's wicked critical wit missing; nor does Mr. Wilson forget the satirical verses of James Russell Lowell and Amy Lowell. The talk of artists is sharply seasoned.

M. V. D.

338. *The Shores of Light*

by EDMUND WILSON

For many years Edmund Wilson (1895-) has been, by common consent, the most eminent literary critic in America. He did not achieve this position by the default of competitors; indeed, one of the characteristics of American literature in the past two decades has been the remarkable rise of literary criticism and the development of many critical reputations.

Nor did Mr. Wilson achieve his eminence by becoming the leader of a literary school. On the contrary, he has gone against the prevailing tendency in criticism and stands alone. The typical critic of the new American movement is likely to be a university teacher, and his work, brilliant and theoretical, is likely to appear in a quarterly journal appealing to a small and special audience. But Mr. Wilson, although a man of superb erudition, has never identified himself with the universities. His critical writing has its roots in journalism and is marked by the best qualities of journalism raised to their highest level—clearness, immediacy, cogency, and strong common sense.

Mr. Wilson's reputation began in the early 1920's when, as literary editor of the *New Republic,* a liberal weekly of considerable influence at the time, he wrote regularly about the books and the literary and general cultural problems of the day. *Shores of Light* is a collection of a large number of Mr. Wilson's contributions to the *New Republic* during the 1920's and 1930's, together with pieces of similar kind published elsewhere in the same period. The collection constitutes, as Mr. Wilson says he means it to, a kind of panorama of books and ideas and the movements of the literary life of the two decades. Far better than any formal literary history, it conveys the actuality of what was being thought and written at the time.

As the prologue to the collection Mr. Wilson has used his recent essay on the late Christian Gauss, professor of French and Italian literature at Princeton University and later dean of the undergraduate college, a teacher who played an important part in the intellectual development of Mr. Wilson and of other young men who worked under him. The epilogue of the volume is a striking and painful memoir of a poet who embodied so much of the characteristic quality of the 1920's, Edna St. Vincent Millay (No. 215).

L. T.

339. *Ruggles of Red Gap*

by HARRY LEON WILSON

There have been at least two ways for Americans to take their westward adventures. They could make folk heroes out of explorers, trappers, prospectors, cowboys, and the more humdrum but equally heroic settlers, or they could adopt the lusty humor of the pioneers and have affectionate fun with the fantastic society on the edges of civilization. Mark Twain (No. 311) was the great exemplar of the second attitude, as Harry E. Maule's collection of *Great Tales of the American West* (No. 130) illustrates the first. The men and women of the West were humorous and heroic; they were both at the same time. Harry Leon Wilson (1867-1939) was an authentic successor to Mark Twain in hiding the heroic qualities in layers of broad humor under which there is a tender irony.

Ruggles tells his own story and no one is required to believe that an English "gentleman's gentleman" would make such a success as Ruggles did in Red Gap in the "cow country." It is not certain that Ruggles himself ever understood what had happened to him, in being translated from the slightly seedy gentility in which the Honorable George kept them both by his mild, conceited profligacy, to his eminence in Red Gap as a leading businessman and the reader of the Declaration of Independence at the local Fourth of July celebration. He would never have expected, in his valet days, even to be interested in that document, to which he gives a commendation typical of his wildest enthusiasm, "It lends itself rather well to reciting."

Red Gap characters, familiar to a whole generation of readers when Wilson was writing for the popular magazines, have their familiar pungency when seen through the eyes of Ruggles, and perhaps more than their usual satirical point. Wilson wrote to amuse as many readers as possible, which was his first business as a humorist. But since he was also a writer of genius, he sent shafts of wicked wit at the pretenders of British and American society—even against the pretenders in Red Gap society, since one of his more heartwarming qualities is his ability to see men and women as fundamentally all alike everywhere, silly, heroic, endearing, exasperating, and always interesting. Wilson had all the qualities of a great satirist except cruelty; it seems likely that he would have been willing to forego Olympus on that disqualification.

L. B.

340. *American Science and Invention*

by MITCHELL WILSON

Though the United States is, to a striking degree, a scientific and mechanical nation, and though myriads of technical and scientific books are published here, there are few books for the nonspecialist that deal with the history of American science and technology. In fact, cultivated and literate people have only recently acknowledged the importance of these forces in the shaping of our culture. By and large historians have stuck to traditional studies of the causes and effects of political and economic events. As Roger Burlingame says in his pioneering history of mass production (No. 45), neither the historians nor anyone else "has kept us in the current of knowledge of our universe." The result has been to surround technology and science with something of the glamorous and terrifying quality of magic, making them things to be worshiped or feared, as the unknown always is.

Like other books described here, including Burlingame's, *American Science and Invention* implies a conviction that an understanding of the "core of technology" is now essential for those who want insight into the way Americans live, "the things they believe and how these things came to be." Significantly, its author-compiler is not an historian, but a best-selling novelist and a research scientist who has worked in the laboratories of several eminent physicists (including that of Enrico Fermi, whose life is told by his wife in No. 110). Significantly, too, he presents his material in the still new and experimental form of the picture-book, in which pictures and text collaborate in exposition and narrative. His emphasis is upon the individuals who created American science and technology, and the reader will no doubt notice that these areas are represented in this collection chiefly in biographical studies —notably Bernard Jaffe's *Men of Science in America* (No. 158) and the lives of Benjamin Franklin (No. 313), Joseph Henry (No. 70), George Washington Carver (No. 153), Michael Pupin (No. 252), and the Mayo brothers (No. 62). This may remind us that such matters, deprived of the aura of mystery and magic with which ignorance surrounds them, are best understood in very human terms.

J. A. K.

341. *The Springs*

by ANNE GOODWIN WINSLOW

Mrs. Winslow's reputation as a novelist is based on an exquisite specialization. She writes about the Southern gentry at the turn of the present century. This might well prove trivial or suffocating if it were not for the author's astonishing power to make life pulse vigorously in the constricted places, situations, and people that she chooses. Her outlook is perhaps best expressed in the contrast between the title of one of her other novels—*A Quiet Neighborhood* (1947)—and the violent events, the passions leading to murder, which inform the work.

Mrs. Winslow belongs to no school, for although some of her perceptions are akin to William Faulkner's (No. 108) and her technique is in the tradition of William Dean Howells (No. 155), her temperament, style, and biography set her in a world apart. A native of Memphis, Tennessee, which is to say a "border state" in the great North-and-South struggle of the past century, Mrs. Winslow married a Northern army engineer and spent many years in New England and abroad. She has returned to live in her home state and it is the distillation of her childhood memories through her traveled mind—emotion recollected in tranquillity—that she gives us in her novels and tales.

The Springs is a study of character which by its subdued atmosphere makes one think of Henry James's *The Europeans*. But the "culture" in which the characters evolve is markedly different, as is the fact that Mrs. Winslow's interest in household detail lends a peculiar vividness, almost a pathos, to the scene. It is as if, suddenly transplanted to those quiet old days we sometimes long for, we discovered their slow terror, which not even conventional happiness could allay.

J. B.

342. *The Virginian*

by Owen Wister

In 1885 Owen Wister (1860-1938) recorded that "it won't be a century before the West is simply the true America, with thought, type, and life of its own" and he wanted "to be the hand that once for all chronicled and laid bare the virtues and the vices of this extraordinary phase of American social progress." He never became that self-envisioned Tolstoi of the old West, but in 1902 *The Virginian* was published. It won instant success and skyrocketed its author to fame. It is still the most popular "Western" novel ever published and the master design for the fiction of the Wild West.

The Virginian established a literary form, a formula popularly known as "horse opera," whose conventions, clichés, and values have reappeared in novels and short stories, in movies and television serials, ever since. The romantic cowboy is the hero and gentleman, one of those "good men in the humbler walks of life," who sees through shams, defends justice and a lady's honor, shoots it out with the villain, and conquers evil. Because of *The Virginian,* motion picture audiences the world over cheer "Westerns" and little boys carry toy pistols to shoot imaginary Indians and desperadoes.

In the Virginian, Wister created a character who is the original type for the Western folk hero. He represents the embodiment of certain American ideals—a man who is equal to all occasions, who shows independence of action, a man who keeps his word and who is "a broad-gauge fellow living among narrow-gauge folk." But the literary device and cowboy code which Wister established dictated that the hero must kill the bad man. This necessity for sanctioning murder and the romanticizing of the cowboy as a gentleman prohibited *The Virginian* and the genre it created from becoming serious fiction, or even an authentic product of the western experience. Instead of achieving his ambition, therefore, Wister gave us a sort of American folk epic, the cowboy story. So successful and popular has it been that few Western writers other than Eugene Manlove Rhodes (see Nos. 130 and 278), A. B. Guthrie (No. 133), and Walter Van Tilburg Clark (No. 130) have ever tried to do anything else.

C. G.

343. *We Who Built America*

by Carl Wittke

With the advent of the quota system shortly after the first World War the story of mass immigration to our shores came to what seems a permanent end. Thus, though this sober, workmanlike study was published as long ago as 1939 it is not in any essential out of date. On the other hand, students of the subject may wish to supplement their researches with the later books of such brilliant scholars as Oscar Handlin (No. 136).

Carl Wittke (1892-), himself the son of a German immigrant, writes sympathetically of the contributions made to the country's political, economic, social and intellectual progress by the three separable waves of immigration: that of the colonial period, sparse but important; "the old immigration," which began to peter out around 1880; and "the new immigration," the reaction to which is notable in such obscurantist movements as Know-Nothingism and the Ku Klux Klan.

While the author's major thesis—"the grand central motif of United States history has been the impact of immigrant tides upon a New World environment"—is debatable, there is no doubt that one of the dominating patterns in our history has been the conflict between our original conception of the United States as a universal refuge, and the later one which, strongly based on fear and a growing love of uniformity, has triumphed in various forms of nativism. The consequence of this triumph is that, since November 1930, more people have been leaving than entering the United States, and we may expect during the next century or two that this trend will become more and more strongly marked.

The author's outlook is, one need hardly say, non-racist; in fact, he tries a little *too* hard to be fair to all groups and to show them in the best possible light. A certain amount of space is devoted to the rather meaningless enumeration of the names of immigrants who have achieved leadership in American life—a "Who's Who" approach of journalistic rather than scholarly coloration. Among his general conclusions is the statement that immigrant stocks have in general been more remarkable for their intellectual and scientific contributions than for their eminence in politics or war—a fact which may in part account for the disfavor in which they are held by the successful upholders of the policy of severely restricted immigration.

"Not many years ago," adds Dean Wittke, "the final play in a World

Series baseball game was made when a Serbian threw wild in an effort to deceive an Italian, thus permitting a native American from the Kentucky hill country to trot across the plate with the winning run." A pleasant sentence, harking back to a tradition of interracial friendliness that sometimes seems to belong to a vanished era.

C. F.

344. *Look Homeward, Angel*

by THOMAS WOLFE

Asheville, the Altamont of *Look Homeward, Angel,* is in the mountains of western North Carolina. At the time of Thomas Wolfe's birth it was a large small town not yet a city. It was also the confluence of three centuries. Up from the low country of the Carolinas had come the planter aristocracy—eighteenth century—for a breath of cool air, and their descendants still came, though now less affluent and in smaller numbers. From the nearer Piedmont section, a spearhead of the Industrial Revolution, the new cotton-mill aristocracy—"sheets and pillowcases" to the low countryman—sent wives, sons, and daughters for the summer.

Westward, less than fifty miles, the seventeenth century was sealed off, by mountains and by choice, from outlandish influence. The natives sang Elizabethan ballads, and Elizabethan words were at home in their language. They were in fact Elizabethans, a little late, except that they did nothing. They took things out in talk, or fight. For they were fierce individualists, each on his island mountainside and quick to discover offense. The only reading, or rather hearing, they ever did was the Bible—the Old Testament, the New being too mild. Not having had any part in the plantation economy, and Negro being hardly more than a word—but inferior of course—they were not Southerners. But they were not Yankees, either. They were, as William Alexander Percy (No. 245) said of some of his Mississippi neighbors, "an alien Anglo-Saxon breed."

These were the discernible streams that flowed and were dammed up in Thomas Wolfe (1900-38). Besides, there was an interminable talker of a mother, sharp of tongue and eye, and greedy, and a father striking madly at invisible foes. At first Thomas Wolfe tried writing poetry. For a while there was a trickle, and then the dam burst and the flood came, of poetry that was prose, prose that suddenly went roaring into something else. It was said, not entirely in jest, that, asked to produce a manuscript, he showed up with a truckload. It is estimated that the original manuscript of *Look Homeward, Angel* ran to a million words, until reduced to size by a patient editor.

Here is a book of taste, smell, hearing, sight, feeling, all clamoring for a place on the page. Thomas Wolfe died in his 30's, under such pressure of life as to bring death.

J. A. R.

345. *The Bonanza Trail*

by MURIEL SIBELL WOLLE

The first notable invasion of the greater part of the American West was made by the hunters of gold and silver. The discovery of the former metal in California in 1848, precipitating the Gold Rush of the Forty-niners, also created the supposition that more deposits of valuable minerals could be found in the region of the Rocky Mountains, and an army of intrepid prospectors explored that difficult country. Some found precious lodes, established camps that were to become such modern cities as Butte, Montana, and Denver, Colorado, opened fields of industry, settled towns, and established roads of approach, clearing the way for the herdsmen and farmers to come. There were many others who left their bones in forgotten valleys. Bearing mute testimony to the passage of these hunters and their turbulent quest are the hundreds of ghost towns and abandoned mining sites still dotting the vast stretches of valley and desert, mountain and plain, in the West today (see also No. 96).

Muriel Sibell Wolle (1898-) of the University of Colorado fine arts department, has had a lifelong interest in visiting and sketching these ghost towns and mining camps. Over the years, she has covered 70,000 miles in her research, and in *The Bonanza Trail* she has accumulated and organized into a coherent whole what is known about the ghost towns of the twelve far western states in which lie significant mining zones. Heavily illustrated and annotated with maps, her own on-the-spot drawings, and a glossary of the terminology of mining and mineralogy, the main text of the book consists of informal, detailed descriptions, state by state, of the places she saw, and reports of their physical aspects, recorded documentation, hearsay anecdotes and legends.

"Mining history," says Mrs. Wolle, "is exhilarating and depressing. It is full of violence and faith, of bravery and chicanery. It is built on extremes—a boom, a crash; a strike, a shut-down." But she sees the ghost towns themselves as "gallant monuments of faith and daring." Behind the present ruins she sees "the once bustling cities whose teeming life made possible the West of today." *The Bonanza Trail* is a valuable book for those who want a factual recording of era and place, and for those who find romantic interest in the story of the search for hidden mineral riches—the search which, though it enriched only the few, did much to accomplish the opening of America's frontier.

C. C.

346. *The Strange Career of Jim Crow*

by C. VANN WOODWARD

One of the central arguments in American society is what might be called the argument between law and nature. On the one hand are those who argue that most relationships—the relationships between buyer and seller, employer and employee, between white and Negro—should not be made the subject of legislation but are best left to nature to work themselves out. The great American sociologist William Graham Sumner (1840-1910) was one of the most famous spokesmen for this point of view (see No. 106); writing in the heyday of Social Darwinism, he declared that such legislation was not only undesirable but impossible to put into effect: "Stateways cannot change folkways." But on the whole American history is a demonstration of how important law can be in shaping society, and European observers have repeatedly been impressed by this fact.

But it would be misleading to give the impression that in this argument between law and nature most Americans occupy a consistent position; they do not. For instance, the man who wants the law to exercise restraint on business freedom may not want it to exercise restraint on academic freedom, and vice versa. Americans also disagree on the degree of legal restraint they think desirable. It is hardly cynical to say that the average American thinks it would do little harm for the law to take in hand most activities except his own, and he will welcome the law's participation in his own activity so long as it confines itself to protection without interference.

Professor C. Vann Woodward (1908-) has made a fascinating study of the "Jim Crow" laws, the laws effecting racial segregation in the Southern states and one of the most vital areas in which "stateways" and "folkways" meet. Legislation, as he shows, has played a highly important part in racial segregation, though the apologists for segregation defend it on the grounds that it is a folkway. The reader would do well to note that in delivering the lectures that make up this book Professor Woodward was speaking as a Southerner to an audience of Southerners. He could trust his audience to know how powerful tradition has been in their region, and therefore he could concentrate his argument on the amount of freedom in race relations that tradition has permitted.

P. P.

347. *Autobiography*

by FRANK LLOYD WRIGHT

Frank Lloyd Wright (1869-) has lived long enough to enjoy, as it has been put, his own posthumous reputation. At the turn of the century he was a successful Chicago suburban architect. By the 1920's he was exercising an international influence, particularly in Europe. There came a time when his fame passed into eclipse, and he waited long years for clients who did not come; but there later came a time when the prophet was honored even in his own country, and he entered his eighth decade with more "work on the boards" than ever before.

Now we are able to concede, even to his own face, that Mr. Wright is one of the master builders. He is continually at odds with society, however. Though generous of his gifts, he knows their worth. He has a matchless sense of publicity combined with an irrepressible desire to reform the manners and morals of his countrymen—that is to say, his is the American character writ large. He has never regarded architecture as anything less than the determining matrix of culture.

There is much of Walt Whitman (No. 333) in Mr. Wright, much also of his mentor, Louis Sullivan (see No. 298). The reader who looks for pictures of Mr. Wright's work (as in Nos. 113, 146, or 229) should remember that he is getting only a faint flavor of the actuality and that much that he sees, more than may appear, is a part of its time. Mr. Wright's genius is to amaze, instruct, and delight the eye in three dimensions, as it moves through and around his buildings. His own account of what he is doing, and why, is less impressive than what he has done.

But he is, at the same time, a marvelous writer—not by skill so much as by dominating language through will power. Mr. Wright composes as he speaks, without the expected amenities but with the fully deployed resources of his personality. He is by turn exasperating, candid, tedious, and deeply moving, but always there. And to the extent that this enormous individuality can convey itself in words, it does so here.

E. L.

348. *How We Invented the Airplane*

by ORVILLE WRIGHT

Of all the books here assembled, this is perhaps the one least in need of introduction. Everyone recognizes the invention of the airplane as being something of an achievement and no one disputes the priority of the Wright brothers—Orville (1871-1948) and Wilbur (1867-1912)—in having constructed a heavier-than-air machine that stayed aloft and landed without killing its occupants—a convenience too often absent from later models.

What is particularly interesting about this small volume is that it contains an account by the inventors of the work that led to their success. A sign of the times is that they did not write this account for a newspaper syndicate or as part of an autobiography stimulated by a publisher, but for the purpose of legal self-justification. The simplicity, almost humility, of the narrative turns in retrospect into an element of irresistible charm. In the absence of intellectual pose or literary flourishes, History herself becomes a stylist. But History here is necessarily incomplete and this unique primary source on the subject of flight must be supplemented by Fred Kelly's biographical work (No. 171).

J. B.

349. *Literary Opinion in America*

edited by MORTON DAUWEN ZABEL

These 77 essays, ranging from 1889 to 1950, the work of 50 critics, illustrate "the status, methods, and problems of criticism in the United States in the twentieth century." Read along with the editor's first-rate summary-introduction, they enable the serious student to learn all he needs to know in a field that has during the past half century undergone a rapid, a fruitful, and in some respects an almost feverish development. Whatever one may think of America's novelists and playwrights, there can be little doubt that on the critical side we have produced several score of intelligences, ranging from the highly competent to the brilliant.

Morton Dauwen Zabel (1901-) divides his selections into five parts. In the first some of the older critics, beginning with the greatest of them, Henry James, lay down a few of the issues which are to concern a later generation. Part II deals with a problem of special import to new countries—that of tradition and responsibility. The third section is occupied with what is usually considered the major function of literary criticism—the assaying of individual writers. Following this is a group of essays that also deal with writers, but from a specifically American point of view. The final section, more abstract, more illustrative of the "new criticism," is concerned with the problems, methods, and prospects of modern criticism.

The prime quality of most of these essays is a high intellectual seriousness. For these men literature is as grave and important a matter as golf or the stock market is for other Americans. Analysis; the making of fine discriminations; an unwillingness to repeat anything already said; the skillful use of insights and knowledge derived from other disciplines, such as philosophy, psychology and sociology; carefully hidden scholarship; thoroughness; elevated morality; rejection of impressionism: these are some of the characteristics of the criticism of the past quarter century. The defect of these qualities is a desiccation of tone, an unwillingness to *love* literature. The great critics of the past have in most cases been able to combine intellect and enthusiasm; but this is a marriage upon which our whole post-T. S. Eliot generation looks with a certain disfavor.

C. F.

350. *As I Remember Him*

by Hans Zinsser

Although Dr. Hans Zinsser (1878-1940) presents his book as the biography of a physician-friend to whom he gives the initials R.S., it is actually an autobiography. The substitution of a fictitious friend for himself as the subject of *As I Remember Him* is merely a device for objectifying the personal narrative, and for permitting Dr. Zinsser omissions and reticences which would have reduced the sense of truth in a conventional autobiography. It also provides Dr. Zinsser with the opportunity for large interpolations of informal comment on his own history.

Much of the charm of *As I Remember Him* stems from this random quality. A distinguished research doctor and epidemiologist, perhaps best known for his part in combatting the scourge of typhoid fever, Dr. Zinsser was also a devoted private scholar who read voraciously in many disparate fields; he was a passionate traveler and social observer; he looked to art to rescue civilization from the depredations of science; he loved the variousness of life, in both people and nature; he had a genius for friendship. If his personal recollections fall short of completeness as an account of his professional development and thus fail to meet a first requirement of traditional autobiography, they more than compensate for this lack by the gusto and humor with which they range a world in which epidemic disease was but one of the challenges to their author's imagination.

As much at the call of adventure as in the service of hygiene, Dr. Zinsser went everywhere and met everyone: his teaching post at Harvard University was simply home base. He was in Serbia during the first World War; in Russia in the early years of the Revolution; in China, Japan, Mexico, wherever a new field for bacteriological research gave him the occasion for a new experience of mankind. And wherever Dr. Zinsser went, curiosity, kindliness, and an essential innocence went with him, lightening the burdens of his public career and laying the ground for an uncommon personal satisfaction.

D. T.

INDEXES

Index of Authors and Titles Included in the Collection of 350 Books

This complete index of authors and titles is a guide to the collection of 350 books and is not intended as an index to the volume, *American Panorama.* Page references to *American Panorama,* however, are included and are for those titles and authors which are described in this volume.

Subject Index of the 350 Books

Page references in this index are to the essays contained in *American Panorama.* However, there are many references to subjects treated only in the books themselves, and readers are advised to consult the indexes of the individual books.